You're Reading the WRONG WAY!

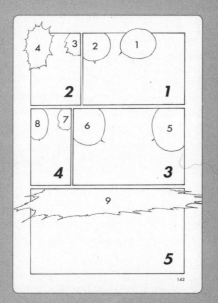

NISEKOI reads from right to left, starting in the upper-right corner. Japanese is read from right to left, meaning that action, sound effects, and word-balloon order are completely reversed from English order.

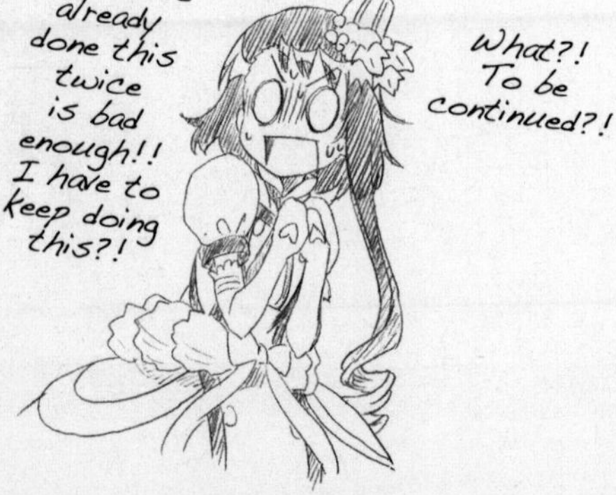
What?! To be continued?!
The fact that we've already done this twice is bad enough!! I have to keep doing this?!

In this volume, Raku and his friends are now second-year students,

and new first-year students join the mix.

It's becoming livelier! How will things shake out by graduation?

I really don't know at this point, but I'm looking forward to finding out!

Naoshi Komi

NAOSHI KOMI was born in Kochi Prefecture, Japan, on March 28, 1986. His first serialized work in *Weekly Shonen Jump* was the series *Double Arts*. His current series, *Nisekoi*, is serialized in *Weekly Shonen Jump*.

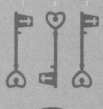

NISEKOI:
False Love
VOLUME 9
SHONEN JUMP Manga Edition

Story and Art by
NAOSHI KOMI

Translation ✐ Camellia Nieh
Touch-Up Art & Lettering ✐ Stephen Dutro
Design ✐ Fawn Lau
Shonen Jump Series Editor ✐ John Bae
Graphic Novel Editor ✐ Amy Yu

NISEKOI © 2011 by Naoshi Komi
All rights reserved.
First published in Japan in 2011
by SHUEISHA Inc., Tokyo.
English translation rights arranged
by SHUEISHA Inc.

The stories, characters and incidents mentioned
in this publication are entirely fictional.

Printed in the U.S.A.

Published by VIZ Media, LLC
P.O. Box 77010
San Francisco, CA 94107

10 9 8 7 6 5 4 3 2 1
First printing, May 2015

www.shonenjump.com   www.viz.com

NISEKOI

False Love

vol. 9: Kamikaze

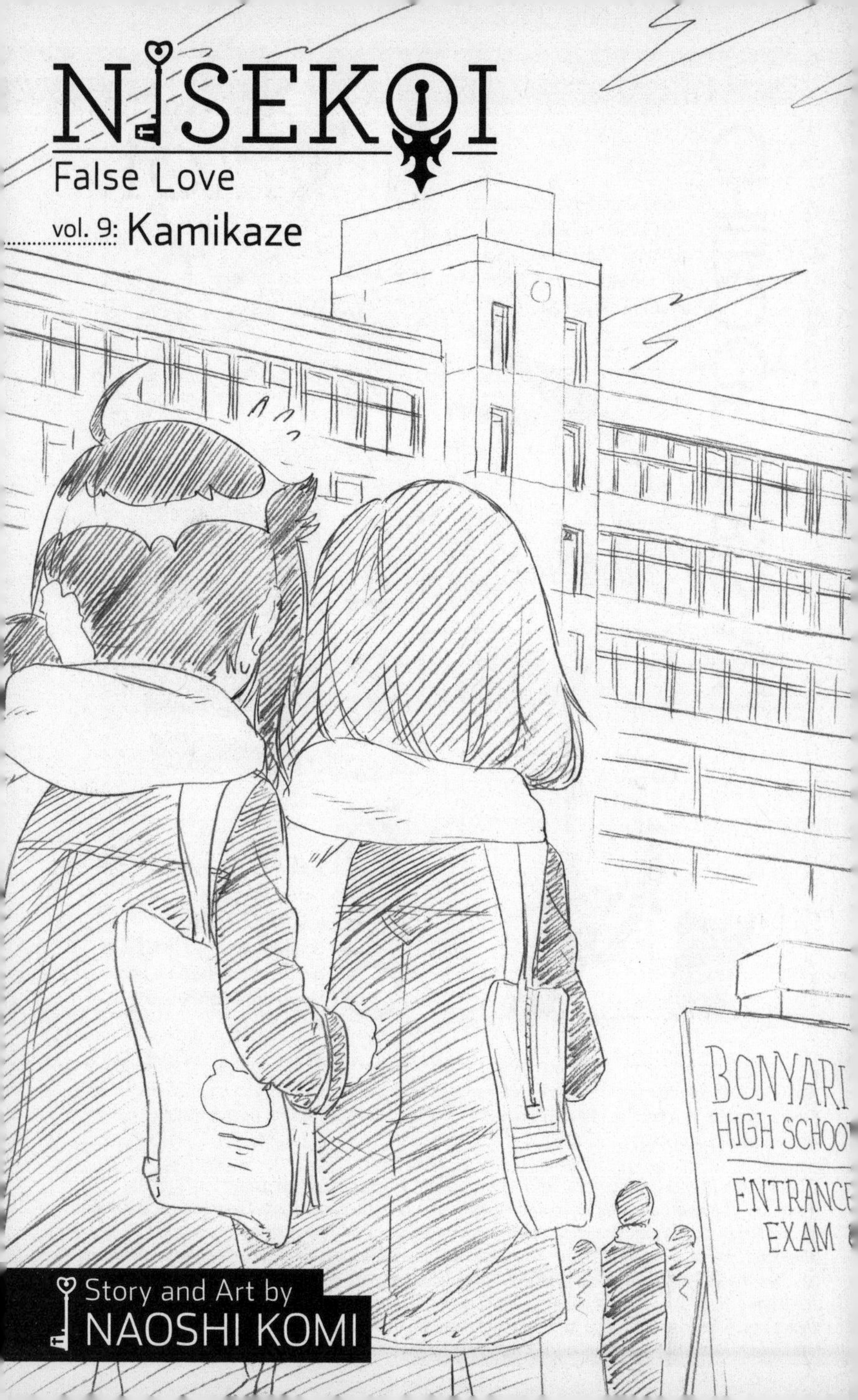
BONYARI
HIGH SCHOO
ENTRANC
EXAM

Story and Art by
NAOSHI KOMI

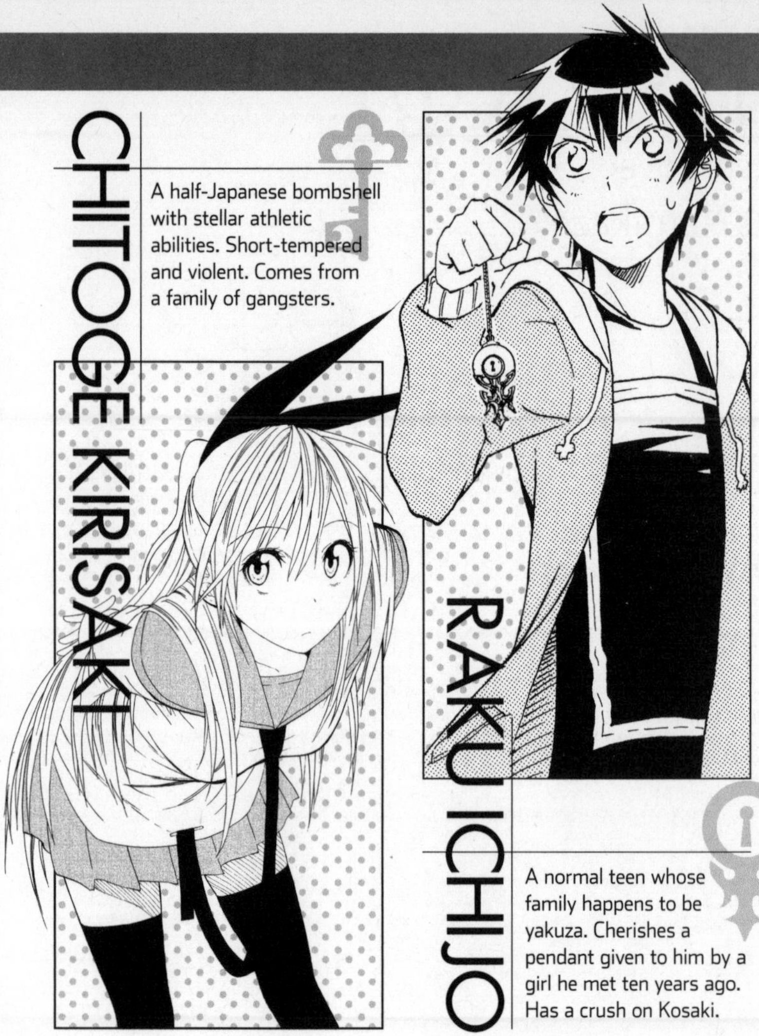

CHITOGE KIRISAKI

A half-Japanese bombshell with stellar athletic abilities. Short-tempered and violent. Comes from a family of gangsters.

RAKU ICHIJO

A normal teen whose family happens to be yakuza. Cherishes a pendant given to him by a girl he met ten years ago. Has a crush on Kosaki.

Raku Ichijo is an ordinary teen...who just happens to come from a family of yakuza! His most treasured item is a pendant he was given ten years ago by a girl whom he promised to meet again one day and marry.

Thanks to family circumstances, Raku is forced into a false relationship with Chitoge, the daughter of a rival gangster, to keep their families from shedding blood. Despite their constant spats, Raku and Chitoge manage to fool everyone. One day, Chitoge discovers an old key, jogging memories of her own first love ten years earlier. Meanwhile, Raku's crush, Kosaki, confesses that she also has a key and made a promise with a boy ten years ago. To complicate matters, Marika Tachibana, a girl who claims to be Raku's fiancée, has a key as well and remembers a promise ten years ago. The mystery keeps getting more complex as Raku and the gang spend time together and grow closer. But what will become of their relationships in the end?

THE STORY THUS FAR

MARIKA TACHIBANA

Daughter of the chief of police, Marika is Raku's fiancée, according to an agreement made by their fathers—an agreement Marika takes very seriously! Also has a key and remembers making a promise with Raku ten years ago.

KOSAKI ONODERA

A girl Raku has a crush on. Beautiful and sweet, Kosaki has no shortage of admirers. She's a terrible cook but makes food that *looks* amazing.

SEISHIRO TSUGUMI

Adopted by Claude as a young child and raised as a top-notch assassin, Seishiro is 100% devoted to Chitoge. Often mistaken for a boy, Tsugumi's really a girl.

SHU MAIKO

Raku's best friend. Outgoing and girl-crazy. Always tuned in to the latest gossip at school.

RURI MIYAMOTO

Kosaki's best gal pal. Comes off as aloof, but is actually a devoted and highly intuitive friend.

Hurry up!!

BONYARI HIGH SCHOOL
Enrollment Ceremony

NISEKOI
False Love

vol. 9: Kamikaze

TABLE OF CONTENTS

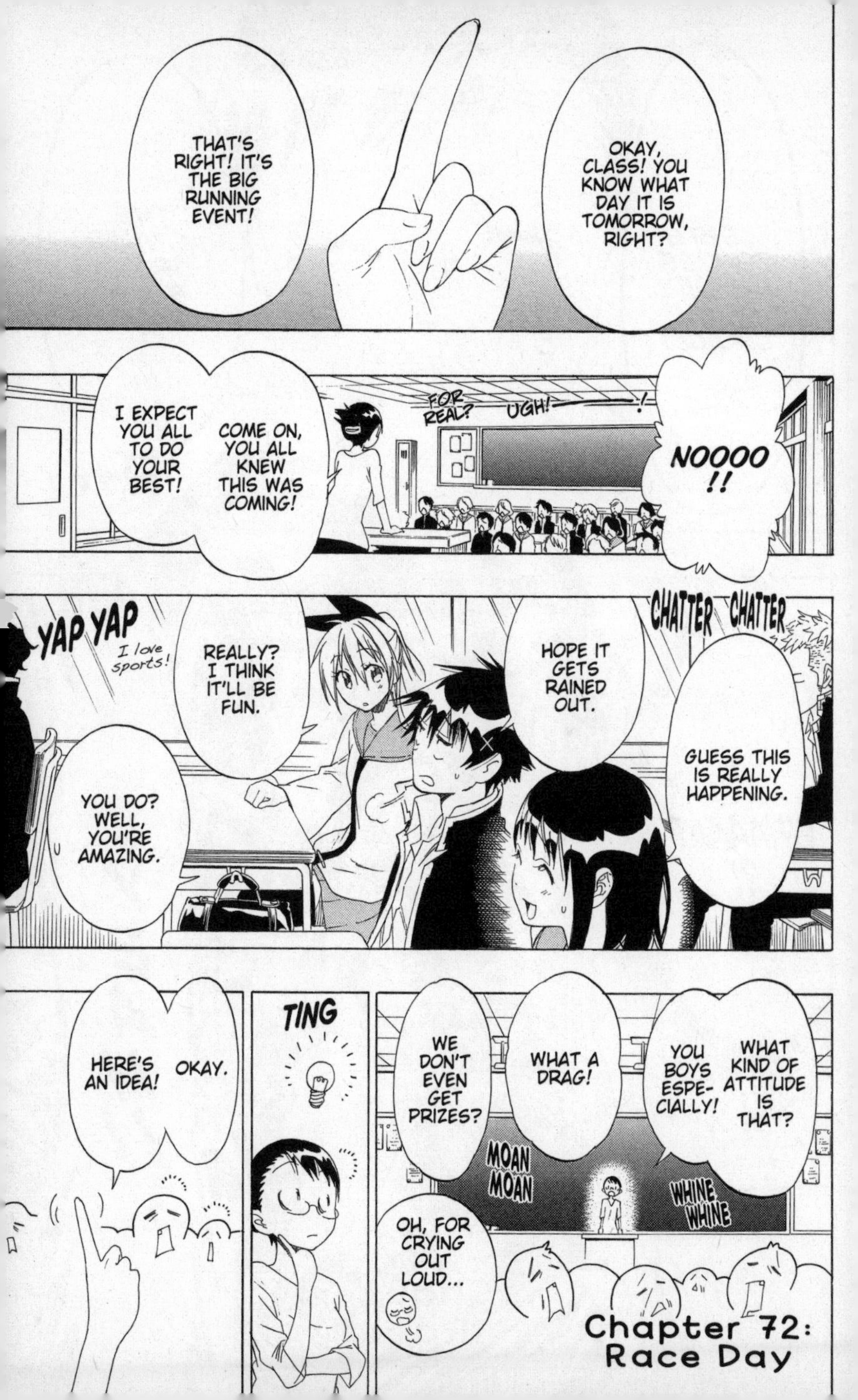
OKAY, CLASS! YOU KNOW WHAT DAY IT IS TOMORROW, RIGHT?
THAT'S RIGHT! IT'S THE BIG RUNNING EVENT!
NOOOO!!
FOR REAL?
UGH!
—!
COME ON, YOU ALL KNEW THIS WAS COMING!
I EXPECT YOU ALL TO DO YOUR BEST!
CHATTER CHATTER
GUESS THIS IS REALLY HAPPENING.
HOPE IT GETS RAINED OUT.
REALLY? I THINK IT'LL BE FUN.
YAP YAP
I love sports!
YOU DO? WELL, YOU'RE AMAZING.
WHAT KIND OF ATTITUDE IS THAT?
YOU BOYS ESPE-CIALLY!
WHAT A DRAG!
WE DON'T EVEN GET PRIZES?
MOAN MOAN
WHINE WHINE
OH, FOR CRYING OUT LOUD...
Chapter 72: Race Day
TING
OKAY.
HERE'S AN IDEA!

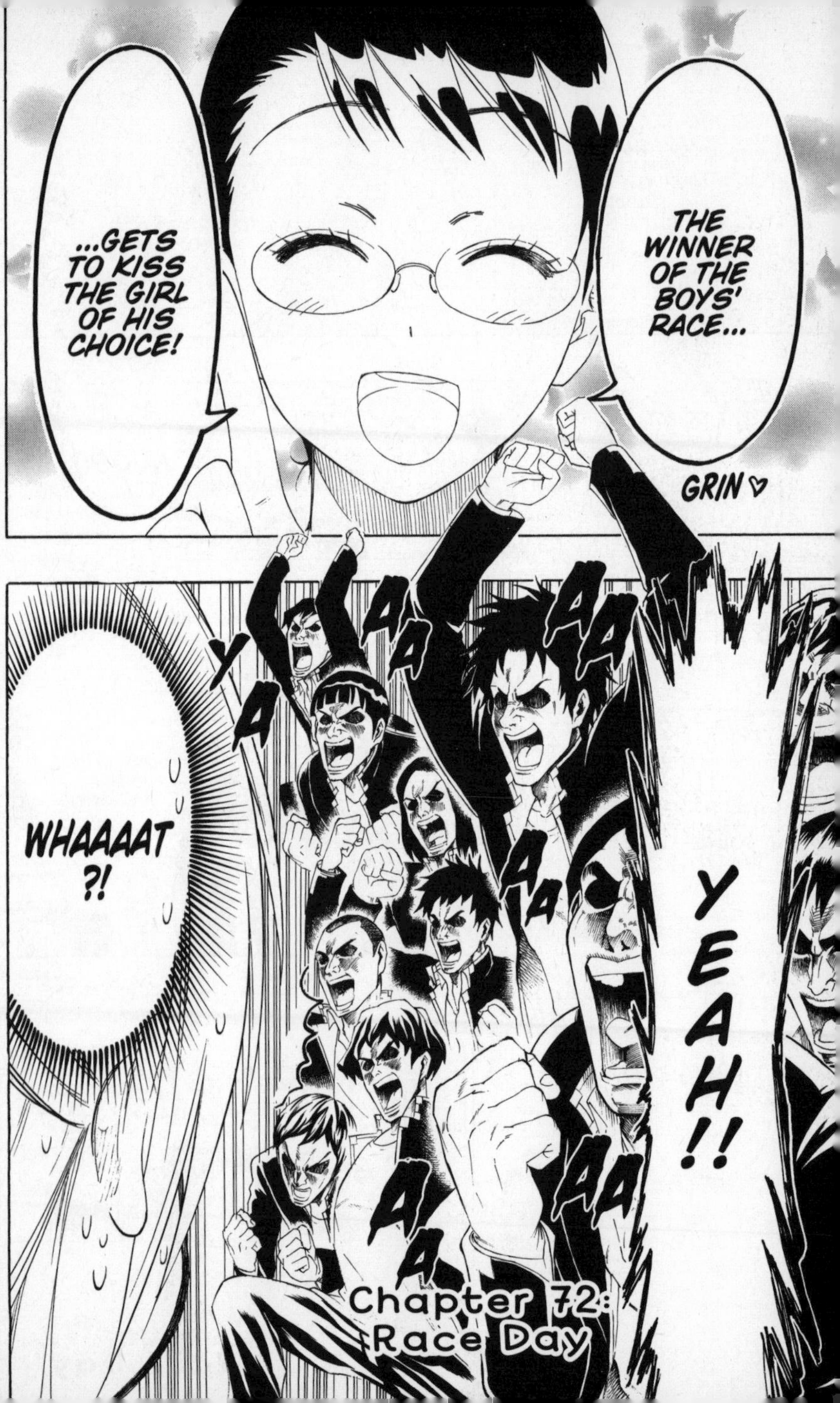
THE WINNER OF THE BOYS' RACE...
...GETS TO KISS THE GIRL OF HIS CHOICE!
GRIN♡
YEAH!!
YAAAAA
WHAAAAT?!
Chapter 72: Race Day

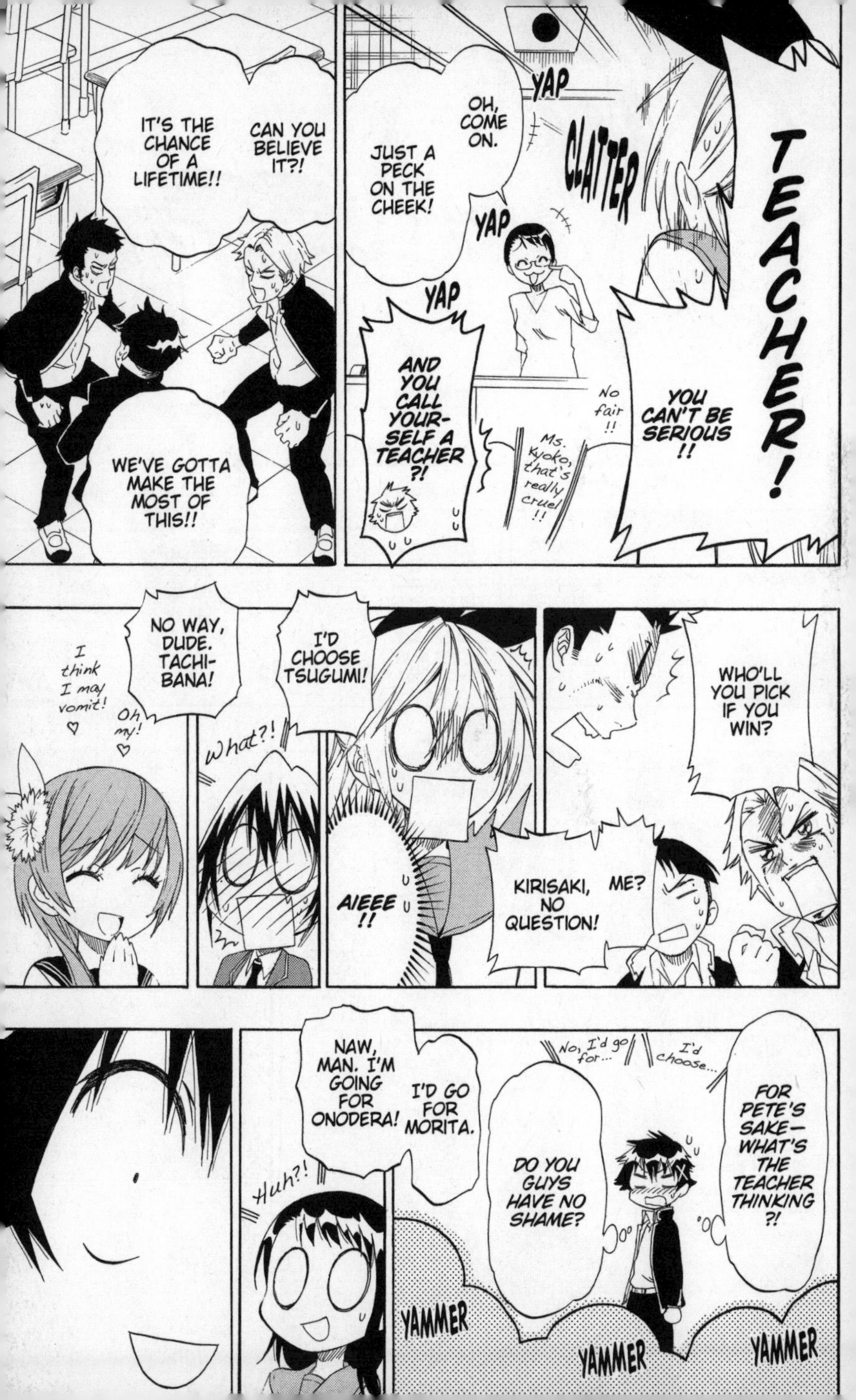
TEACHER!
YOU CAN'T BE SERIOUS!!
CLATTER
YAP
OH, COME ON.
JUST A PECK ON THE CHEEK!
YAP
YAP
AND YOU CALL YOURSELF A TEACHER?!
No fair!!
Ms. Kyoko, that's really cruel!!
CAN YOU BELIEVE IT?!
IT'S THE CHANCE OF A LIFETIME!!
WE'VE GOTTA MAKE THE MOST OF THIS!!
WHO'LL YOU PICK IF YOU WIN?
ME?
KIRISAKI, NO QUESTION!
AIEEE!!
I'D CHOOSE TSUGUMI!
What?!
NO WAY, DUDE. TACHIBANA!
Oh my! ♥
I think I may vomit! ♥
FOR PETE'S SAKE—WHAT'S THE TEACHER THINKING?!
I'd choose...
No, I'd go for...
DO YOU GUYS HAVE NO SHAME?
I'D GO FOR MORITA.
NAW, MAN. I'M GOING FOR ONODERA!
Huh?!
YAMMER
YAMMER
YAMMER

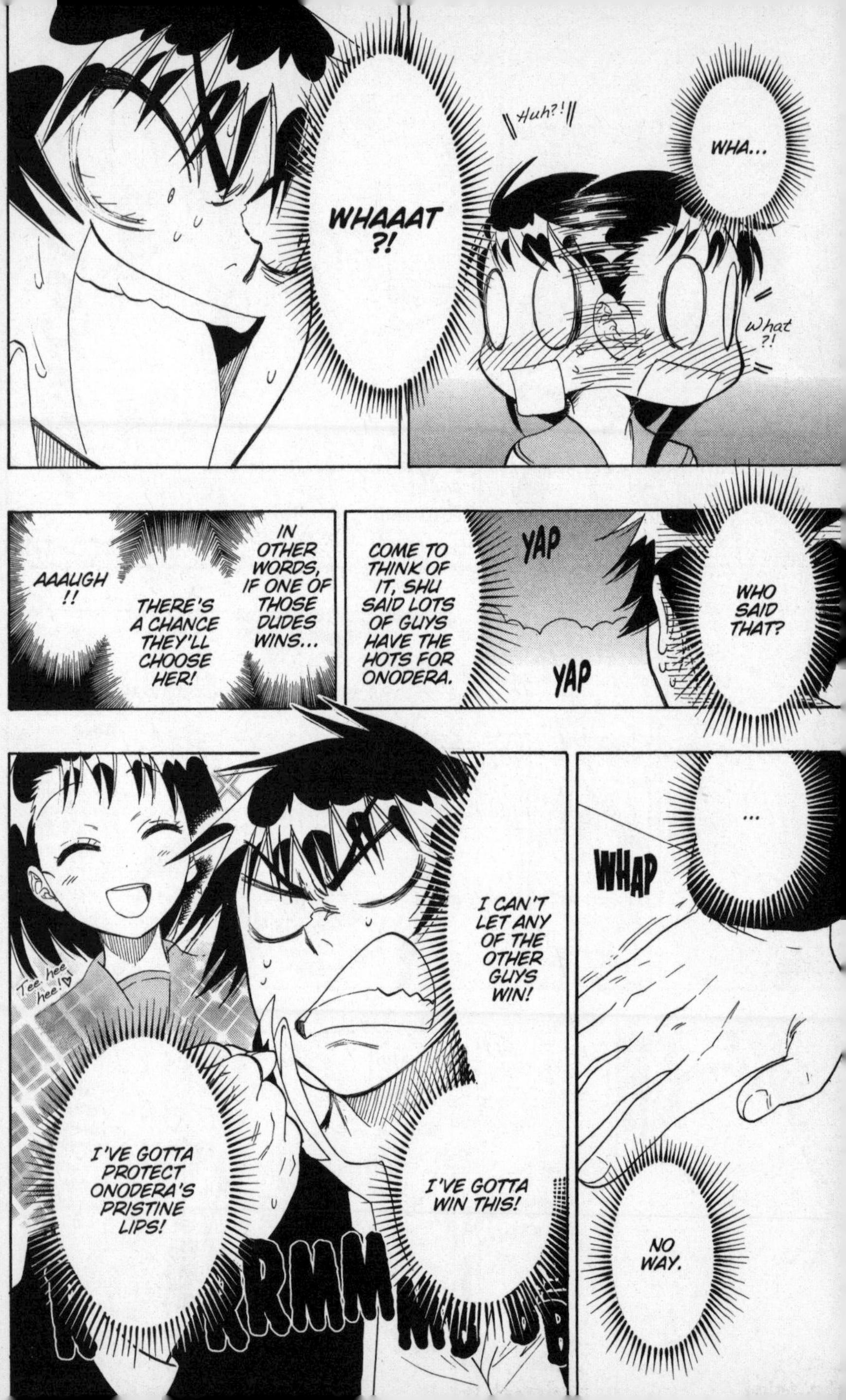
WHA...
Huh?!
What ?!
WHAAAT ?!
WHO SAID THAT?
YAP
YAP
COME TO THINK OF IT, SHU SAID LOTS OF GUYS HAVE THE HOTS FOR ONODERA.
IN OTHER WORDS, IF ONE OF THOSE DUDES WINS...
THERE'S A CHANCE THEY'LL CHOOSE HER!
AAAUGH !!
...
WHAP
NO WAY.
I CAN'T LET ANY OF THE OTHER GUYS WIN!
I'VE GOTTA WIN THIS!
I'VE GOTTA PROTECT ONODERA'S PRISTINE LIPS!
Tee hee hee!♡

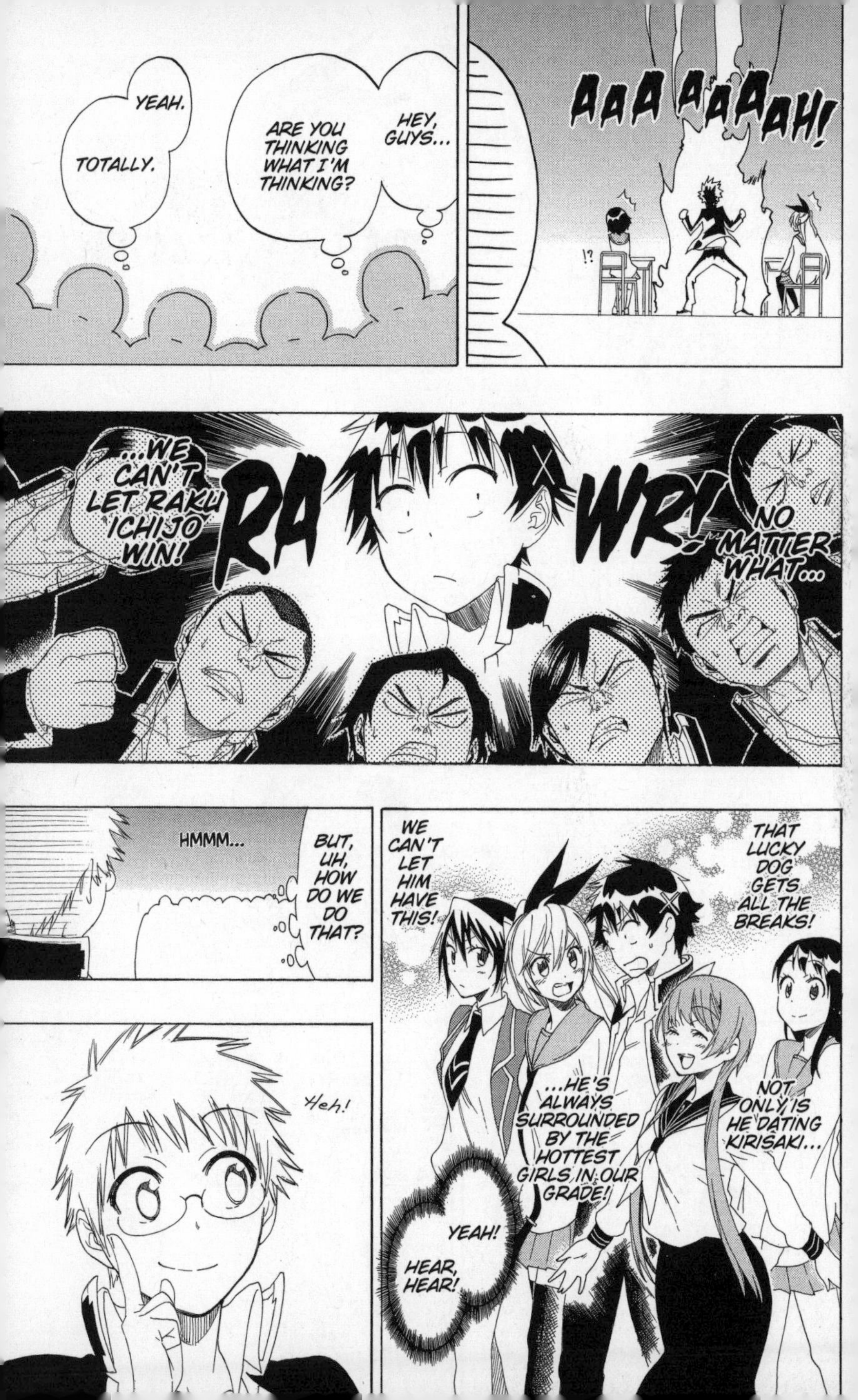
AAAAAAAAH!
!?
HEY, GUYS...
ARE YOU THINKING WHAT I'M THINKING?
YEAH.
TOTALLY.
NO MATTER WHAT...
...WE CAN'T LET RAKU ICHIJO WIN!
RAWR!
THAT LUCKY DOG GETS ALL THE BREAKS!
NOT ONLY IS HE DATING KIRISAKI...
...HE'S ALWAYS SURROUNDED BY THE HOTTEST GIRLS IN OUR GRADE!
WE CAN'T LET HIM HAVE THIS!
YEAH!
HEAR, HEAR!
BUT, UH, HOW DO WE DO THAT?
HMMM...
Heh!

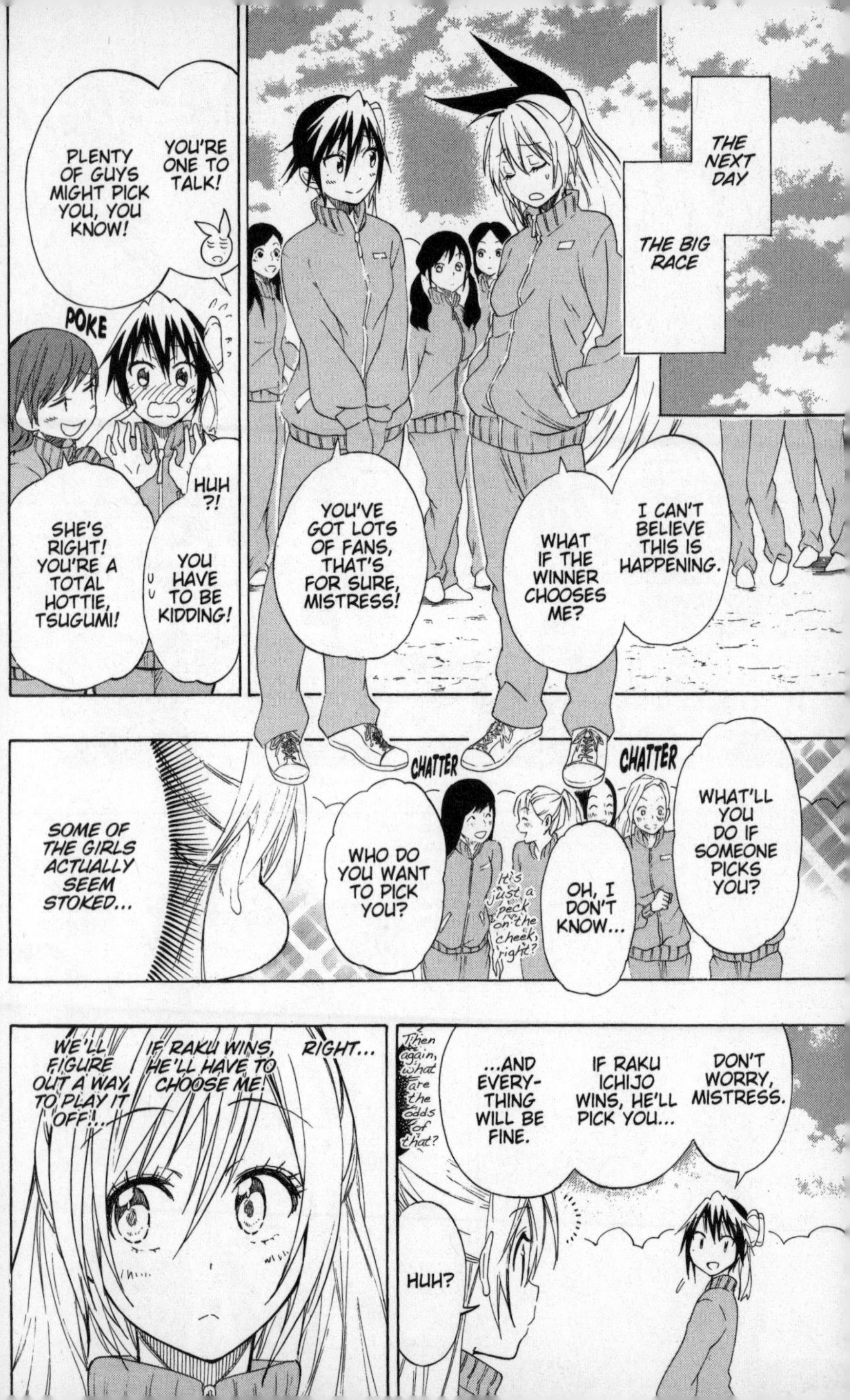
THE NEXT DAY
THE BIG RACE
I CAN'T BELIEVE THIS IS HAPPENING. WHAT IF THE WINNER CHOOSES ME?
YOU'VE GOT LOTS OF FANS, THAT'S FOR SURE, MISTRESS!
YOU'RE ONE TO TALK! PLENTY OF GUYS MIGHT PICK YOU, YOU KNOW!
POKE
HUH?! YOU HAVE TO BE KIDDING!
SHE'S RIGHT! YOU'RE A TOTAL HOTTIE, TSUGUMI!
WHAT'LL YOU DO IF SOMEONE PICKS YOU?
CHATTER
OH, I DON'T KNOW...
It's just a peck on the cheek, right?
WHO DO YOU WANT TO PICK YOU?
CHATTER
SOME OF THE GIRLS ACTUALLY SEEM STOKED...
DON'T WORRY, MISTRESS. IF RAKU ICHIJO WINS, HE'LL PICK YOU... ...AND EVERYTHING WILL BE FINE.
Then again, what are the odds of that?
HUH?
RIGHT... IF RAKU WINS, HE'LL HAVE TO CHOOSE ME! WE'LL FIGURE OUT A WAY TO PLAY IT OFF!...

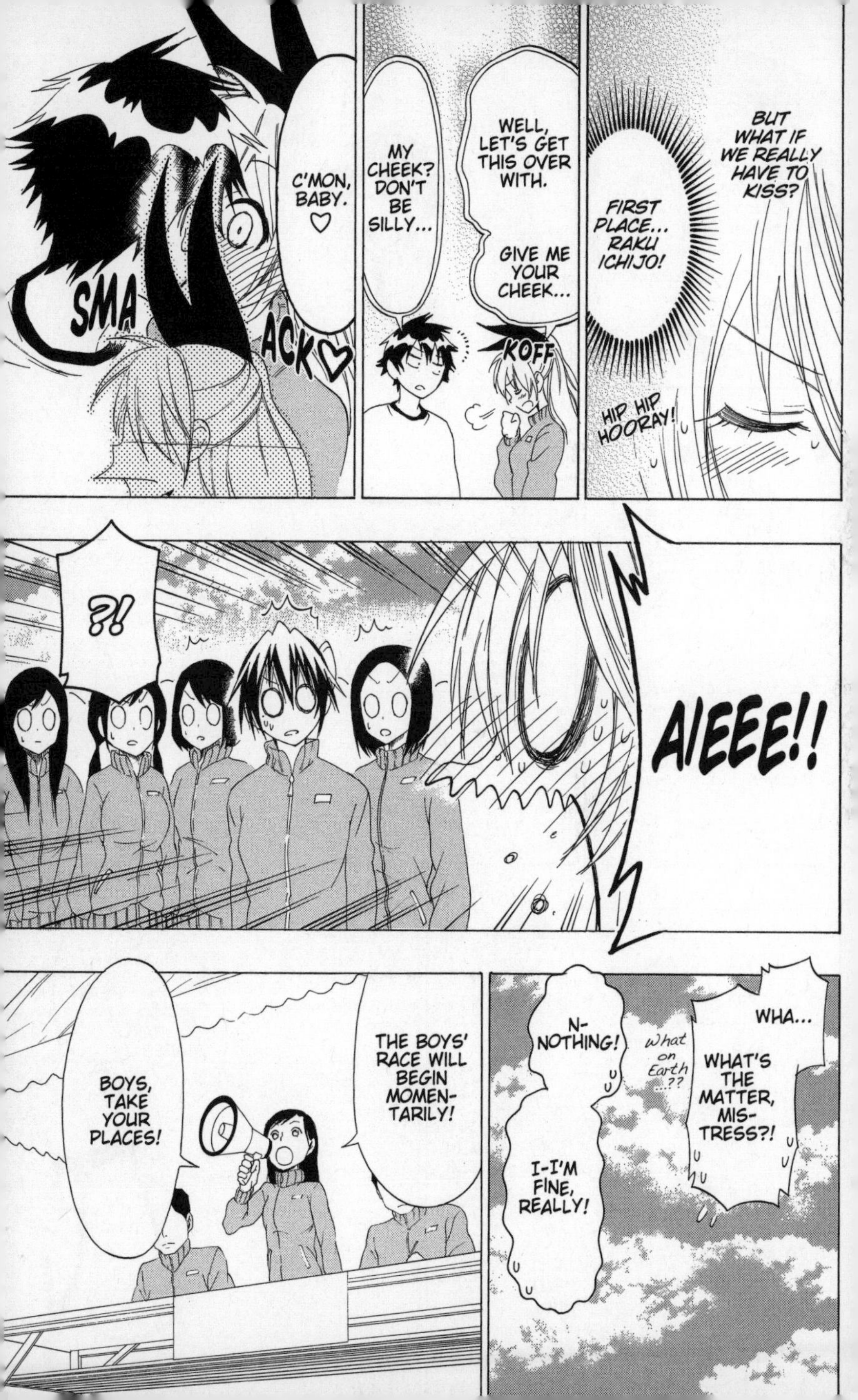
BUT WHAT IF WE REALLY HAVE TO KISS?
FIRST PLACE... RAKU ICHIJO!
HIP HIP HOORAY!
WELL, LET'S GET THIS OVER WITH.
GIVE ME YOUR CHEEK...
KOFF
MY CHEEK? DON'T BE SILLY...
C'MON, BABY. ♡
SMA
ACK♡
AIEEE!!
?!
WHA...
WHAT'S THE MATTER, MIS-TRESS?!
What on Earth...??
N-NOTHING!
I-I'M FINE, REALLY!
THE BOYS' RACE WILL BEGIN MOMEN-TARILY!
BOYS, TAKE YOUR PLACES!

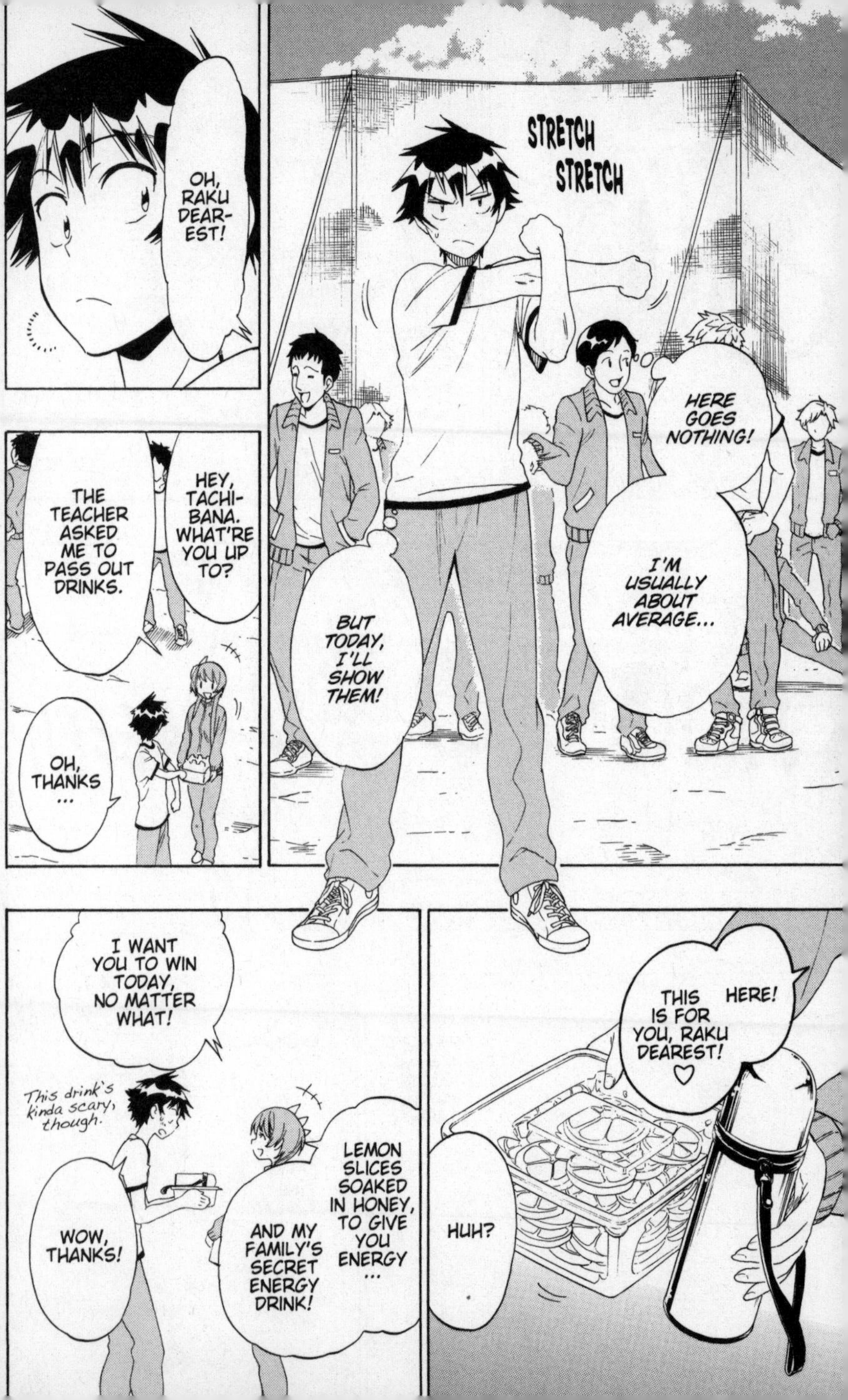
STRETCH STRETCH
HERE GOES NOTHING!
I'M USUALLY ABOUT AVERAGE...
BUT TODAY, I'LL SHOW THEM!
OH, RAKU DEAREST!
HEY, TACHIBANA. WHAT'RE YOU UP TO?
THE TEACHER ASKED ME TO PASS OUT DRINKS.
OH, THANKS...
HERE!
THIS IS FOR YOU, RAKU DEAREST! ♡
HUH?
LEMON SLICES SOAKED IN HONEY, TO GIVE YOU ENERGY...
AND MY FAMILY'S SECRET ENERGY DRINK!
I WANT YOU TO WIN TODAY, NO MATTER WHAT!
WOW, THANKS!
This drink's kinda scary, though.

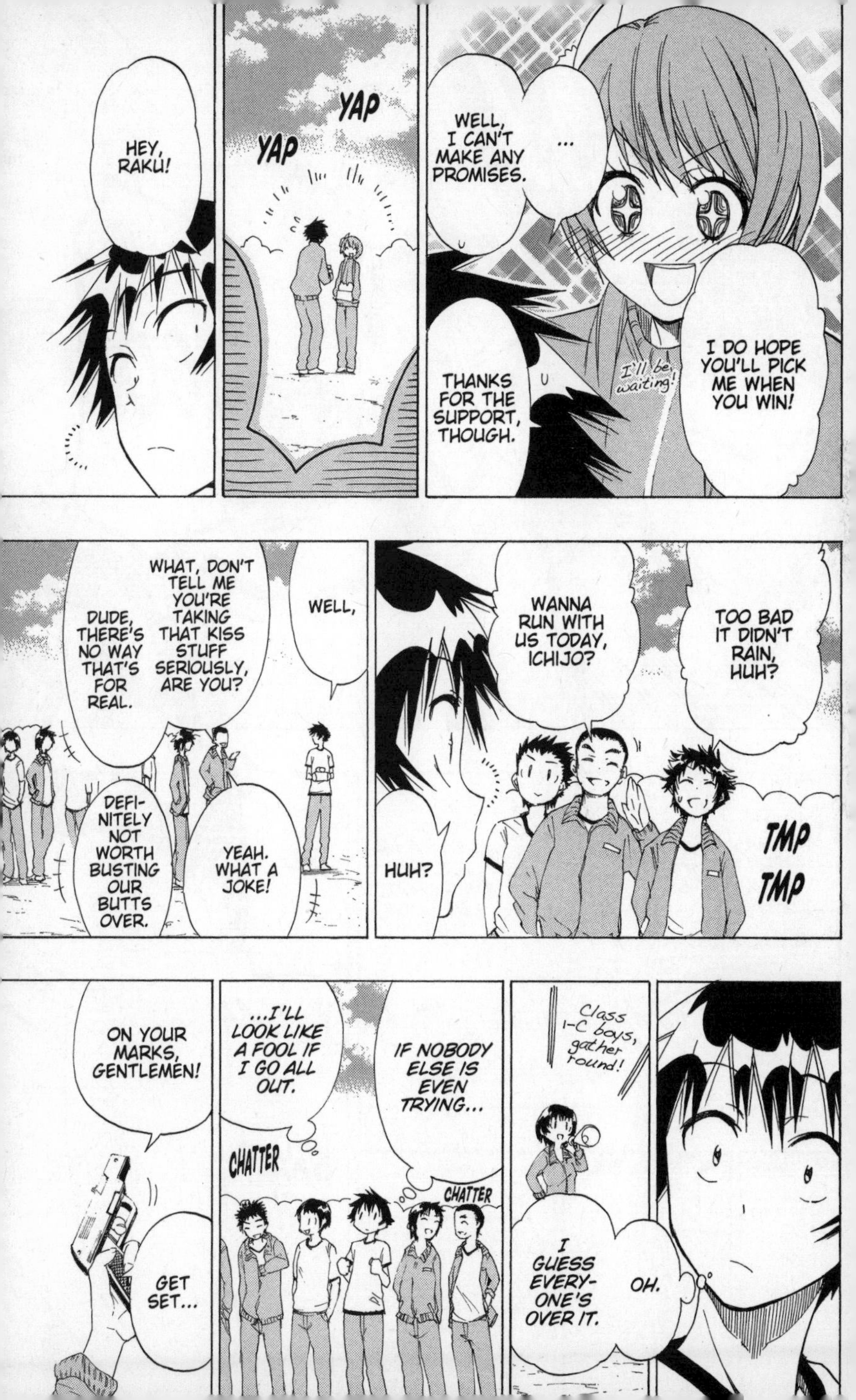
I DO HOPE YOU'LL PICK ME WHEN YOU WIN!
I'll be waiting!
...
WELL, I CAN'T MAKE ANY PROMISES.
THANKS FOR THE SUPPORT, THOUGH.
YAP
YAP
HEY, RAKU!
TOO BAD IT DIDN'T RAIN, HUH?
WANNA RUN WITH US TODAY, ICHIJO?
TMP
TMP
HUH?
WELL,
WHAT, DON'T TELL ME YOU'RE TAKING THAT KISS STUFF SERIOUSLY, ARE YOU?
DUDE, THERE'S NO WAY THAT'S FOR REAL.
YEAH. WHAT A JOKE!
DEFI-NITELY NOT WORTH BUSTING OUR BUTTS OVER.
Class 1-C boys, gather round!
OH.
I GUESS EVERY-ONE'S OVER IT.
IF NOBODY ELSE IS EVEN TRYING...
...I'LL LOOK LIKE A FOOL IF I GO ALL OUT.
CHATTER
CHATTER
ON YOUR MARKS, GENTLEMEN!
GET SET...

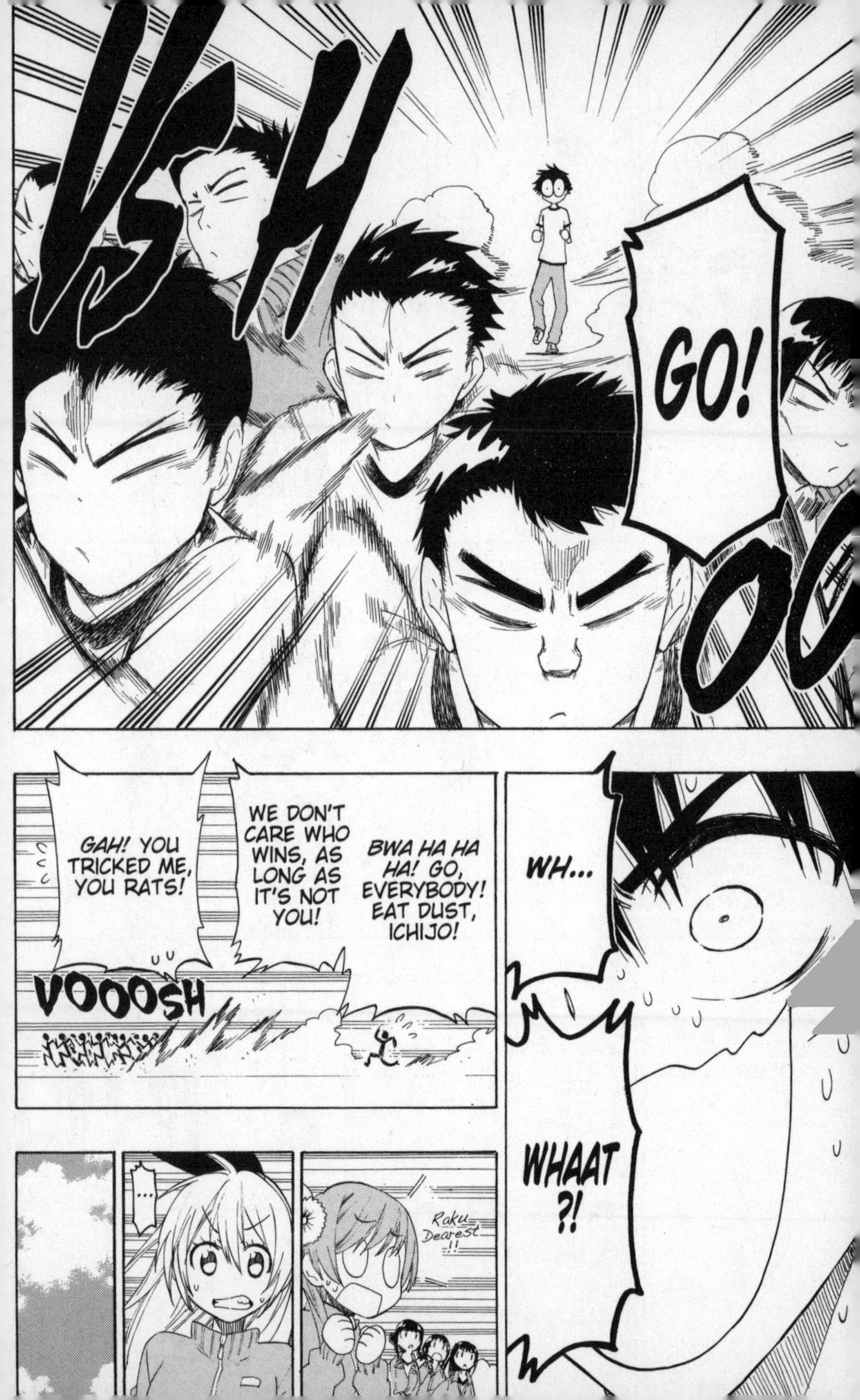
GO!
OO
VSH
WH...
WHAAT?!
BWA HA HA HA! GO, EVERYBODY! EAT DUST, ICHIJO!
WE DON'T CARE WHO WINS, AS LONG AS IT'S NOT YOU!
GAH! YOU TRICKED ME, YOU RATS!
VOOOSH
Raku Dearest!!
...

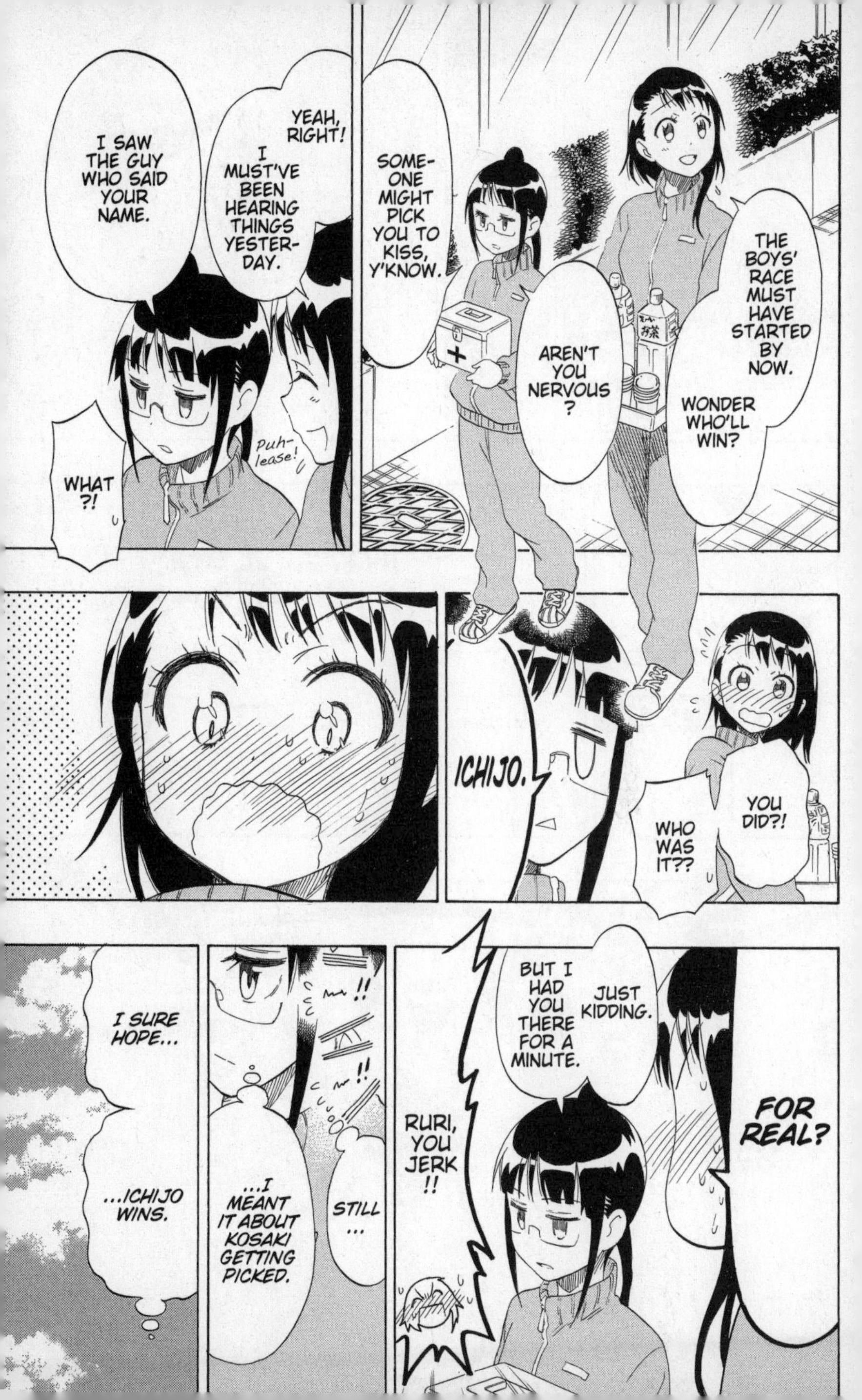
THE BOYS' RACE MUST HAVE STARTED BY NOW.
WONDER WHO'LL WIN?
AREN'T YOU NERVOUS?
SOME-ONE MIGHT PICK YOU TO KISS, Y'KNOW.
YEAH, RIGHT! I MUST'VE BEEN HEARING THINGS YESTER-DAY.
Puh-lease!
I SAW THE GUY WHO SAID YOUR NAME.
WHAT?!
YOU DID?!
WHO WAS IT??
ICHIJO.
FOR REAL?
JUST KIDDING.
BUT I HAD YOU THERE FOR A MINUTE.
RURI, YOU JERK!!
STILL...
...I MEANT IT ABOUT KOSAKI GETTING PICKED.
I SURE HOPE...
...ICHIJO WINS.

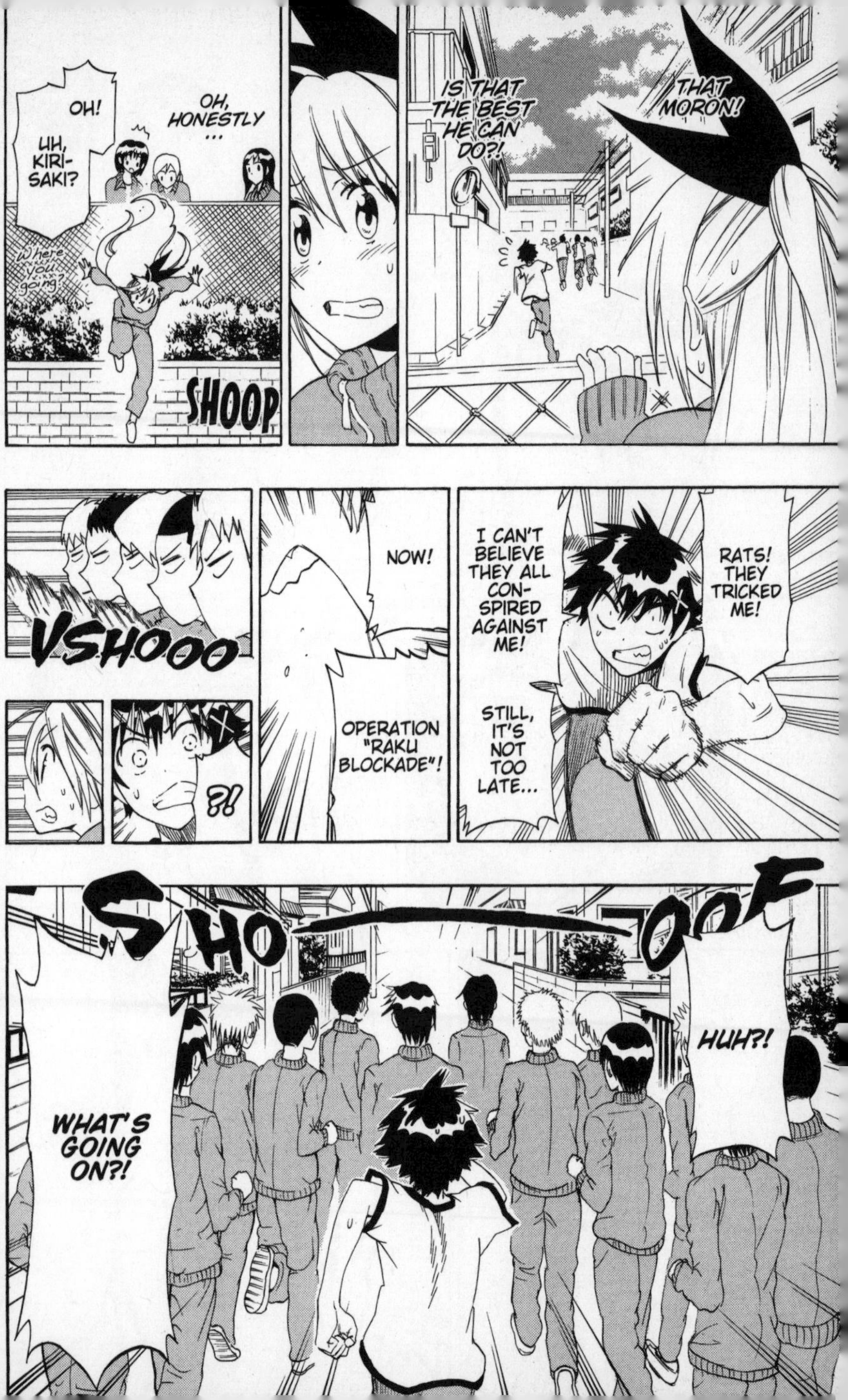
THAT MORON!
IS THAT THE BEST HE CAN DO?!
OH, HONESTLY ...
OH!
UH, KIRI-SAKI?
Where you going?
SHOOP
RATS! THEY TRICKED ME!
I CAN'T BELIEVE THEY ALL CON-SPIRED AGAINST ME!
STILL, IT'S NOT TOO LATE...
NOW!
OPERATION "RAKU BLOCKADE"!
VSHOOO
?!
SHO———OOF
HUH?!
WHAT'S GOING ON?!

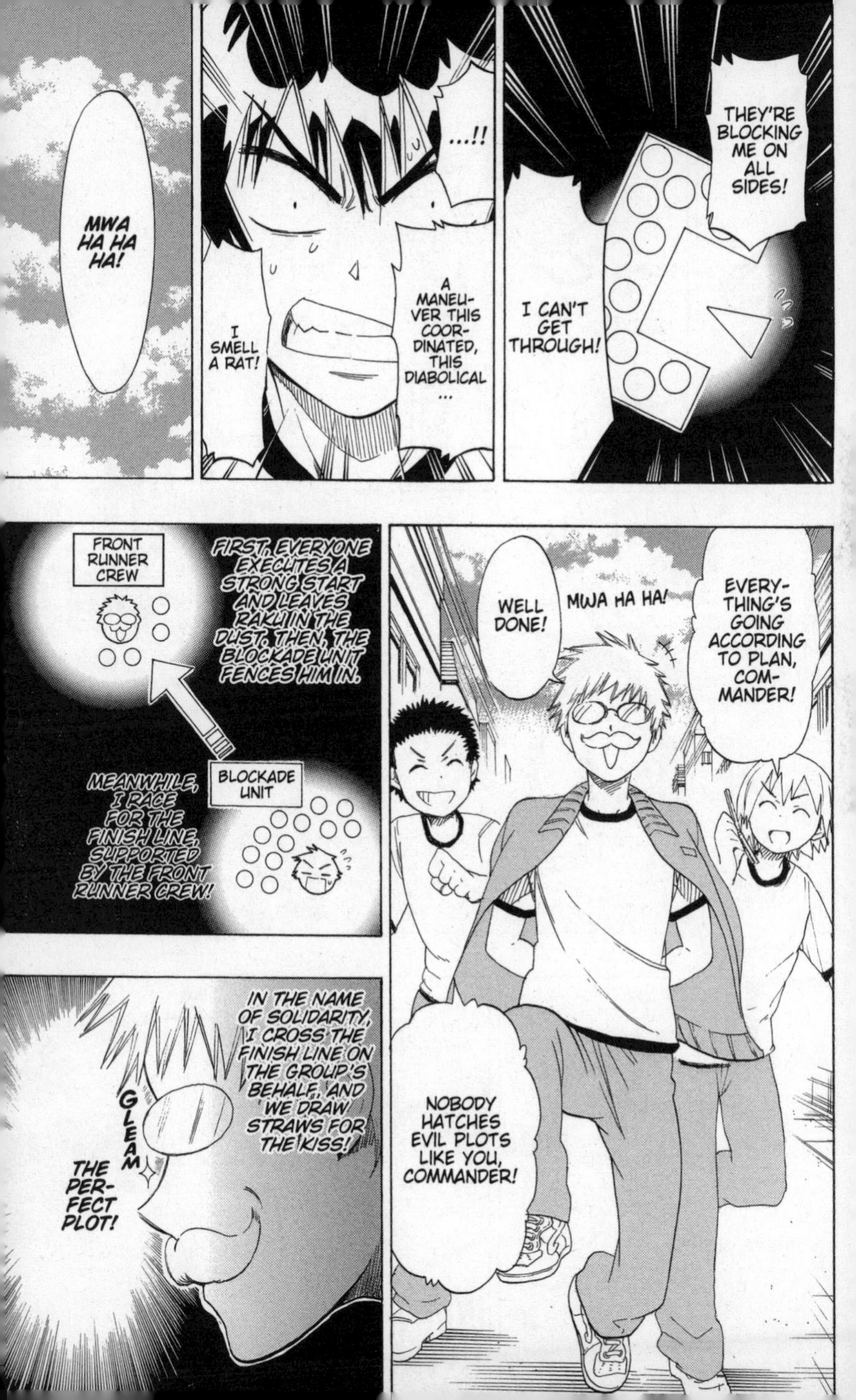
THEY'RE BLOCKING ME ON ALL SIDES!
I CAN'T GET THROUGH!
...!!
A MANEUVER THIS COORDINATED, THIS DIABOLICAL...
I SMELL A RAT!
MWA HA HA HA!
EVERYTHING'S GOING ACCORDING TO PLAN, COMMANDER!
MWA HA HA!
WELL DONE!
NOBODY HATCHES EVIL PLOTS LIKE YOU, COMMANDER!
FIRST, EVERYONE EXECUTES A STRONG START AND LEAVES RAKU IN THE DUST. THEN, THE BLOCKADE UNIT FENCES HIM IN.
FRONT RUNNER CREW
BLOCKADE UNIT
MEANWHILE, I RACE FOR THE FINISH LINE, SUPPORTED BY THE FRONT RUNNER CREW!
IN THE NAME OF SOLIDARITY, I CROSS THE FINISH LINE ON THE GROUP'S BEHALF, AND WE DRAW STRAWS FOR THE KISS!
GLEAM
THE PERFECT PLOT!

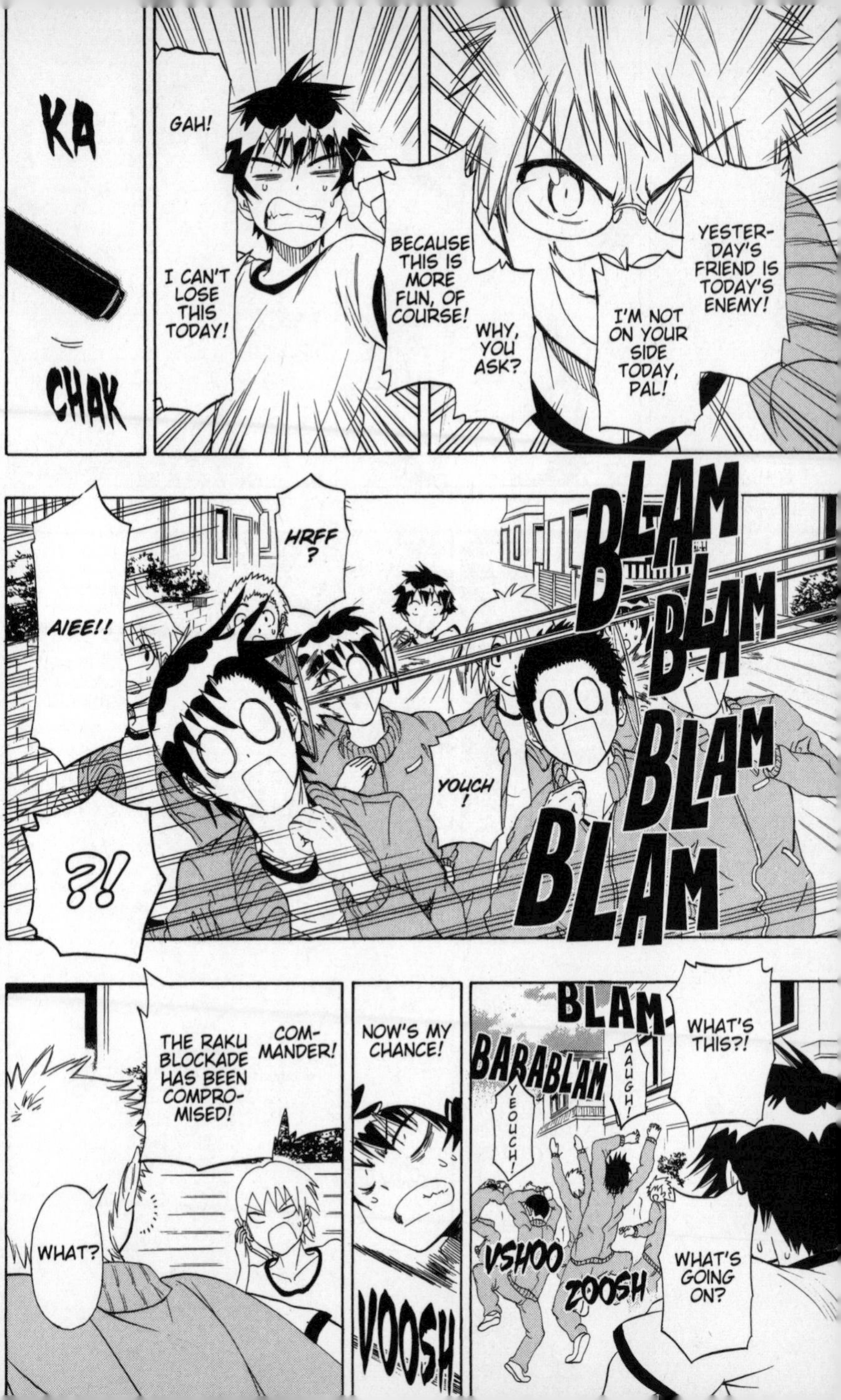
YESTER-DAY'S FRIEND IS TODAY'S ENEMY!
I'M NOT ON YOUR SIDE TODAY, PAL!
WHY, YOU ASK?
BECAUSE THIS IS MORE FUN, OF COURSE!
GAH!
I CAN'T LOSE THIS TODAY!
KA
CHAK
BLAM
BLAM
BLAM
BLAM
HRFF?
YOUCH!
AIEE!!
?!
WHAT'S THIS?!
BLAM-
BABABLAM
AAUGH!
YEOUCH!
VSHOO
ZOOSH
WHAT'S GOING ON?
NOW'S MY CHANCE!
VOOSH
COM-MANDER!
THE RAKU BLOCKADE HAS BEEN COMPROMISED!
WHAT?

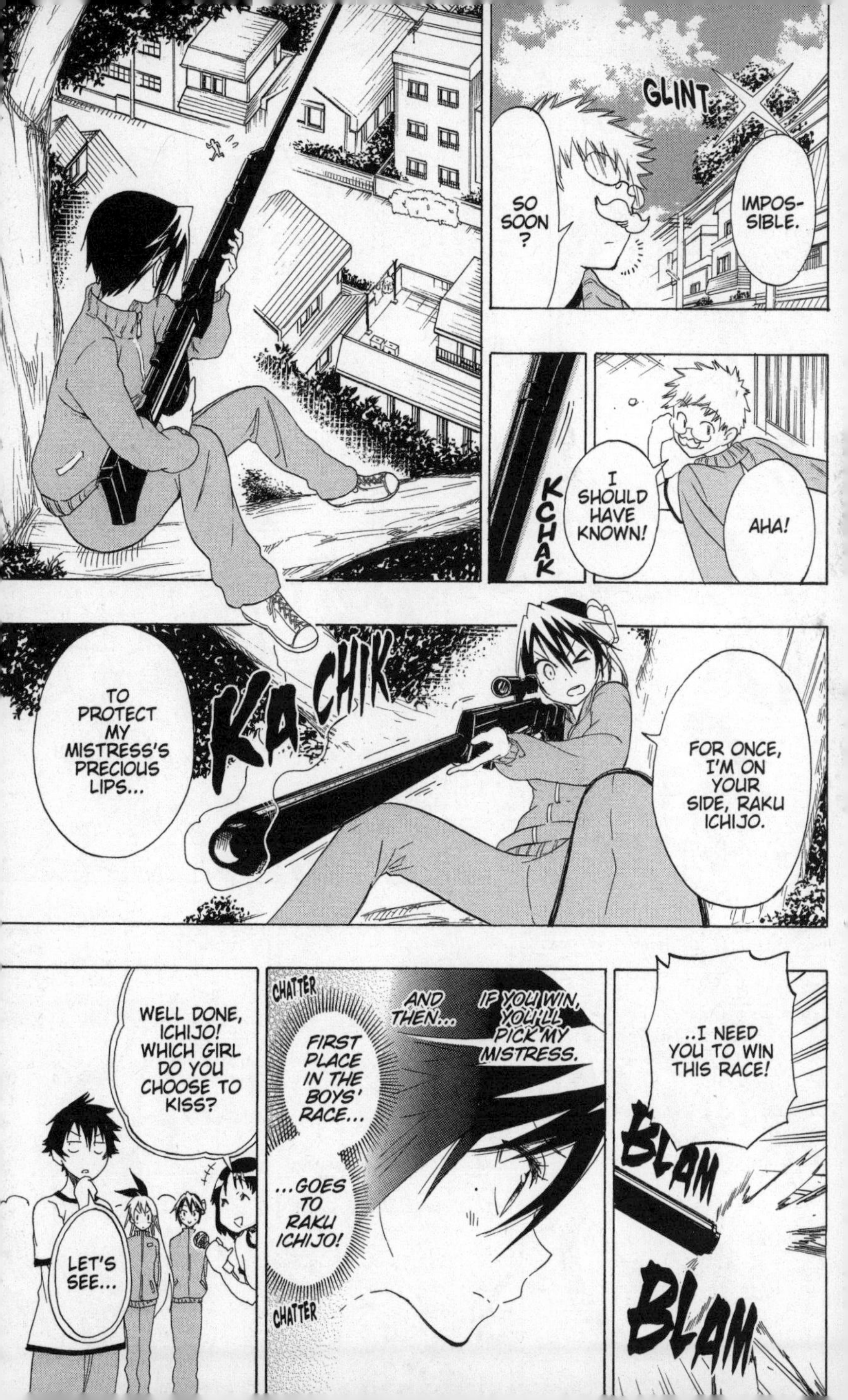
GLINT
IMPOSSIBLE.
SO SOON?
AHA!
I SHOULD HAVE KNOWN!
KCHAK
FOR ONCE, I'M ON YOUR SIDE, RAKU ICHIJO.
KA CHIK
TO PROTECT MY MISTRESS'S PRECIOUS LIPS...
..I NEED YOU TO WIN THIS RACE!
BLAM
BLAM
IF YOU WIN, YOU'LL PICK MY MISTRESS.
AND THEN...
CHATTER
FIRST PLACE IN THE BOYS' RACE...
...GOES TO RAKU ICHIJO!
CHATTER
WELL DONE, ICHIJO! WHICH GIRL DO YOU CHOOSE TO KISS?
LET'S SEE...

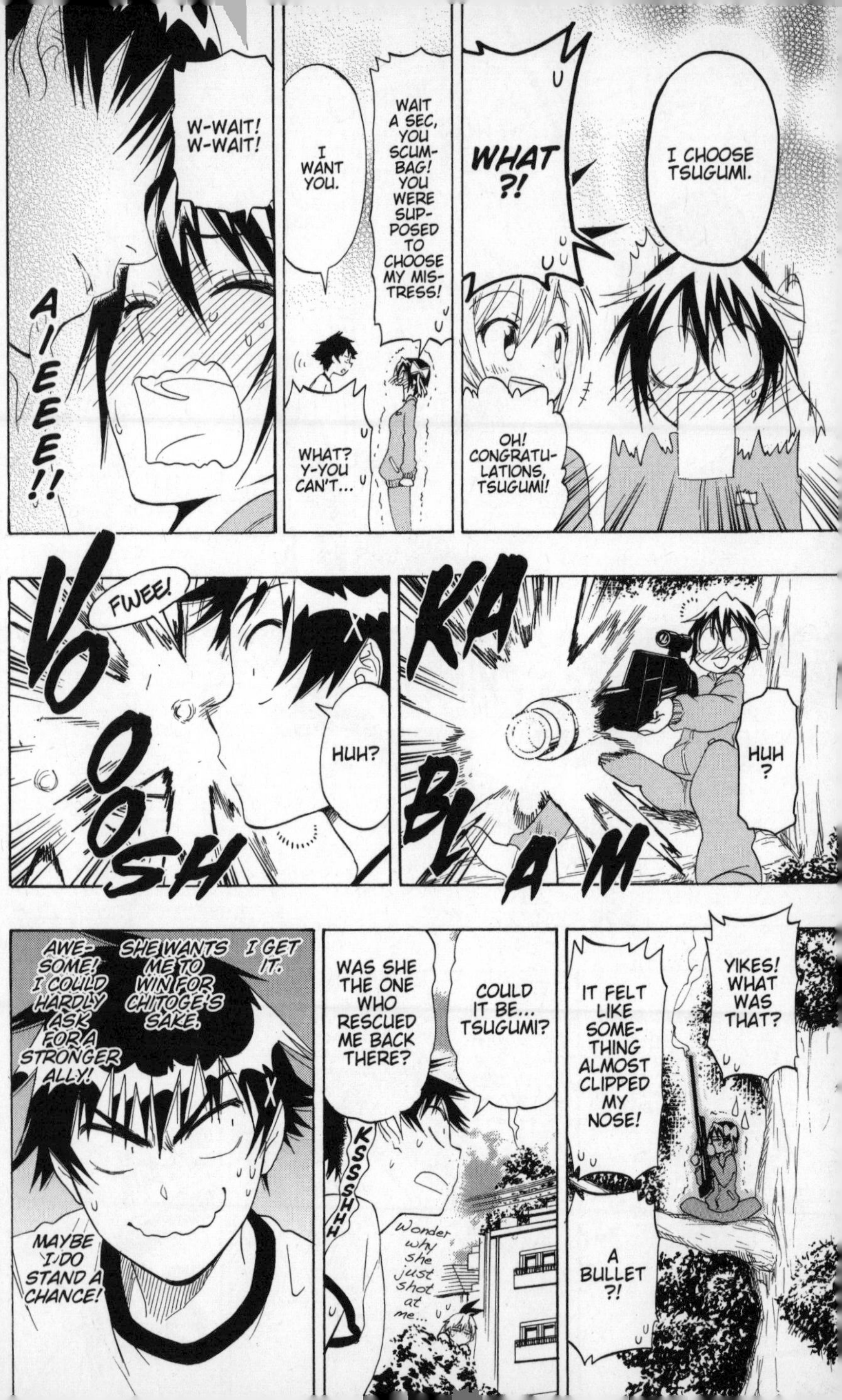
I CHOOSE TSUGUMI.
WHAT?!
OH! CONGRATULATIONS, TSUGUMI!
WAIT A SEC, YOU SCUMBAG! YOU WERE SUPPOSED TO CHOOSE MY MISTRESS!
I WANT YOU.
WHAT? Y-YOU CAN'T...
W-WAIT! W-WAIT!
AIEEEE!!
KA BLAM
HUH?
VOOOSH
FWEE!
HUH?
YIKES! WHAT WAS THAT?
IT FELT LIKE SOMETHING ALMOST CLIPPED MY NOSE!
A BULLET?!
COULD IT BE... TSUGUMI?
WAS SHE THE ONE WHO RESCUED ME BACK THERE?
KSSSHHH
Wonder why she just shot at me...
I GET IT.
SHE WANTS ME TO WIN FOR CHITOGE'S SAKE.
AWESOME! I COULD HARDLY ASK FOR A STRONGER ALLY!
MAYBE I DO STAND A CHANCE!

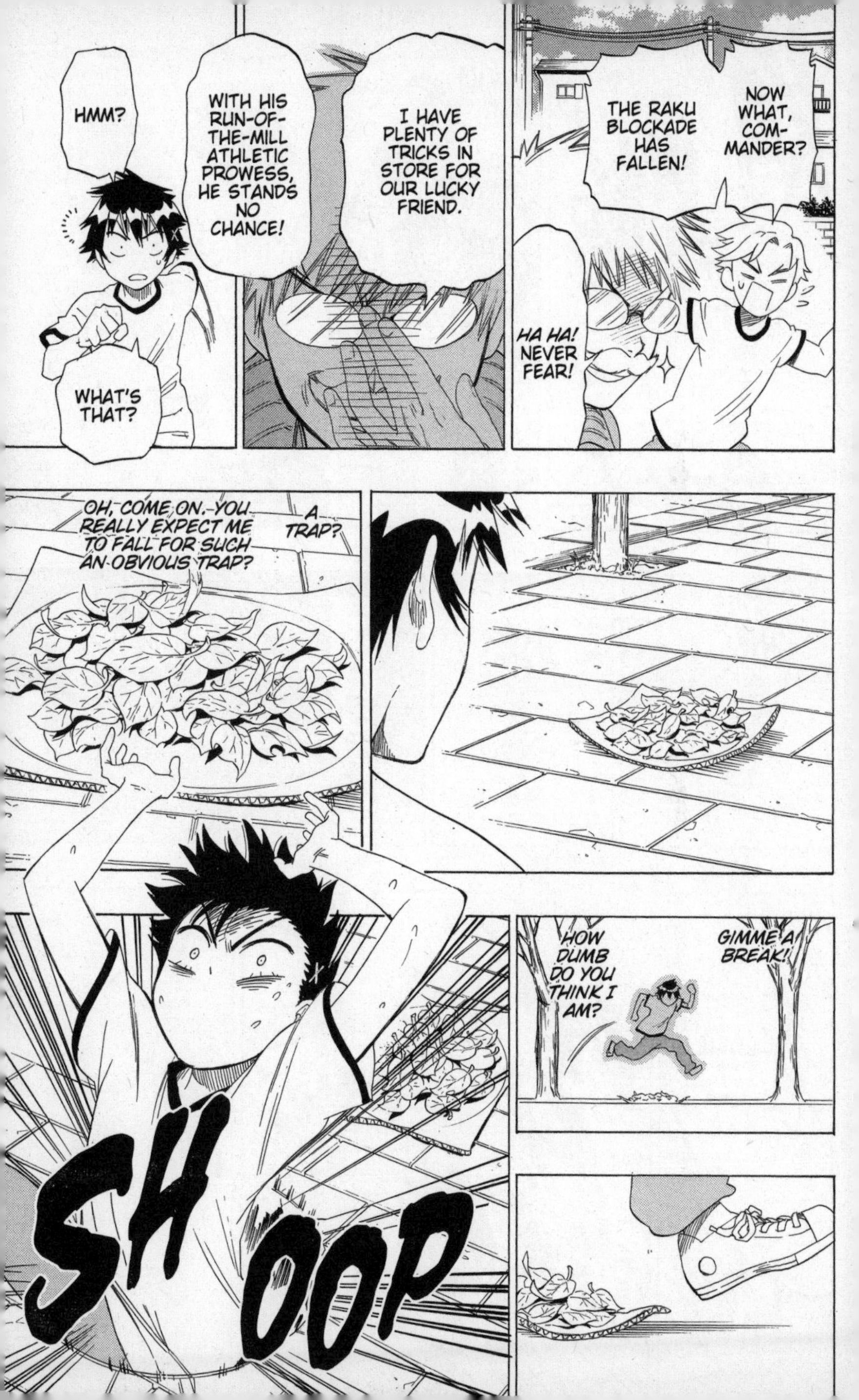
NOW WHAT, COM-MANDER?
THE RAKU BLOCKADE HAS FALLEN!
HA HA! NEVER FEAR!
I HAVE PLENTY OF TRICKS IN STORE FOR OUR LUCKY FRIEND.
WITH HIS RUN-OF-THE-MILL ATHLETIC PROWESS, HE STANDS NO CHANCE!
HMM?
WHAT'S THAT?
A TRAP?
OH, COME ON. YOU REALLY EXPECT ME TO FALL FOR SUCH AN OBVIOUS TRAP?
GIMME A BREAK!
HOW DUMB DO YOU THINK I AM?
SHOOP

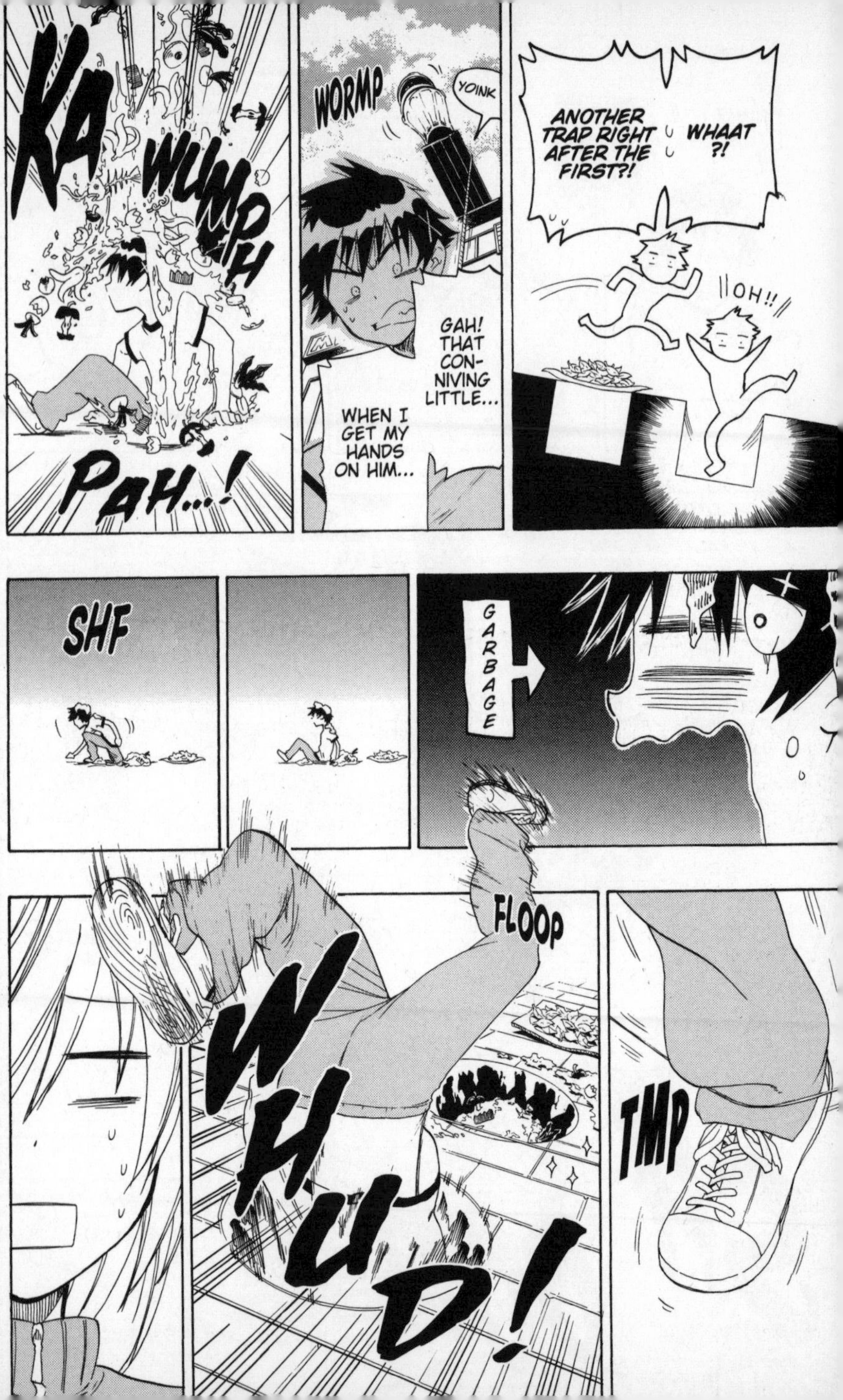
WHAAT?!
ANOTHER TRAP RIGHT AFTER THE FIRST?!
OH!!
YOINK
WORMP
GAH! THAT CON-NIVING LITTLE...
WHEN I GET MY HANDS ON HIM...
KA WUMPH
PAH...!
GARBAGE
SHF
TMP
FLOOP
WHUD!

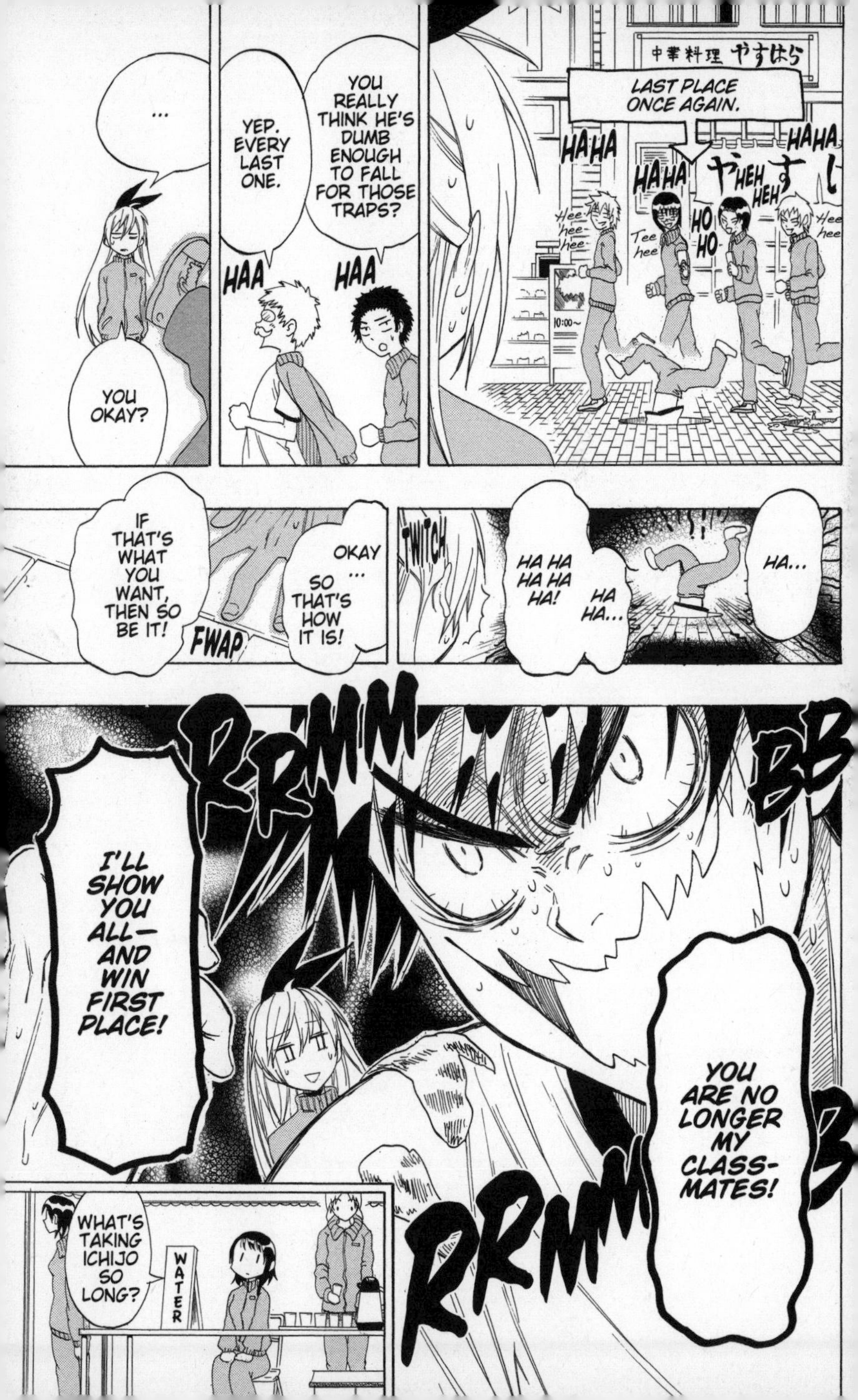
中華料理 やすはら
LAST PLACE ONCE AGAIN.
HAHA
HAHA
HEH HEH
HO HO
Hee hee
Tee hee
HAHA
Hee hee-hee
HAHA
YOU REALLY THINK HE'S DUMB ENOUGH TO FALL FOR THOSE TRAPS?
HAA
YEP. EVERY LAST ONE.
HAA
...
YOU OKAY?
HA...
HA HA HA HA HA!
HA HA...
TWITCH
OKAY... SO THAT'S HOW IT IS!
FWAP
IF THAT'S WHAT YOU WANT, THEN SO BE IT!
RRMMBB
YOU ARE NO LONGER MY CLASSMATES!
I'LL SHOW YOU ALL—AND WIN FIRST PLACE!
RRMMBB
WATER
WHAT'S TAKING ICHIJO SO LONG?

Tachibana's Legendary
Vitality Tonic

☆ Recipe ☆

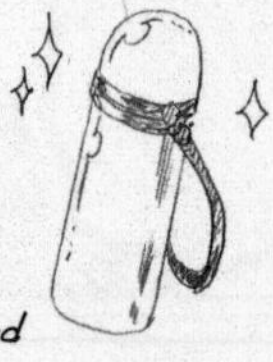

- Lemon
- Honey
- Garlic
- Sweet Potato
- Blackened Lizard
- Surströmming
- Trinidad Scorpion Butch T Pepper

Etc...

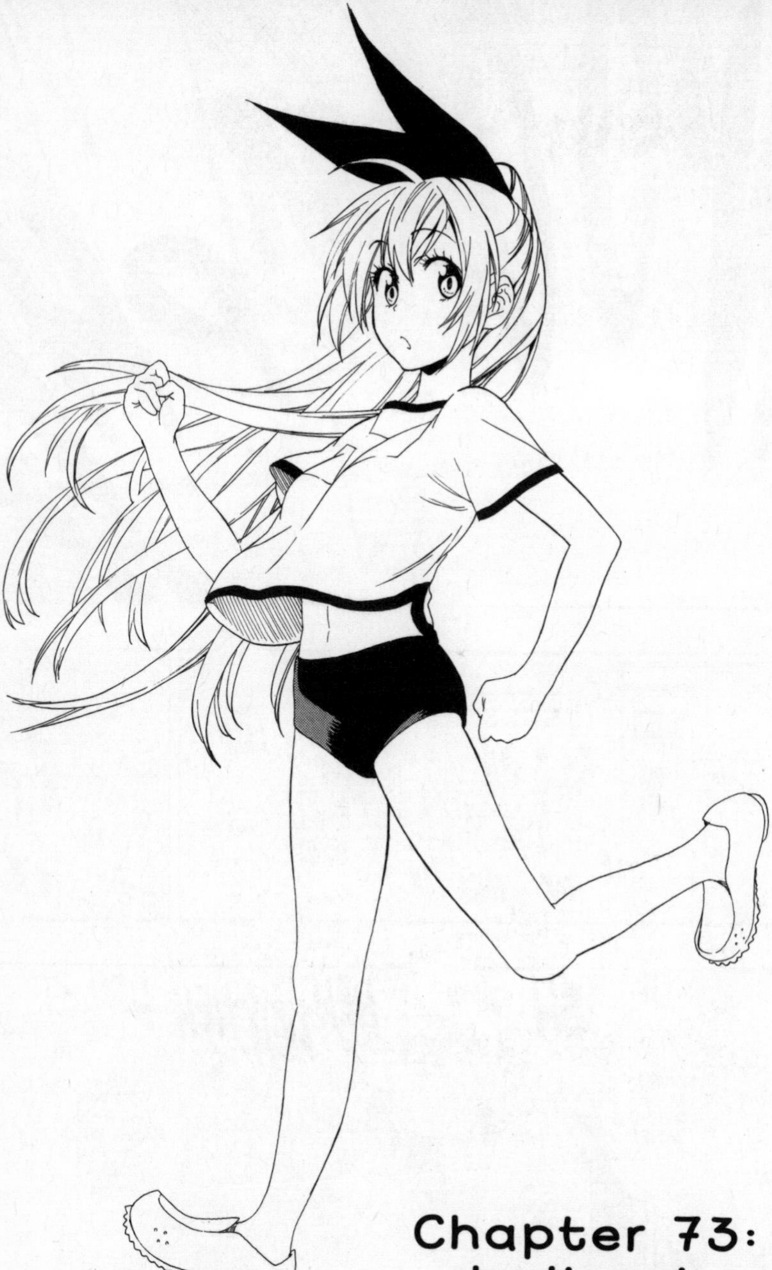

Chapter 73: Indirect

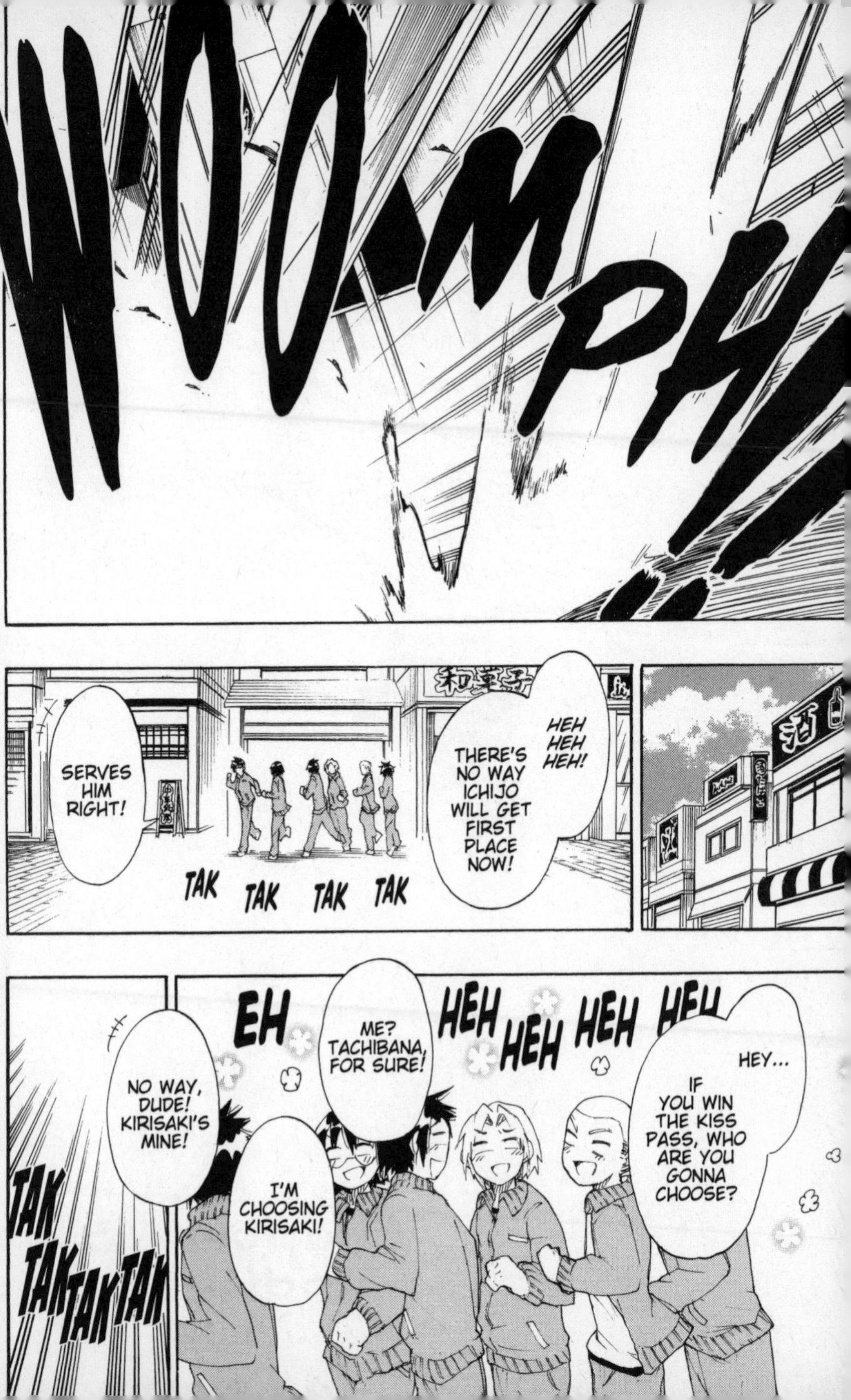
WOOMPH!!
HEH HEH HEH!
THERE'S NO WAY ICHIJO WILL GET FIRST PLACE NOW!
SERVES HIM RIGHT!
TAK TAK TAK TAK
HEY... IF YOU WIN THE KISS PASS, WHO ARE YOU GONNA CHOOSE?
HEH HEH HEH
ME? TACHIBANA, FOR SURE!
EH
I'M CHOOSING KIRISAKI!
NO WAY, DUDE! KIRISAKI'S MINE!
TAK TAK TAK TAK

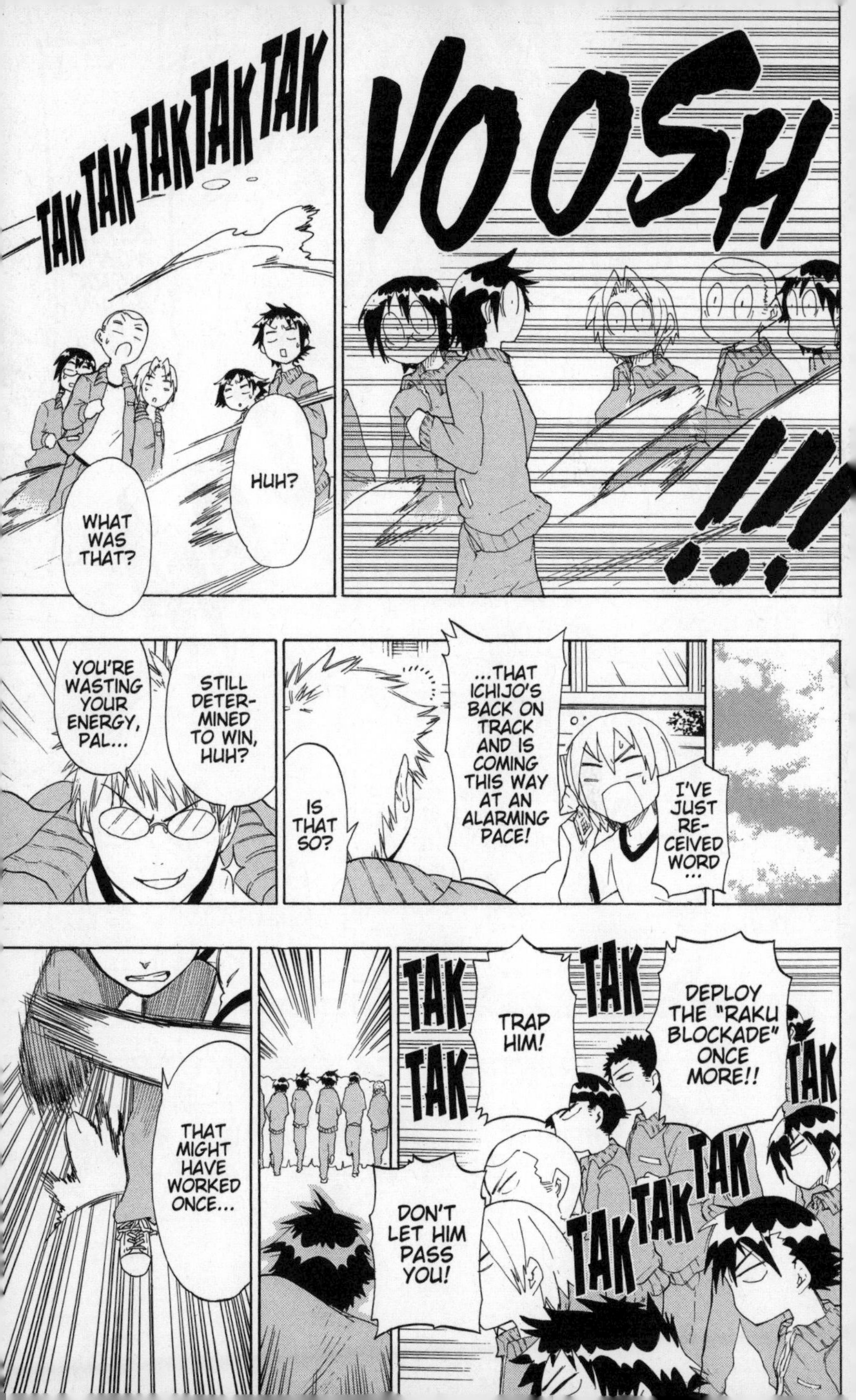
VOOSH
!!!
TAK TAK TAK TAK TAK
HUH?
WHAT WAS THAT?
I'VE JUST RE-CEIVED WORD...
...THAT ICHIJO'S BACK ON TRACK AND IS COMING THIS WAY AT AN ALARMING PACE!
IS THAT SO?
STILL DETER-MINED TO WIN, HUH?
YOU'RE WASTING YOUR ENERGY, PAL...
DEPLOY THE "RAKU BLOCKADE" ONCE MORE!!
TAK
TAK
TRAP HIM!
TAK TAK
TAK TAK TAK
DON'T LET HIM PASS YOU!
THAT MIGHT HAVE WORKED ONCE...

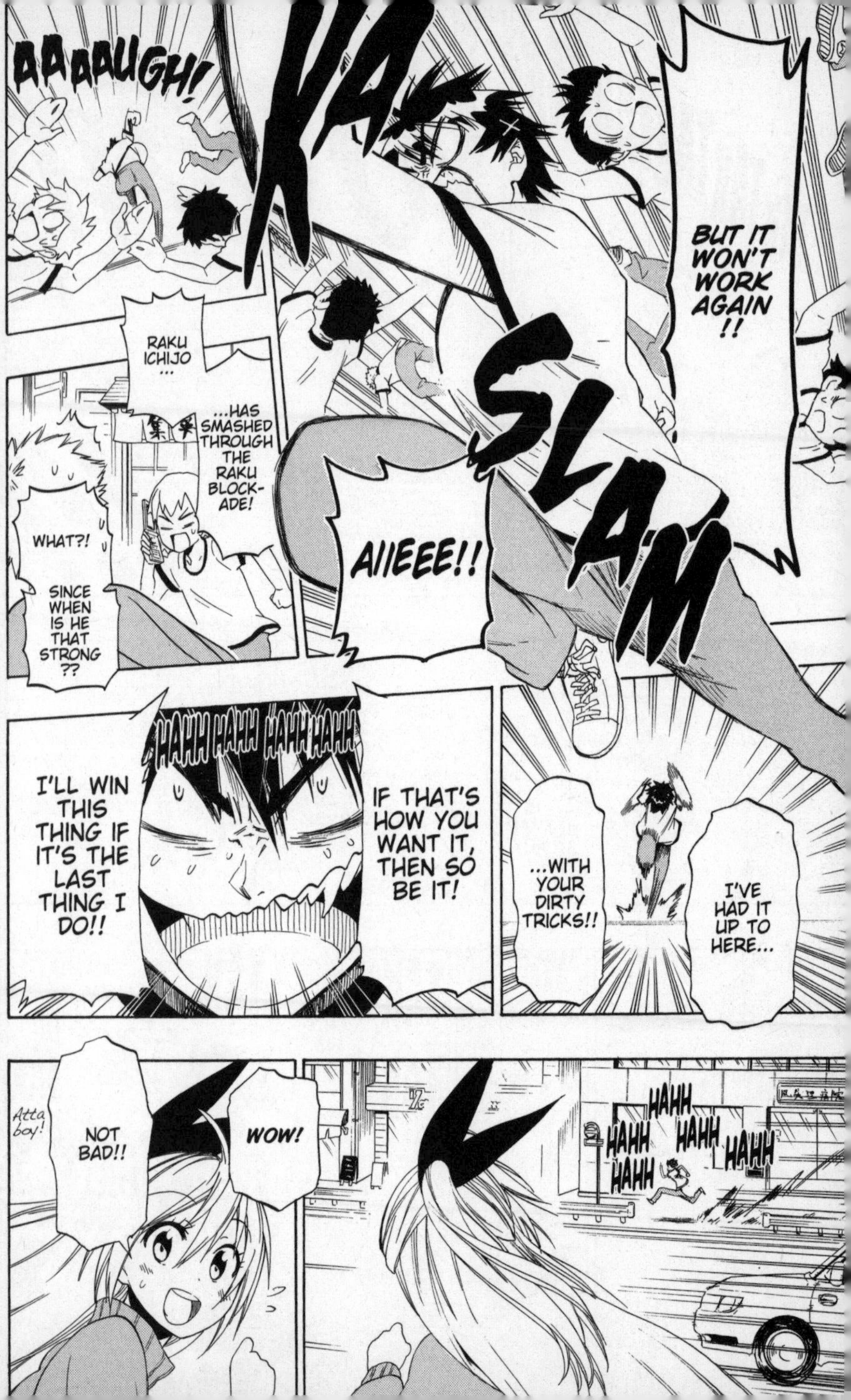
BUT IT WON'T WORK AGAIN!!
WA
SLAM
AIIEEE!!
AAAAUGH!
RAKU ICHIJO...
...HAS SMASHED THROUGH THE RAKU BLOCKADE!
WHAT?!
SINCE WHEN IS HE THAT STRONG??
I'VE HAD IT UP TO HERE...
...WITH YOUR DIRTY TRICKS!!
HAHH HAHH HAHH HAHH
IF THAT'S HOW YOU WANT IT, THEN SO BE IT!
I'LL WIN THIS THING IF IT'S THE LAST THING I DO!!
HAHH HAHH HAHH HAHH HAHH HAHH
WOW!
NOT BAD!!
Atta boy!

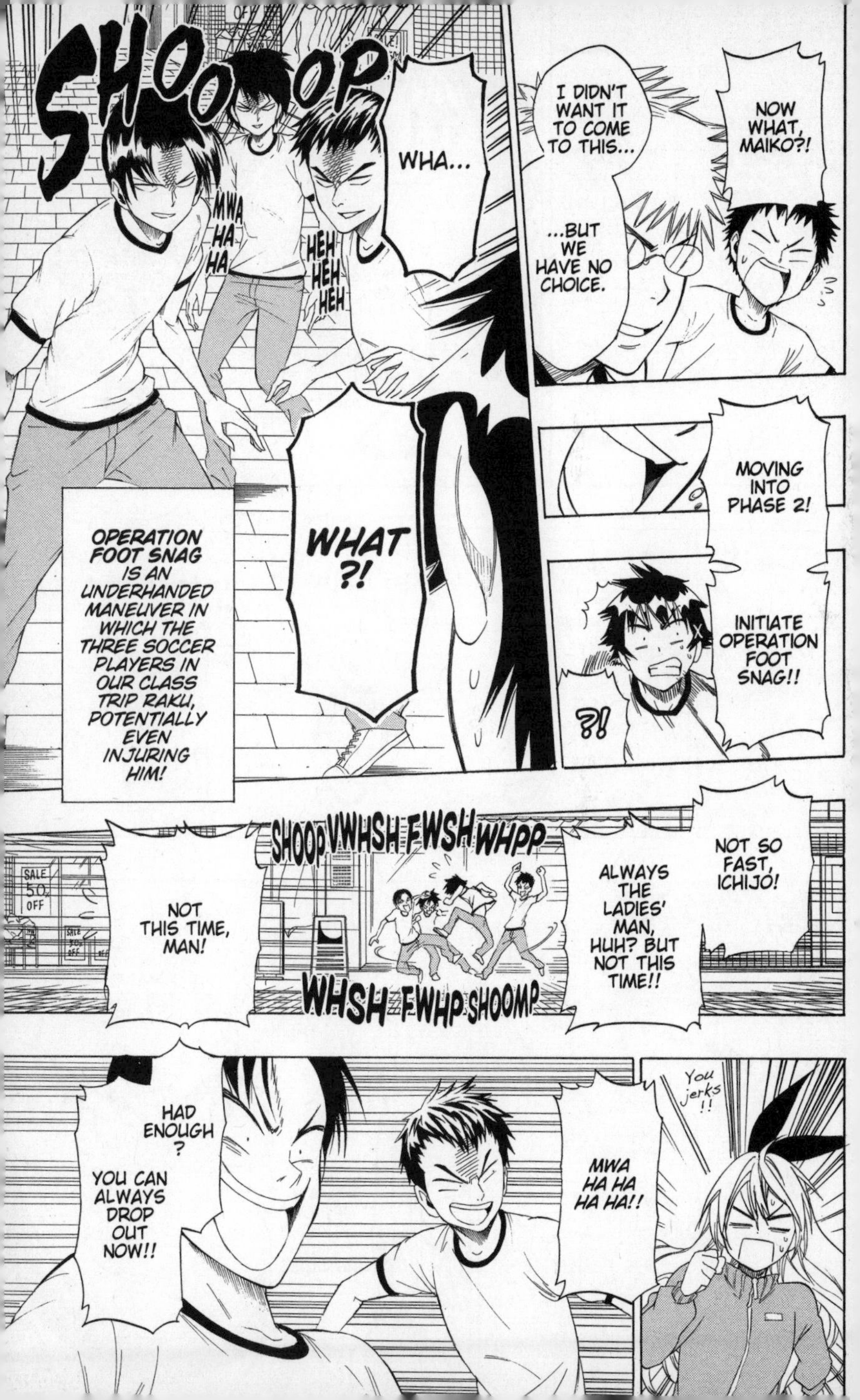
NOW WHAT, MAIKO?!
I DIDN'T WANT IT TO COME TO THIS...
...BUT WE HAVE NO CHOICE.
MOVING INTO PHASE 2!
INITIATE OPERATION FOOT SNAG!!
?!
WHA...
SHOOOOP
HEH HEH HEH
MWA HA HA
WHAT?!
OPERATION FOOT SNAG IS AN UNDERHANDED MANEUVER IN WHICH THE THREE SOCCER PLAYERS IN OUR CLASS TRIP RAKU, POTENTIALLY EVEN INJURING HIM!
NOT SO FAST, ICHIJO!
ALWAYS THE LADIES' MAN, HUH? BUT NOT THIS TIME!!
SHOOP VWHSH FWSH WHPP
WHSH FWHP SHOOMP
SALE 50% OFF
NOT THIS TIME, MAN!
You jerks!!
MWA HA HA HA HA!!
HAD ENOUGH?
YOU CAN ALWAYS DROP OUT NOW!!

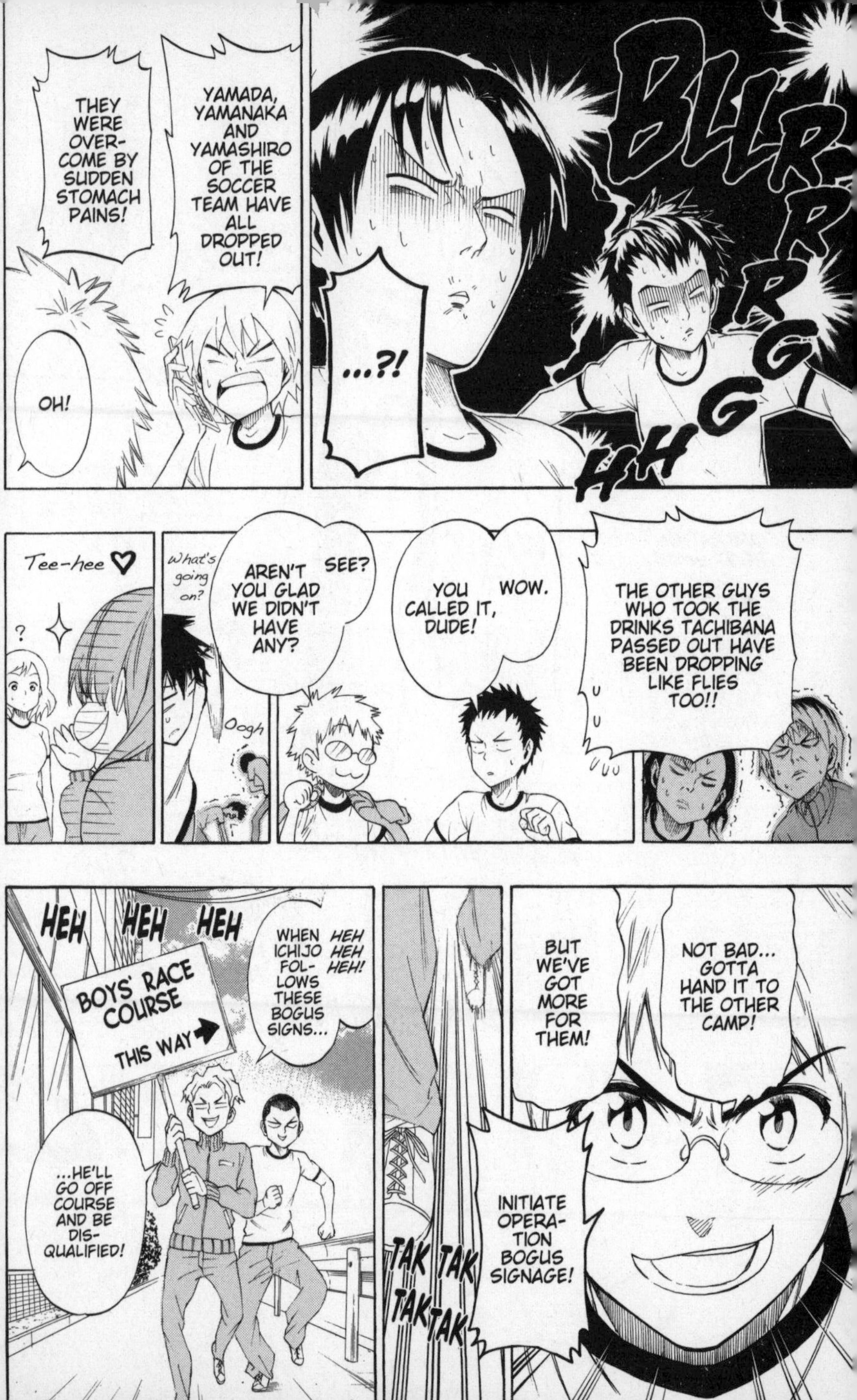
BLLRRRGGHH
...?!
YAMADA, YAMANAKA AND YAMASHIRO OF THE SOCCER TEAM HAVE ALL DROPPED OUT!
THEY WERE OVERCOME BY SUDDEN STOMACH PAINS!
OH!
THE OTHER GUYS WHO TOOK THE DRINKS TACHIBANA PASSED OUT HAVE BEEN DROPPING LIKE FLIES TOO!!
WOW.
YOU CALLED IT, DUDE!
SEE?
AREN'T YOU GLAD WE DIDN'T HAVE ANY?
What's going on?
Oogh
Tee-hee ♥
?
NOT BAD... GOTTA HAND IT TO THE OTHER CAMP!
BUT WE'VE GOT MORE FOR THEM!
INITIATE OPERA-TION BOGUS SIGNAGE!
TAK TAK TAK TAK
HEH HEH HEH
BOYS' RACE COURSE THIS WAY
WHEN ICHIJO FOL-LOWS THESE BOGUS SIGNS...
HEH HEH HEH!
...HE'LL GO OFF COURSE AND BE DIS-QUALIFIED!

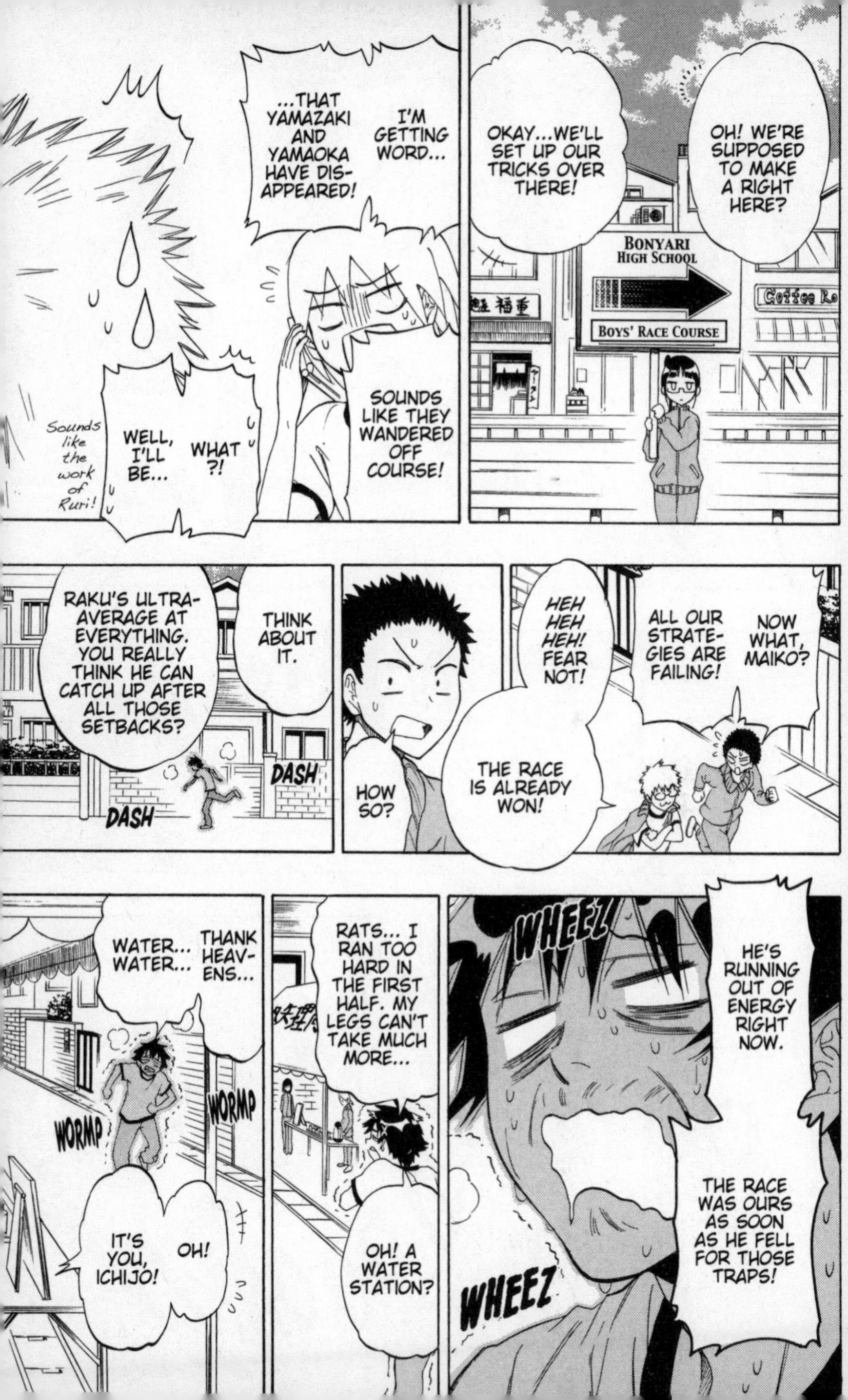

OH! WE'RE SUPPOSED TO MAKE A RIGHT HERE?
OKAY...WE'LL SET UP OUR TRICKS OVER THERE!
BONYARI HIGH SCHOOL
BOYS' RACE COURSE
I'M GETTING WORD...
...THAT YAMAZAKI AND YAMAOKA HAVE DIS-APPEARED!
SOUNDS LIKE THEY WANDERED OFF COURSE!
WHAT?!
WELL, I'LL BE...
Sounds like the work of Ruri!
NOW WHAT, MAIKO?
ALL OUR STRATE-GIES ARE FAILING!
HEH HEH HEH! FEAR NOT!
THE RACE IS ALREADY WON!
HOW SO?
THINK ABOUT IT.
RAKU'S ULTRA-AVERAGE AT EVERYTHING. YOU REALLY THINK HE CAN CATCH UP AFTER ALL THOSE SETBACKS?
DASH
DASH
HE'S RUNNING OUT OF ENERGY RIGHT NOW.
WHEEZ
WHEEZ
THE RACE WAS OURS AS SOON AS HE FELL FOR THOSE TRAPS!
RATS... I RAN TOO HARD IN THE FIRST HALF. MY LEGS CAN'T TAKE MUCH MORE...
OH! A WATER STATION?
THANK HEAV-ENS...
WATER... WATER...
WORMP
WORMP
OH!
IT'S YOU, ICHIJO!

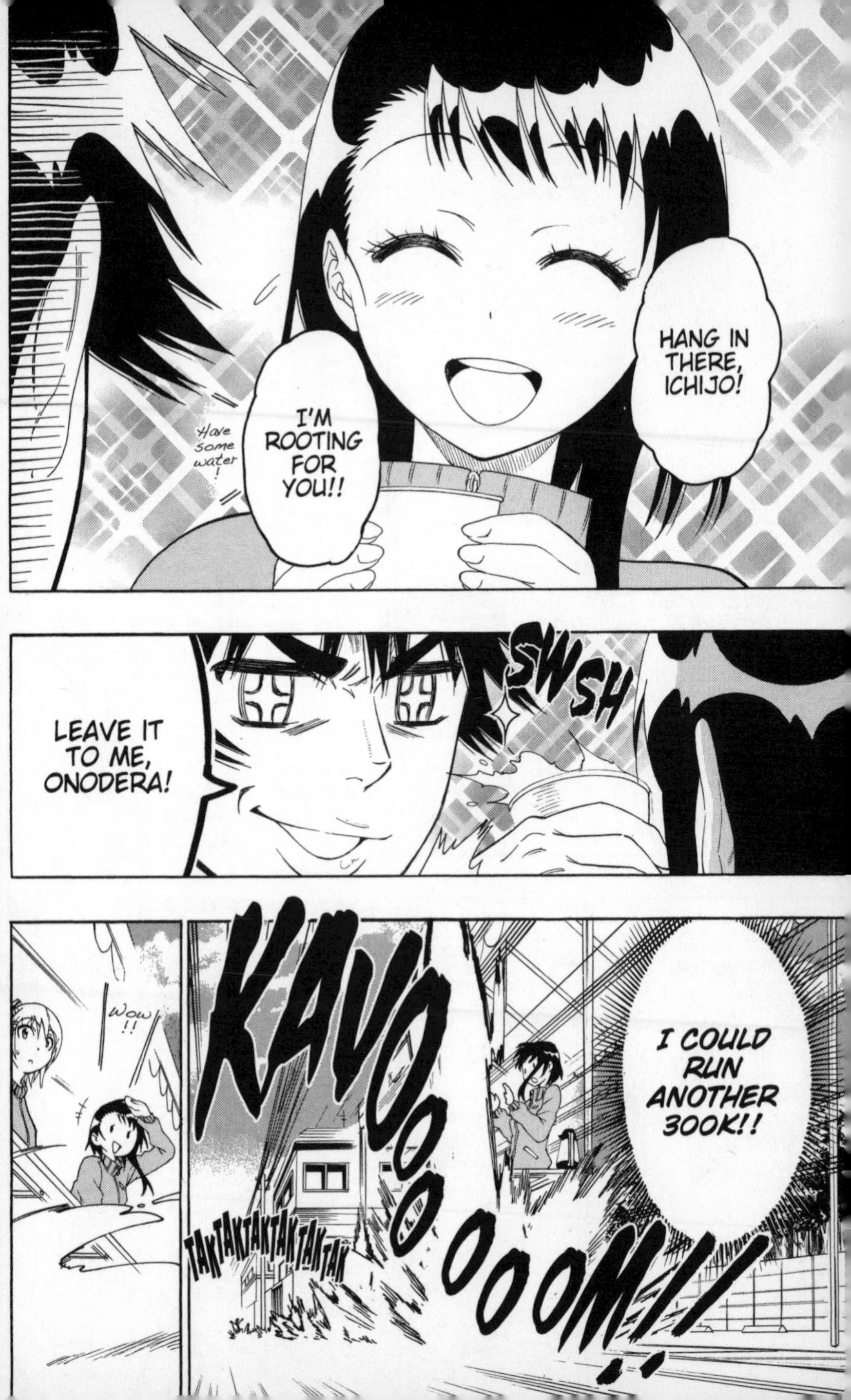
HANG IN THERE, ICHIJO!
I'M ROOTING FOR YOU!!
Have some water!
SWSH
LEAVE IT TO ME, ONODERA!
I COULD RUN ANOTHER 300K!!
KAVOOOOOOOM!!
TAKTAKTAKTAKTAKTAK
Wow!!

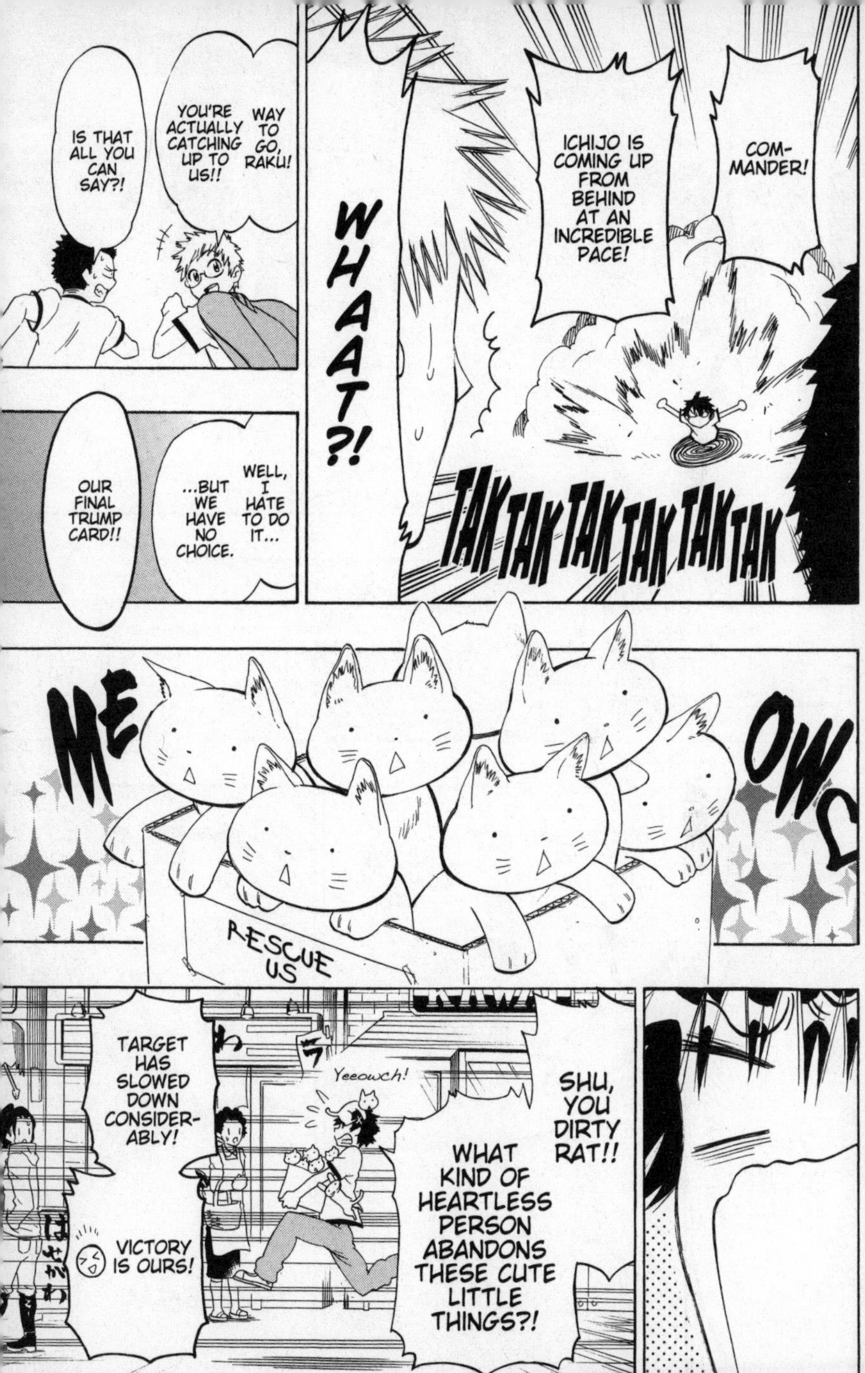
COM-MANDER!
ICHIJO IS COMING UP FROM BEHIND AT AN INCREDIBLE PACE!
WHAAT?!
TAK TAK TAK TAK TAK TAK
WAY TO GO, RAKU!
YOU'RE ACTUALLY CATCHING UP TO US!!
IS THAT ALL YOU CAN SAY?!
WELL, I HATE TO DO IT...
...BUT WE HAVE NO CHOICE.
OUR FINAL TRUMP CARD!!
ME
OW
RESCUE US
SHU, YOU DIRTY RAT!!
WHAT KIND OF HEARTLESS PERSON ABANDONS THESE CUTE LITTLE THINGS?!
Yeeowch!
TARGET HAS SLOWED DOWN CONSIDERABLY!
VICTORY IS OURS!
はせがわ

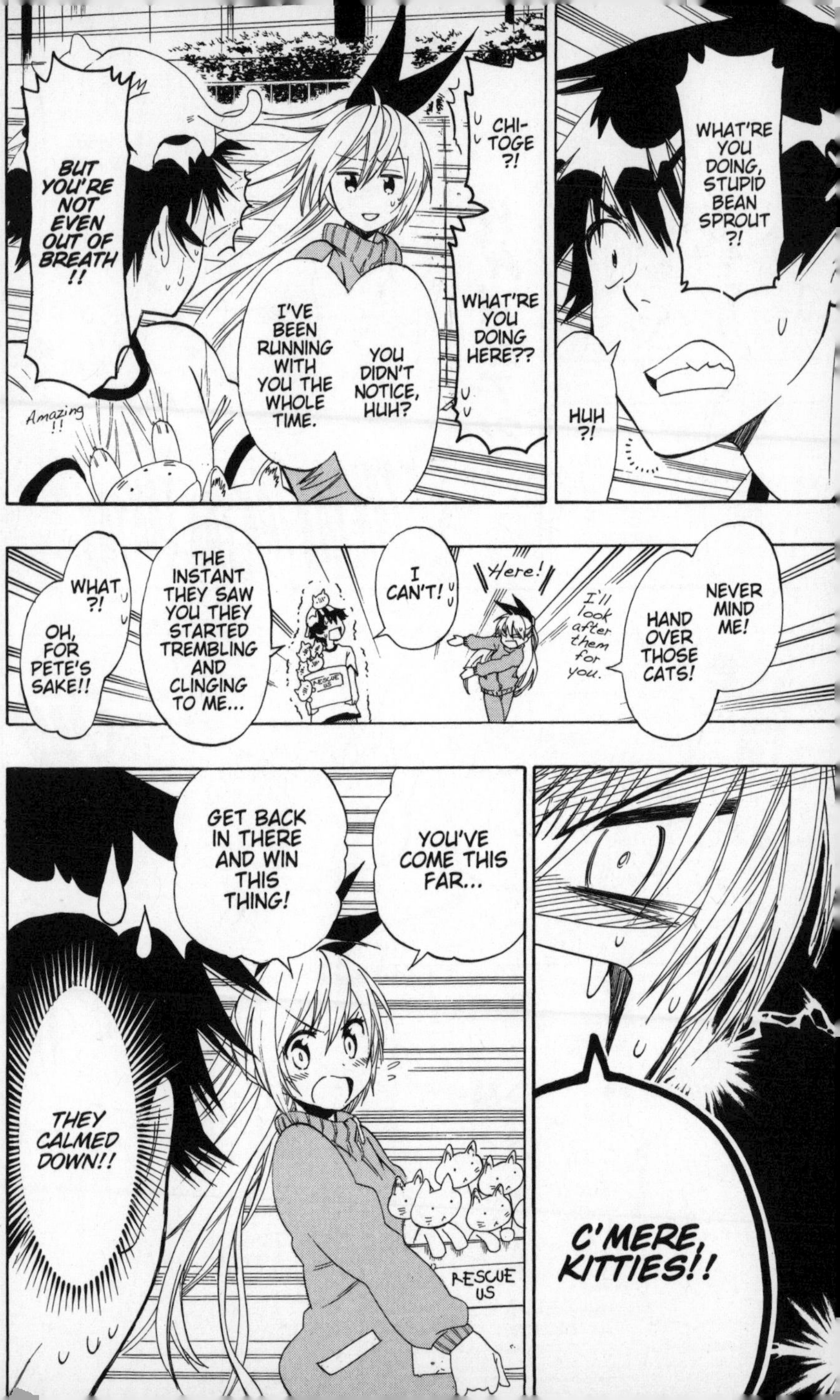
WHAT'RE YOU DOING, STUPID BEAN SPROUT?!
HUH?!
CHI-TOGE?!
WHAT'RE YOU DOING HERE??
YOU DIDN'T NOTICE, HUH?
I'VE BEEN RUNNING WITH YOU THE WHOLE TIME.
BUT YOU'RE NOT EVEN OUT OF BREATH!!
Amazing!!
NEVER MIND ME!
HAND OVER THOSE CATS!
I'll look after them for you.
Here!
I CAN'T!
THE INSTANT THEY SAW YOU THEY STARTED TREMBLING AND CLINGING TO ME...
RESCUE US
WHAT?!
OH, FOR PETE'S SAKE!!
C'MERE, KITTIES!!
YOU'VE COME THIS FAR...
GET BACK IN THERE AND WIN THIS THING!
THEY CALMED DOWN!!
RESCUE US

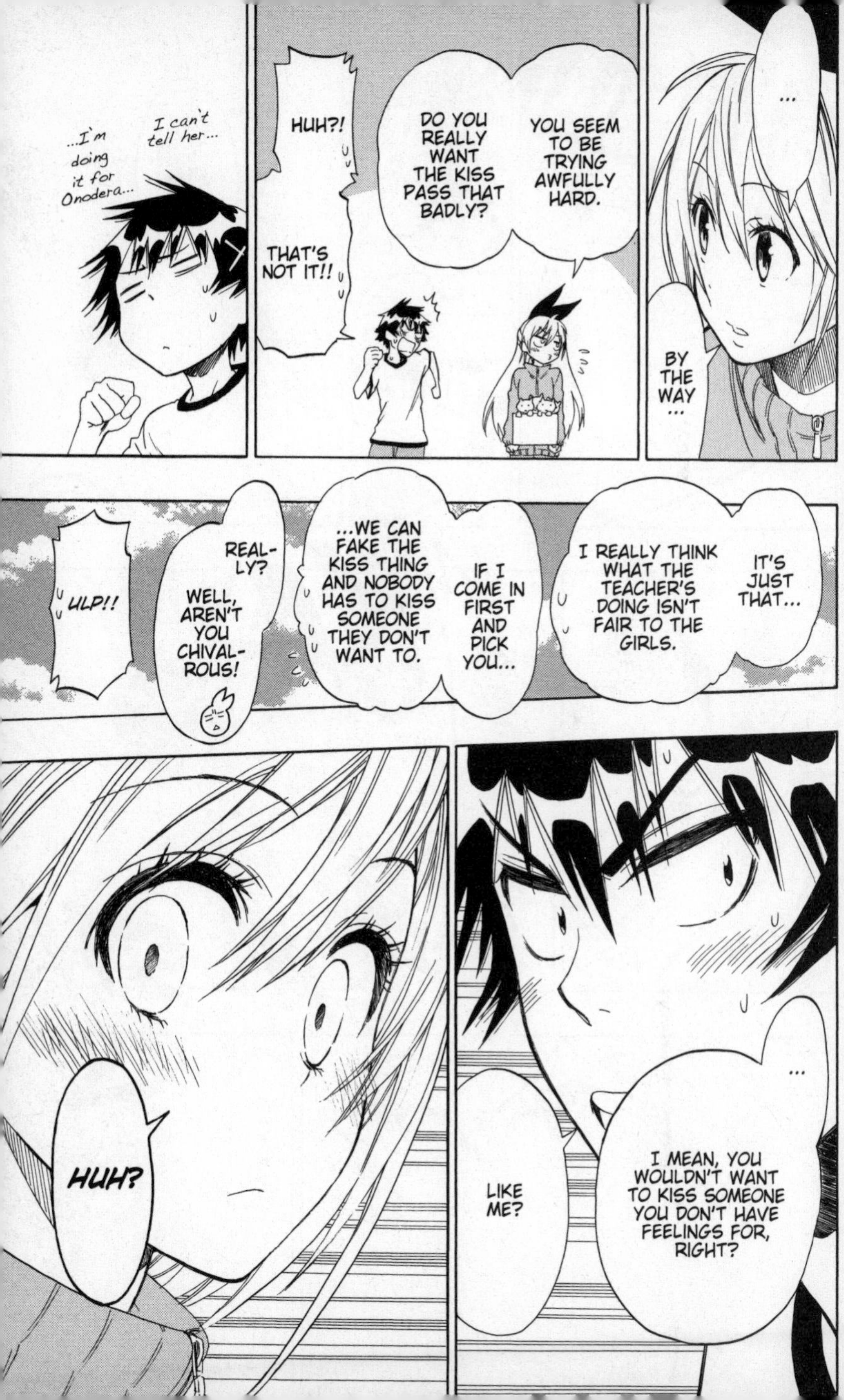
...
BY THE WAY...
YOU SEEM TO BE TRYING AWFULLY HARD.
DO YOU REALLY WANT THE KISS PASS THAT BADLY?
HUH?!
THAT'S NOT IT!!
I can't tell her...
...I'm doing it for Onodera...
IT'S JUST THAT...
I REALLY THINK WHAT THE TEACHER'S DOING ISN'T FAIR TO THE GIRLS.
IF I COME IN FIRST AND PICK YOU...
...WE CAN FAKE THE KISS THING AND NOBODY HAS TO KISS SOMEONE THEY DON'T WANT TO.
REAL-LY?
WELL, AREN'T YOU CHIVAL-ROUS!
ULP!!
...
I MEAN, YOU WOULDN'T WANT TO KISS SOMEONE YOU DON'T HAVE FEELINGS FOR, RIGHT?
LIKE ME?
HUH?

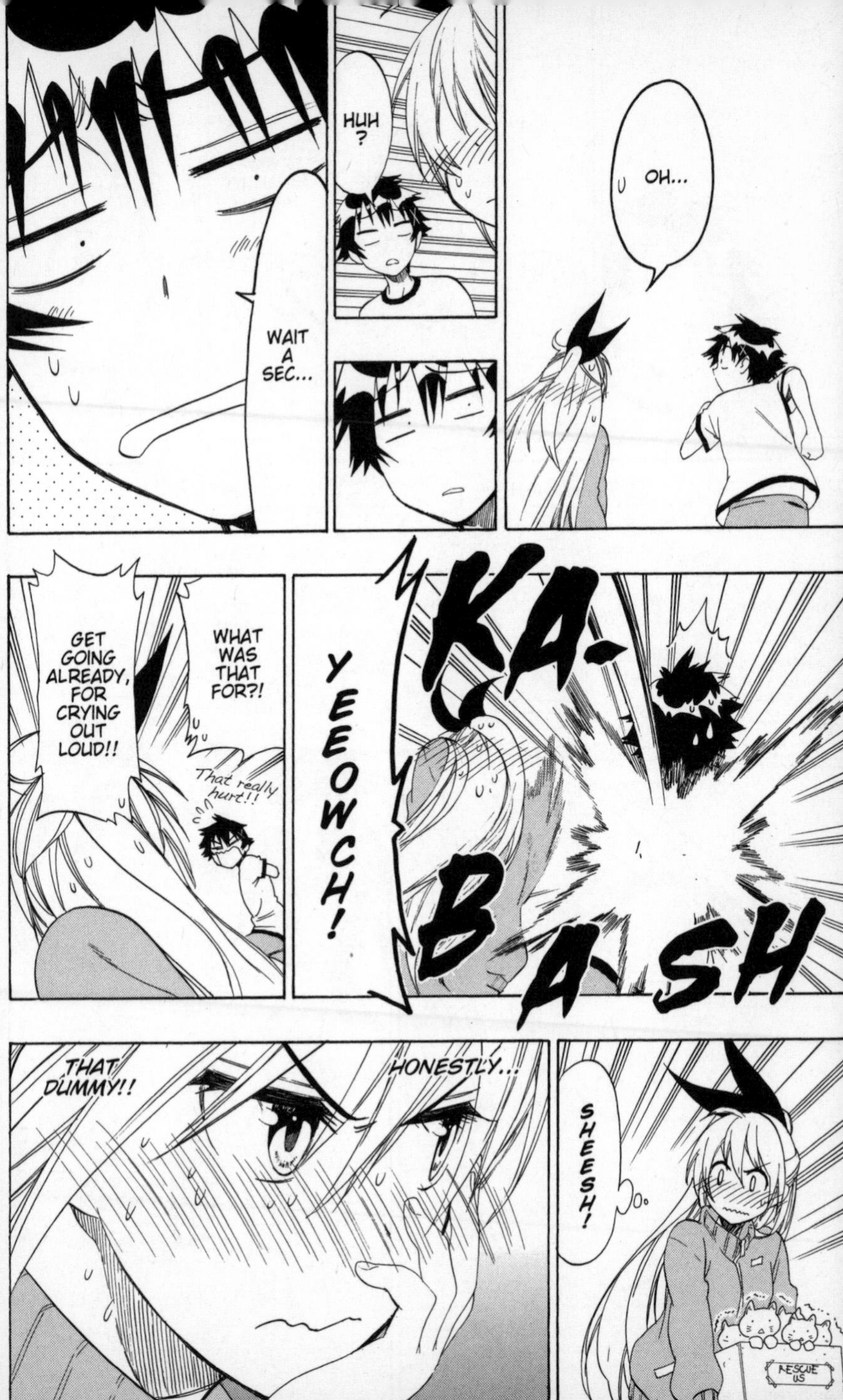
OH...
HUH ?
WAIT A SEC...
KA-BASH
YEEOWCH!
WHAT WAS THAT FOR?!
GET GOING ALREADY, FOR CRYING OUT LOUD!!
That really hurt!!
SHEESH!
RESCUE US
HONESTLY...
THAT DUMMY!!

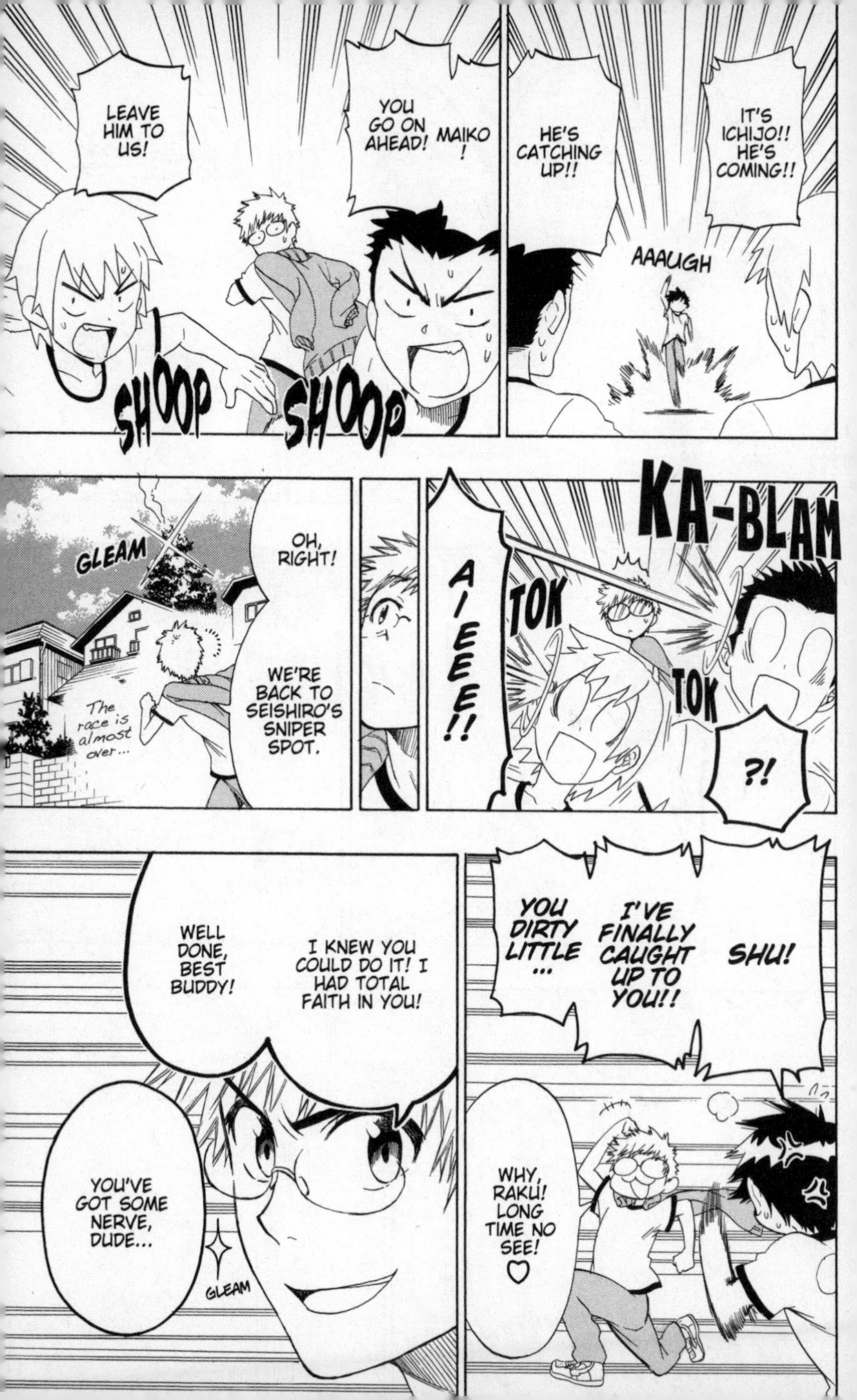
IT'S ICHIJO!! HE'S COMING!!
HE'S CATCHING UP!!
AAAUGH
MAIKO!
YOU GO ON AHEAD!
LEAVE HIM TO US!
SHOOP
SHOOP
KA-BLAM
AIEEE!!
TOK
TOK
?!
OH, RIGHT!
WE'RE BACK TO SEISHIRO'S SNIPER SPOT.
GLEAM
The race is almost over...
SHU!
I'VE FINALLY CAUGHT UP TO YOU!!
YOU DIRTY LITTLE...
WHY, RAKU! LONG TIME NO SEE! ♡
I KNEW YOU COULD DO IT! I HAD TOTAL FAITH IN YOU!
WELL DONE, BEST BUDDY!
YOU'VE GOT SOME NERVE, DUDE...
GLEAM

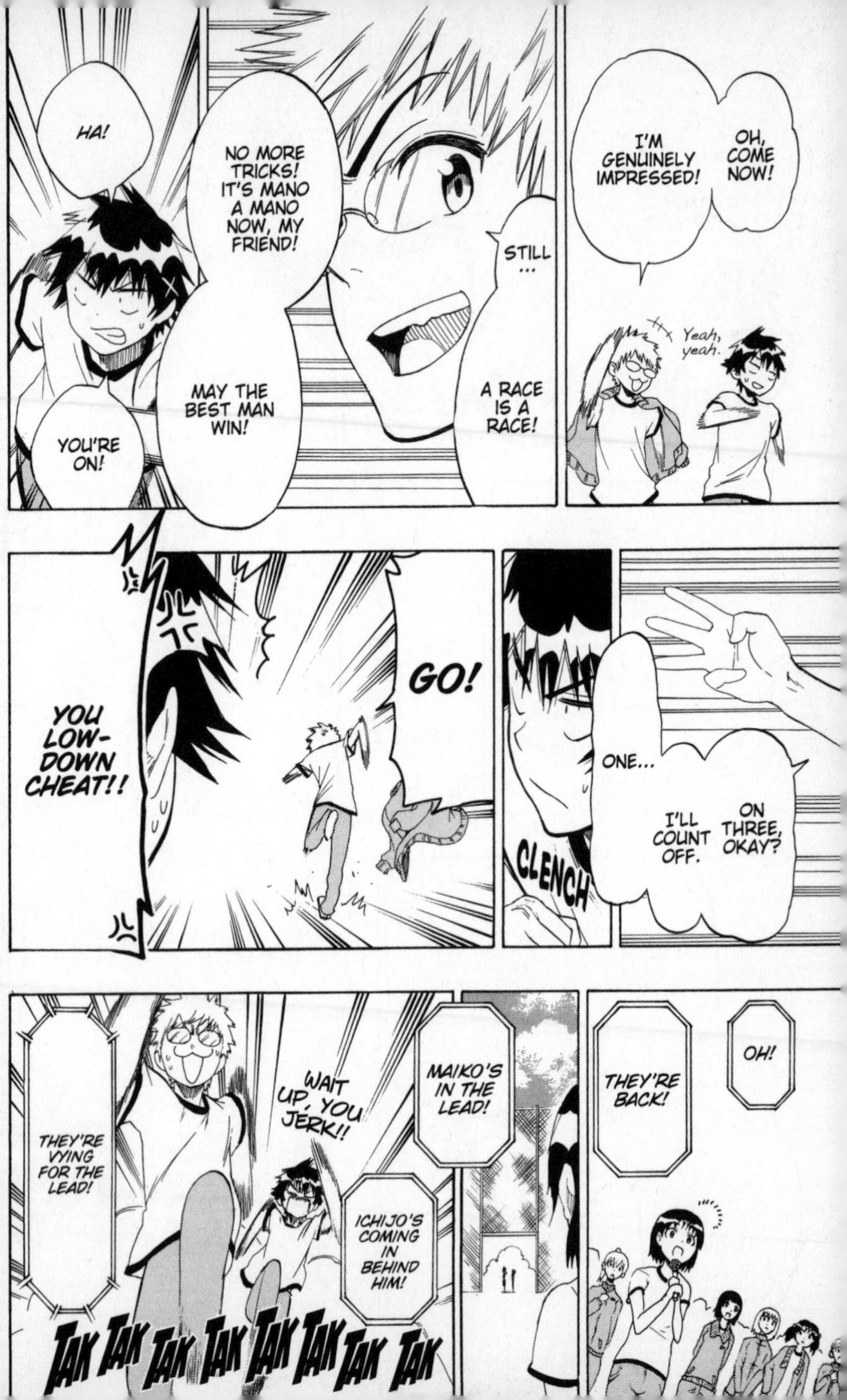
OH, COME NOW!
I'M GENUINELY IMPRESSED!
Yeah, yeah.
STILL...
A RACE IS A RACE!
NO MORE TRICKS! IT'S MANO A MANO NOW, MY FRIEND!
MAY THE BEST MAN WIN!
HA!
YOU'RE ON!
ON THREE, OKAY?
I'LL COUNT OFF.
ONE...
CLENCH
GO!
YOU LOW-DOWN CHEAT!!
OH!
THEY'RE BACK!
MAIKO'S IN THE LEAD!
ICHIJO'S COMING IN BEHIND HIM!
WAIT UP, YOU JERK!!
THEY'RE VYING FOR THE LEAD!
TAK TAK TAK TAK TAK TAK TAK TAK

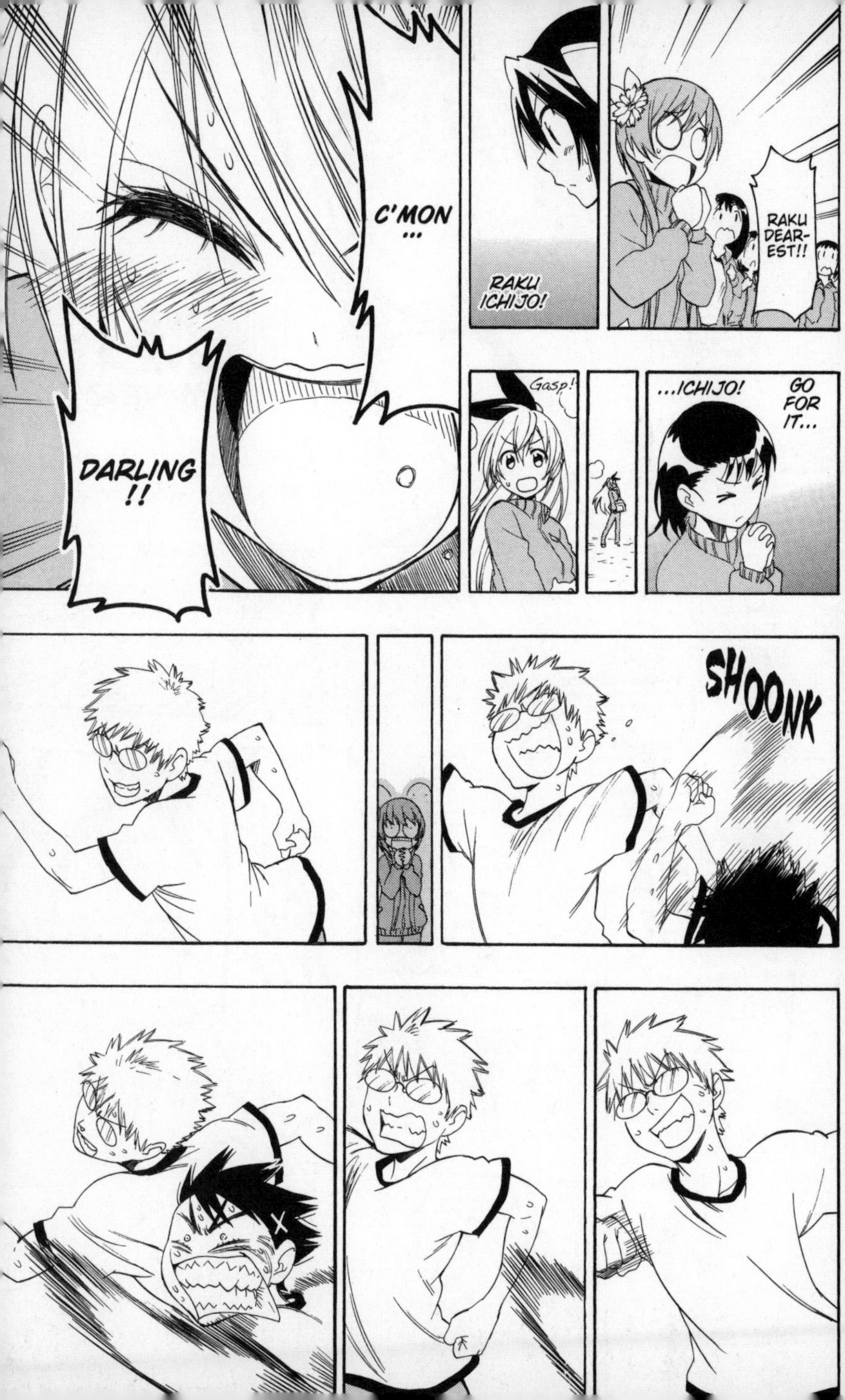
RAKU DEAREST!!
RAKU ICHIJO!
GO FOR IT...
...ICHIJO!
Gasp!
C'MON ...
DARLING !!
SHOONK

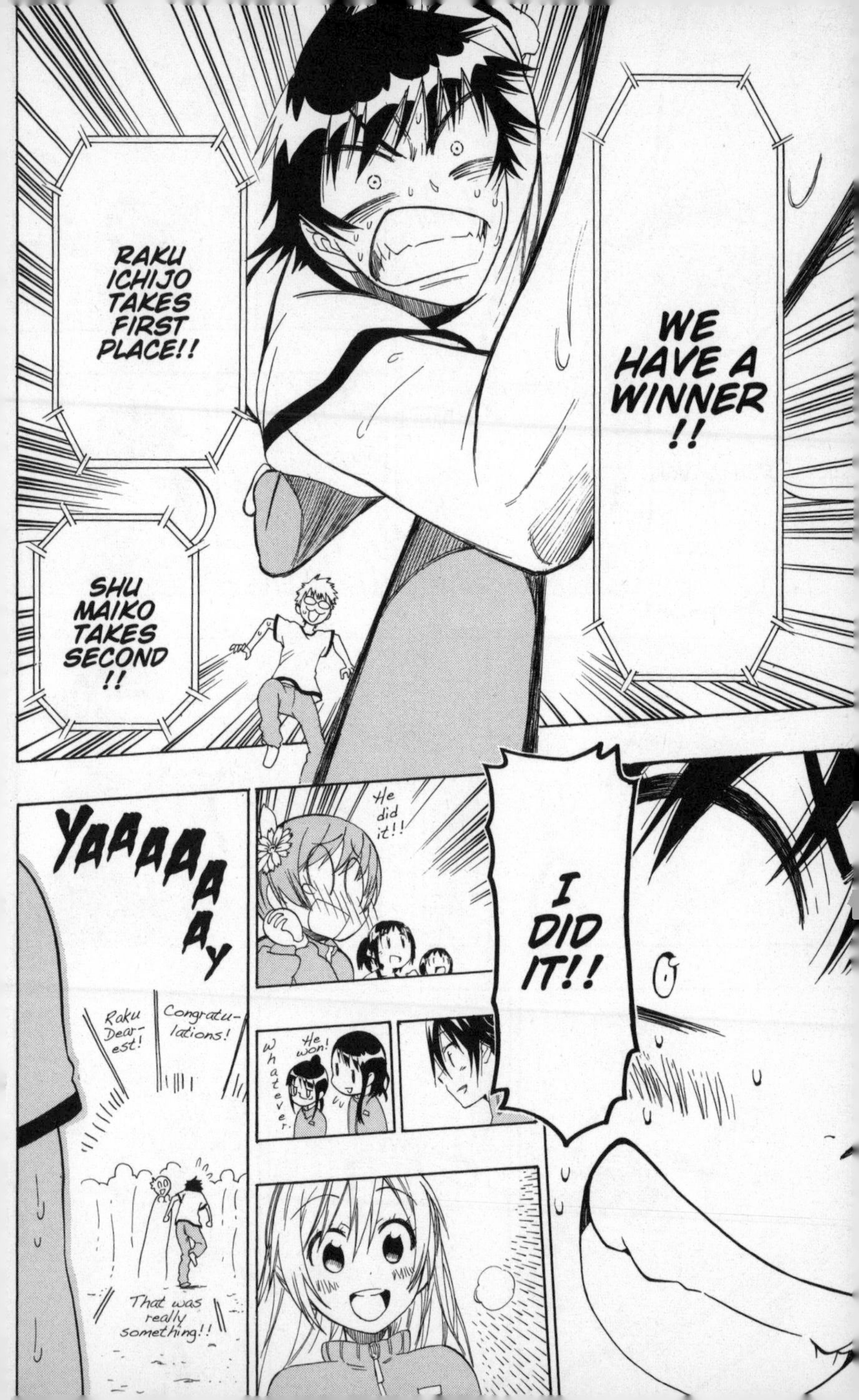

WE HAVE A WINNER!!
RAKU ICHIJO TAKES FIRST PLACE!!
SHU MAIKO TAKES SECOND!!
I DID IT!!
He did it!!
He won!
Whatever.
Yaaaaaaay
Congratulations!
Raku Dearest!
That was really something!!

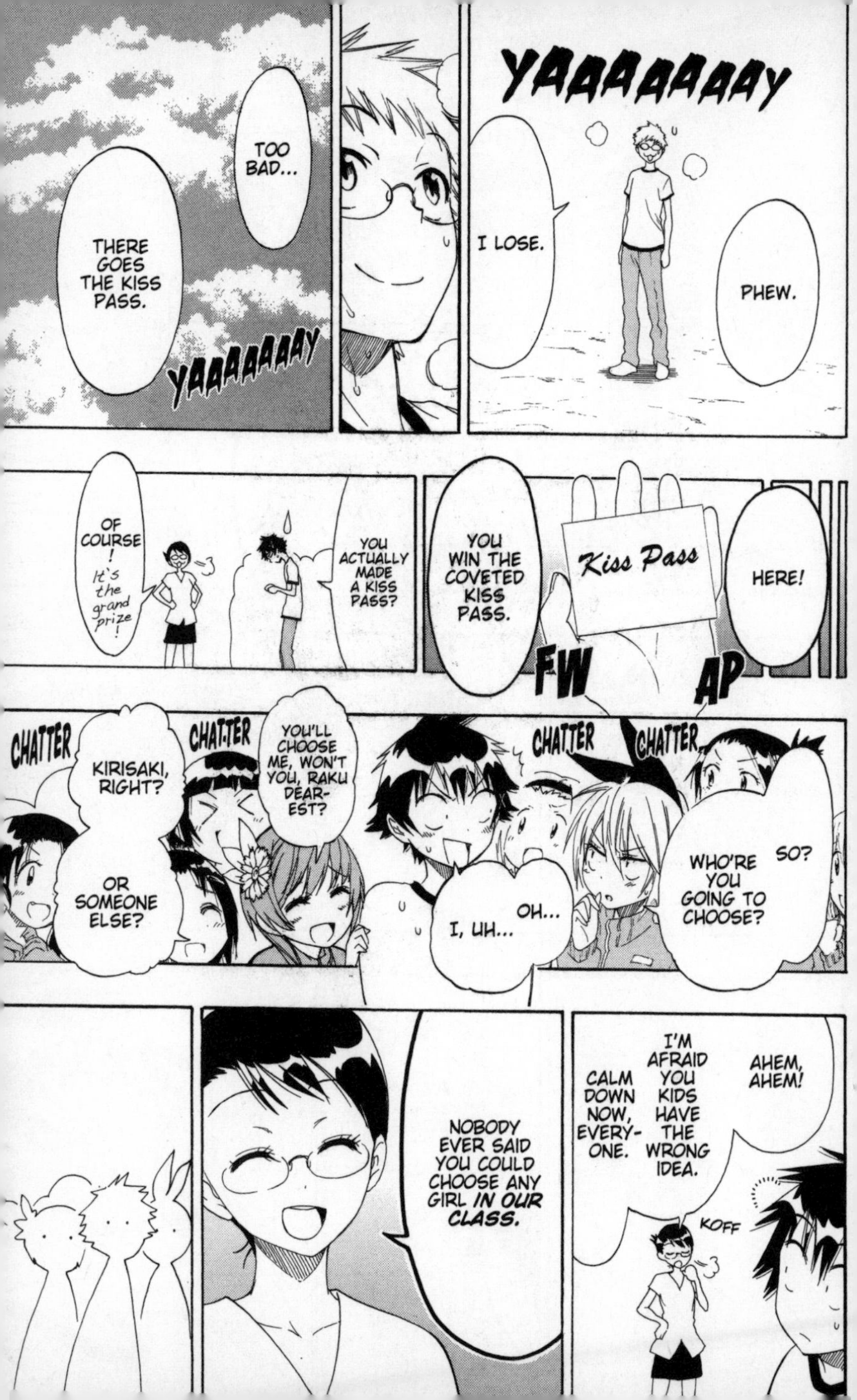
YAAAAAAAY
PHEW.
I LOSE.
TOO BAD...
THERE GOES THE KISS PASS.
YAAAAAAAY
HERE!
FWAP
Kiss Pass
YOU WIN THE COVETED KISS PASS.
YOU ACTUALLY MADE A KISS PASS?
OF COURSE! It's the grand prize!
CHATTER
CHATTER
SO? WHO'RE YOU GOING TO CHOOSE?
OH... I, UH...
CHATTER
YOU'LL CHOOSE ME, WON'T YOU, RAKU DEAREST?
KIRISAKI, RIGHT? OR SOMEONE ELSE?
CHATTER
AHEM, AHEM!
I'M AFRAID YOU KIDS HAVE THE WRONG IDEA.
CALM DOWN NOW, EVERYONE.
KOFF
NOBODY EVER SAID YOU COULD CHOOSE ANY GIRL ***IN OUR CLASS.***

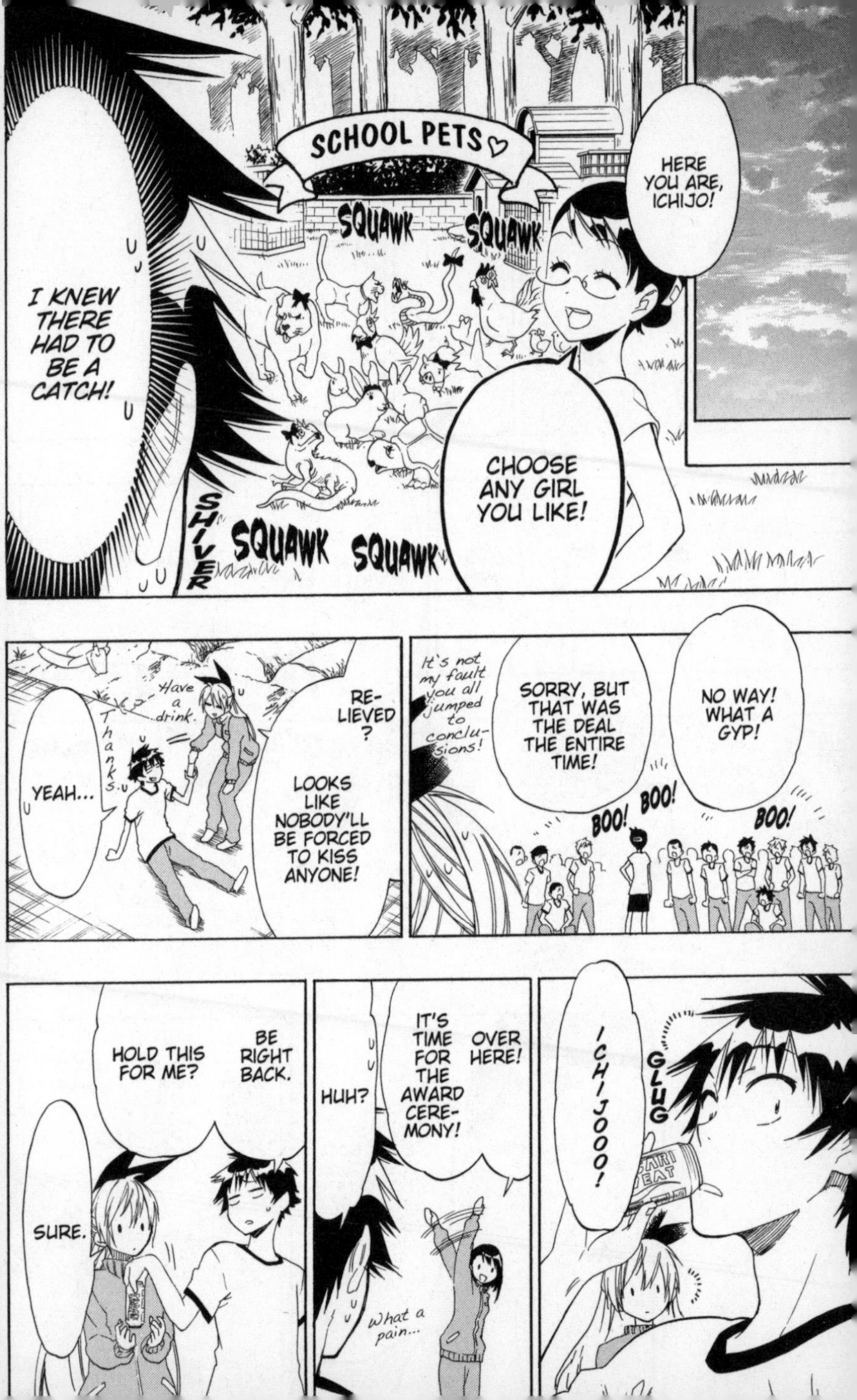
HERE YOU ARE, ICHIJO!
CHOOSE ANY GIRL YOU LIKE!
SCHOOL PETS♡
SQUAWK
SQUAWK
I KNEW THERE HAD TO BE A CATCH!
SHIVER
SQUAWK
SQUAWK
NO WAY! WHAT A GYP!
SORRY, BUT THAT WAS THE DEAL THE ENTIRE TIME!
It's not my fault you all jumped to conclu-sions!
BOO!
BOO!
BOO!
RE-LIEVED?
LOOKS LIKE NOBODY'LL BE FORCED TO KISS ANYONE!
Have a drink.
Thanks.
YEAH...
ICHIJOOO!
GLUG
OVER HERE!
IT'S TIME FOR THE AWARD CERE-MONY!
HUH?
What a pain...
BE RIGHT BACK.
HOLD THIS FOR ME?
SURE.

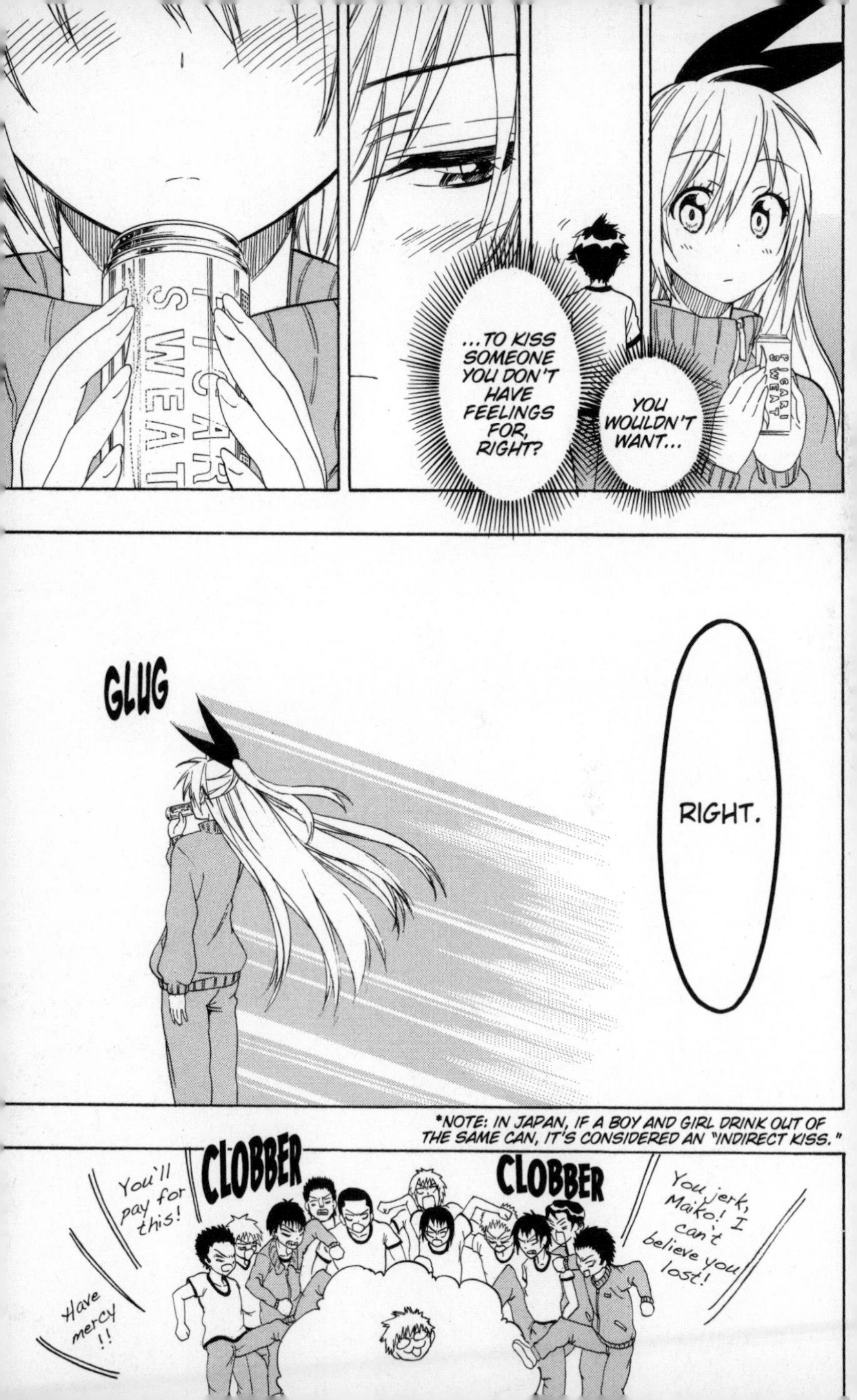
YOU WOULDN'T WANT...
...TO KISS SOMEONE YOU DON'T HAVE FEELINGS FOR, RIGHT?
PIGARI SWEAT
RIGHT.
GLUG
*NOTE: IN JAPAN, IF A BOY AND GIRL DRINK OUT OF THE SAME CAN, IT'S CONSIDERED AN "INDIRECT KISS."
You jerk, Maiko! I can't believe you lost!
CLOBBER
CLOBBER
You'll pay for this!
Have mercy!!

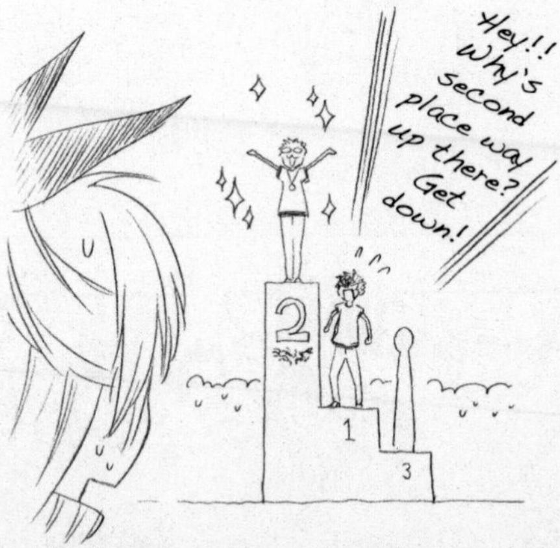
Hey!! Why's second place way up there? Get down!
2
1
3

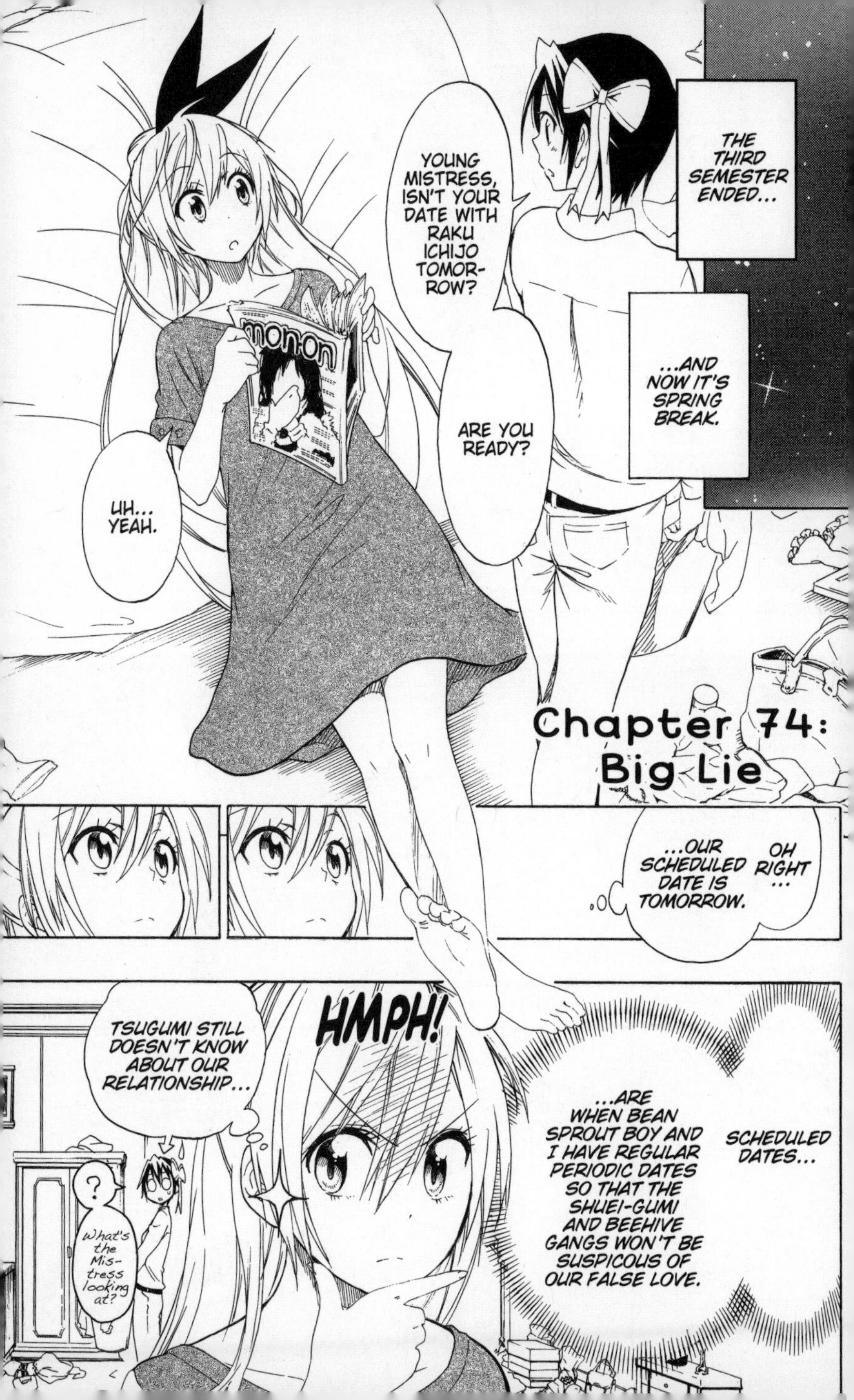
THE THIRD SEMESTER ENDED...
...AND NOW IT'S SPRING BREAK.
YOUNG MISTRESS, ISN'T YOUR DATE WITH RAKU ICHIJO TOMORROW?
ARE YOU READY?
UH... YEAH.
Chapter 74: Big Lie
OH RIGHT...
...OUR SCHEDULED DATE IS TOMORROW.
SCHEDULED DATES...
...ARE WHEN BEAN SPROUT BOY AND I HAVE REGULAR PERIODIC DATES SO THAT THE SHUEI-GUMI AND BEEHIVE GANGS WON'T BE SUSPICOUS OF OUR FALSE LOVE.
HMPH!
TSUGUMI STILL DOESN'T KNOW ABOUT OUR RELATIONSHIP...
?
What's the Mistress looking at?

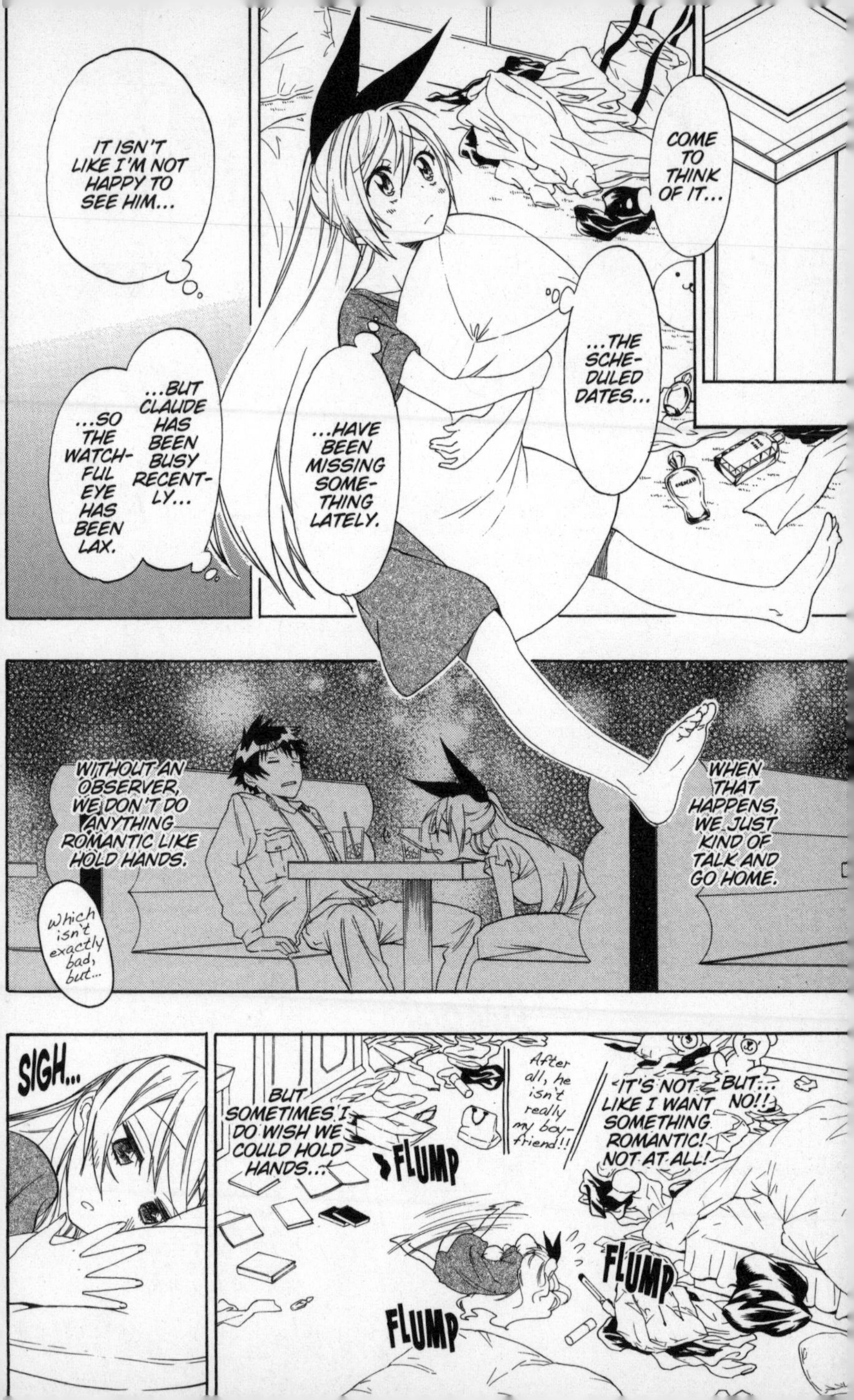
COME TO THINK OF IT...
...THE SCHEDULED DATES...
...HAVE BEEN MISSING SOMETHING LATELY.
IT ISN'T LIKE I'M NOT HAPPY TO SEE HIM...
...BUT CLAUDE HAS BEEN BUSY RECENTLY...
...SO THE WATCHFUL EYE HAS BEEN LAX.
WHEN THAT HAPPENS, WE JUST KIND OF TALK AND GO HOME.
WITHOUT AN OBSERVER, WE DON'T DO ANYTHING ROMANTIC LIKE HOLD HANDS.
Which isn't exactly bad, but...
BUT... NO!!
IT'S NOT LIKE I WANT SOMETHING ROMANTIC! NOT AT ALL!
After all, he isn't really my boyfriend!!
BUT SOMETIMES I DO WISH WE COULD HOLD HANDS...
FLUMP
FLUMP
FLUMP
SIGH...

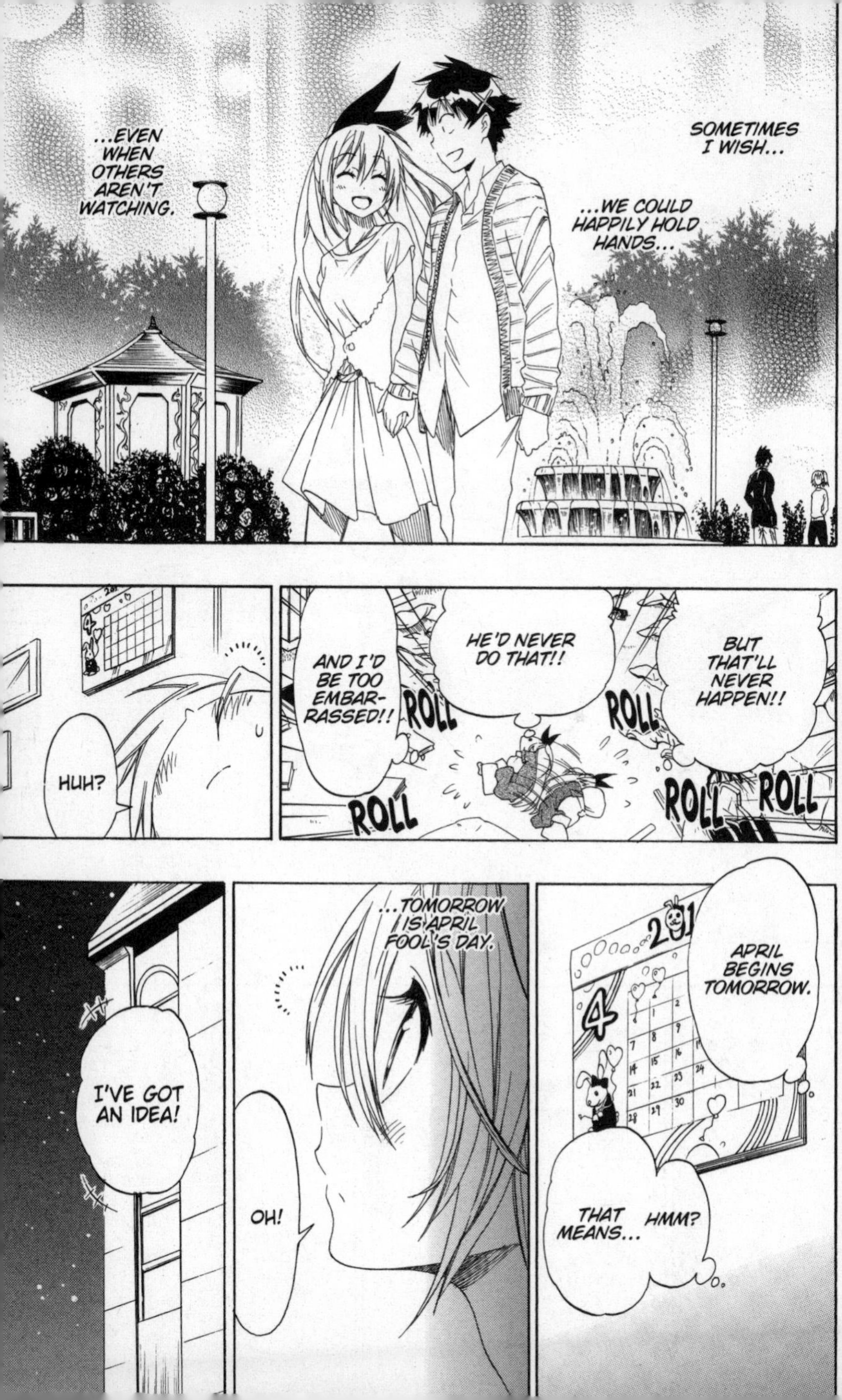
SOMETIMES I WISH...
...WE COULD HAPPILY HOLD HANDS...
...EVEN WHEN OTHERS AREN'T WATCHING.
BUT THAT'LL NEVER HAPPEN!!
HE'D NEVER DO THAT!!
ROLL
AND I'D BE TOO EMBAR-RASSED!!
ROLL
ROLL ROLL
ROLL
HUH?
APRIL BEGINS TOMORROW.
HMM?
THAT MEANS...
...TOMORROW IS APRIL FOOL'S DAY.
OH!
I'VE GOT AN IDEA!

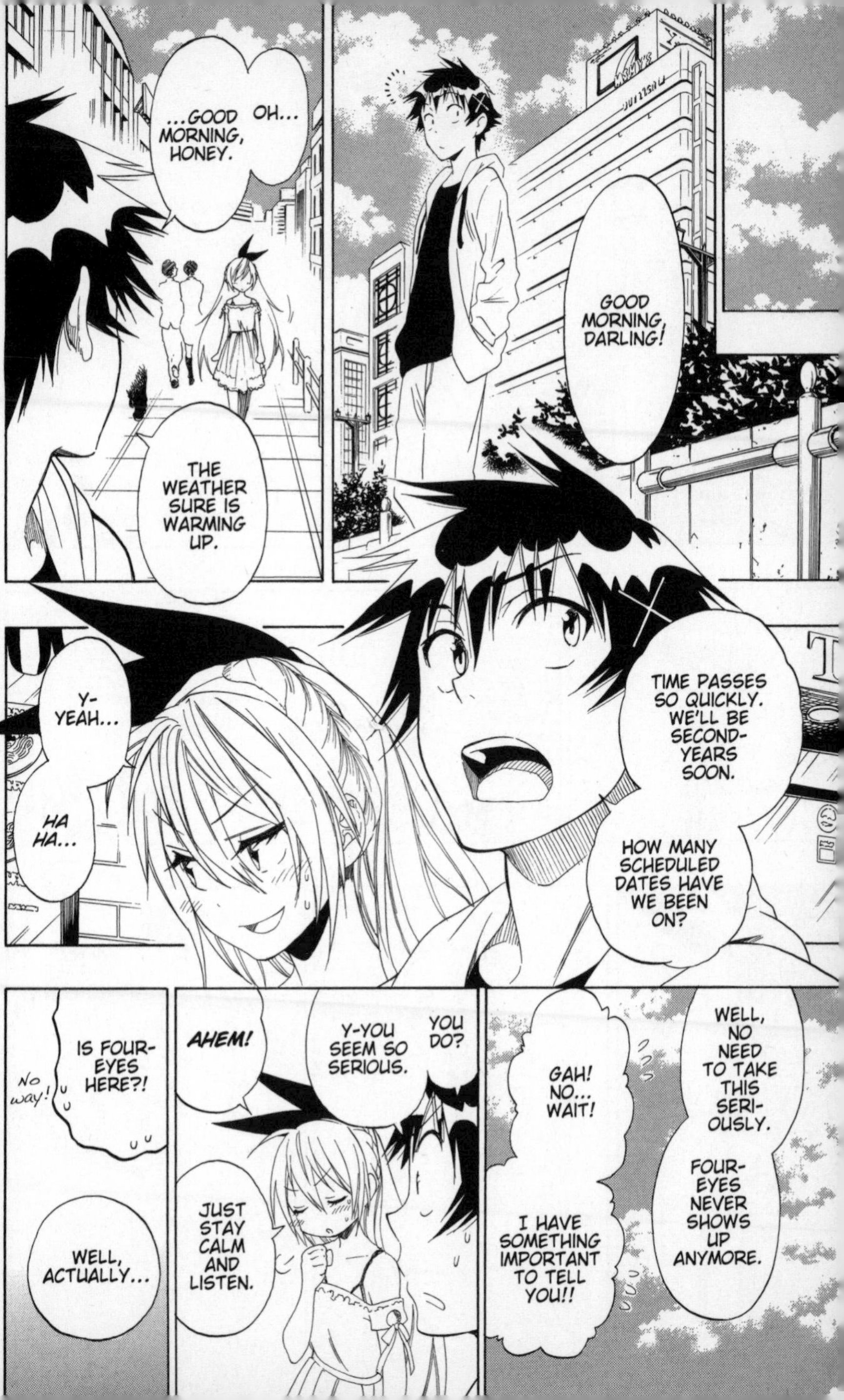
GOOD MORNING, DARLING!
OH...
...GOOD MORNING, HONEY.
THE WEATHER SURE IS WARMING UP.
TIME PASSES SO QUICKLY. WE'LL BE SECOND-YEARS SOON.
HOW MANY SCHEDULED DATES HAVE WE BEEN ON?
Y-YEAH...
HA HA...
WELL, NO NEED TO TAKE THIS SERIOUSLY.
FOUR-EYES NEVER SHOWS UP ANYMORE.
GAH! NO... WAIT!
I HAVE SOMETHING IMPORTANT TO TELL YOU!!
YOU DO?
Y-YOU SEEM SO SERIOUS.
AHEM!
JUST STAY CALM AND LISTEN.
IS FOUR-EYES HERE?!
No way!
WELL, ACTUALLY...

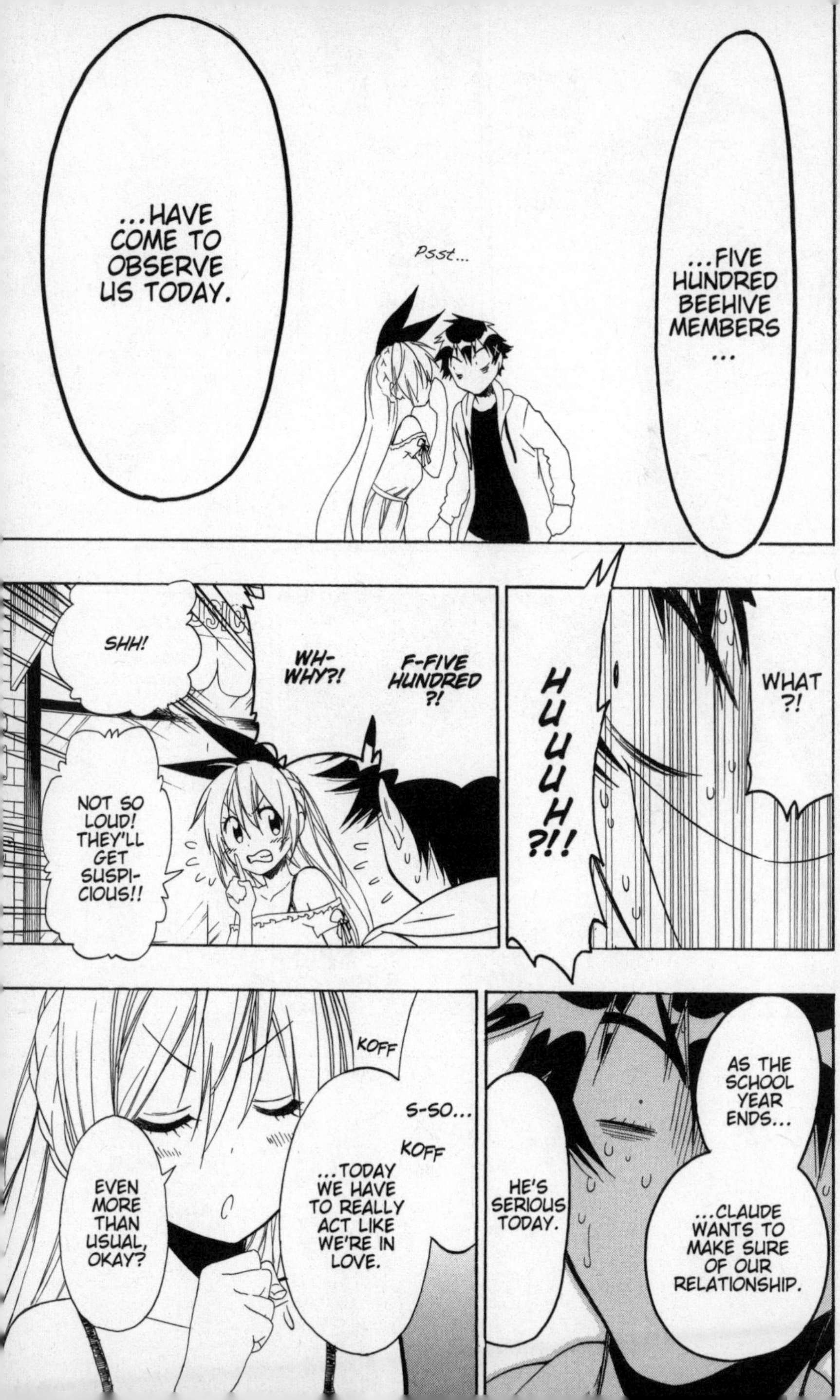
...FIVE HUNDRED BEEHIVE MEMBERS ...
Psst...
...HAVE COME TO OBSERVE US TODAY.
WHAT?!
HUUUUH?!!
F-FIVE HUNDRED?!
WH-WHY?!
SHH!
NOT SO LOUD! THEY'LL GET SUSPICIOUS!!
AS THE SCHOOL YEAR ENDS...
...CLAUDE WANTS TO MAKE SURE OF OUR RELATIONSHIP.
HE'S SERIOUS TODAY.
KOFF
S-SO...
KOFF
...TODAY WE HAVE TO REALLY ACT LIKE WE'RE IN LOVE.
EVEN MORE THAN USUAL, OKAY?

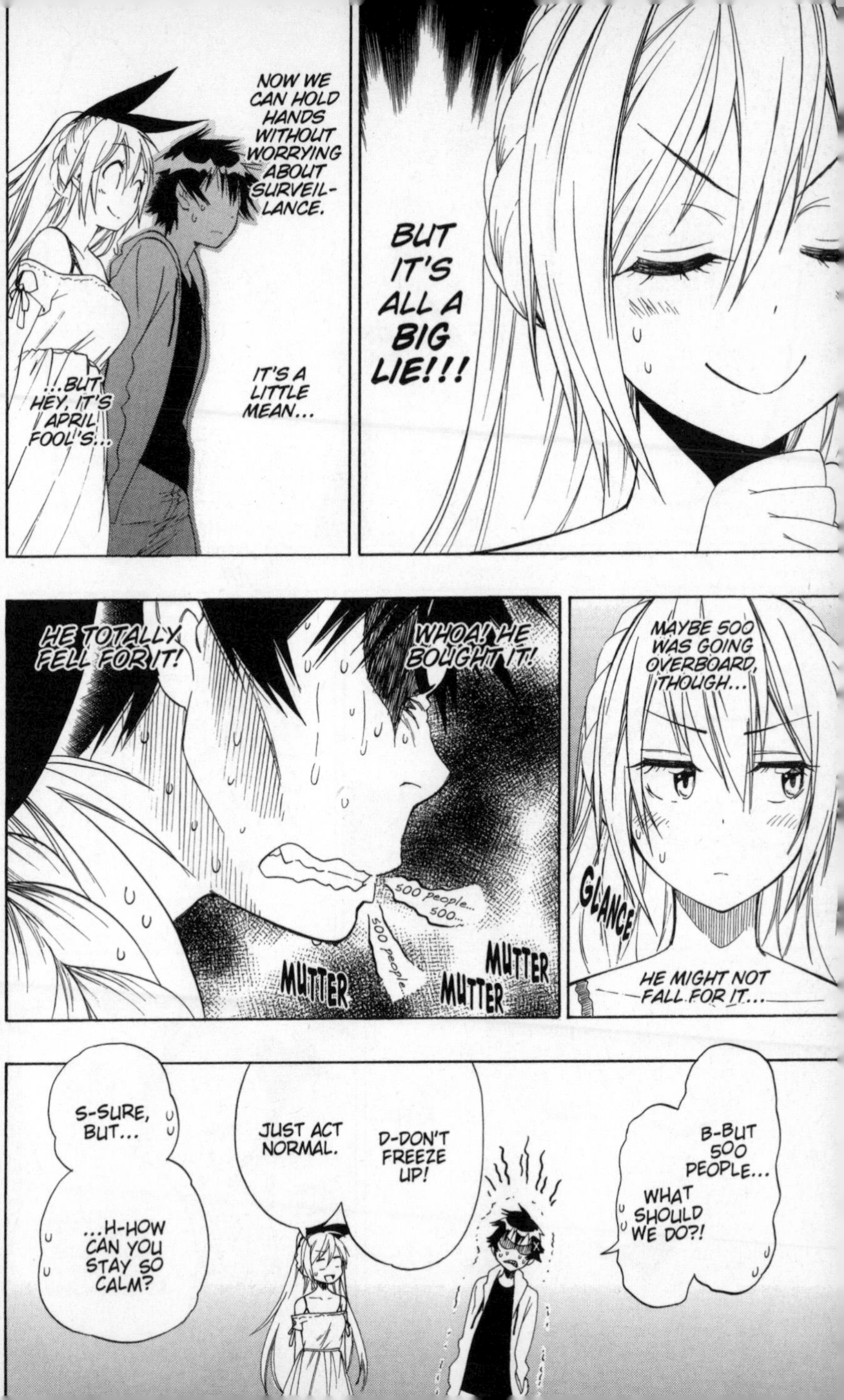
BUT IT'S ALL A BIG LIE!!!
NOW WE CAN HOLD HANDS WITHOUT WORRYING ABOUT SURVEIL-LANCE.
IT'S A LITTLE MEAN...
...BUT HEY, IT'S APRIL FOOL'S...
MAYBE 500 WAS GOING OVERBOARD, THOUGH...
GLANCE
HE MIGHT NOT FALL FOR IT...
WHOA! HE BOUGHT IT!
HE TOTALLY FELL FOR IT!
500 people... 500...
500 people...
MUTTER
MUTTER
MUTTER
B-BUT 500 PEOPLE...
WHAT SHOULD WE DO?!
D-DON'T FREEZE UP!
JUST ACT NORMAL.
S-SURE, BUT...
...H-HOW CAN YOU STAY SO CALM?

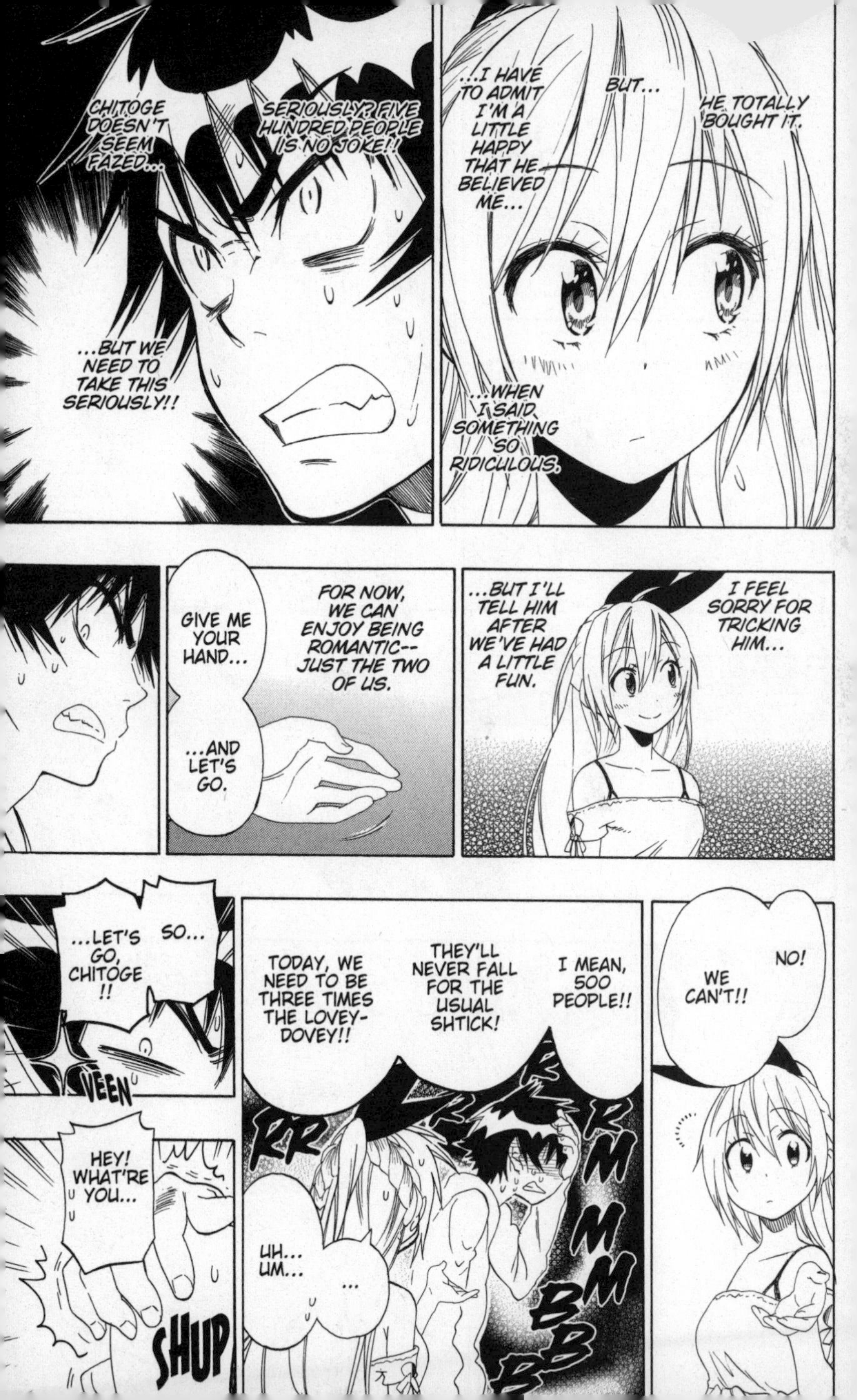
HE TOTALLY BOUGHT IT.
BUT...
...I HAVE TO ADMIT I'M A LITTLE HAPPY THAT HE BELIEVED ME...
...WHEN I SAID SOMETHING SO RIDICULOUS.
SERIOUSLY? FIVE HUNDRED PEOPLE IS NO JOKE!!
CHITOGE DOESN'T SEEM FAZED...
...BUT WE NEED TO TAKE THIS SERIOUSLY!!
I FEEL SORRY FOR TRICKING HIM...
...BUT I'LL TELL HIM AFTER WE'VE HAD A LITTLE FUN.
FOR NOW, WE CAN ENJOY BEING ROMANTIC--JUST THE TWO OF US.
GIVE ME YOUR HAND...
...AND LET'S GO.
NO!
WE CAN'T!!
I MEAN, 500 PEOPLE!!
THEY'LL NEVER FALL FOR THE USUAL SHTICK!
TODAY, WE NEED TO BE THREE TIMES THE LOVEY-DOVEY!!
RR
RRMMMMBBB
UH... UM...
...
SO...
...LET'S GO, CHITOGE!!
VEEN
HEY! WHAT'RE YOU...
SHUP

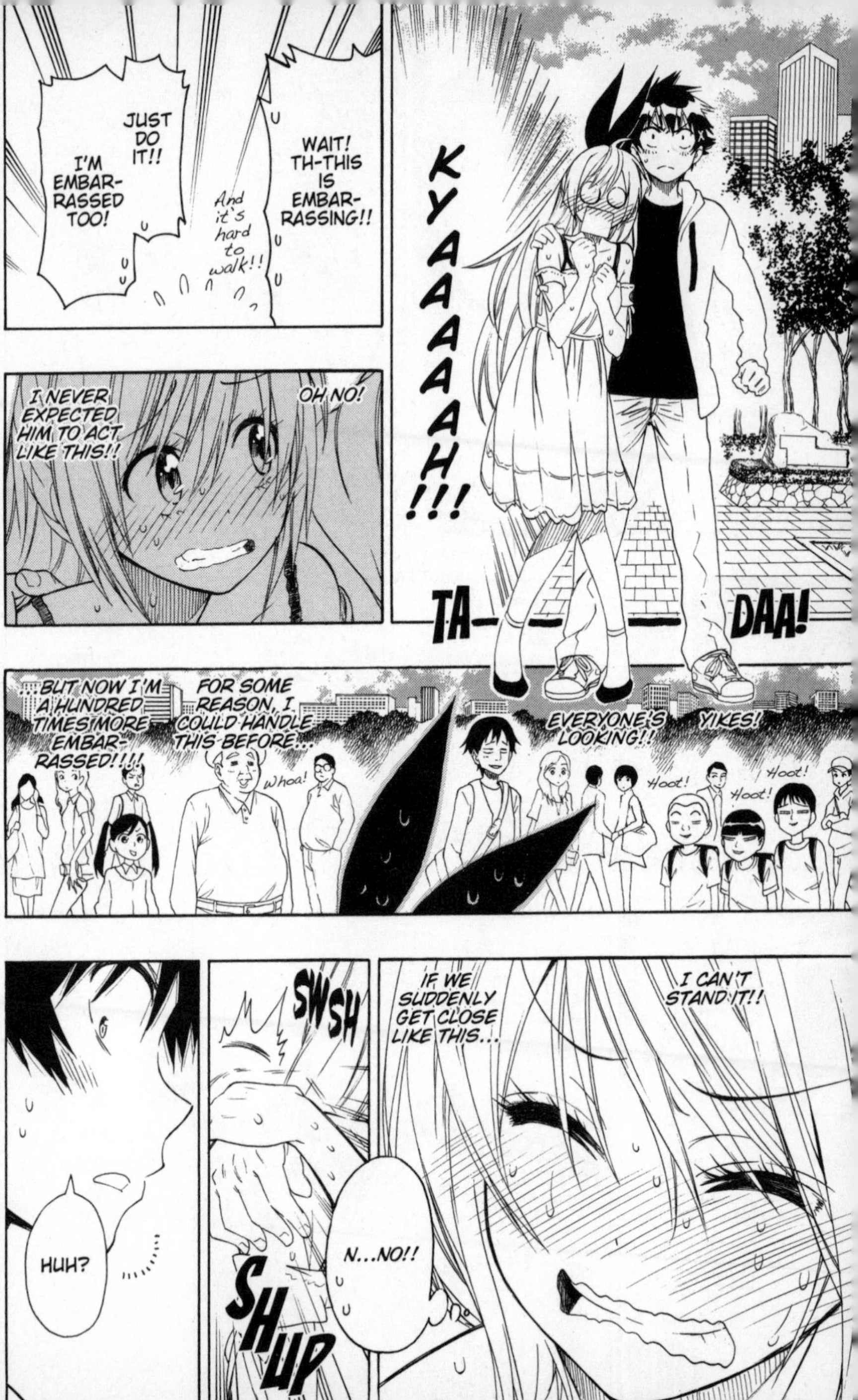
KYAAAAAH!!!
TA-DAA!
WAIT! TH-THIS IS EMBARRASSING!!
And it's hard to walk!!
JUST DO IT!!
I'M EMBARRASSED TOO!
OH NO!
I NEVER EXPECTED HIM TO ACT LIKE THIS!!
YIKES!
EVERYONE'S LOOKING!!
Hoot!
Hoot!
Hoot!
Whoa!
FOR SOME REASON, I COULD HANDLE THIS BEFORE...
...BUT NOW I'M A HUNDRED TIMES MORE EMBARRASSED!!!!
I CAN'T STAND IT!!
IF WE SUDDENLY GET CLOSE LIKE THIS...
SWSH
N...NO!!
SHUP
......
HUH?

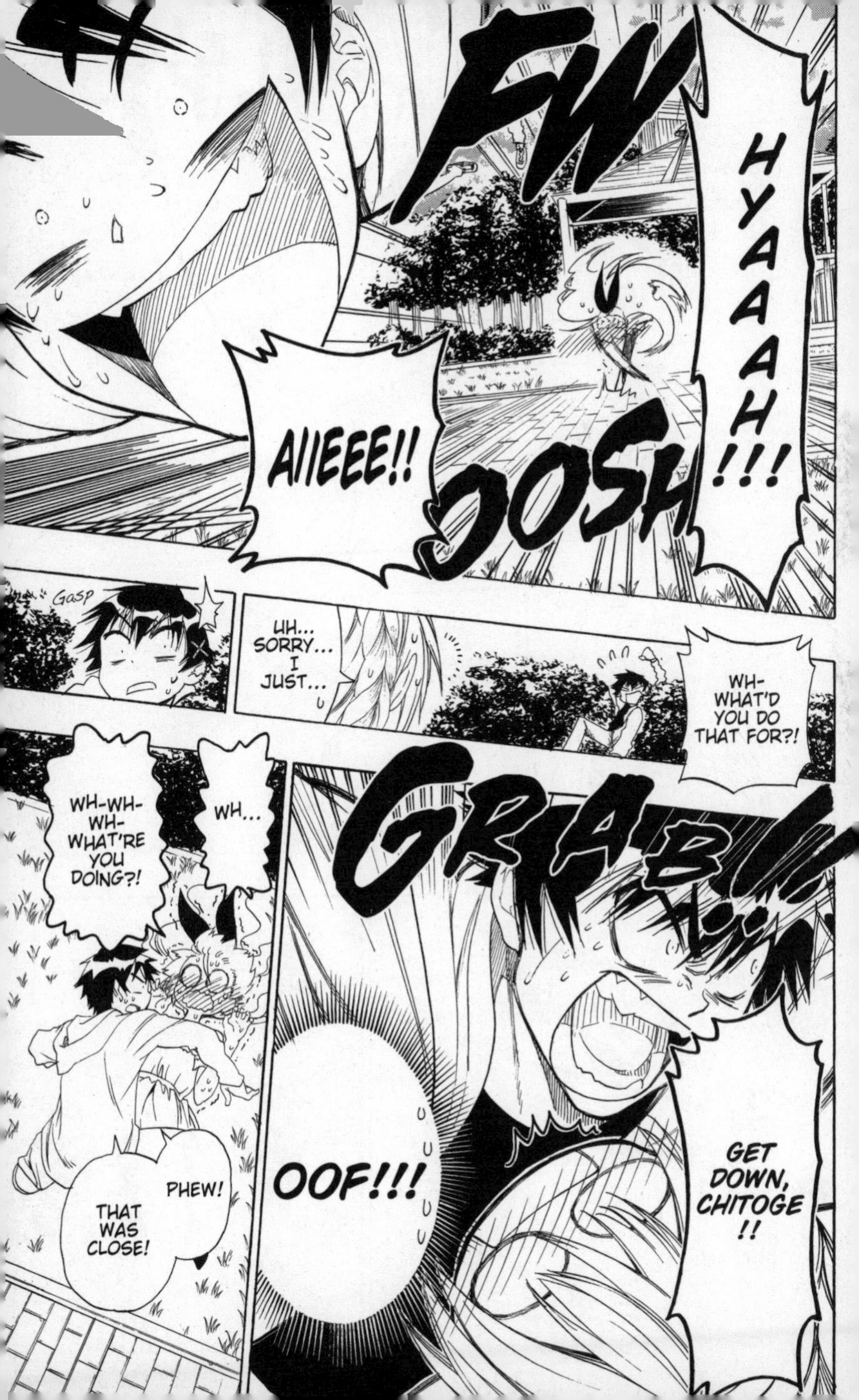
HYAAAAH!!!
FW
DOSH
AIIEEE!!
WH-WHAT'D YOU DO THAT FOR?!
UH... SORRY... I JUST...
Gasp
GRAB
GET DOWN, CHITOGE!!
OOF!!!
WH...
WH-WH-WH-WHAT'RE YOU DOING?!
PHEW! THAT WAS CLOSE!

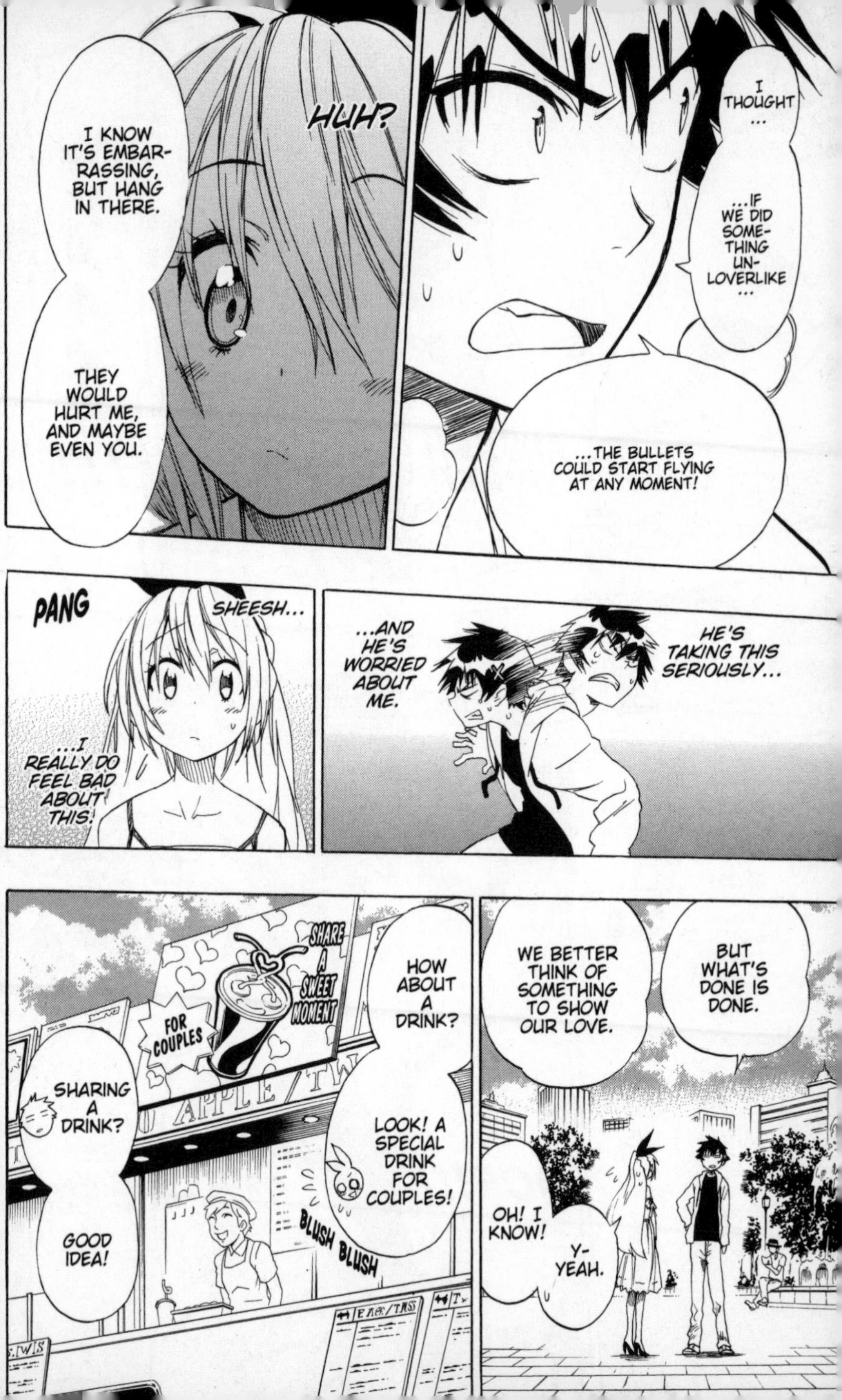
I THOUGHT...
...IF WE DID SOMETHING UN-LOVERLIKE...
...THE BULLETS COULD START FLYING AT ANY MOMENT!
HUH?
I KNOW IT'S EMBARRASSING, BUT HANG IN THERE.
THEY WOULD HURT ME, AND MAYBE EVEN YOU.
HE'S TAKING THIS SERIOUSLY...
...AND HE'S WORRIED ABOUT ME.
PANG
SHEESH...
...I REALLY DO FEEL BAD ABOUT THIS!
BUT WHAT'S DONE IS DONE.
WE BETTER THINK OF SOMETHING TO SHOW OUR LOVE.
Y-YEAH.
OH! I KNOW!
HOW ABOUT A DRINK?
LOOK! A SPECIAL DRINK FOR COUPLES!
SHARE A SWEET MOMENT
FOR COUPLES
BLUSH BLUSH
SHARING A DRINK?
GOOD IDEA!

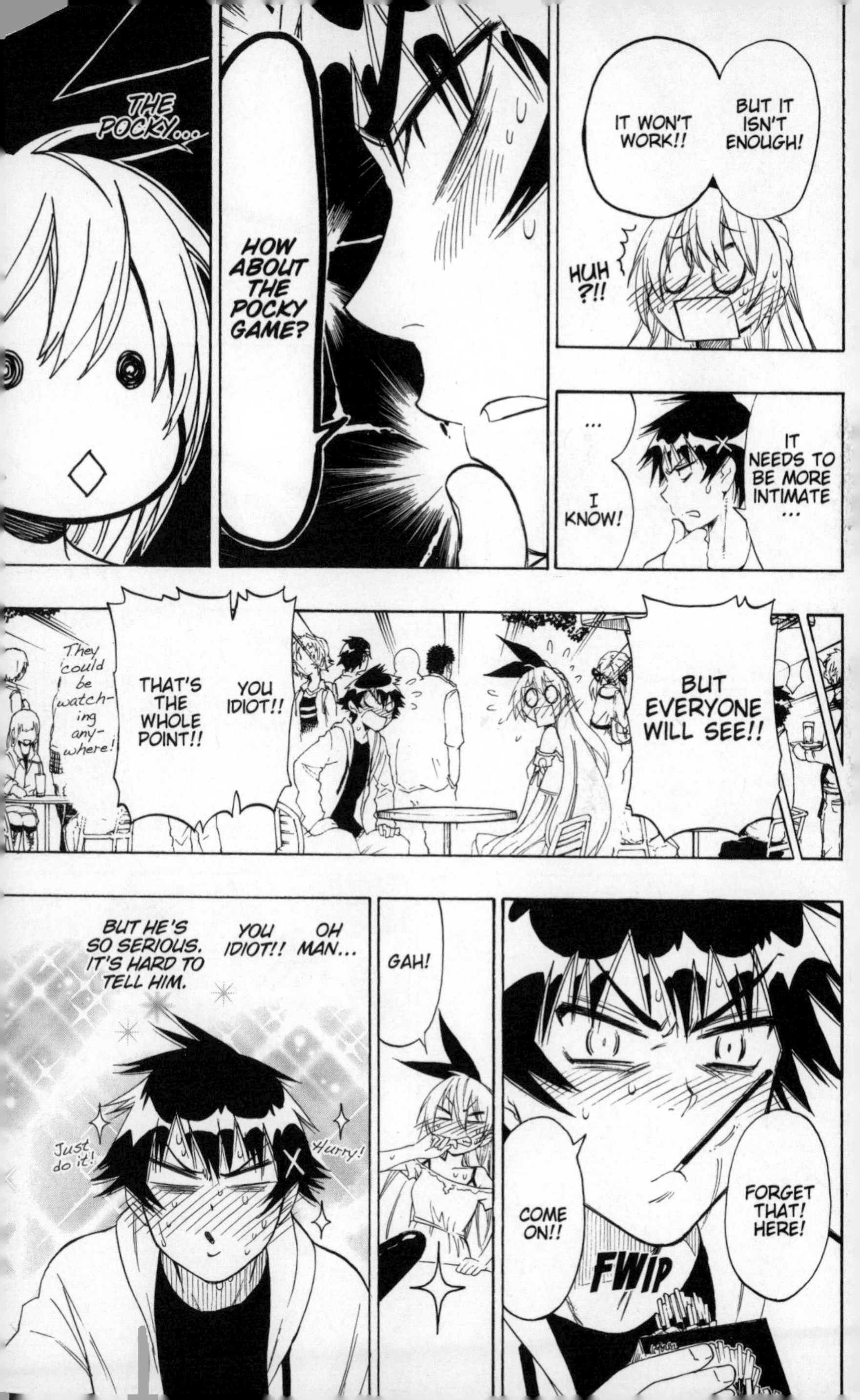
BUT IT ISN'T ENOUGH!
IT WON'T WORK!!
HUH ?!!
IT NEEDS TO BE MORE INTIMATE ...
... I KNOW!
HOW ABOUT THE POCKY GAME?
THE POCKY...
BUT EVERYONE WILL SEE!!
YOU IDIOT!!
THAT'S THE WHOLE POINT!!
They could be watching anywhere!
FORGET THAT! HERE!
FWIP
COME ON!!
GAH!
OH MAN...
YOU IDIOT!!
BUT HE'S SO SERIOUS. IT'S HARD TO TELL HIM.
Hurry!
Just do it!

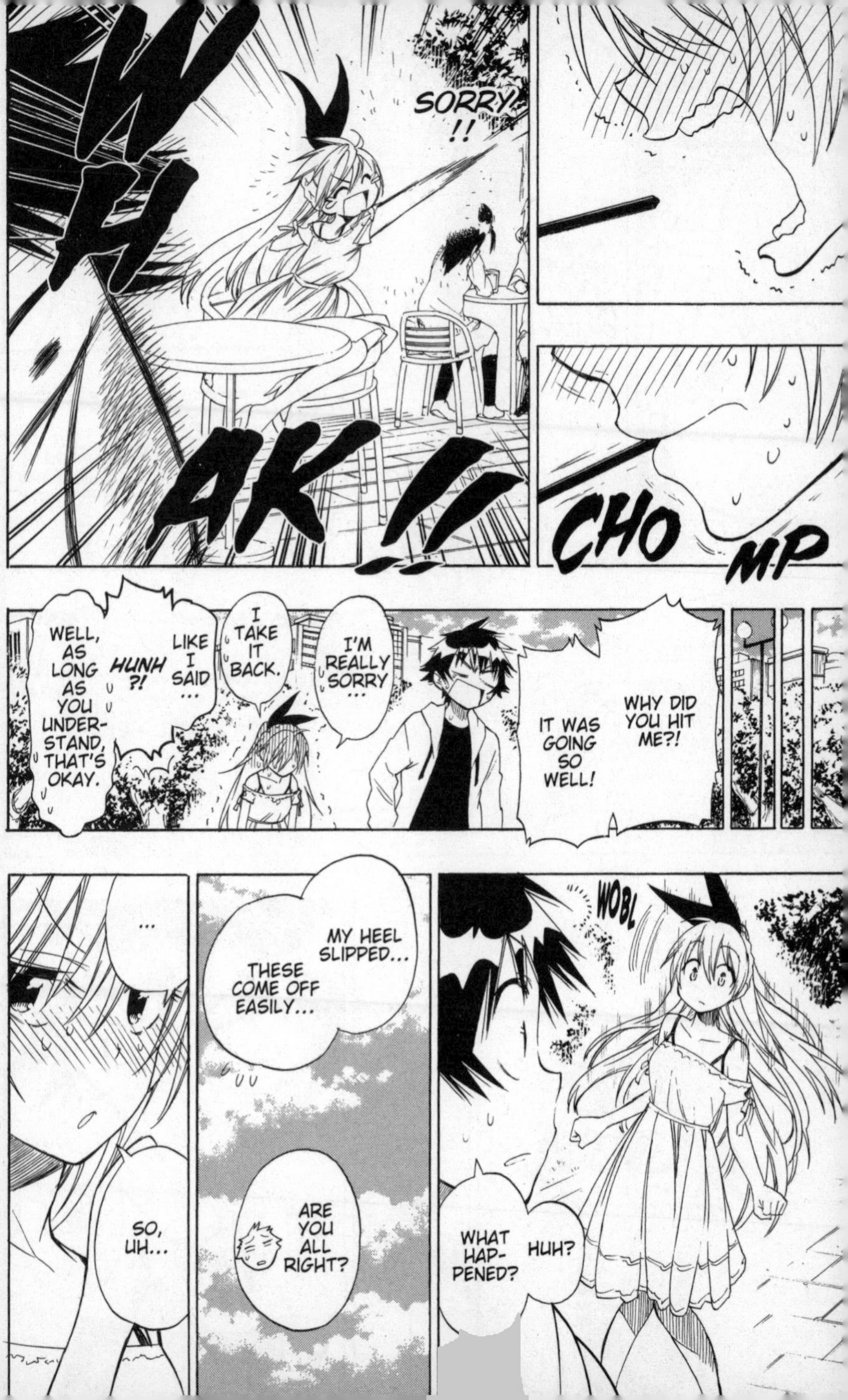
CHOMP
WHAK!!
SORRY!!
WHY DID YOU HIT ME?!
IT WAS GOING SO WELL!
I'M REALLY SORRY...
I TAKE IT BACK.
LIKE I SAID...
HUNH?!
WELL, AS LONG AS YOU UNDER-STAND, THAT'S OKAY.
WOBL
HUH?
WHAT HAP-PENED?
MY HEEL SLIPPED...
THESE COME OFF EASILY...
ARE YOU ALL RIGHT?
...
SO, UH...

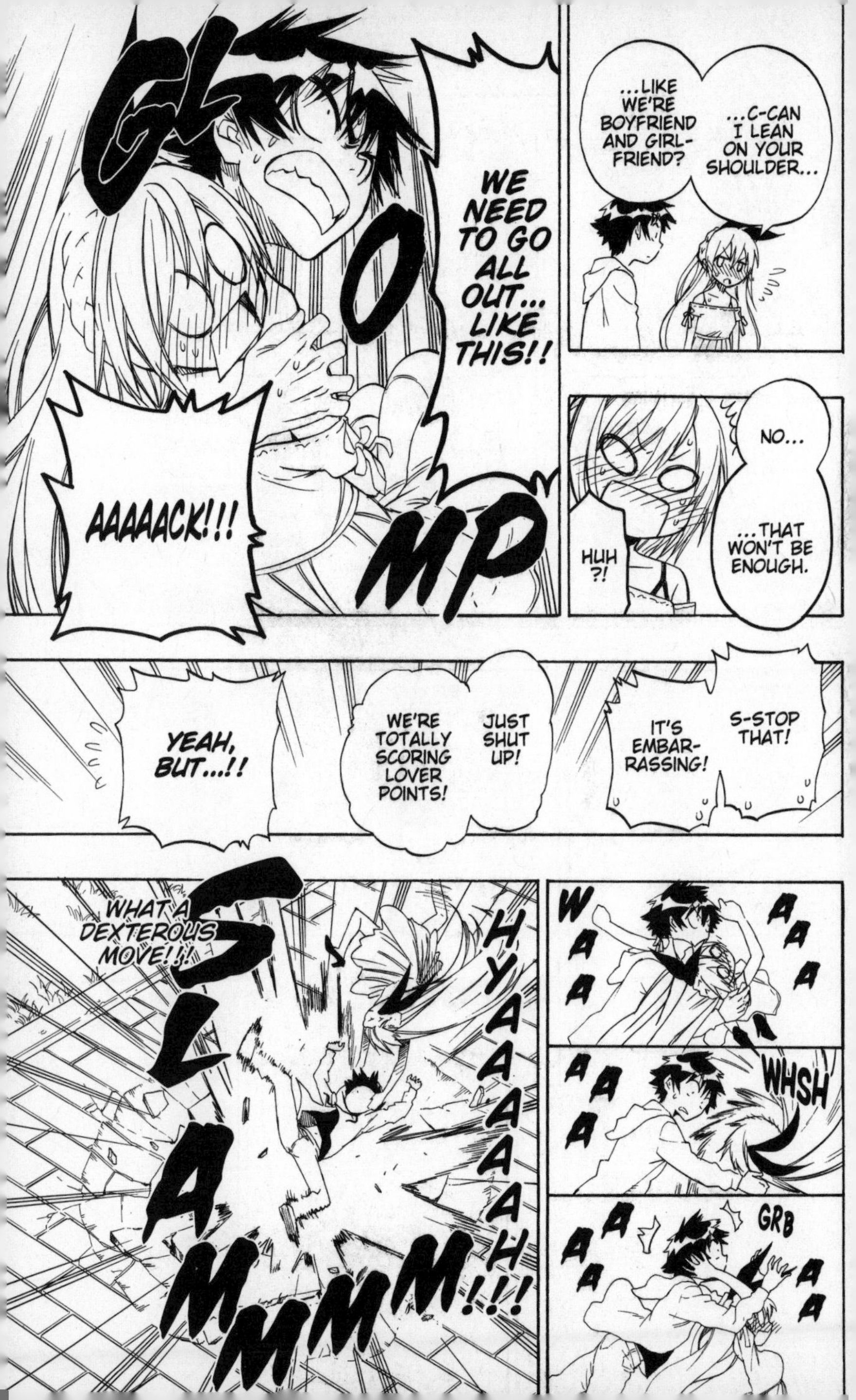
...C-CAN I LEAN ON YOUR SHOULDER...
...LIKE WE'RE BOYFRIEND AND GIRL-FRIEND?
NO...
...THAT WON'T BE ENOUGH.
HUH?!
WE NEED TO GO ALL OUT... LIKE THIS!!
GLOMP
AAAAACK!!!
S-STOP THAT!
IT'S EMBAR-RASSING!
JUST SHUT UP!
WE'RE TOTALLY SCORING LOVER POINTS!
YEAH, BUT...!!
WAAAAAAA
AAAA
WHSH
AAAAAAAA
GRB
HYAAAAAAAAH!!!
SLAMMMM
WHAT A DEXTEROUS MOVE!!!

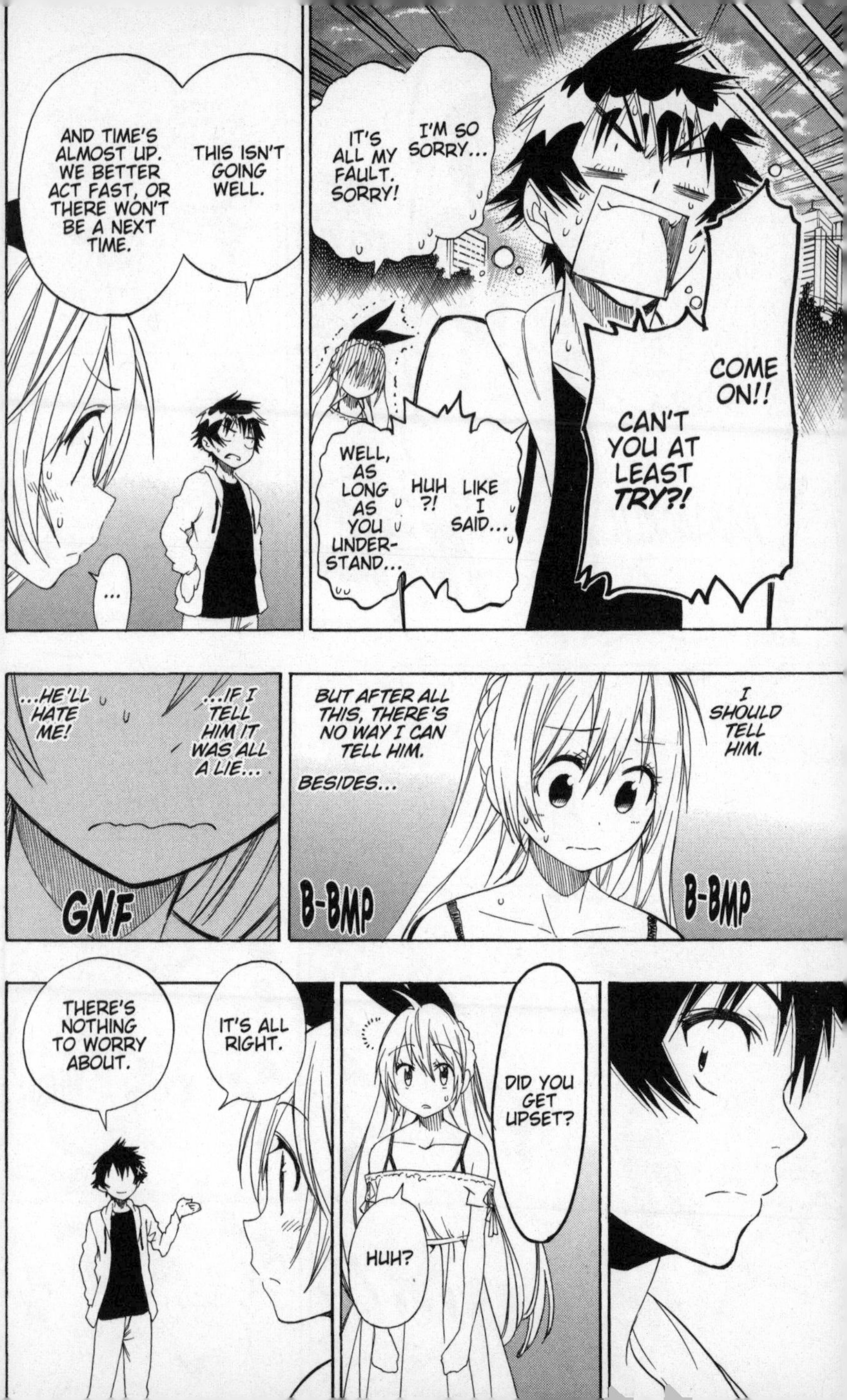
COME ON!!
CAN'T YOU AT LEAST TRY?!
I'M SO SORRY...
IT'S ALL MY FAULT. SORRY!
LIKE I SAID...
HUH ?!
WELL, AS LONG AS YOU UNDER-STAND...
THIS ISN'T GOING WELL.
AND TIME'S ALMOST UP. WE BETTER ACT FAST, OR THERE WON'T BE A NEXT TIME.
...
I SHOULD TELL HIM.
B-BMP
BUT AFTER ALL THIS, THERE'S NO WAY I CAN TELL HIM.
BESIDES...
B-BMP
...IF I TELL HIM IT WAS ALL A LIE...
...HE'LL HATE ME!
GNF
DID YOU GET UPSET?
HUH?
IT'S ALL RIGHT.
THERE'S NOTHING TO WORRY ABOUT.

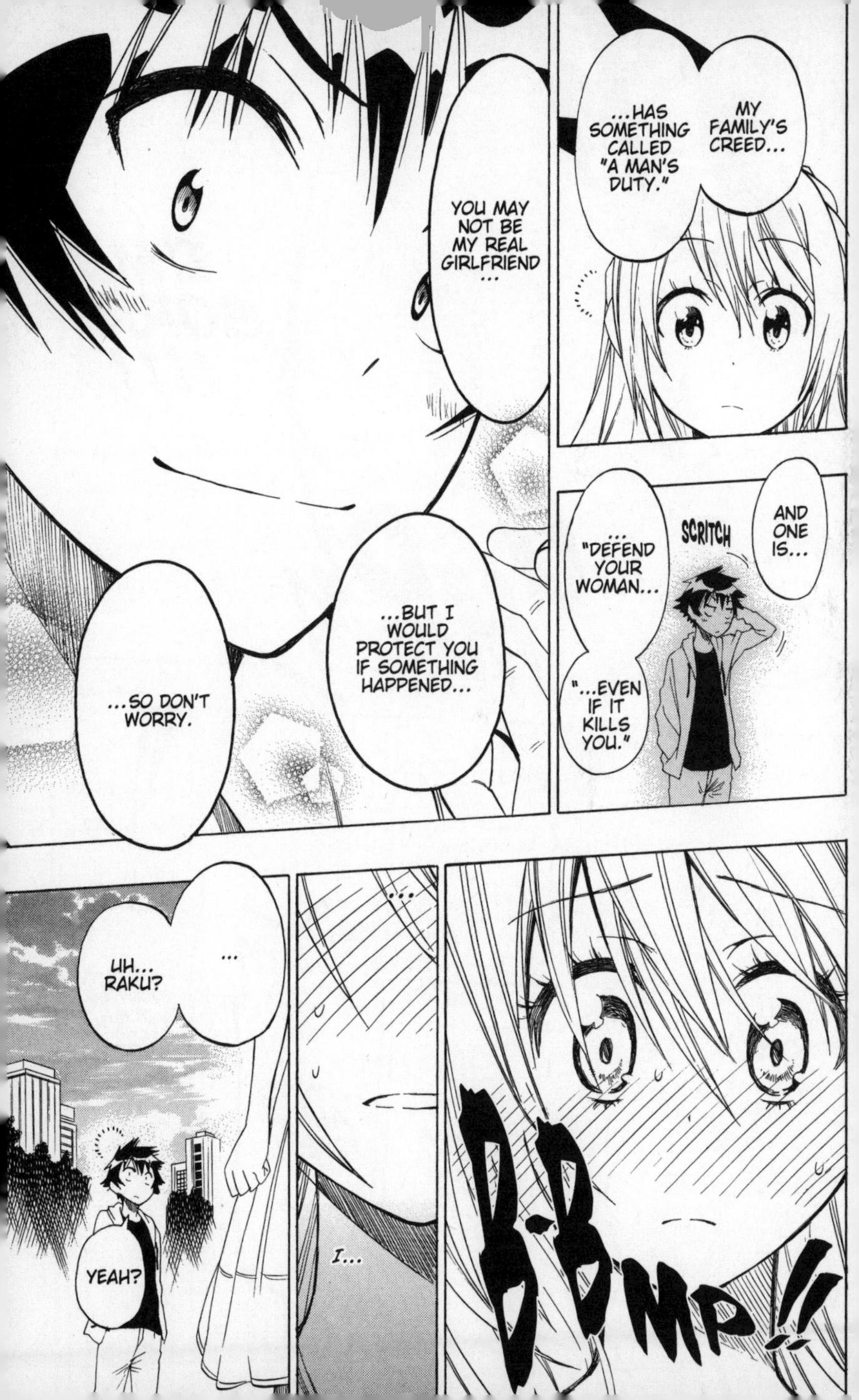
MY FAMILY'S CREED...
...HAS SOMETHING CALLED "A MAN'S DUTY."
AND ONE IS...
SCRITCH
..."DEFEND YOUR WOMAN...
"...EVEN IF IT KILLS YOU."
YOU MAY NOT BE MY REAL GIRLFRIEND...
...BUT I WOULD PROTECT YOU IF SOMETHING HAPPENED...
...SO DON'T WORRY.
B-BMP!!
...
I...
...
UH... RAKU?
YEAH?

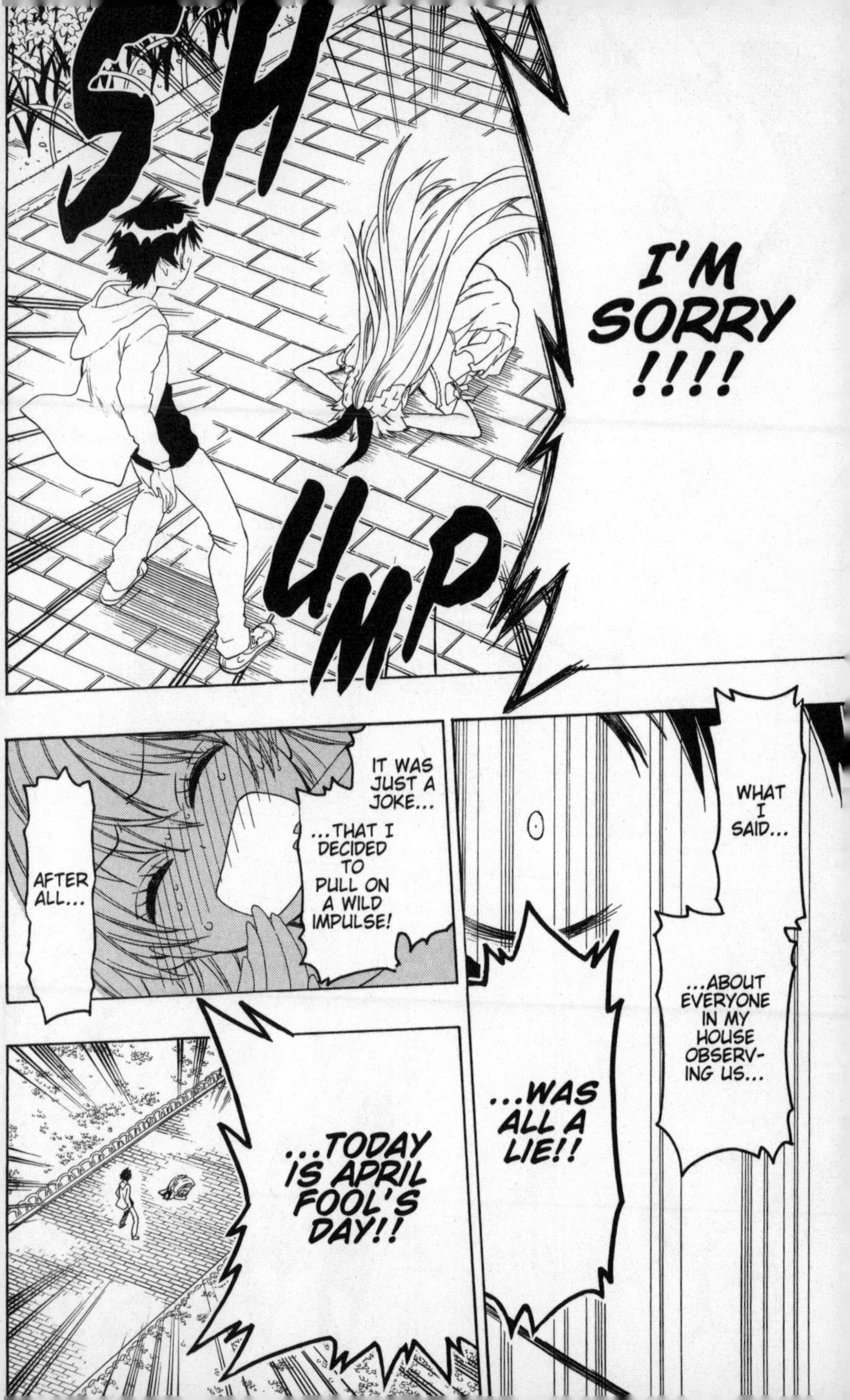
I'M SORRY!!!!
SH
UMP
WHAT I SAID...
...ABOUT EVERYONE IN MY HOUSE OBSERV-ING US...
...WAS ALL A LIE!!
IT WAS JUST A JOKE...
...THAT I DECIDED TO PULL ON A WILD IMPULSE!
AFTER ALL...
...TODAY IS APRIL FOOL'S DAY!!

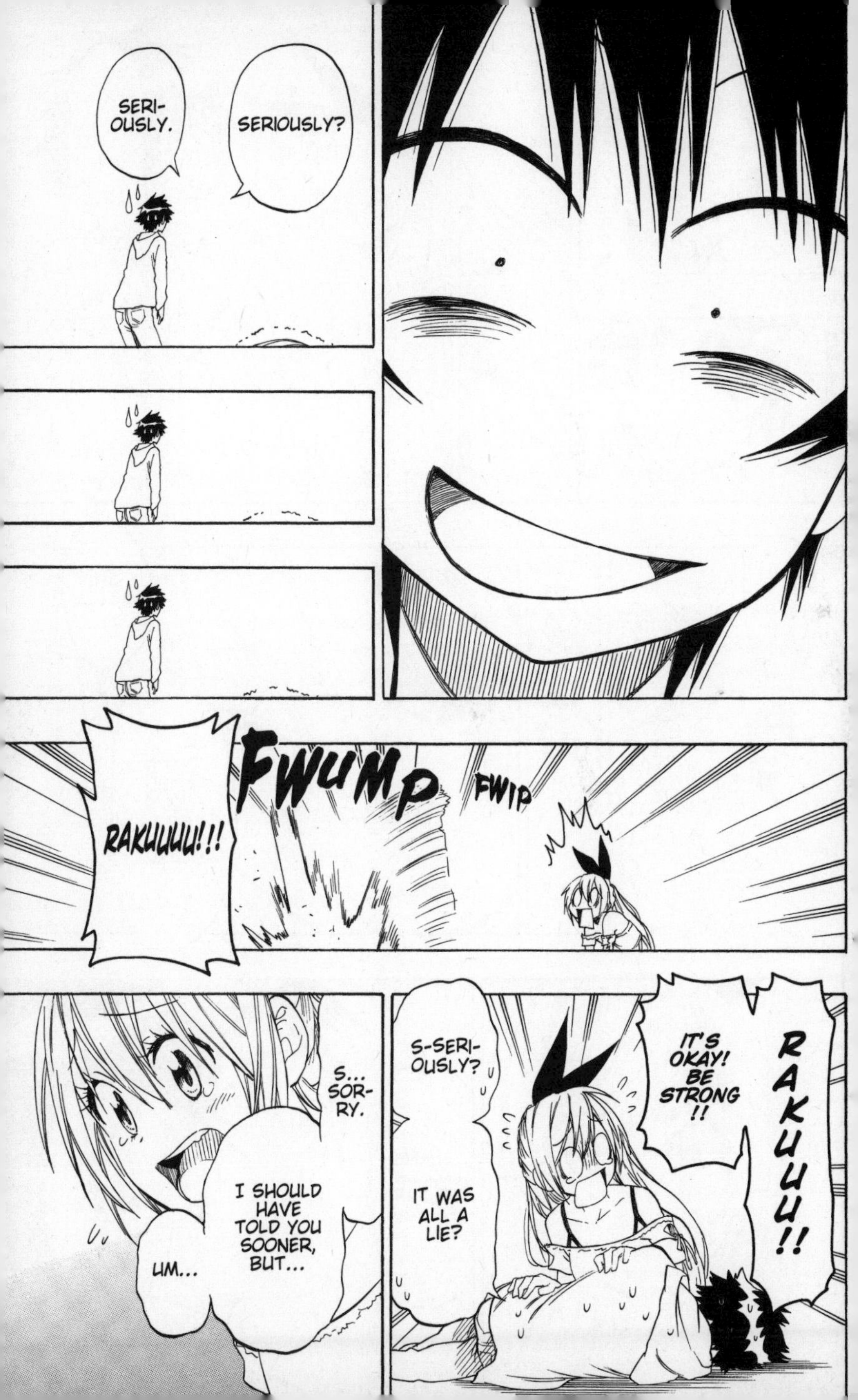
SERIOUSLY?
SERI-OUSLY.
FWIP
FWUMP
RAKUUUU!!!
RAKUUU!!
IT'S OKAY! BE STRONG!!
S-SERI-OUSLY?
IT WAS ALL A LIE?
S... SORRY.
I SHOULD HAVE TOLD YOU SOONER, BUT...
UM...

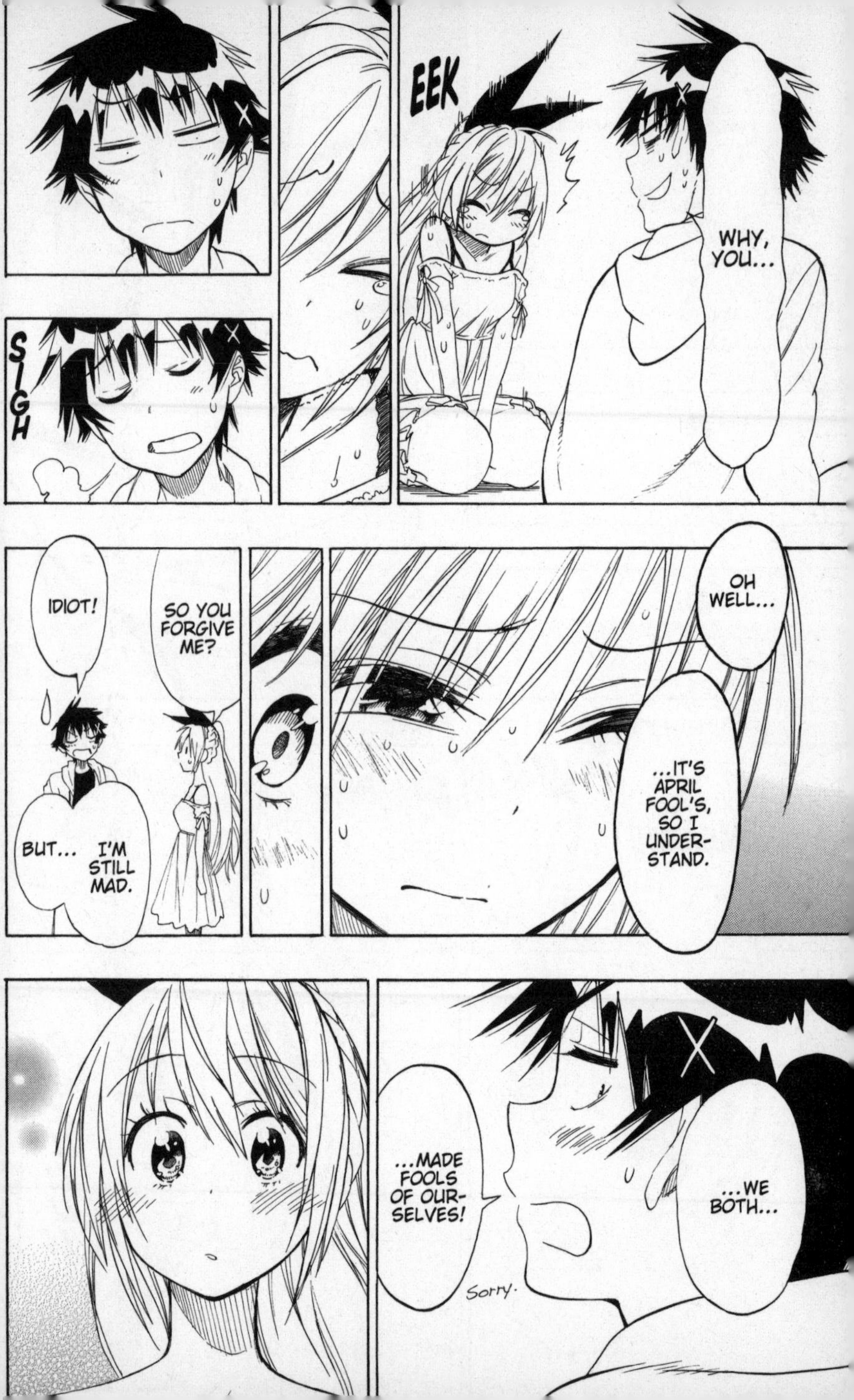
WHY, YOU...
EEK
SIGH
OH WELL...
...IT'S APRIL FOOL'S, SO I UNDER-STAND.
SO YOU FORGIVE ME?
IDIOT!
BUT... I'M STILL MAD.
...WE BOTH...
...MADE FOOLS OF OUR-SELVES!
Sorry.

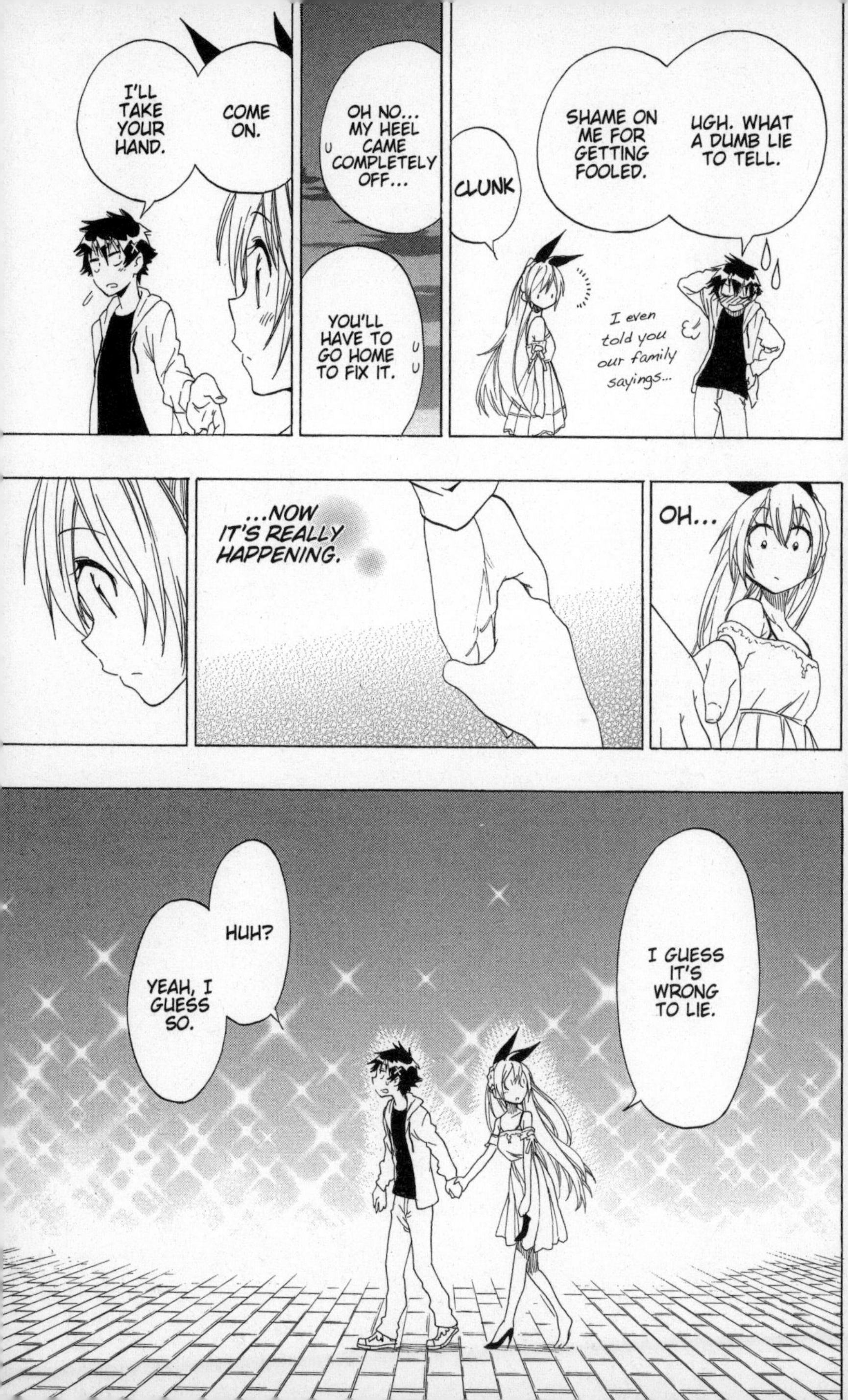
UGH. WHAT A DUMB LIE TO TELL.
SHAME ON ME FOR GETTING FOOLED.
CLUNK
I even told you our family sayings...
OH NO... MY HEEL CAME COMPLETELY OFF...
YOU'LL HAVE TO GO HOME TO FIX IT.
COME ON.
I'LL TAKE YOUR HAND.
OH...
...NOW IT'S REALLY HAPPENING.
I GUESS IT'S WRONG TO LIE.
HUH?
YEAH, I GUESS SO.

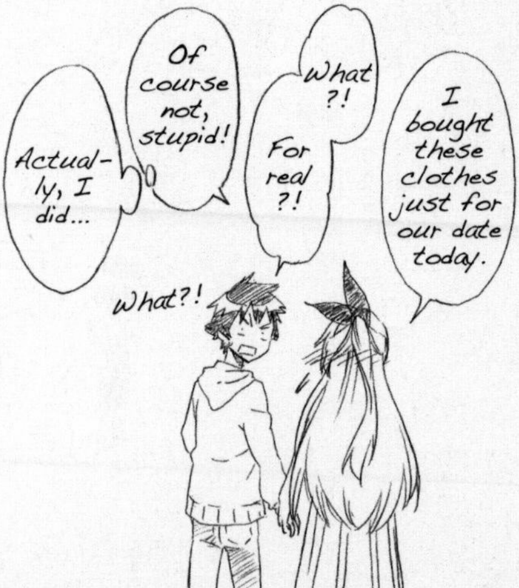
I bought these clothes just for our date today.
What?!
For real?!
Of course not, stupid!
Actual-ly, I did...
What?!

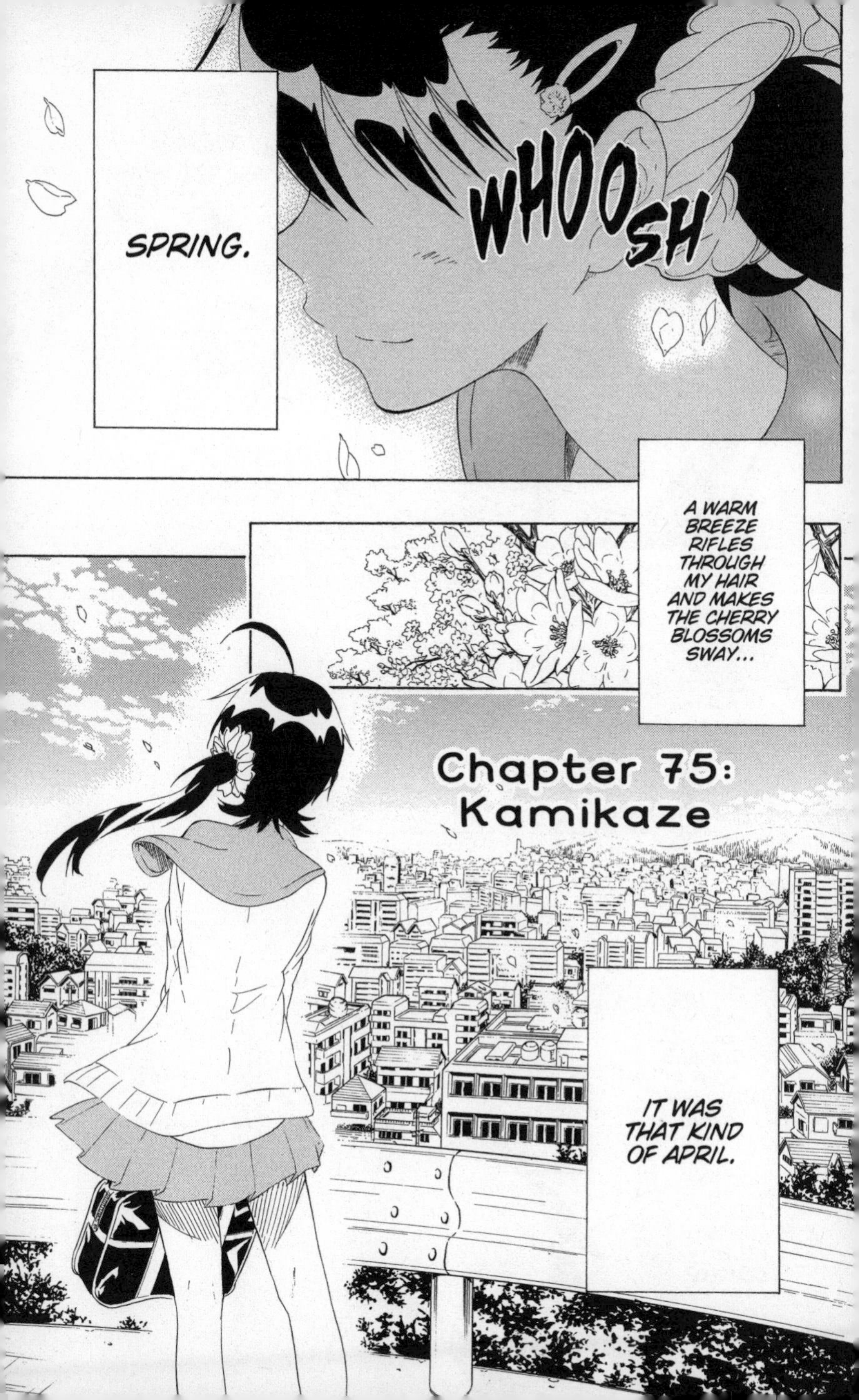
WHOOSH
SPRING.
A WARM BREEZE RIFLES THROUGH MY HAIR AND MAKES THE CHERRY BLOSSOMS SWAY...
Chapter 75: Kamikaze
IT WAS THAT KIND OF APRIL.

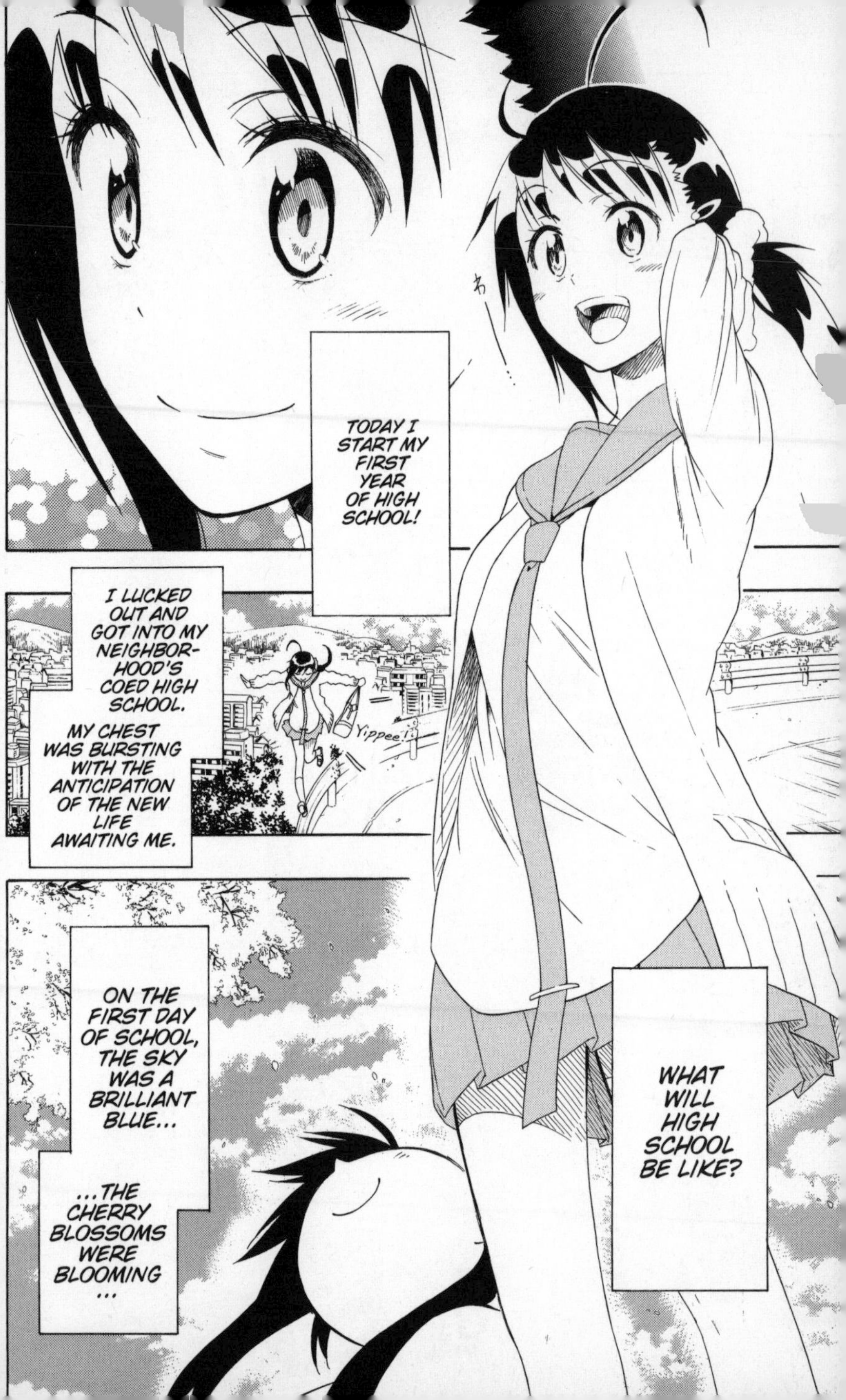
わ
TODAY I START MY FIRST YEAR OF HIGH SCHOOL!
I LUCKED OUT AND GOT INTO MY NEIGHBOR-HOOD'S COED HIGH SCHOOL.
MY CHEST WAS BURSTING WITH THE ANTICIPATION OF THE NEW LIFE AWAITING ME.
Yippee!
ON THE FIRST DAY OF SCHOOL, THE SKY WAS A BRILLIANT BLUE...
...THE CHERRY BLOSSOMS WERE BLOOMING...
WHAT WILL HIGH SCHOOL BE LIKE?

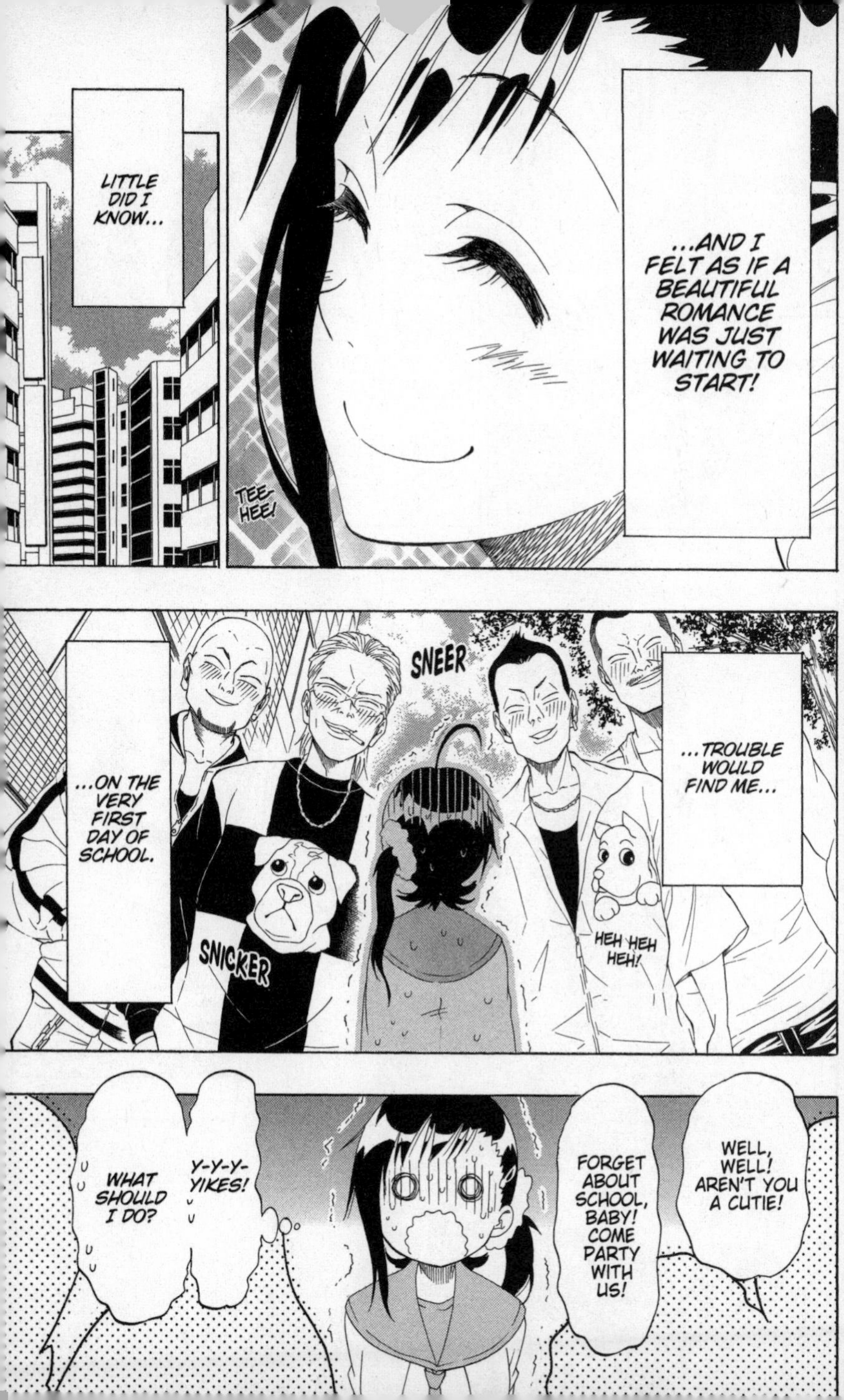
...AND I FELT AS IF A BEAUTIFUL ROMANCE WAS JUST WAITING TO START!
TEE-HEE!
LITTLE DID I KNOW...
...TROUBLE WOULD FIND ME...
SNEER
HEH HEH HEH!
SNICKER
...ON THE VERY FIRST DAY OF SCHOOL.
WELL, WELL! AREN'T YOU A CUTIE!
FORGET ABOUT SCHOOL, BABY! COME PARTY WITH US!
Y-Y-Y-YIKES!
WHAT SHOULD I DO?

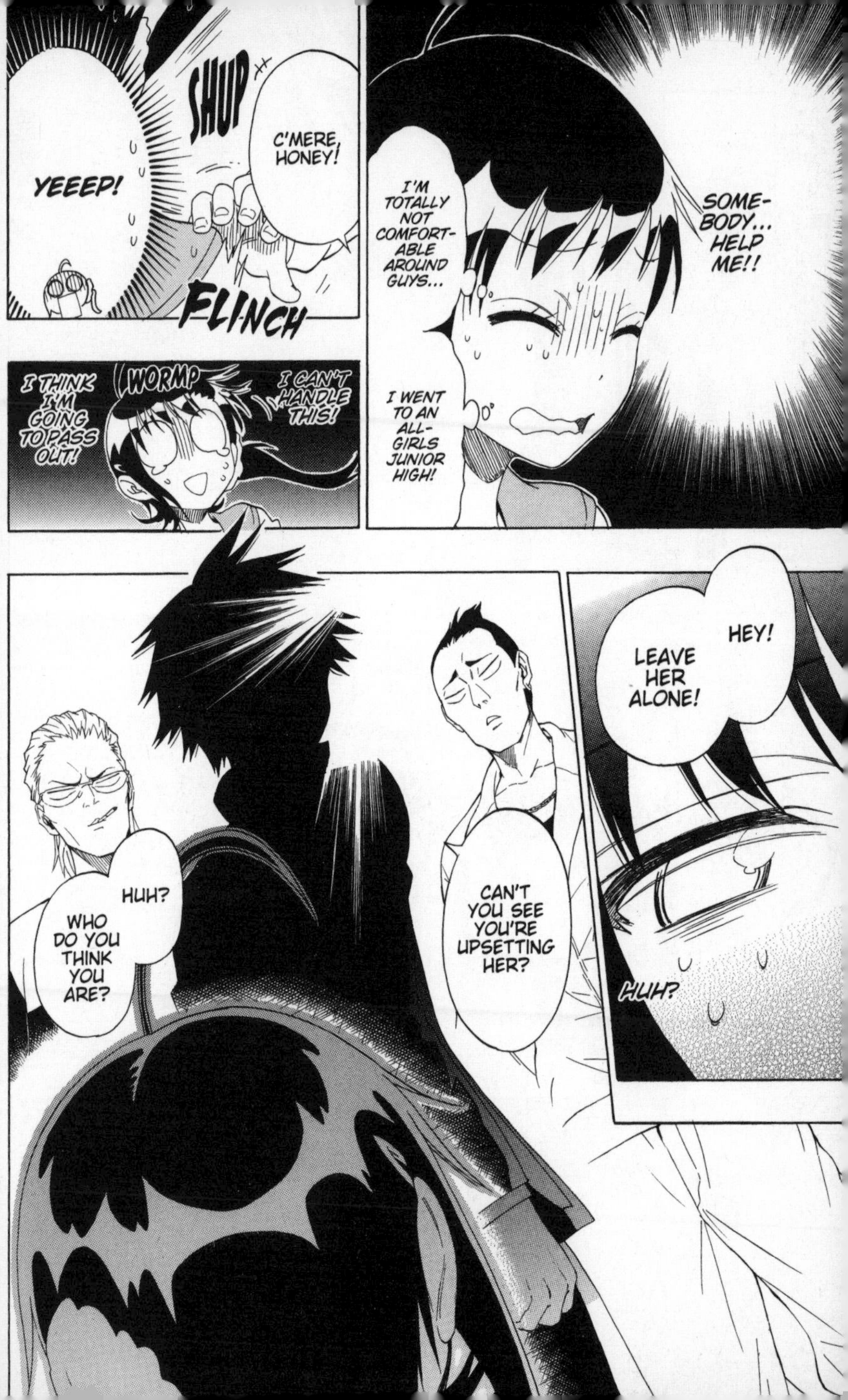
SOME-BODY... HELP ME!!
I'M TOTALLY NOT COMFORT-ABLE AROUND GUYS...
I WENT TO AN ALL-GIRLS JUNIOR HIGH!
C'MERE, HONEY!
SHUP
YEEEP!
FLINCH
WORMP
I CAN'T HANDLE THIS!
I THINK I'M GOING TO PASS OUT!
HEY!
LEAVE HER ALONE!
HUH?
CAN'T YOU SEE YOU'RE UPSETTING HER?
HUH?
WHO DO YOU THINK YOU ARE?

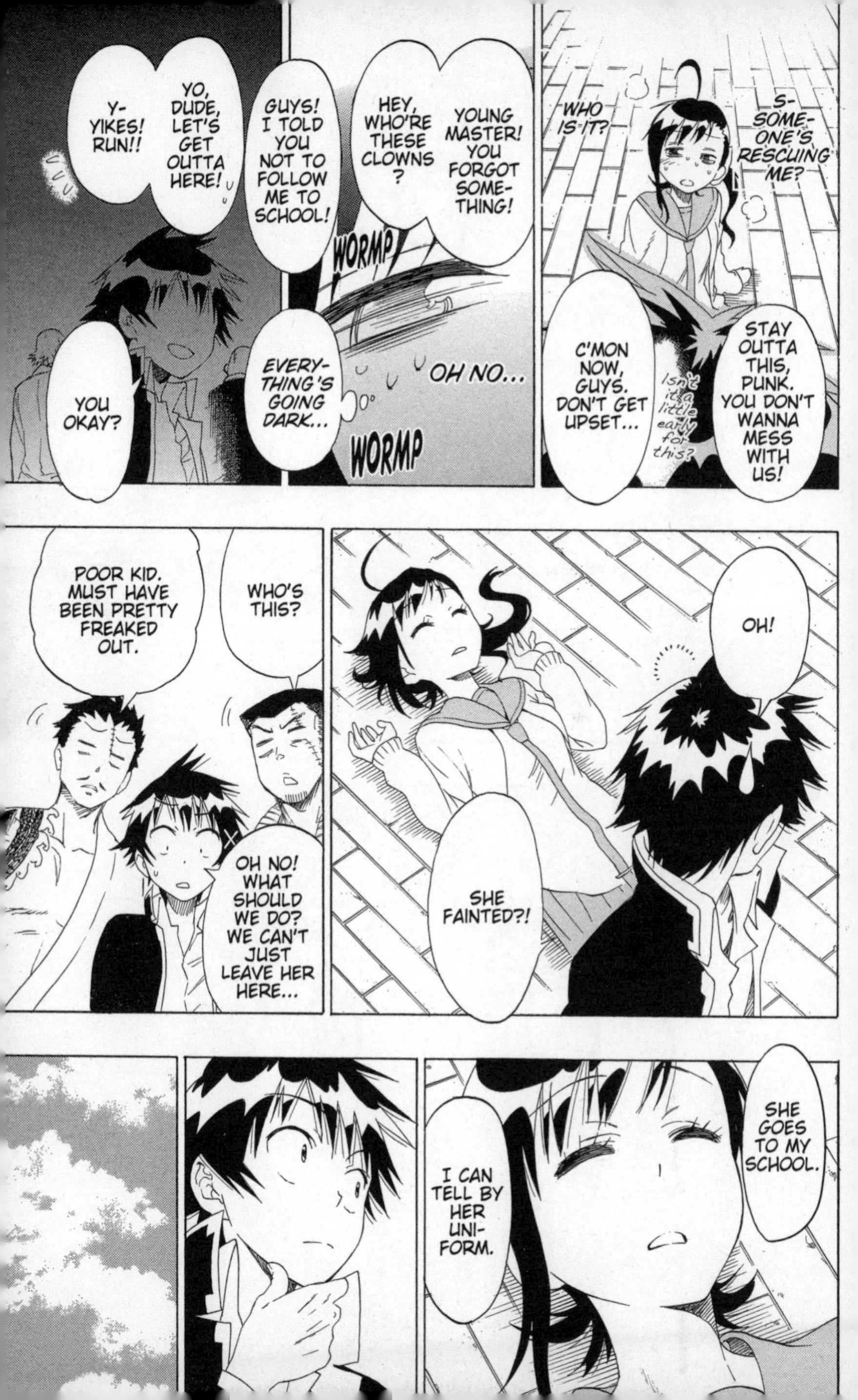

S-SOMEONE'S RESCUING ME?
WHO IS IT?
STAY OUTTA THIS, PUNK. YOU DON'T WANNA MESS WITH US!
Isn't it a little early for this?
C'MON NOW, GUYS. DON'T GET UPSET...
YOUNG MASTER! YOU FORGOT SOMETHING!
HEY, WHO'RE THESE CLOWNS?
GUYS! I TOLD YOU NOT TO FOLLOW ME TO SCHOOL!
WORMP
OH NO...
EVERYTHING'S GOING DARK...
WORMP
YO, DUDE, LET'S GET OUTTA HERE!
Y-YIKES! RUN!!
YOU OKAY?
OH!
SHE FAINTED?!
WHO'S THIS?
POOR KID. MUST HAVE BEEN PRETTY FREAKED OUT.
OH NO! WHAT SHOULD WE DO? WE CAN'T JUST LEAVE HER HERE...
SHE GOES TO MY SCHOOL.
I CAN TELL BY HER UNIFORM.

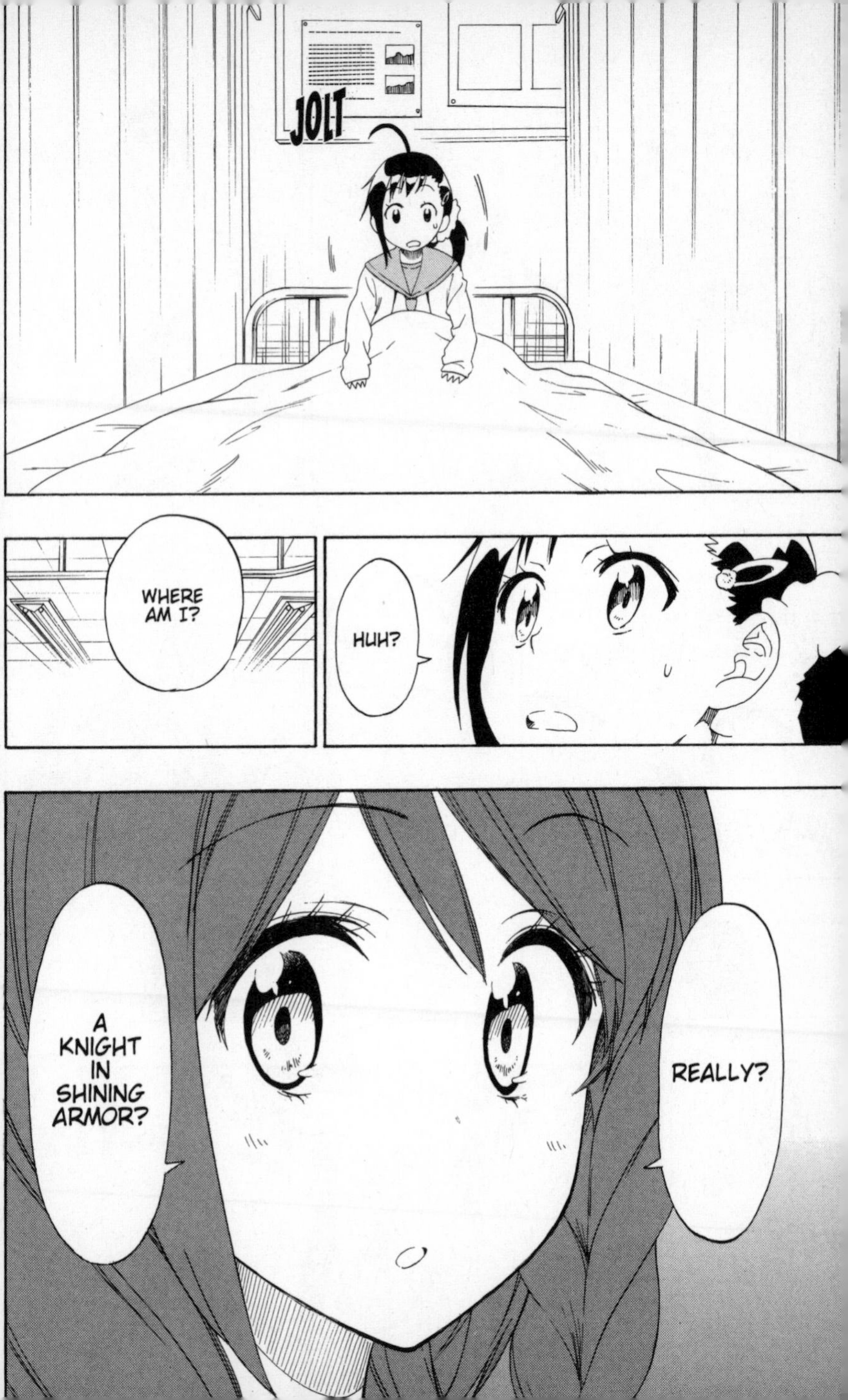
JOLT
HUH?
WHERE AM I?
REALLY?
A KNIGHT IN SHINING ARMOR?

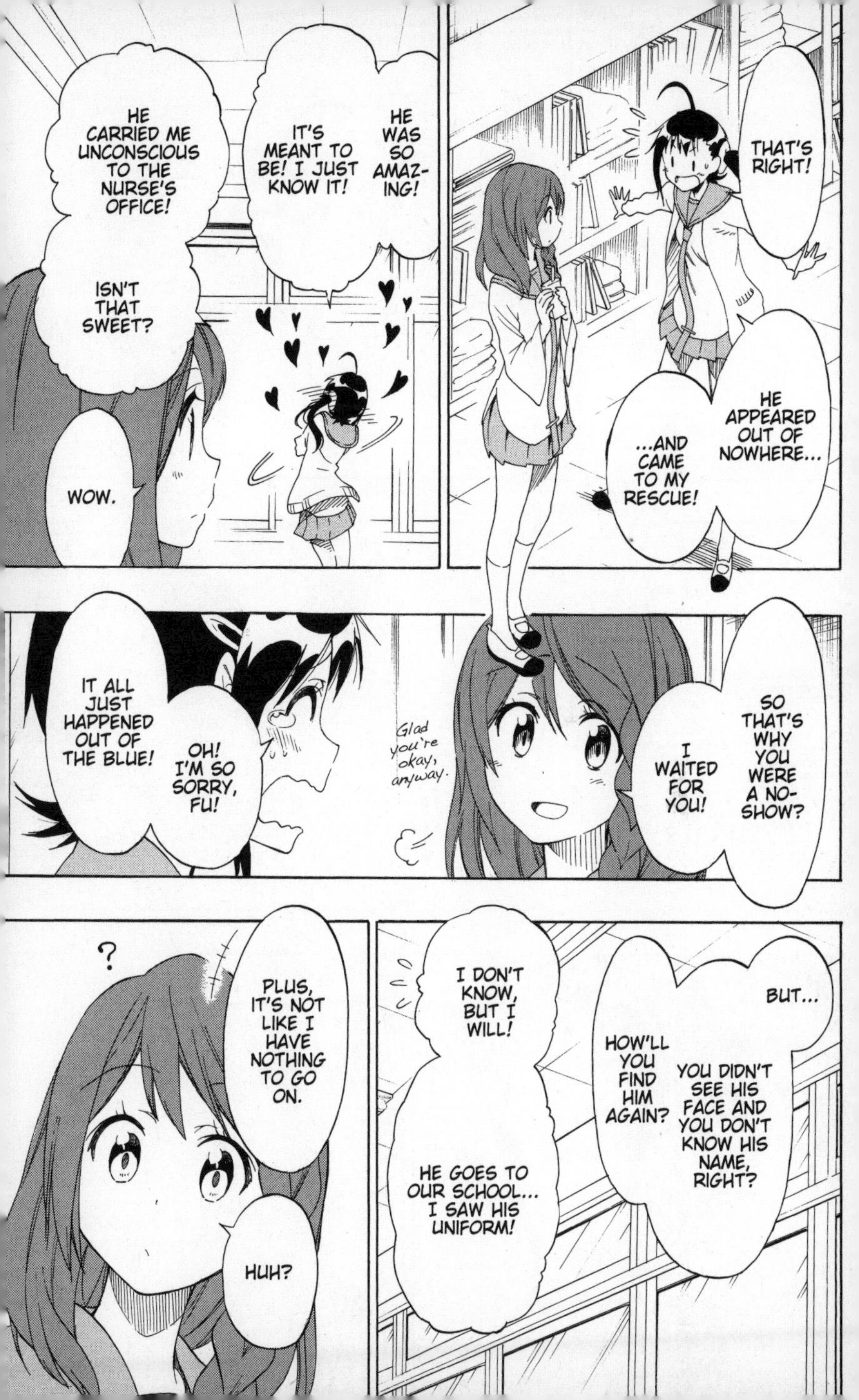
THAT'S RIGHT!
HE APPEARED OUT OF NOWHERE...
...AND CAME TO MY RESCUE!
HE WAS SO AMAZ-ING!
IT'S MEANT TO BE! I JUST KNOW IT!
HE CARRIED ME UNCONSCIOUS TO THE NURSE'S OFFICE!
ISN'T THAT SWEET?
WOW.
SO THAT'S WHY YOU WERE A NO-SHOW?
I WAITED FOR YOU!
Glad you're okay, anyway.
OH! I'M SO SORRY, FU!
IT ALL JUST HAPPENED OUT OF THE BLUE!
BUT...
YOU DIDN'T SEE HIS FACE AND YOU DON'T KNOW HIS NAME, RIGHT?
HOW'LL YOU FIND HIM AGAIN?
I DON'T KNOW, BUT I WILL!
HE GOES TO OUR SCHOOL... I SAW HIS UNIFORM!
?
PLUS, IT'S NOT LIKE I HAVE NOTHING TO GO ON.
HUH?

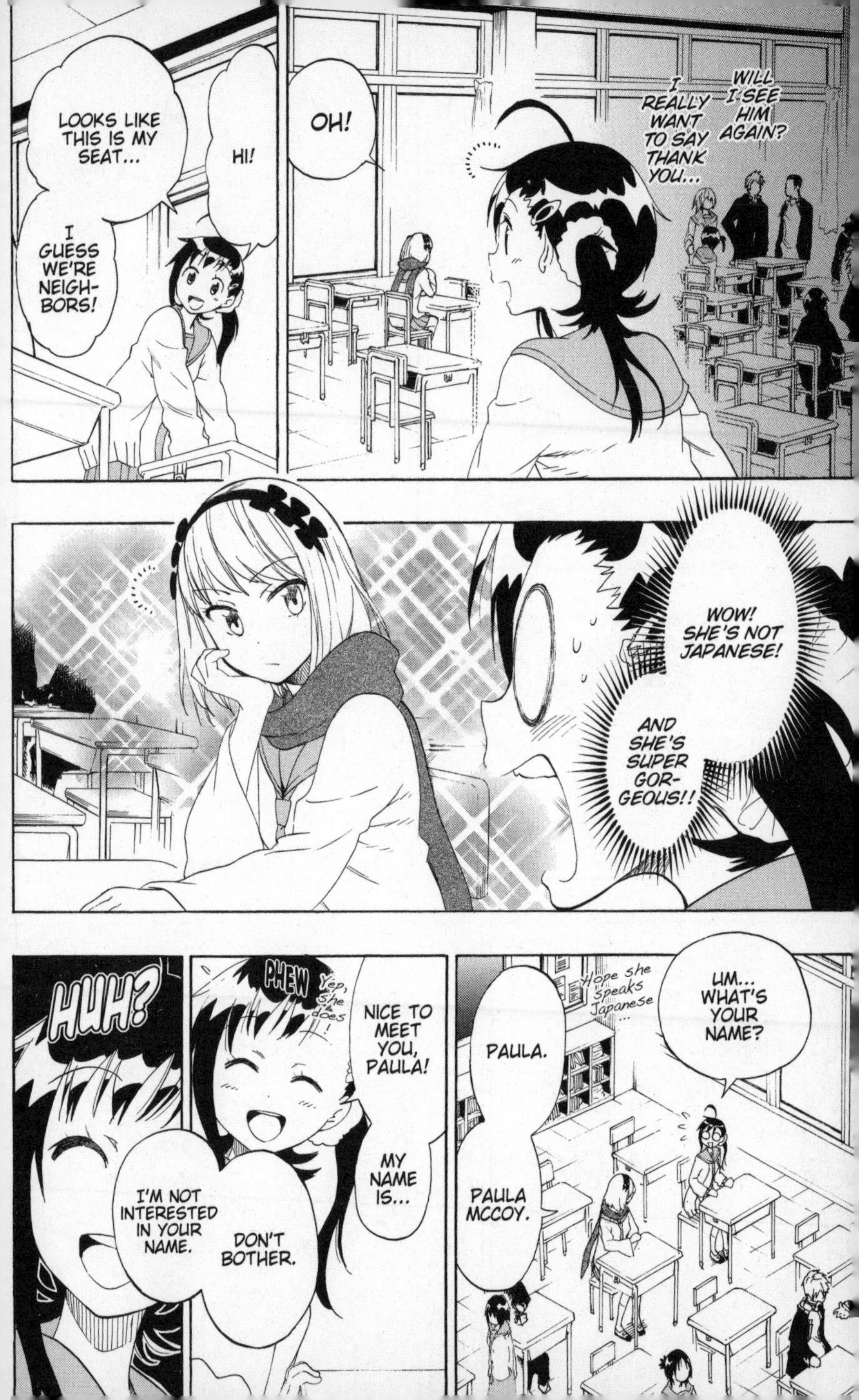
WILL I SEE HIM AGAIN?
I REALLY WANT TO SAY THANK YOU...
OH!
HI!
LOOKS LIKE THIS IS MY SEAT...
I GUESS WE'RE NEIGHBORS!
WOW! SHE'S NOT JAPANESE!
AND SHE'S SUPER GORGEOUS!!
UM... WHAT'S YOUR NAME?
Hope she speaks Japanese...
PAULA.
PAULA MCCOY.
Yep, she does!
PHEW
NICE TO MEET YOU, PAULA!
MY NAME IS...
DON'T BOTHER.
I'M NOT INTERESTED IN YOUR NAME.
HUH?

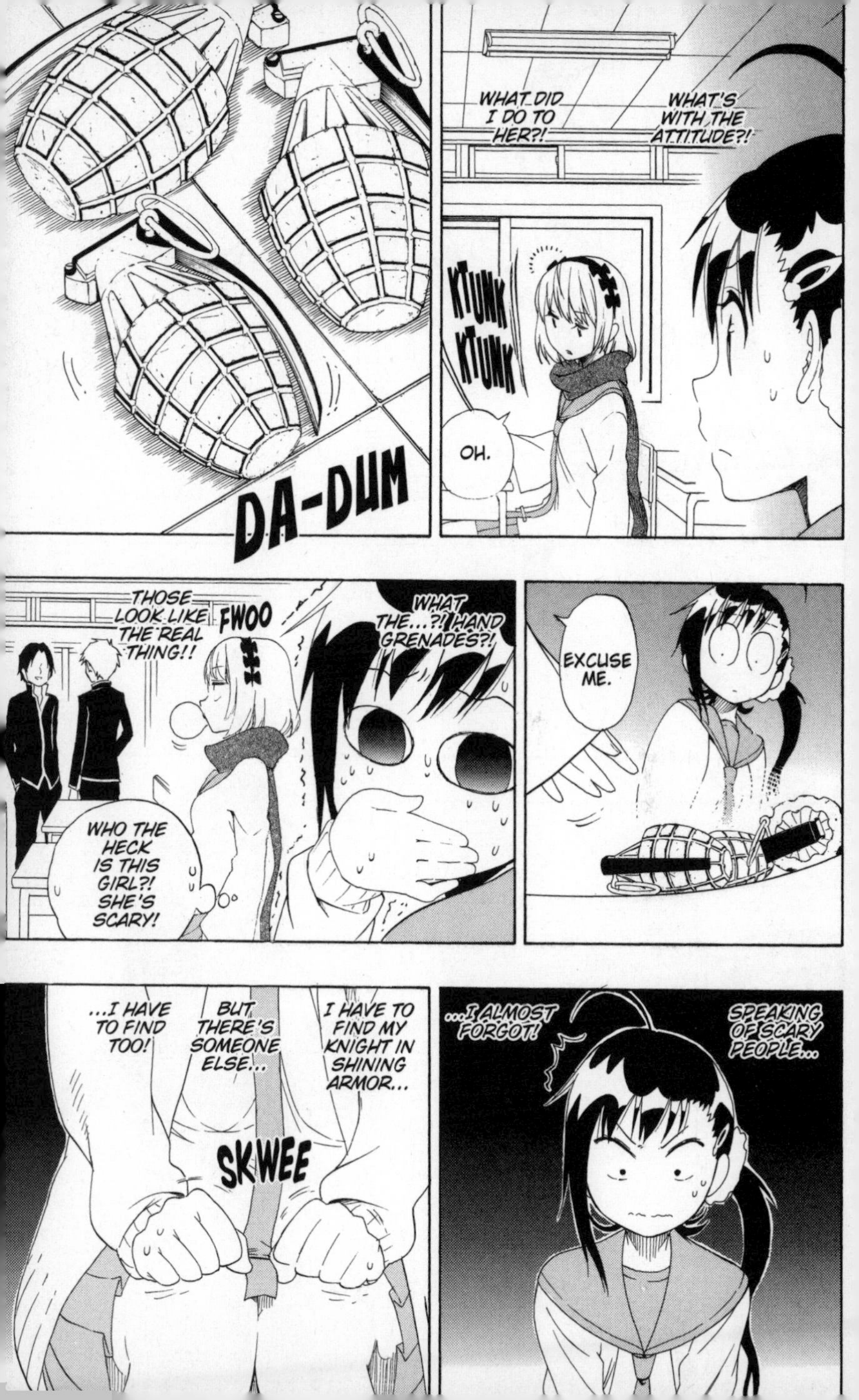
WHAT'S WITH THE ATTITUDE?!
WHAT DID I DO TO HER?!
KTUNK KTUNK
OH.
DA-DUM
EXCUSE ME.
WHAT THE...?! HAND GRENADES?!
FWOO
THOSE LOOK LIKE THE REAL THING!!
WHO THE HECK IS THIS GIRL?! SHE'S SCARY!
SPEAKING OF SCARY PEOPLE...
...I ALMOST FORGOT!
I HAVE TO FIND MY KNIGHT IN SHINING ARMOR...
BUT THERE'S SOMEONE ELSE...
...I HAVE TO FIND TOO!
SKWEE

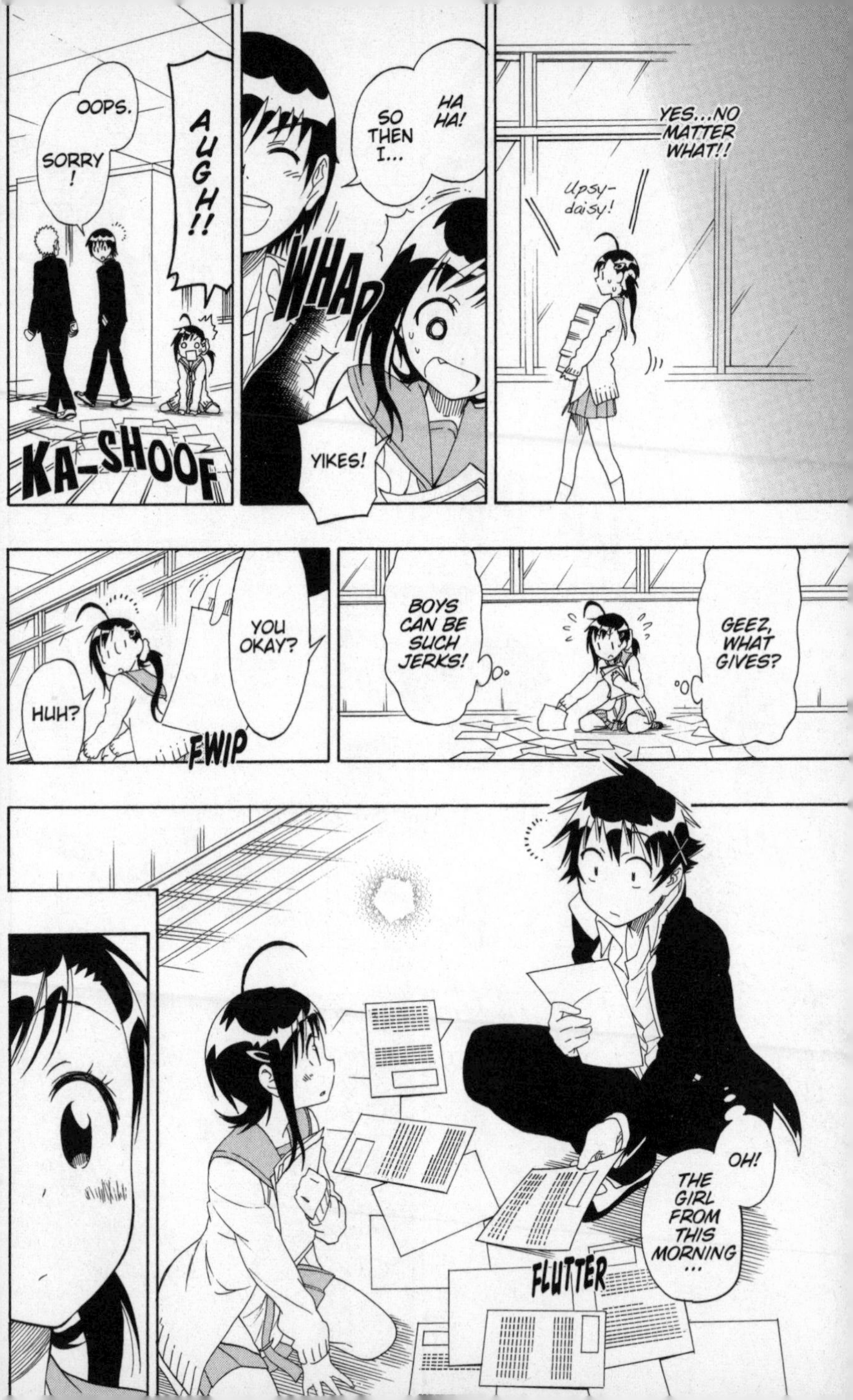
YES...NO MATTER WHAT!!
Upsy-daisy!
HA HA!
SO THEN I...
WHAP
YIKES!
AUGH!!
OOPS.
SORRY!
KA-SHOOF
GEEZ, WHAT GIVES?
BOYS CAN BE SUCH JERKS!
YOU OKAY?
FWIP
HUH?
OH!
THE GIRL FROM THIS MORNING...
FLUTTER

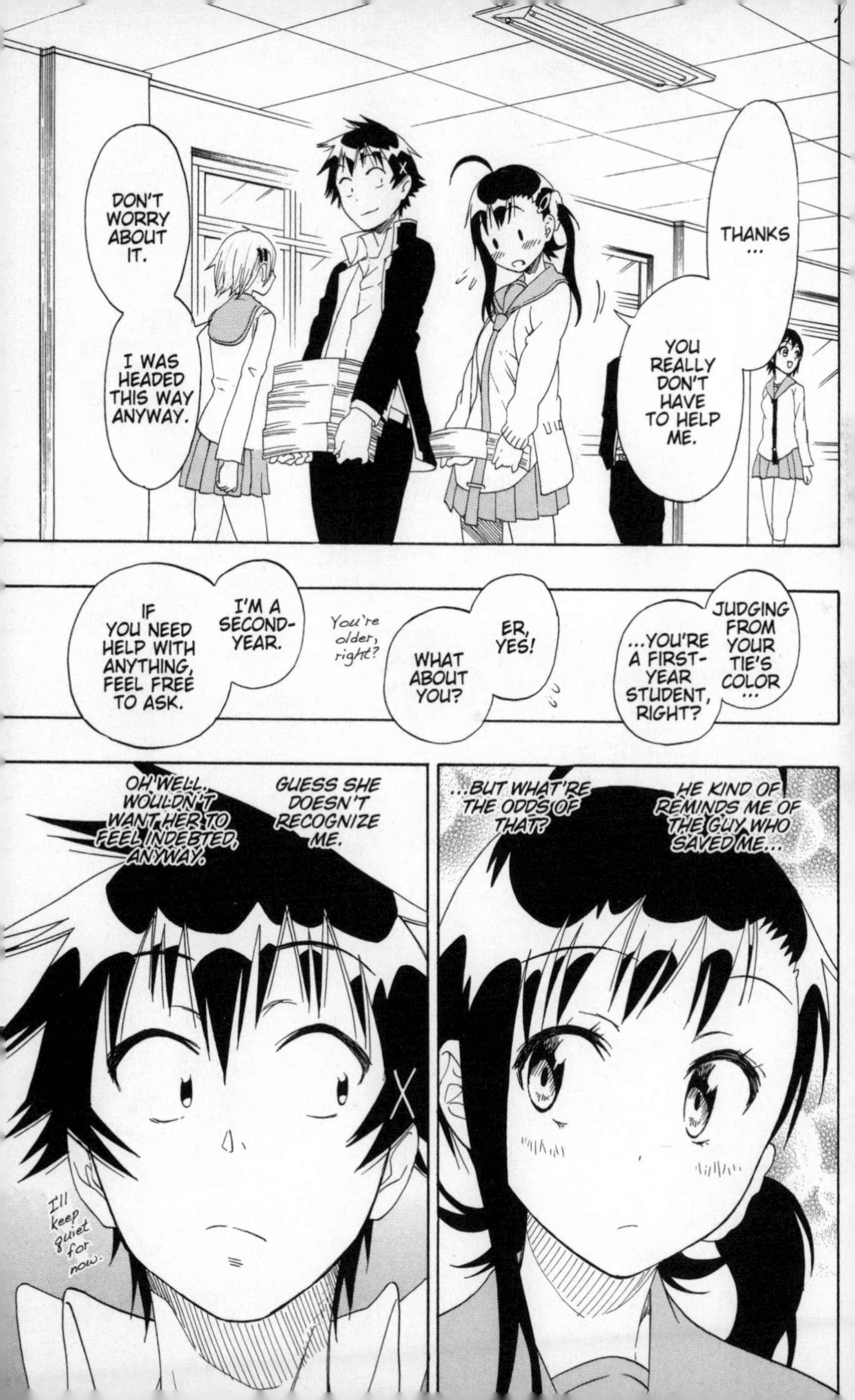
THANKS ...
YOU REALLY DON'T HAVE TO HELP ME.
DON'T WORRY ABOUT IT.
I WAS HEADED THIS WAY ANYWAY.
JUDGING FROM YOUR TIE'S COLOR ...
...YOU'RE A FIRST-YEAR STUDENT, RIGHT?
ER, YES!
WHAT ABOUT YOU?
You're older, right?
I'M A SECOND-YEAR.
IF YOU NEED HELP WITH ANYTHING, FEEL FREE TO ASK.
HE KIND OF REMINDS ME OF THE GUY WHO SAVED ME...
...BUT WHAT'RE THE ODDS OF THAT?
GUESS SHE DOESN'T RECOGNIZE ME.
OH WELL. WOULDN'T WANT HER TO FEEL INDEBTED, ANYWAY.
I'll keep quiet for now.

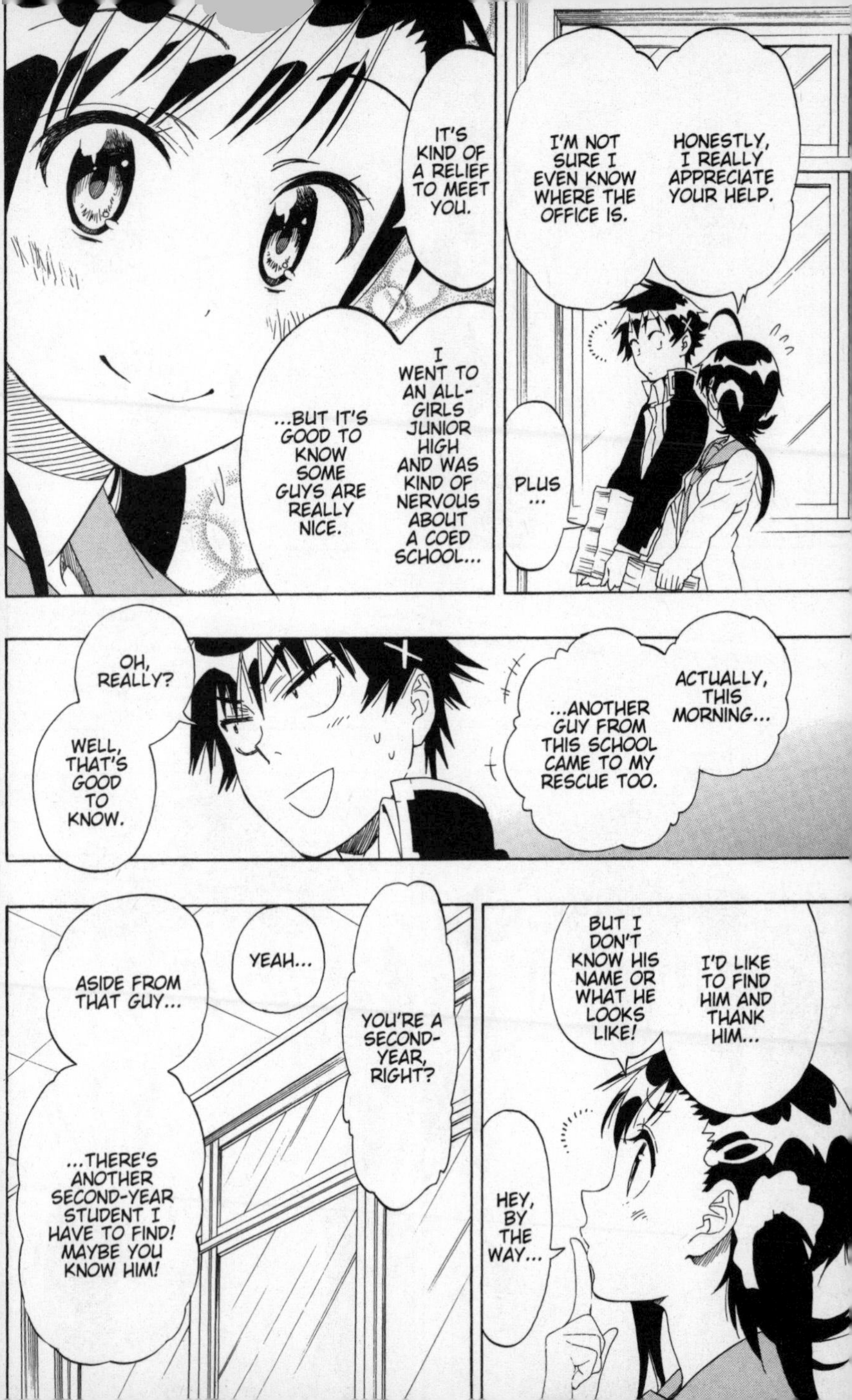
HONESTLY, I REALLY APPRECIATE YOUR HELP.
I'M NOT SURE I EVEN KNOW WHERE THE OFFICE IS.
PLUS ...
IT'S KIND OF A RELIEF TO MEET YOU.
I WENT TO AN ALL-GIRLS JUNIOR HIGH AND WAS KIND OF NERVOUS ABOUT A COED SCHOOL...
...BUT IT'S GOOD TO KNOW SOME GUYS ARE REALLY NICE.
ACTUALLY, THIS MORNING...
...ANOTHER GUY FROM THIS SCHOOL CAME TO MY RESCUE TOO.
OH, REALLY?
WELL, THAT'S GOOD TO KNOW.
I'D LIKE TO FIND HIM AND THANK HIM...
BUT I DON'T KNOW HIS NAME OR WHAT HE LOOKS LIKE!
HEY, BY THE WAY...
YOU'RE A SECOND-YEAR, RIGHT?
YEAH...
ASIDE FROM THAT GUY...
...THERE'S ANOTHER SECOND-YEAR STUDENT I HAVE TO FIND! MAYBE YOU KNOW HIM!

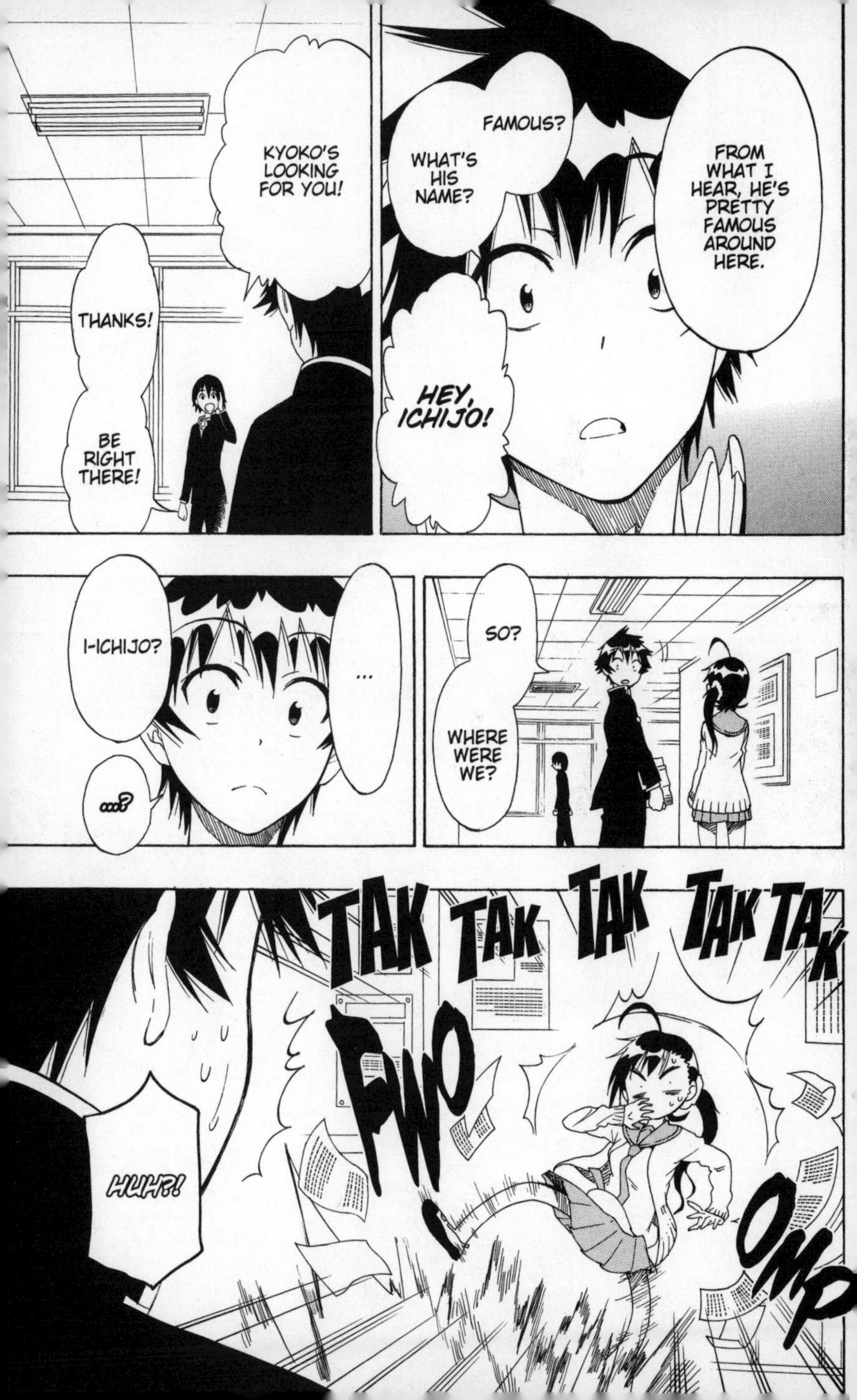

FROM WHAT I HEAR, HE'S PRETTY FAMOUS AROUND HERE.
FAMOUS? WHAT'S HIS NAME?
HEY, ICHIJO!
KYOKO'S LOOKING FOR YOU!
THANKS! BE RIGHT THERE!
SO? WHERE WERE WE?
...
I-ICHIJO?
...?
TAK TAK TAK TAK TAK
PWO
HUH?!
OMP

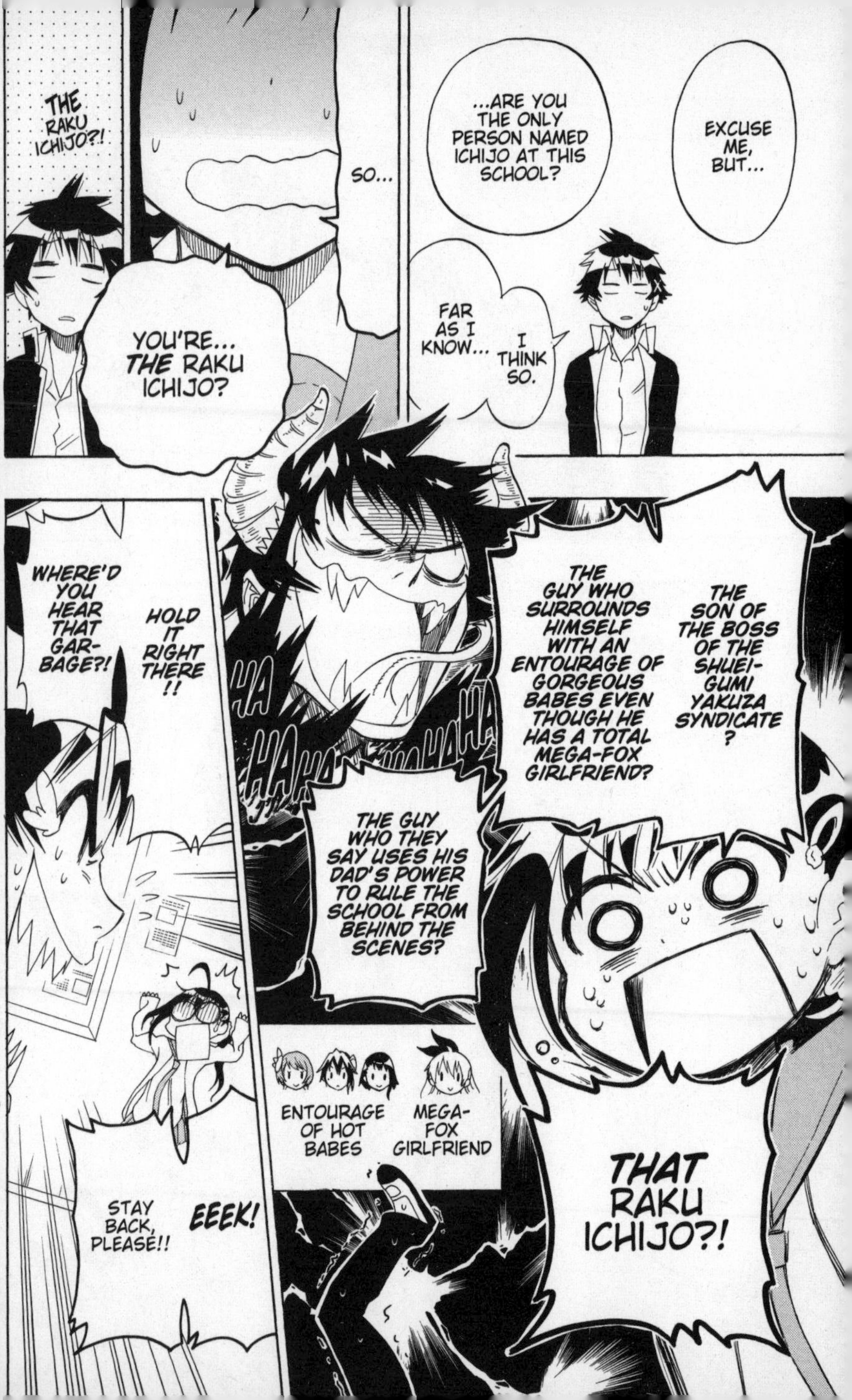
EXCUSE ME, BUT...
...ARE YOU THE ONLY PERSON NAMED ICHIJO AT THIS SCHOOL?
FAR AS I KNOW... I THINK SO.
SO...
YOU'RE... *THE* RAKU ICHIJO?
THE RAKU ICHIJO?!
THE SON OF THE BOSS OF THE SHUEI-GUMI YAKUZA SYNDICATE?
THE GUY WHO SURROUNDS HIMSELF WITH AN ENTOURAGE OF GORGEOUS BABES EVEN THOUGH HE HAS A TOTAL MEGA-FOX GIRLFRIEND?
THE GUY WHO THEY SAY USES HIS DAD'S POWER TO RULE THE SCHOOL FROM BEHIND THE SCENES?
MEGA-FOX GIRLFRIEND
ENTOURAGE OF HOT BABES
THAT RAKU ICHIJO?!
HOLD IT RIGHT THERE!!
WHERE'D YOU HEAR THAT GARBAGE?!
EEEK!
STAY BACK, PLEASE!!

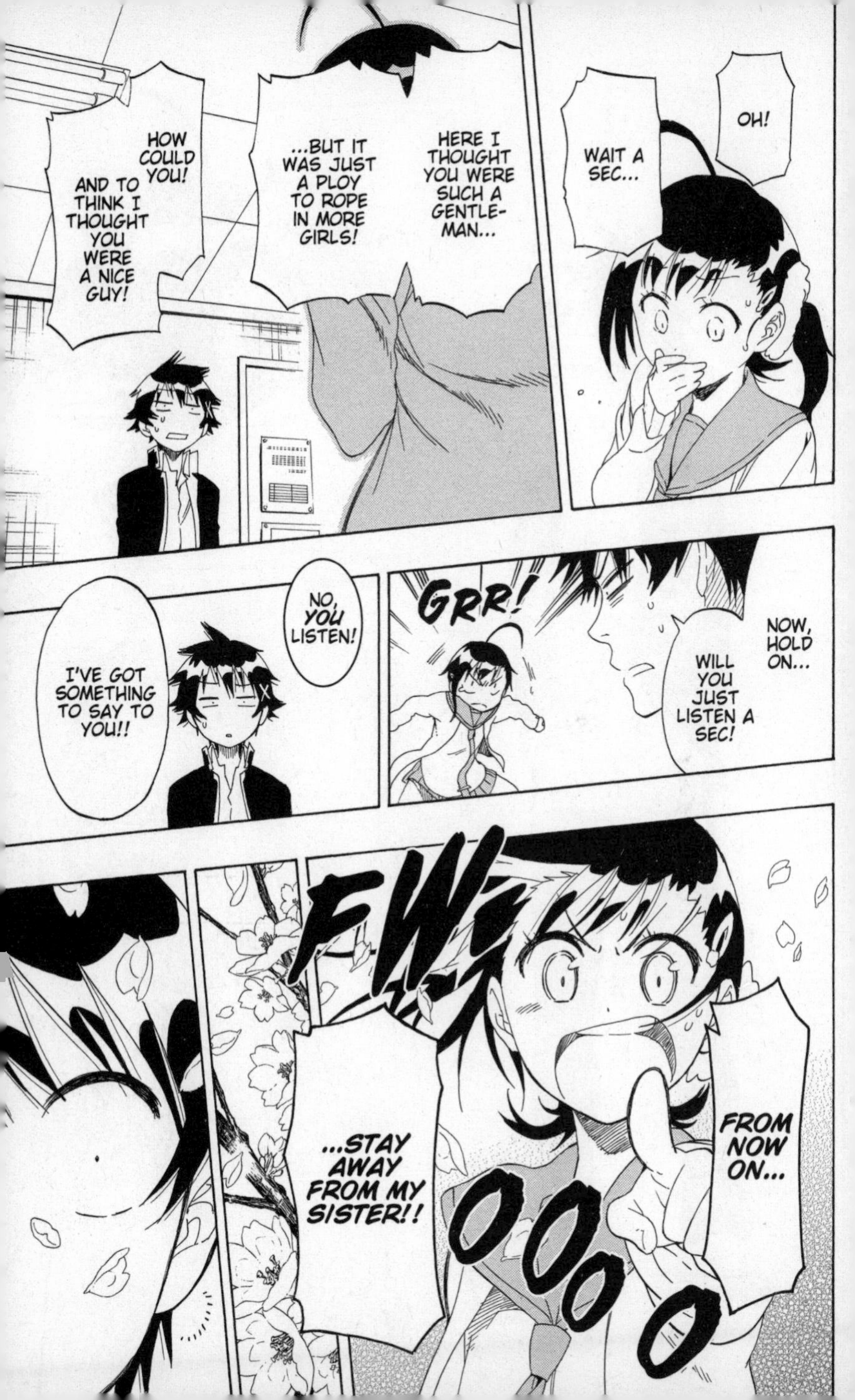
OH!
WAIT A SEC...
HERE I THOUGHT YOU WERE SUCH A GENTLE-MAN...
...BUT IT WAS JUST A PLOY TO ROPE IN MORE GIRLS!
HOW COULD YOU!
AND TO THINK I THOUGHT YOU WERE A NICE GUY!
NOW, HOLD ON...
WILL YOU JUST LISTEN A SEC!
GRR!
NO, YOU LISTEN!
I'VE GOT SOMETHING TO SAY TO YOU!!
FWOOOO
FROM NOW ON...
...STAY AWAY FROM MY SISTER!!

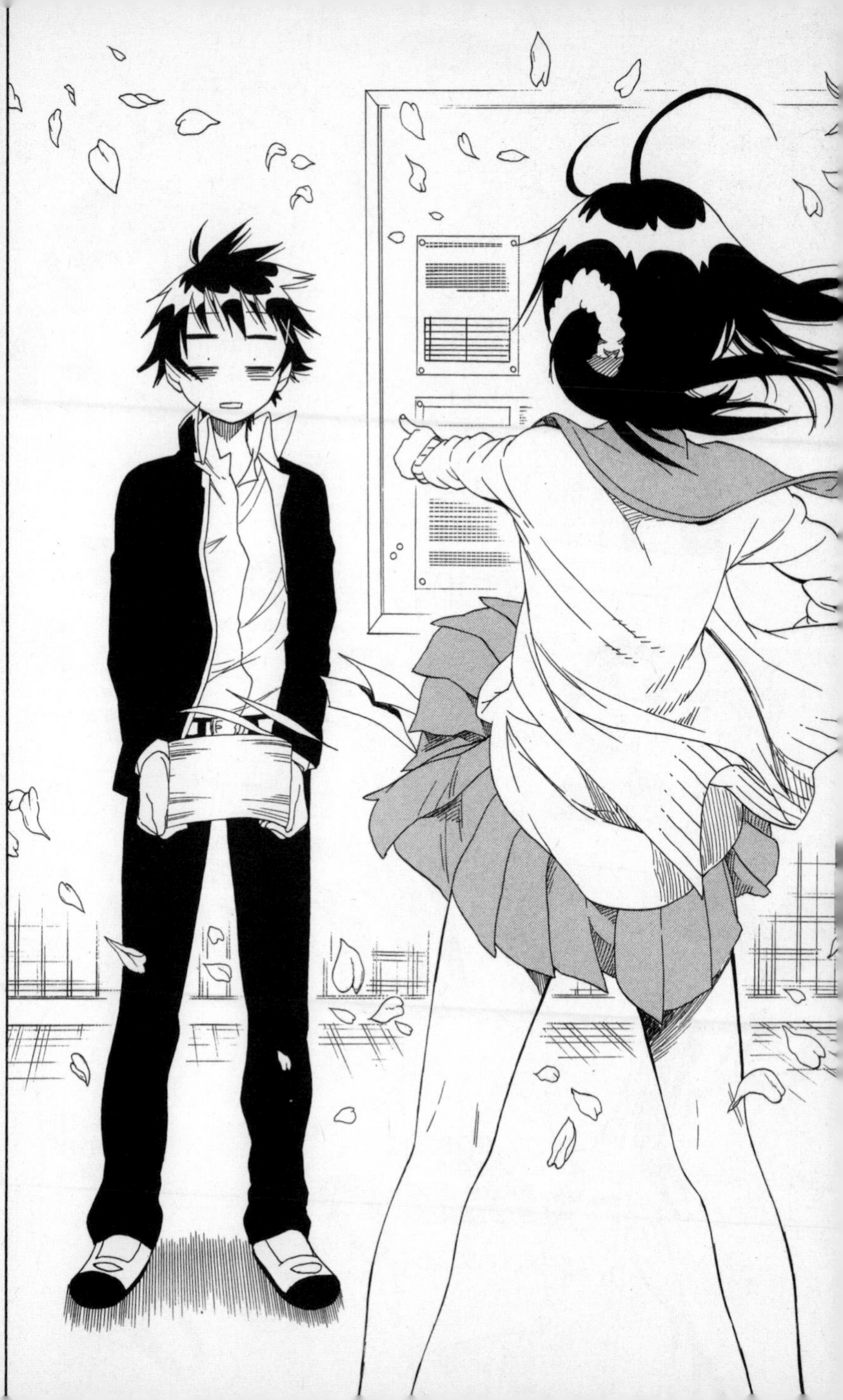

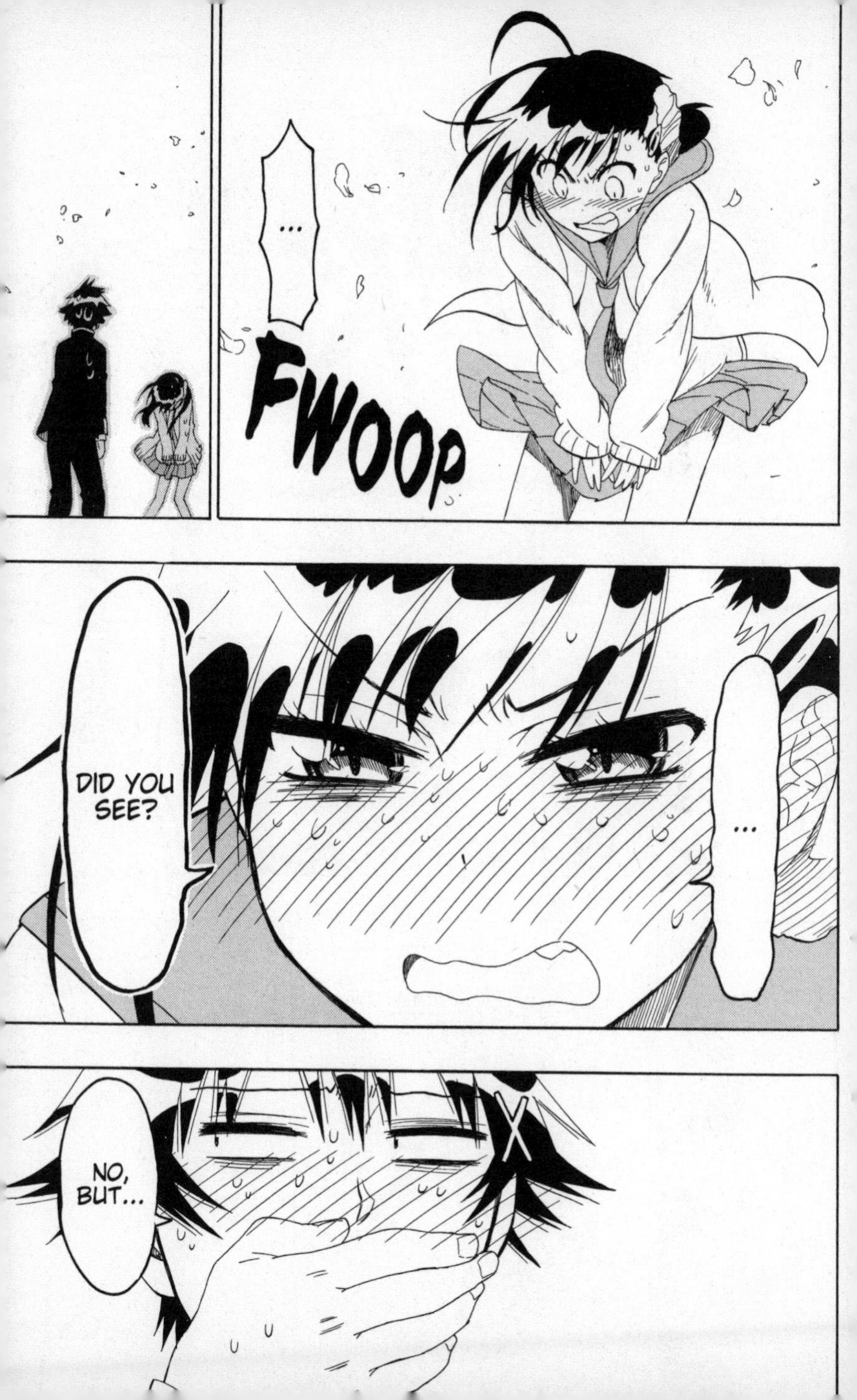
...
FWOOP
...
DID YOU SEE?
NO, BUT...

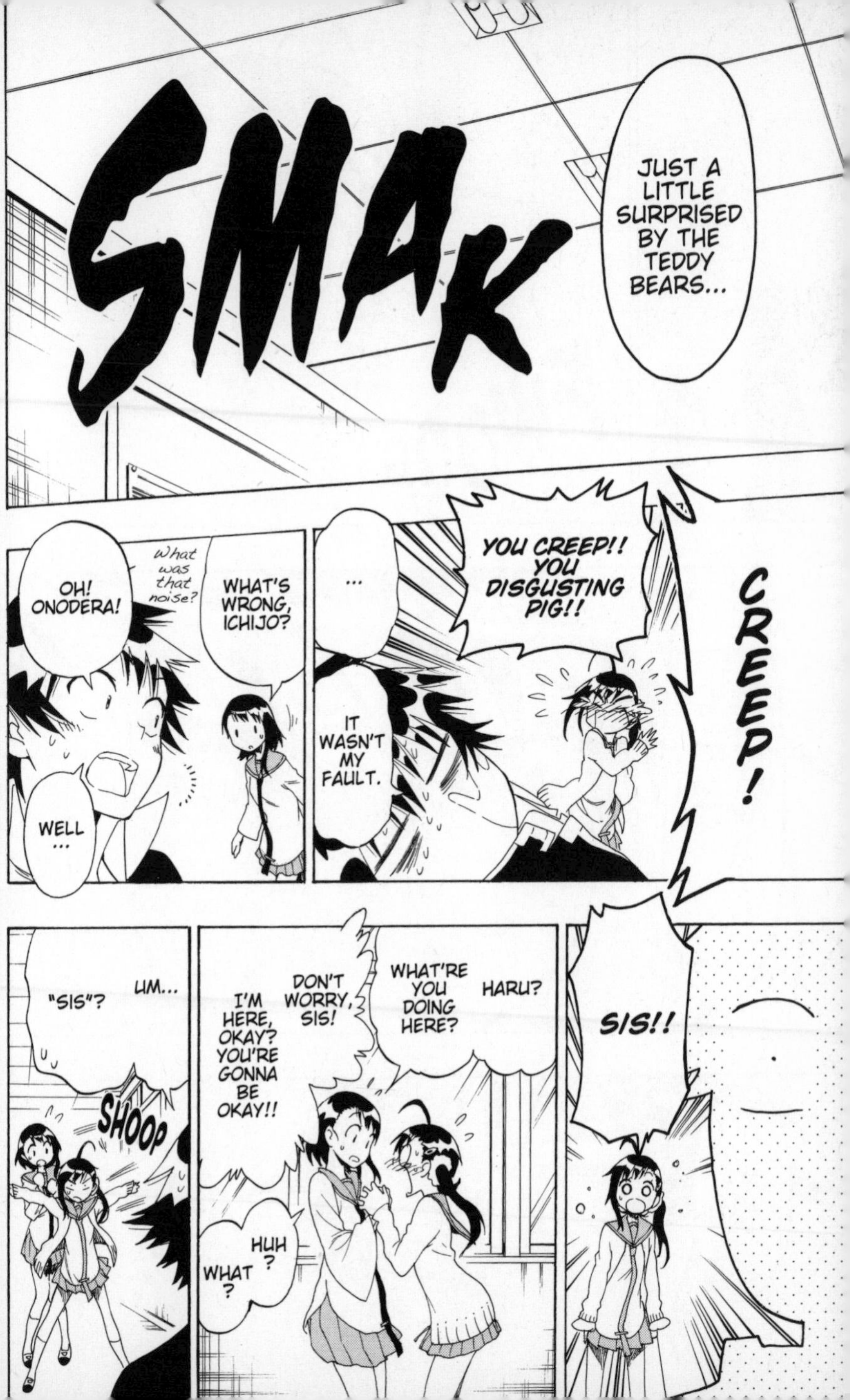
JUST A LITTLE SURPRISED BY THE TEDDY BEARS...
SMAK
YOU CREEP!! YOU DISGUSTING PIG!!
CREEP CREEP!
...
IT WASN'T MY FAULT.
What was that noise?
WHAT'S WRONG, ICHIJO?
OH! ONODERA!
WELL ...
SIS!!
HARU?
WHAT'RE YOU DOING HERE?
DON'T WORRY, SIS!
I'M HERE, OKAY? YOU'RE GONNA BE OKAY!!
HUH?
WHAT?
UM...
"SIS"?
SHOOP

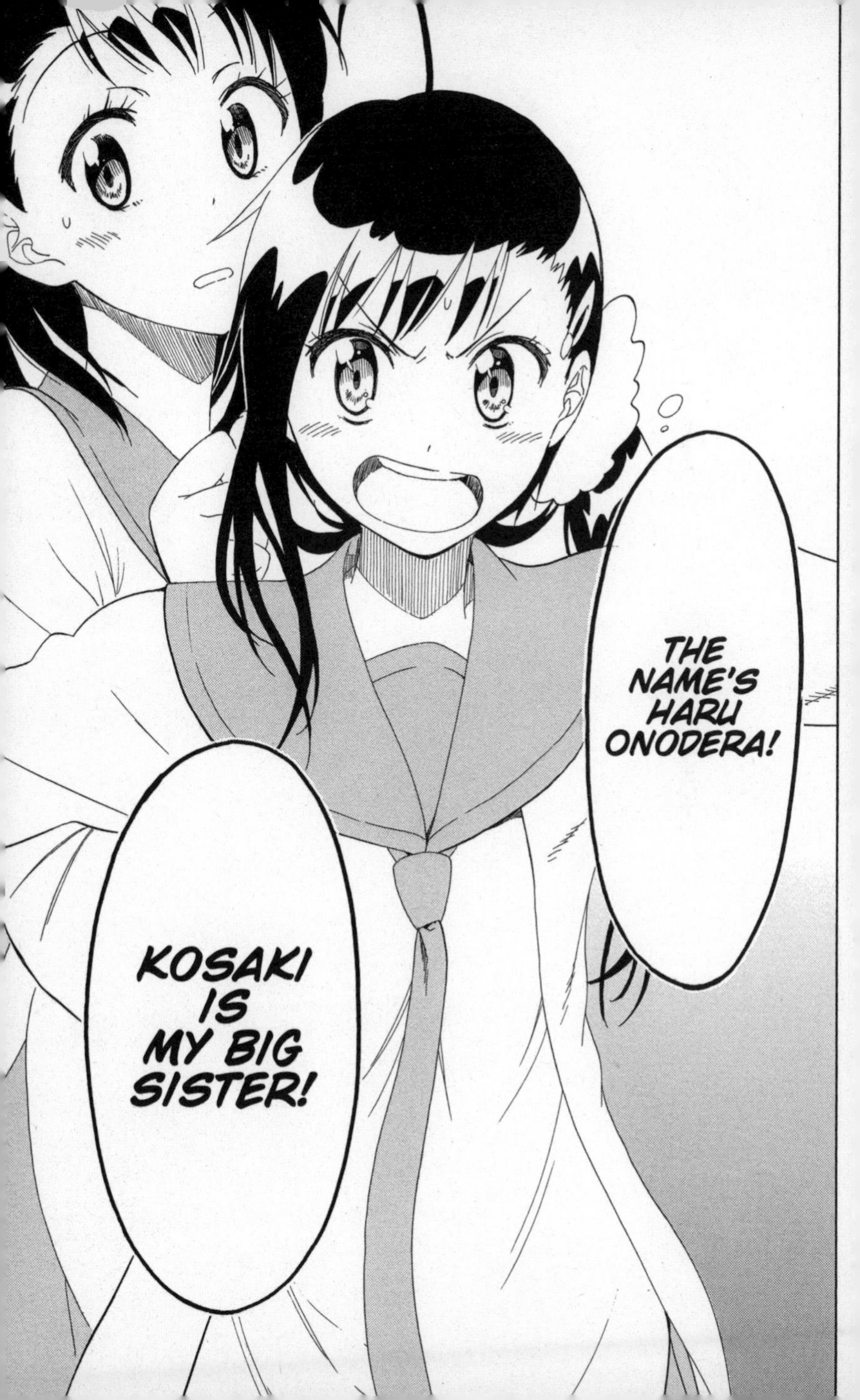
THE NAME'S HARU ONODERA!
KOSAKI IS MY BIG SISTER!

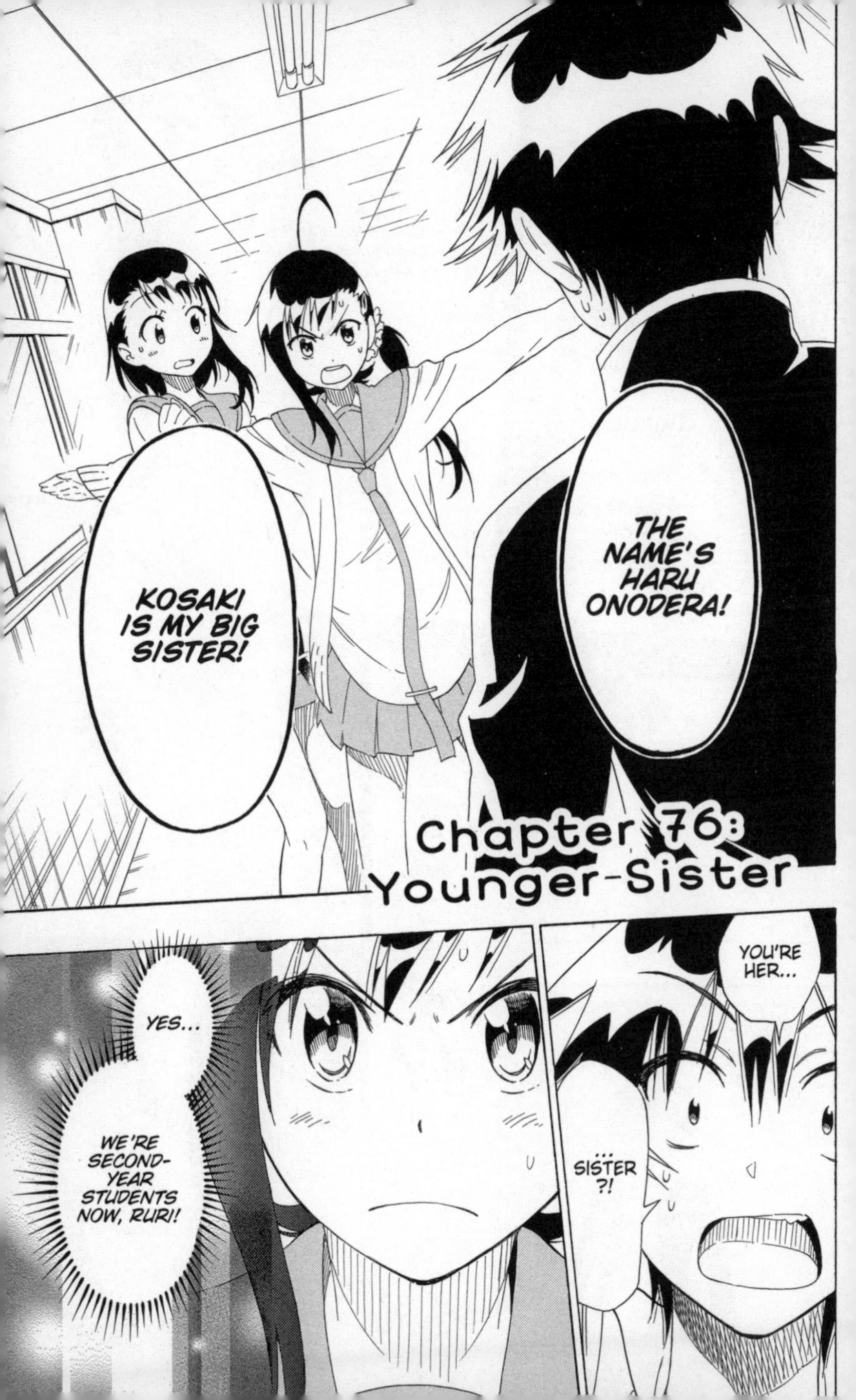
THE NAME'S HARU ONODERA!
KOSAKI IS MY BIG SISTER!
Chapter 76: Younger-Sister
YOU'RE HER...
...SISTER?!
YES...
WE'RE SECOND-YEAR STUDENTS NOW, RURI!

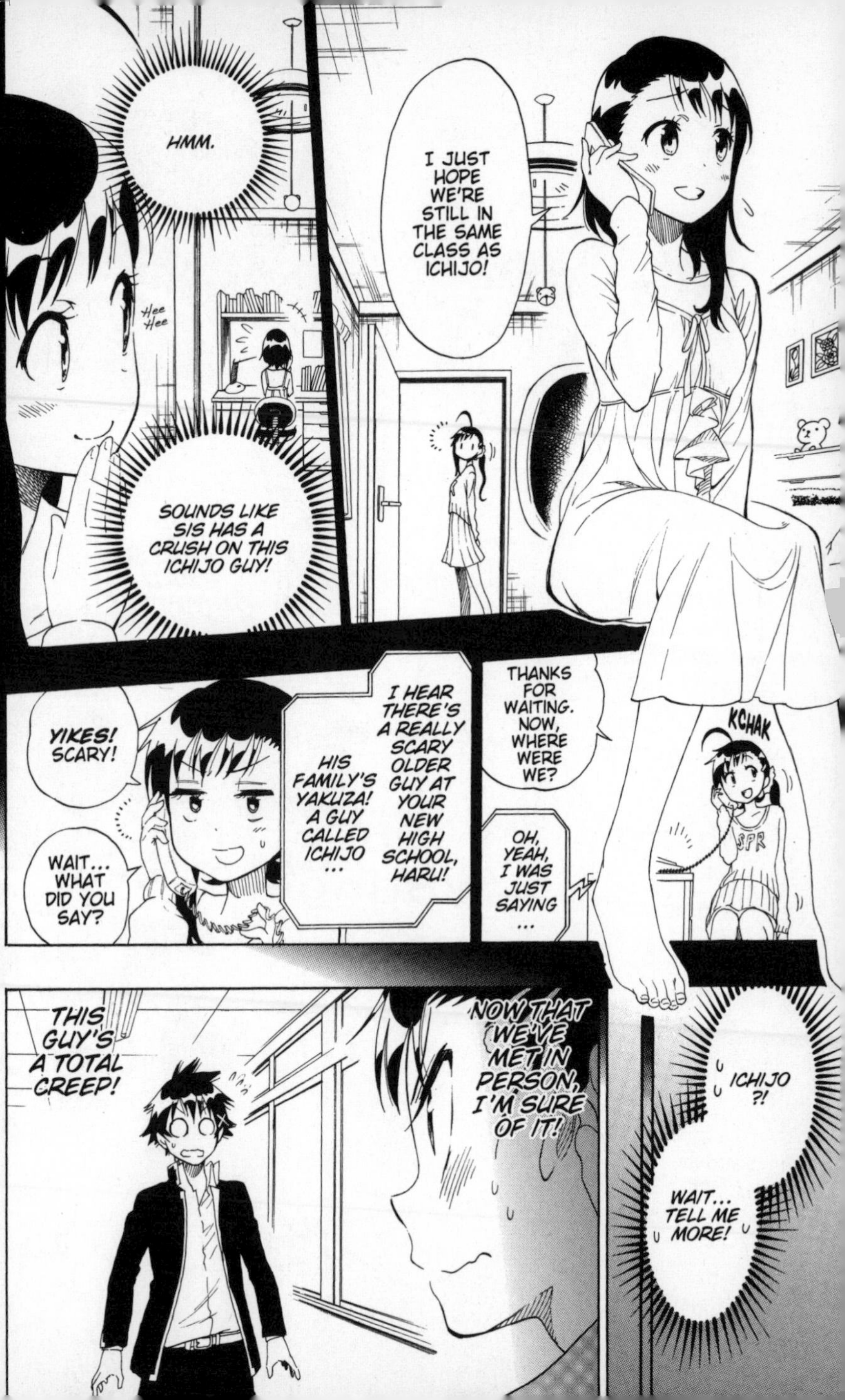
I JUST HOPE WE'RE STILL IN THE SAME CLASS AS ICHIJO!
HMM.
Hee Hee
SOUNDS LIKE SIS HAS A CRUSH ON THIS ICHIJO GUY!
KCHAK
THANKS FOR WAITING. NOW, WHERE WERE WE?
OH, YEAH, I WAS JUST SAYING...
I HEAR THERE'S A REALLY SCARY OLDER GUY AT YOUR NEW HIGH SCHOOL, HARU!
HIS FAMILY'S YAKUZA! A GUY CALLED ICHIJO...
YIKES! SCARY!
WAIT... WHAT DID YOU SAY?
ICHIJO?!
WAIT... TELL ME MORE!
NOW THAT WE'VE MET IN PERSON, I'M SURE OF IT!
THIS GUY'S A TOTAL CREEP!

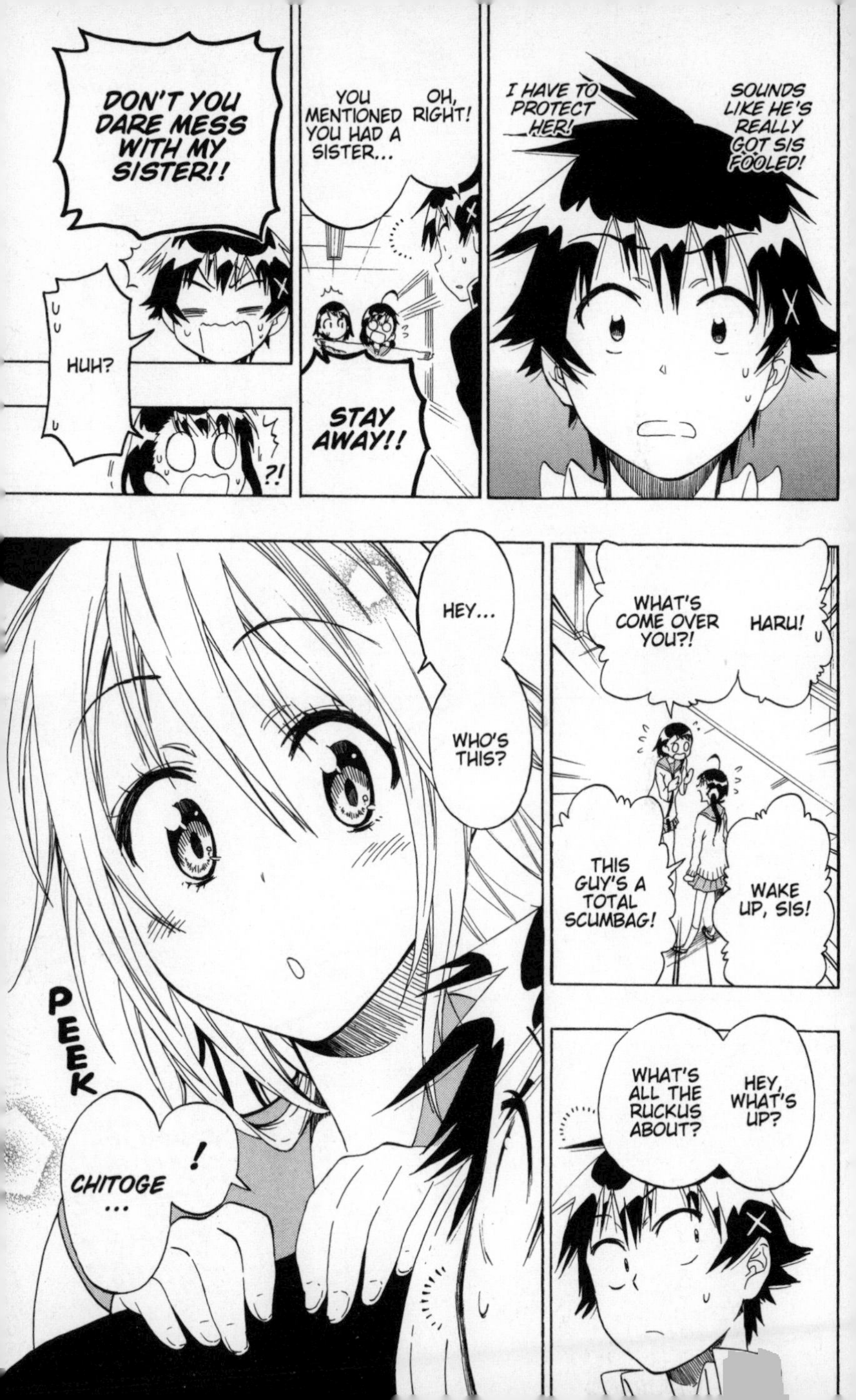
SOUNDS LIKE HE'S REALLY GOT SIS FOOLED!
I HAVE TO PROTECT HER!
OH, RIGHT!
YOU MENTIONED YOU HAD A SISTER...
STAY AWAY!!
DON'T YOU DARE MESS WITH MY SISTER!!
HUH?
?!
HARU!
WHAT'S COME OVER YOU?!
WAKE UP, SIS!
THIS GUY'S A TOTAL SCUMBAG!
HEY, WHAT'S UP?
WHAT'S ALL THE RUCKUS ABOUT?
HEY...
WHO'S THIS?
PEEK
CHITOGE ...!

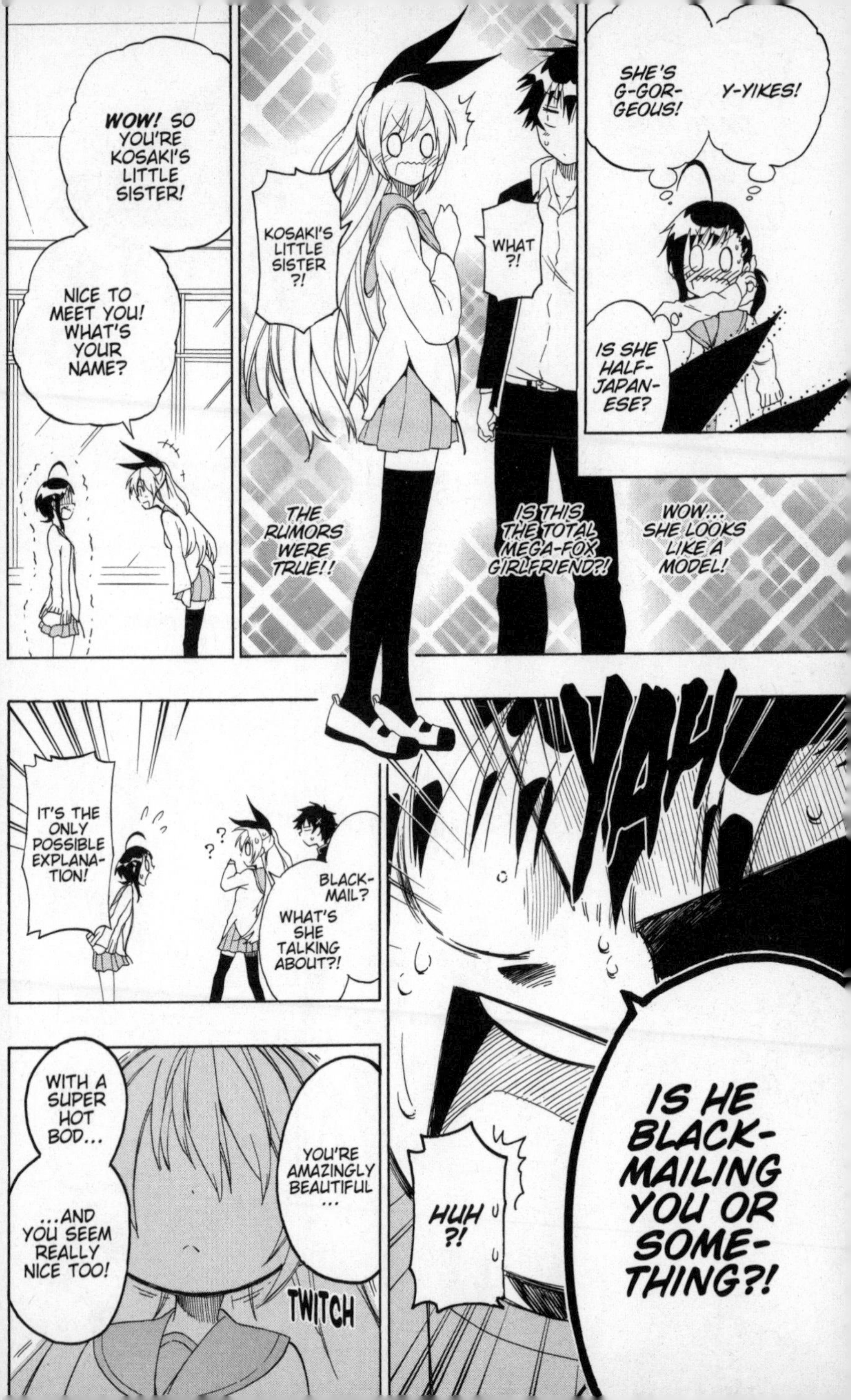
Y-YIKES!
SHE'S G-GORGEOUS!
IS SHE HALF-JAPANESE?
WHAT ?!
KOSAKI'S LITTLE SISTER ?!
WOW... SHE LOOKS LIKE A MODEL!
IS THIS THE TOTAL MEGA-FOX GIRLFRIEND?!
THE RUMORS WERE TRUE!!
WOW! SO YOU'RE KOSAKI'S LITTLE SISTER!
NICE TO MEET YOU! WHAT'S YOUR NAME?
YAH!
HUH ?!
IS HE BLACKMAILING YOU OR SOMETHING?!
BLACKMAIL? WHAT'S SHE TALKING ABOUT?!
IT'S THE ONLY POSSIBLE EXPLANATION!
YOU'RE AMAZINGLY BEAUTIFUL...
WITH A SUPER HOT BOD...
...AND YOU SEEM REALLY NICE TOO!
TWITCH

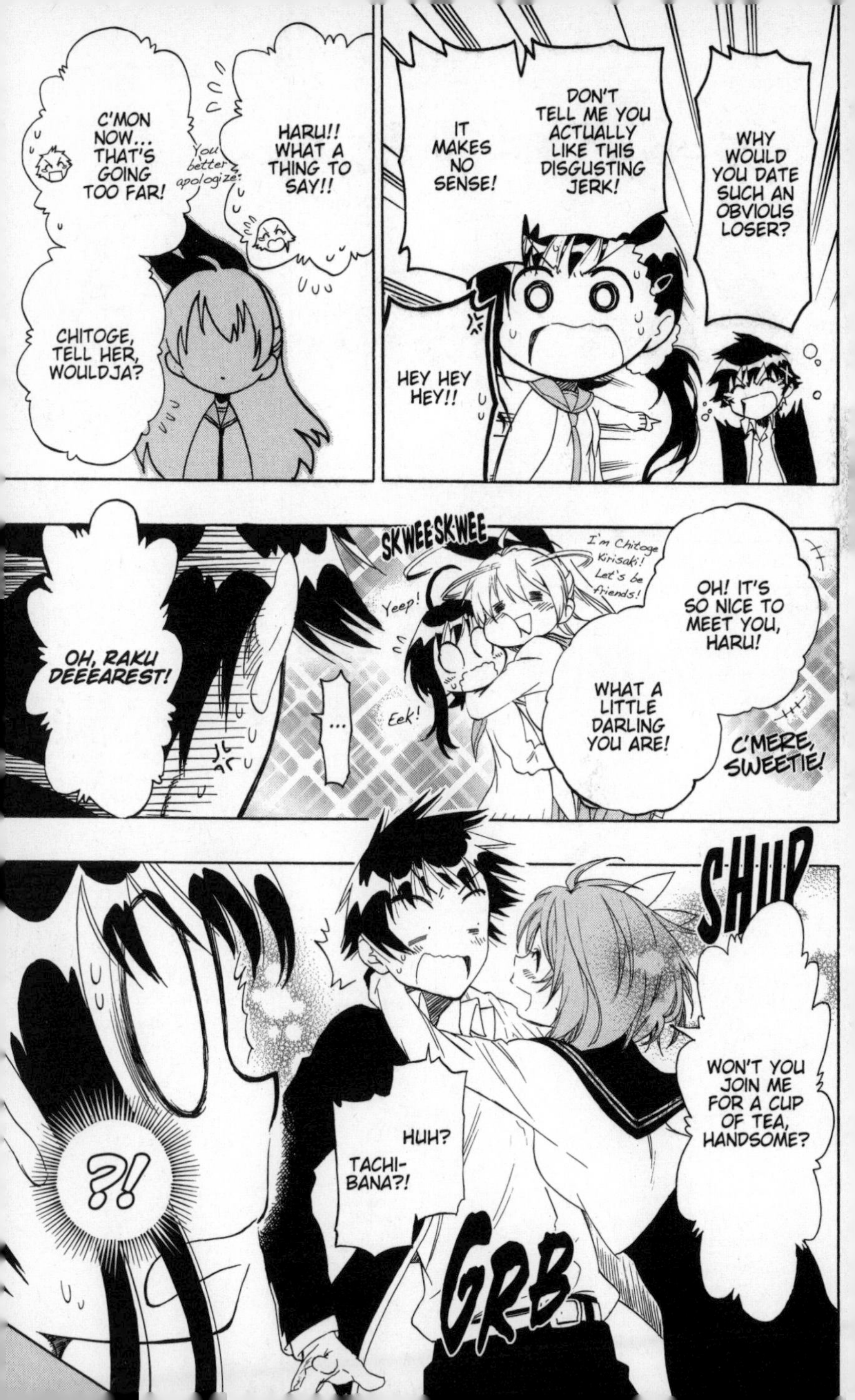
WHY WOULD YOU DATE SUCH AN OBVIOUS LOSER?
DON'T TELL ME YOU ACTUALLY LIKE THIS DISGUSTING JERK!
IT MAKES NO SENSE!
HEY HEY HEY!!
HARU!! WHAT A THING TO SAY!!
You better apologize!
C'MON NOW... THAT'S GOING TOO FAR!
CHITOGE, TELL HER, WOULDJA?
OH! IT'S SO NICE TO MEET YOU, HARU!
I'm Chitoge Kirisaki! Let's be friends!
SKWEE SKWEE
C'MERE, SWEETIE!
WHAT A LITTLE DARLING YOU ARE!
Yeep!
Eek!
...
OH, RAKU DEEEAREST!
SHUP
WON'T YOU JOIN ME FOR A CUP OF TEA, HANDSOME?
HUH? TACHIBANA?!
GRB
?!

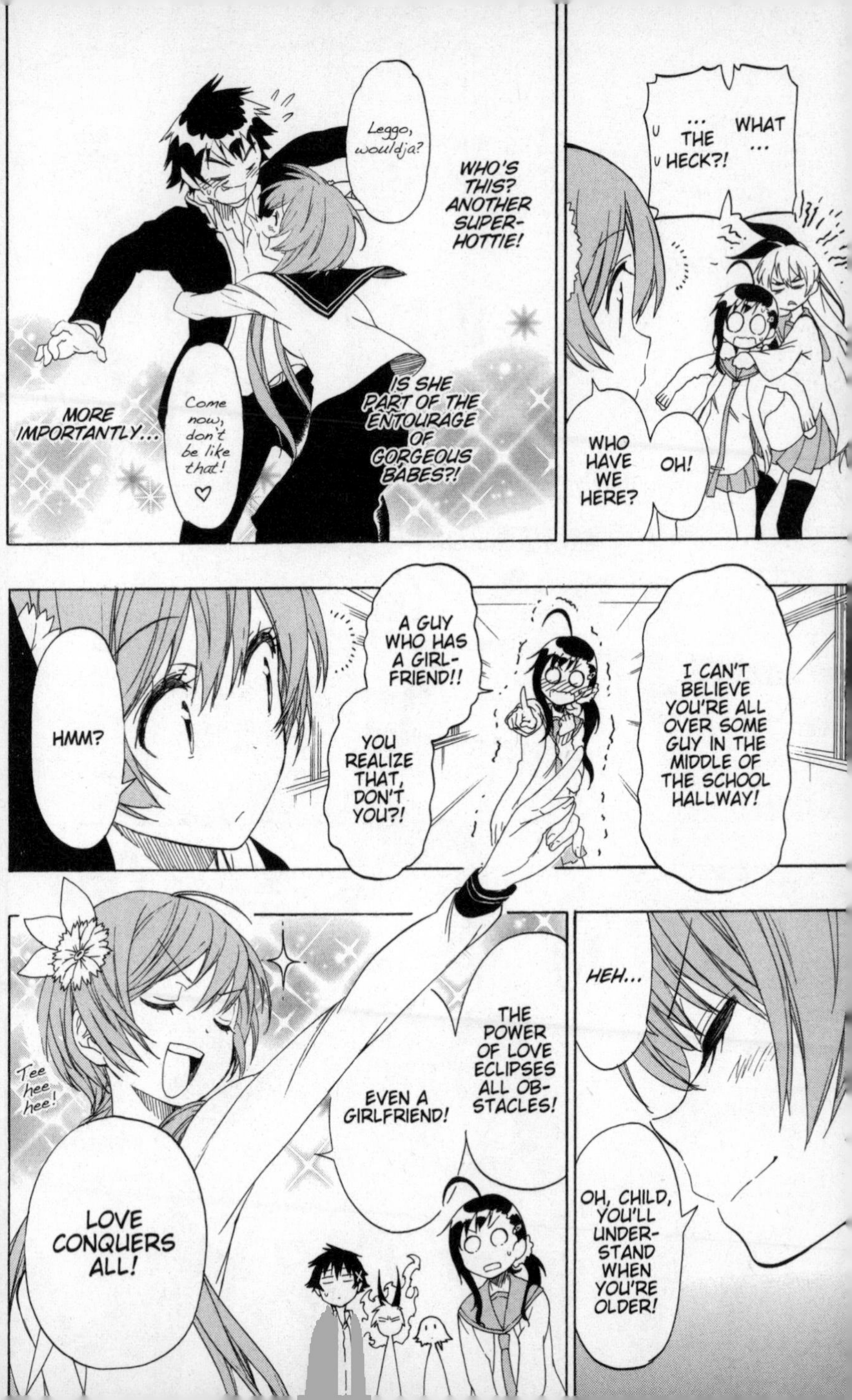
... WHAT ... THE HECK?!
OH!
WHO HAVE WE HERE?
Leggo, wouldja?
WHO'S THIS? ANOTHER SUPER-HOTTIE!
IS SHE PART OF THE ENTOURAGE OF GORGEOUS BABES?!
Come now, don't be like that! ♡
MORE IMPORTANTLY...
I CAN'T BELIEVE YOU'RE ALL OVER SOME GUY IN THE MIDDLE OF THE SCHOOL HALLWAY!
A GUY WHO HAS A GIRL-FRIEND!!
YOU REALIZE THAT, DON'T YOU?!
HMM?
HEH...
OH, CHILD, YOU'LL UNDER-STAND WHEN YOU'RE OLDER!
THE POWER OF LOVE ECLIPSES ALL OB-STACLES!
EVEN A GIRLFRIEND!
LOVE CONQUERS ALL!
Tee hee hee!

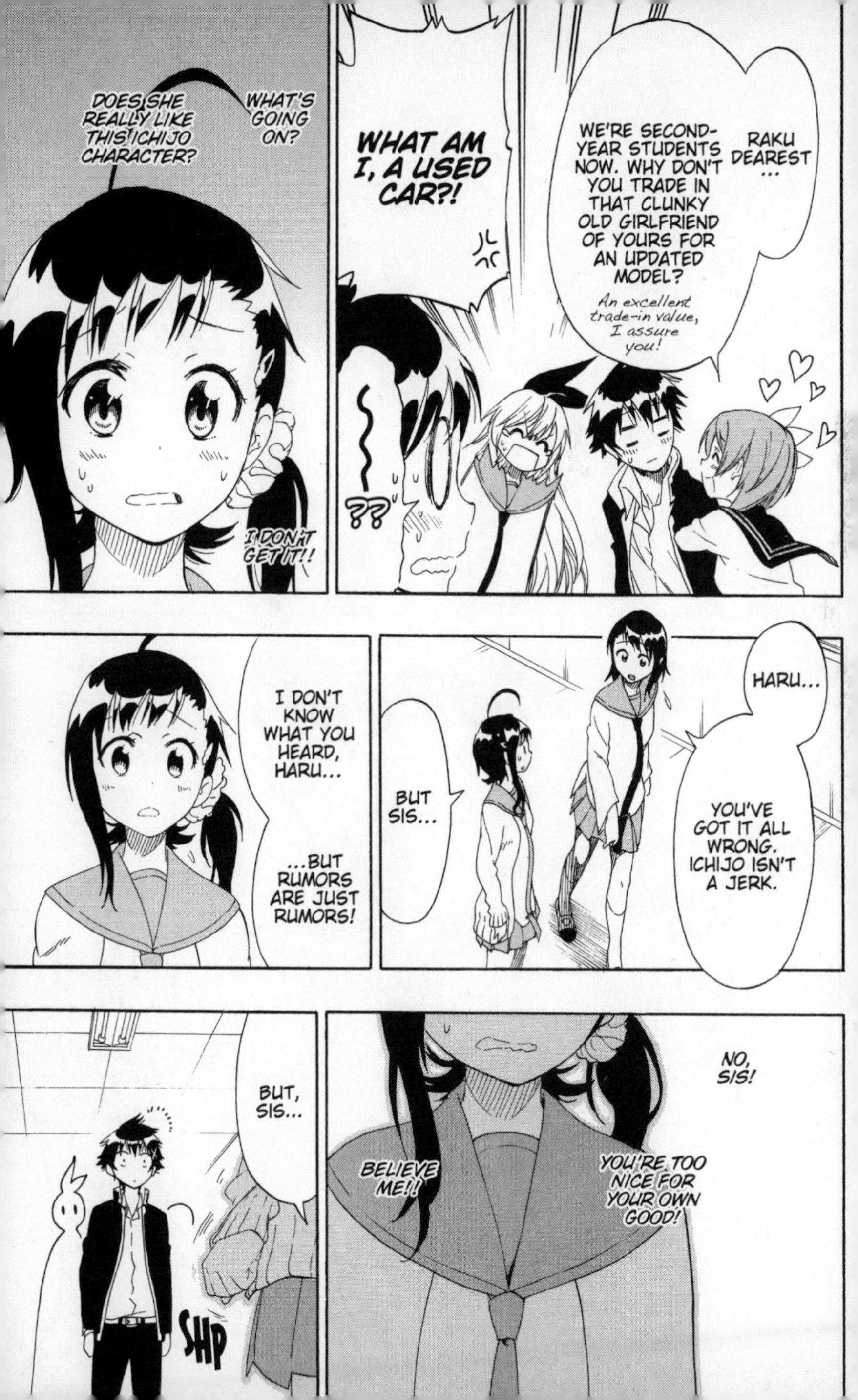
RAKU DEAREST...
WE'RE SECOND-YEAR STUDENTS NOW. WHY DON'T YOU TRADE IN THAT CLUNKY OLD GIRLFRIEND OF YOURS FOR AN UPDATED MODEL?
An excellent trade-in value, I assure you!
WHAT AM I, A USED CAR?!
??
WHAT'S GOING ON?
DOES SHE REALLY LIKE THIS ICHIJO CHARACTER?
I DON'T GET IT!!
HARU...
YOU'VE GOT IT ALL WRONG. ICHIJO ISN'T A JERK.
BUT SIS...
I DON'T KNOW WHAT YOU HEARD, HARU...
...BUT RUMORS ARE JUST RUMORS!
NO, SIS!
YOU'RE TOO NICE FOR YOUR OWN GOOD!
BELIEVE ME!!
BUT, SIS...
SHP

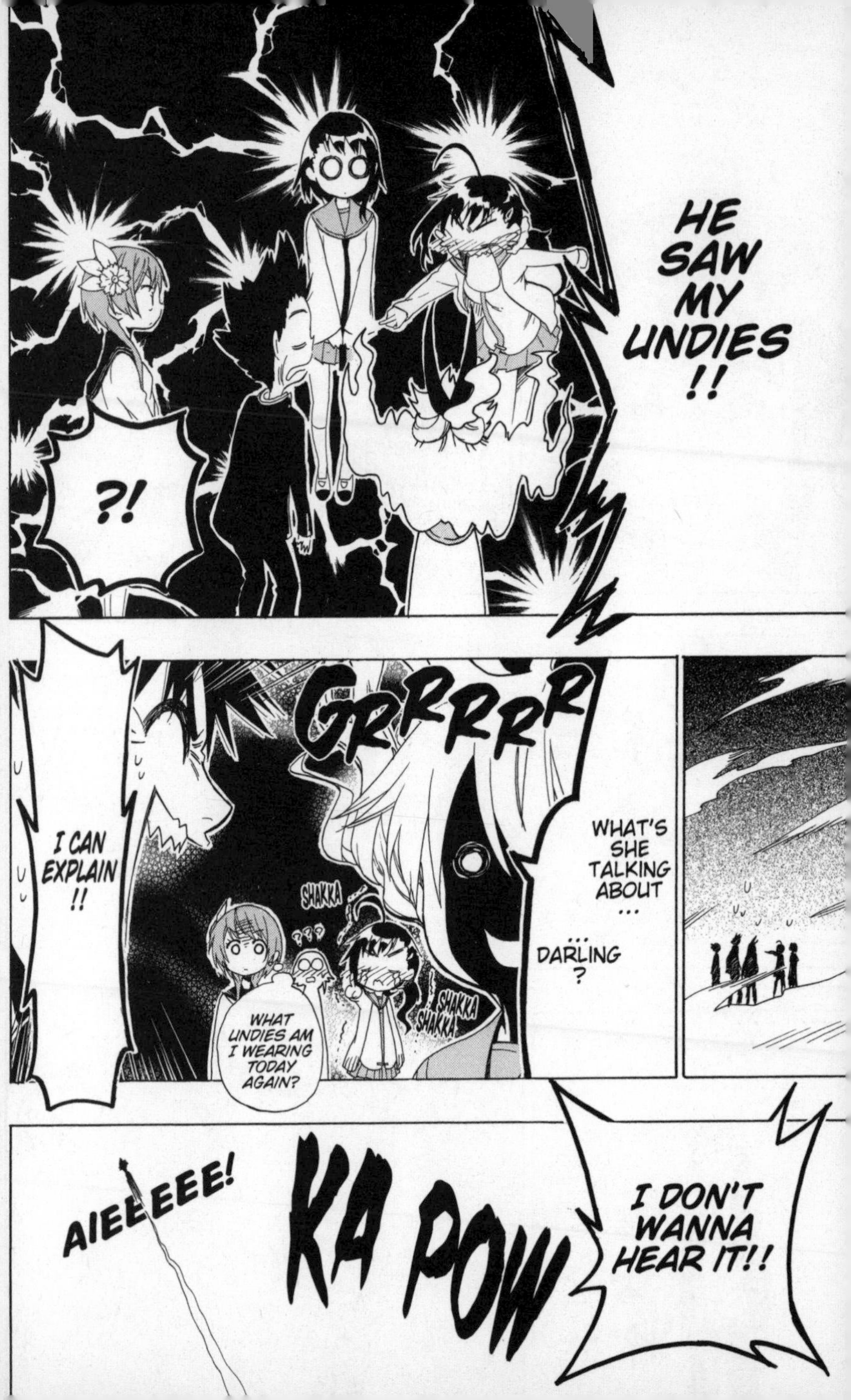
HE SAW MY UNDIES!!
?!
GRRRRRR
WHAT'S SHE TALKING ABOUT...
...DARLING?
I CAN EXPLAIN!!
SHAKKA
SHAKKA SHAKKA
WHAT UNDIES AM I WEARING TODAY AGAIN?
I DON'T WANNA HEAR IT!!
KA POW
AIEEEEE!

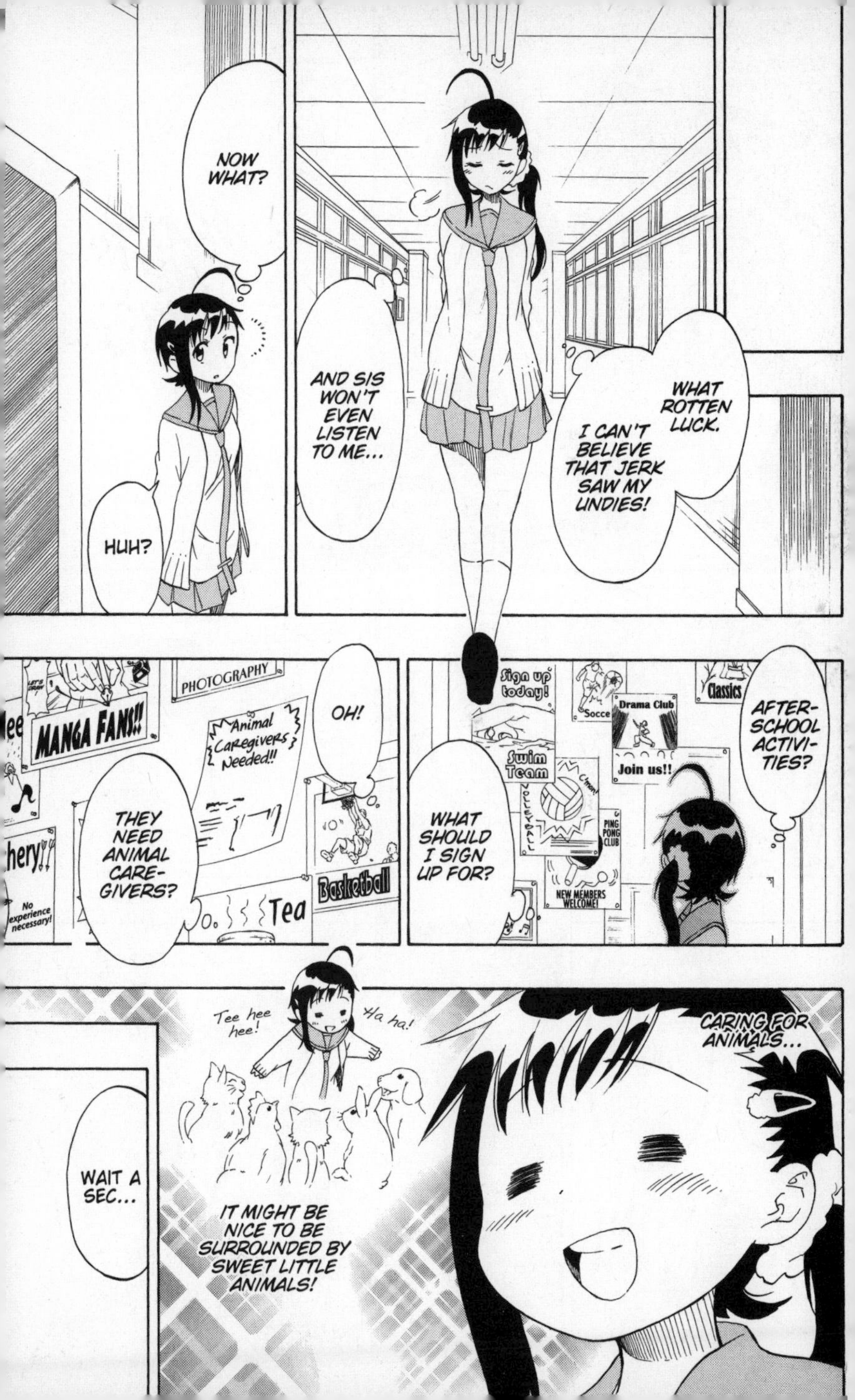

WHAT ROTTEN LUCK.
I CAN'T BELIEVE THAT JERK SAW MY UNDIES!
AND SIS WON'T EVEN LISTEN TO ME...
NOW WHAT?
HUH?
AFTER-SCHOOL ACTIVI-TIES?
Classics
Drama Club
Join us!!
Socce
Sign up today!
Swim Team
C'mon!
VOLLEYBALL
PING PONG CLUB
NEW MEMBERS WELCOME!
WHAT SHOULD I SIGN UP FOR?
OH!
PHOTOGRAPHY
MANGA FANS!!
Animal Caregivers Needed!!
Basketball
Tea
THEY NEED ANIMAL CARE-GIVERS?
No experience necessary!
CARING FOR ANIMALS...
Ha ha!
Tee hee hee!
IT MIGHT BE NICE TO BE SURROUNDED BY SWEET LITTLE ANIMALS!
WAIT A SEC...

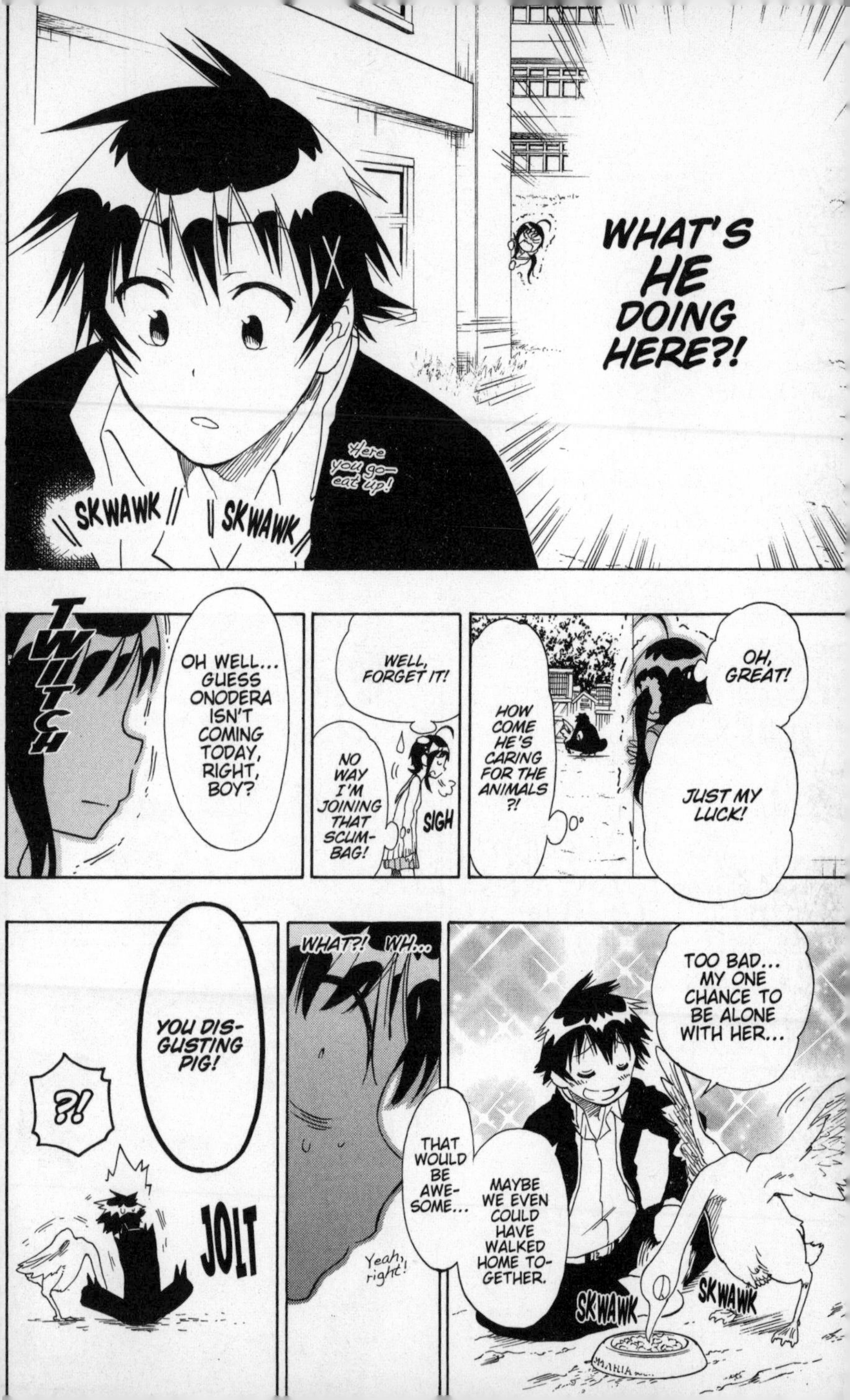
WHAT'S HE DOING HERE?!
Here you go—eat up!
SKWAWK
SKWAWK
OH, GREAT!
JUST MY LUCK!
HOW COME HE'S CARING FOR THE ANIMALS?!
WELL, FORGET IT!
NO WAY I'M JOINING THAT SCUM-BAG!
SIGH
OH WELL... GUESS ONODERA ISN'T COMING TODAY, RIGHT, BOY?
TWITCH
TOO BAD... MY ONE CHANCE TO BE ALONE WITH HER...
MAYBE WE EVEN COULD HAVE WALKED HOME TO-GETHER.
THAT WOULD BE AWE-SOME...
SKWAWK
SKWAWK
WHAT?! WH...
Yeah, right!
YOU DIS-GUSTING PIG!
?!
JOLT

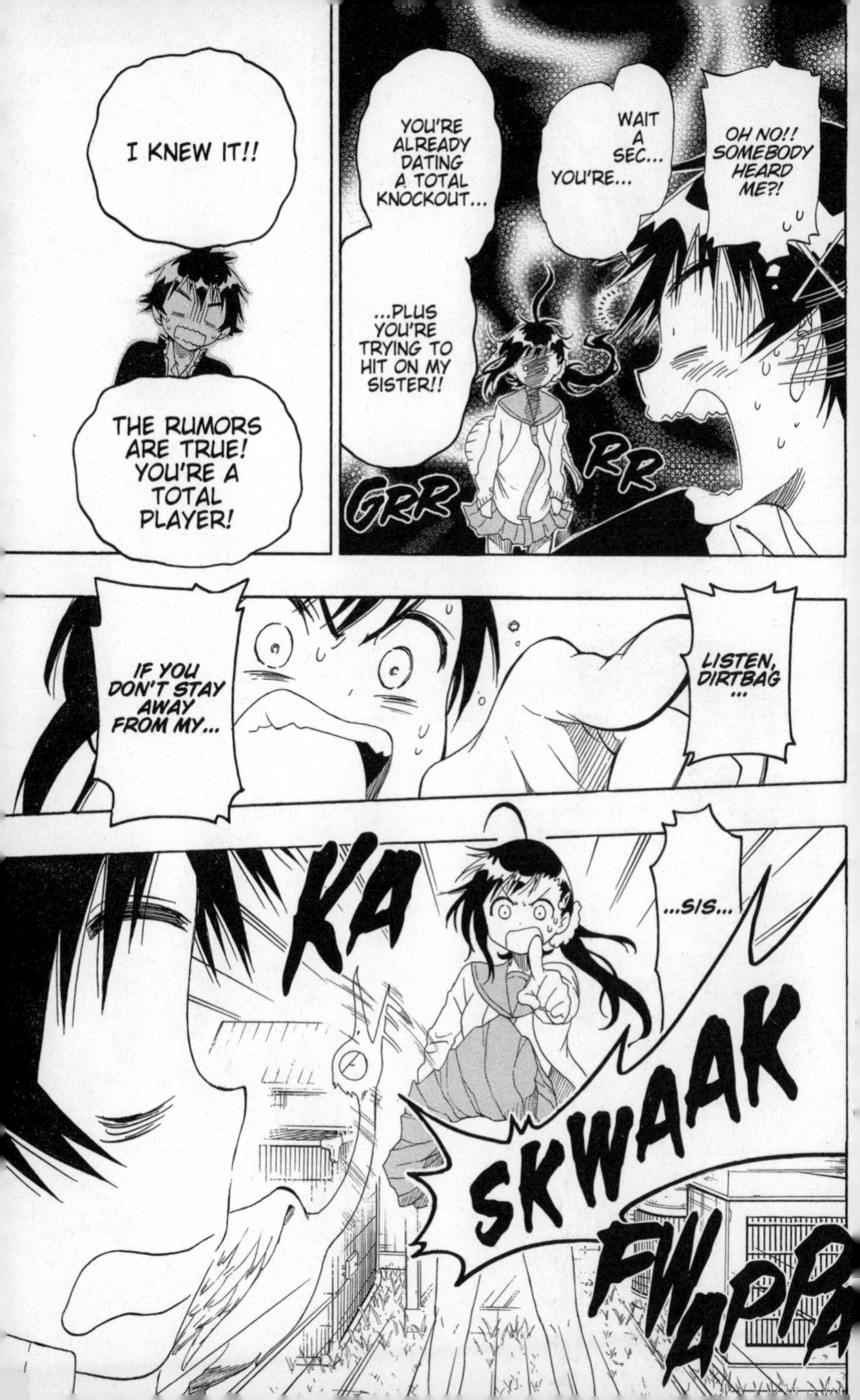
OH NO!! SOMEBODY HEARD ME?!
WAIT A SEC... YOU'RE...
YOU'RE ALREADY DATING A TOTAL KNOCKOUT...
...PLUS YOU'RE TRYING TO HIT ON MY SISTER!!
RR
GRR
I KNEW IT!!
THE RUMORS ARE TRUE! YOU'RE A TOTAL PLAYER!
LISTEN, DIRTBAG ...
IF YOU DON'T STAY AWAY FROM MY...
...SIS...
KA
SKWAAK
FWAPPA

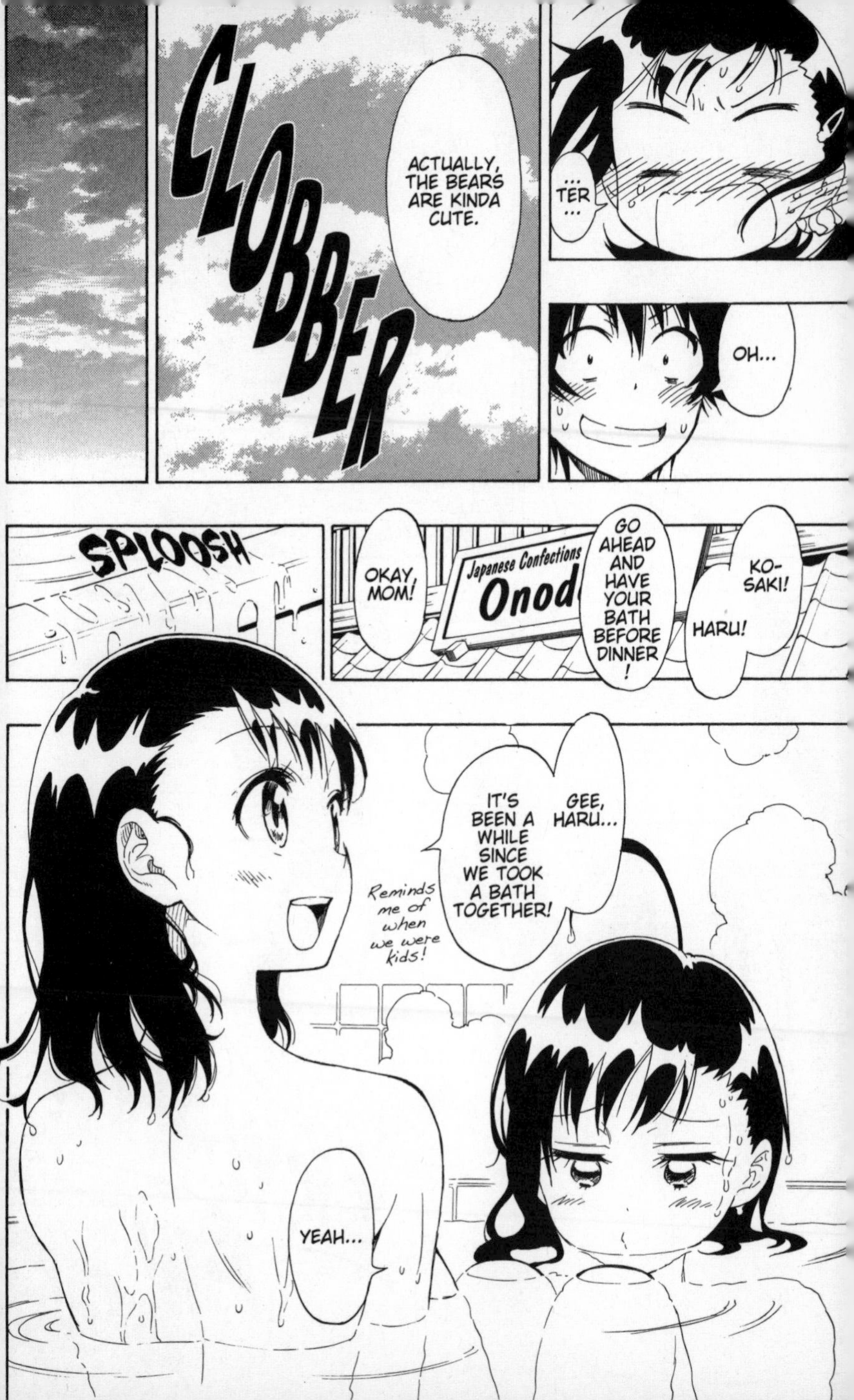

...TER...
OH...
ACTUALLY, THE BEARS ARE KINDA CUTE.
CLOBBER
KO-SAKI!
HARU!
GO AHEAD AND HAVE YOUR BATH BEFORE DINNER!
Japanese Confections
Onod
OKAY, MOM!
SPLOOSH
GEE, HARU...
IT'S BEEN A WHILE SINCE WE TOOK A BATH TOGETHER!
Reminds me of when we were kids!
YEAH...

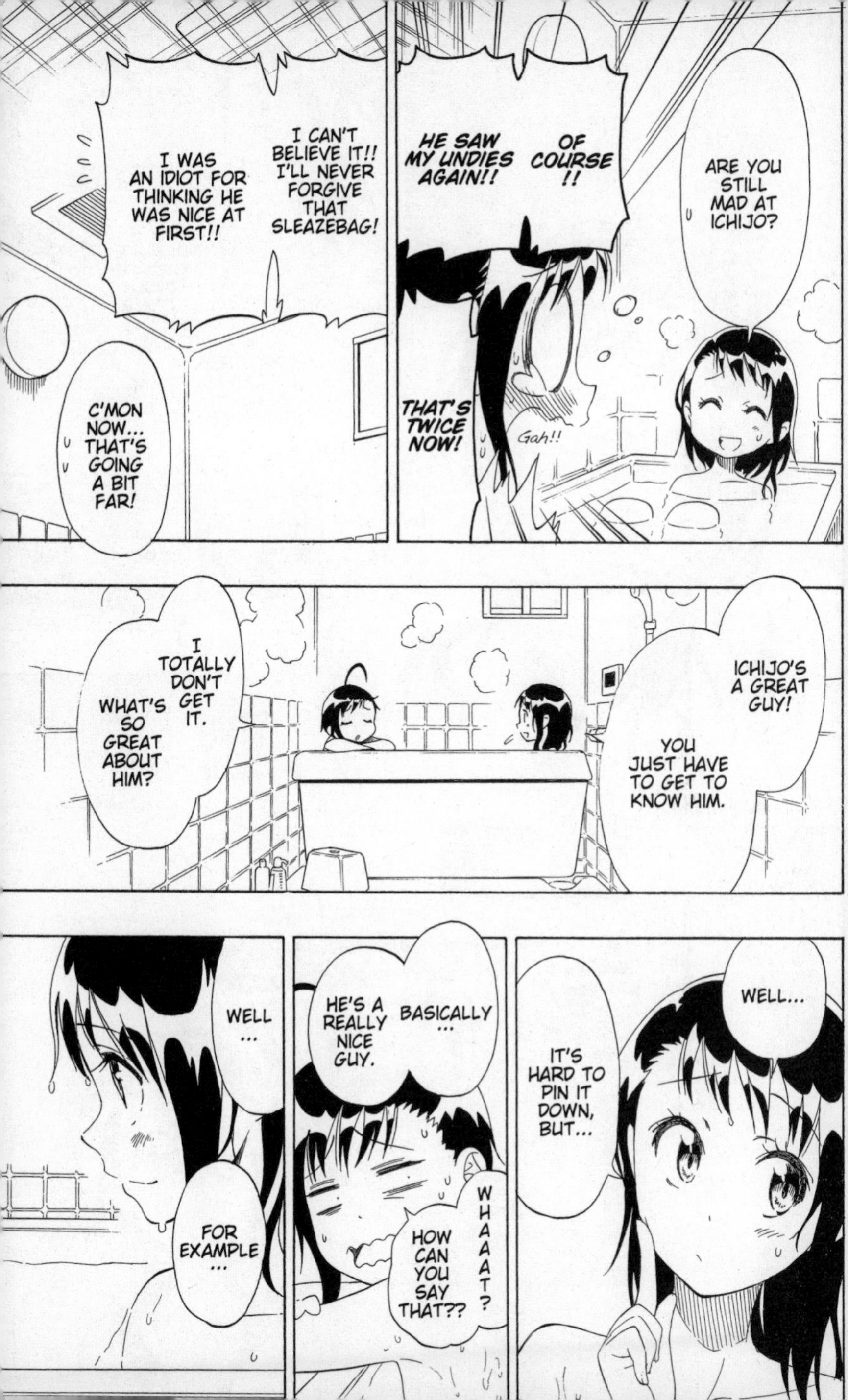
ARE YOU STILL MAD AT ICHIJO?
OF COURSE!!
HE SAW MY UNDIES AGAIN!!
THAT'S TWICE NOW!
Gah!!
I CAN'T BELIEVE IT!! I'LL NEVER FORGIVE THAT SLEAZEBAG!
I WAS AN IDIOT FOR THINKING HE WAS NICE AT FIRST!!
C'MON NOW... THAT'S GOING A BIT FAR!
ICHIJO'S A GREAT GUY!
YOU JUST HAVE TO GET TO KNOW HIM.
I TOTALLY DON'T GET IT.
WHAT'S SO GREAT ABOUT HIM?
WELL...
IT'S HARD TO PIN IT DOWN, BUT...
BASICALLY...
HE'S A REALLY NICE GUY.
WHAAAAT?
HOW CAN YOU SAY THAT??
WELL...
FOR EXAMPLE...

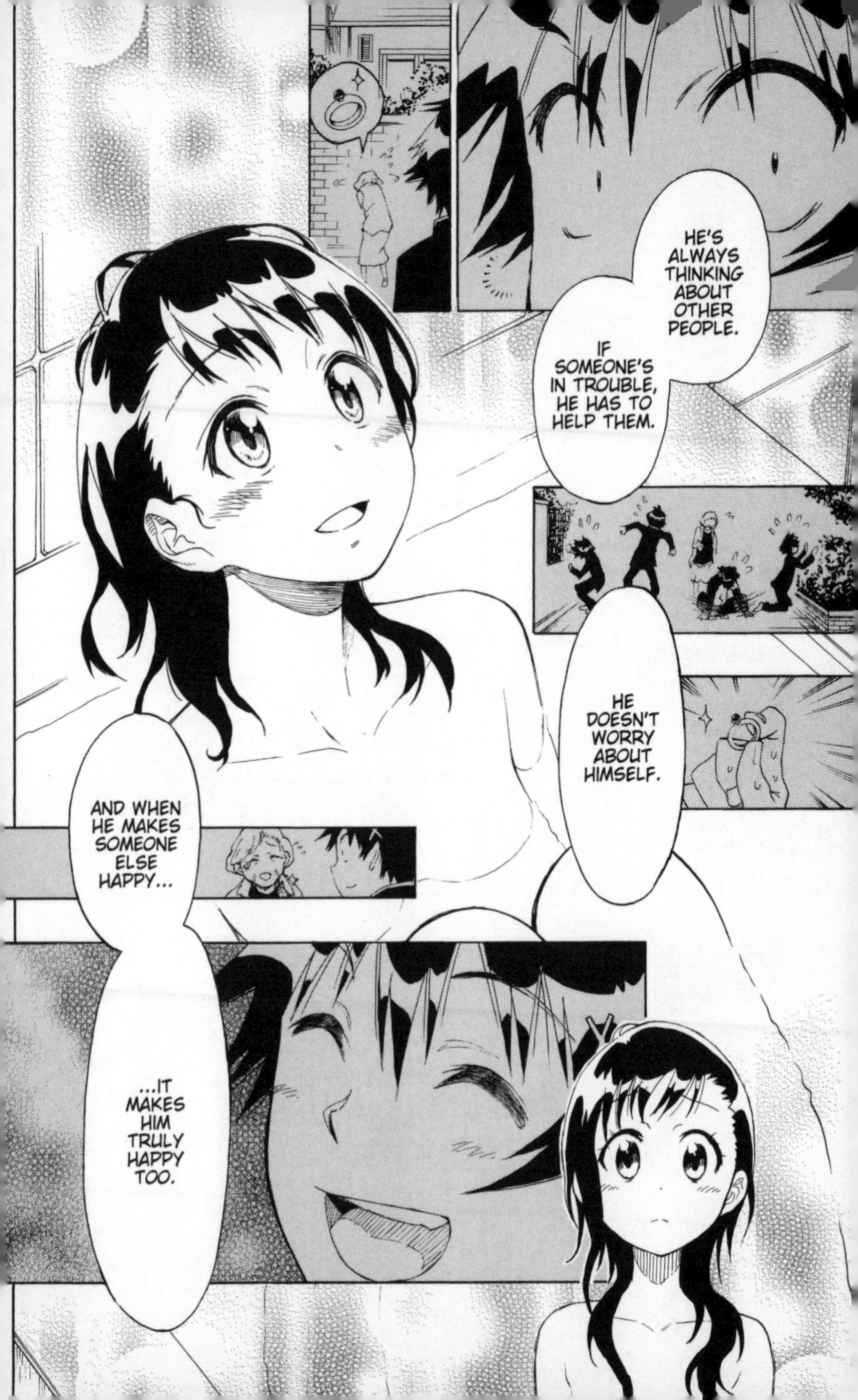
HE'S ALWAYS THINKING ABOUT OTHER PEOPLE.
IF SOMEONE'S IN TROUBLE, HE HAS TO HELP THEM.
HE DOESN'T WORRY ABOUT HIMSELF.
AND WHEN HE MAKES SOMEONE ELSE HAPPY...
...IT MAKES HIM TRULY HAPPY TOO.

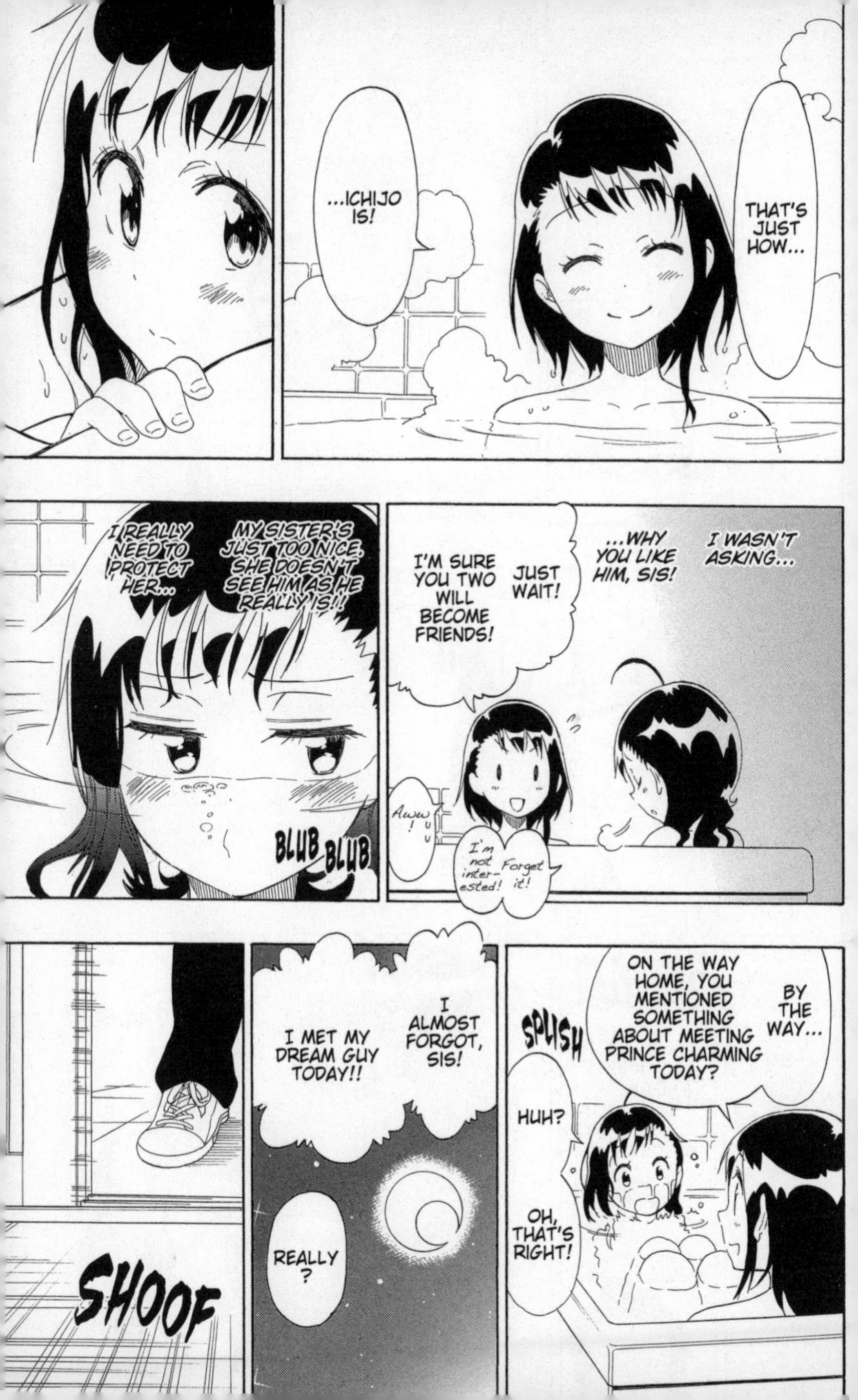
THAT'S JUST HOW...
...ICHIJO IS!
I WASN'T ASKING...
...WHY YOU LIKE HIM, SIS!
JUST WAIT!
I'M SURE YOU TWO WILL BECOME FRIENDS!
Forget it!
I'm not interested!
Aww!
MY SISTER'S JUST TOO NICE, SHE DOESN'T SEE HIM AS HE REALLY IS!!
I REALLY NEED TO PROTECT HER...
BLUB BLUB
BY THE WAY...
ON THE WAY HOME, YOU MENTIONED SOMETHING ABOUT MEETING PRINCE CHARMING TODAY?
SPLISH
HUH?
OH, THAT'S RIGHT!
I ALMOST FORGOT, SIS!
I MET MY DREAM GUY TODAY!!
REALLY?
SHOOF

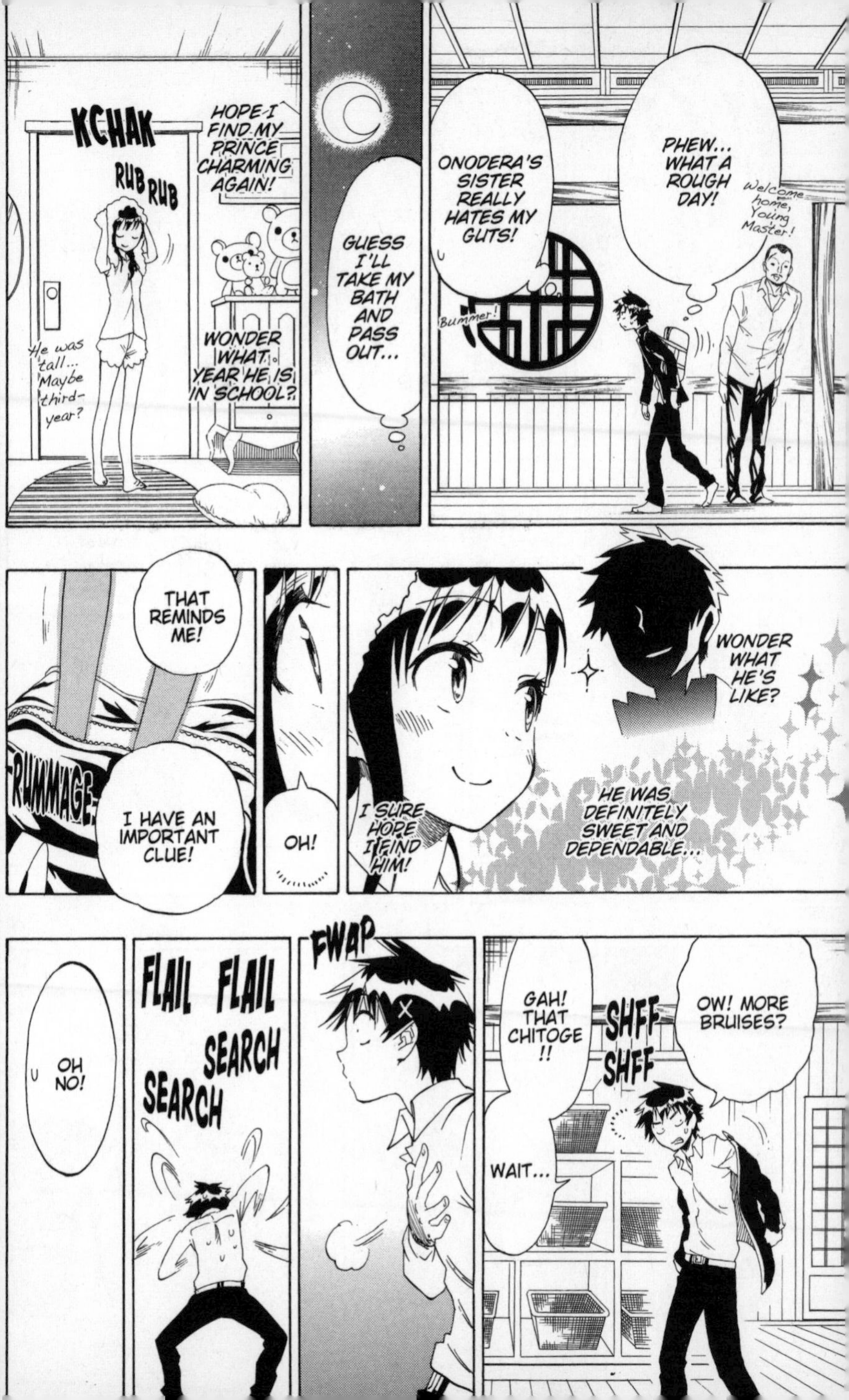
PHEW... WHAT A ROUGH DAY!
Welcome home, Young Master!
ONODERA'S SISTER REALLY HATES MY GUTS!
Bummer!
GUESS I'LL TAKE MY BATH AND PASS OUT...
KCHAK
HOPE I FIND MY PRINCE CHARMING AGAIN!
RUB RUB
WONDER WHAT YEAR HE IS IN SCHOOL?
He was tall... Maybe third-year?
WONDER WHAT HE'S LIKE?
HE WAS DEFINITELY SWEET AND DEPENDABLE...
I SURE HOPE I FIND HIM!
OH!
THAT REMINDS ME!
RUMMAGE
I HAVE AN IMPORTANT CLUE!
OW! MORE BRUISES?
SHFF SHFF
GAH! THAT CHITOGE !!
WAIT...
FWAP
FLAIL FLAIL
SEARCH SEARCH
OH NO!

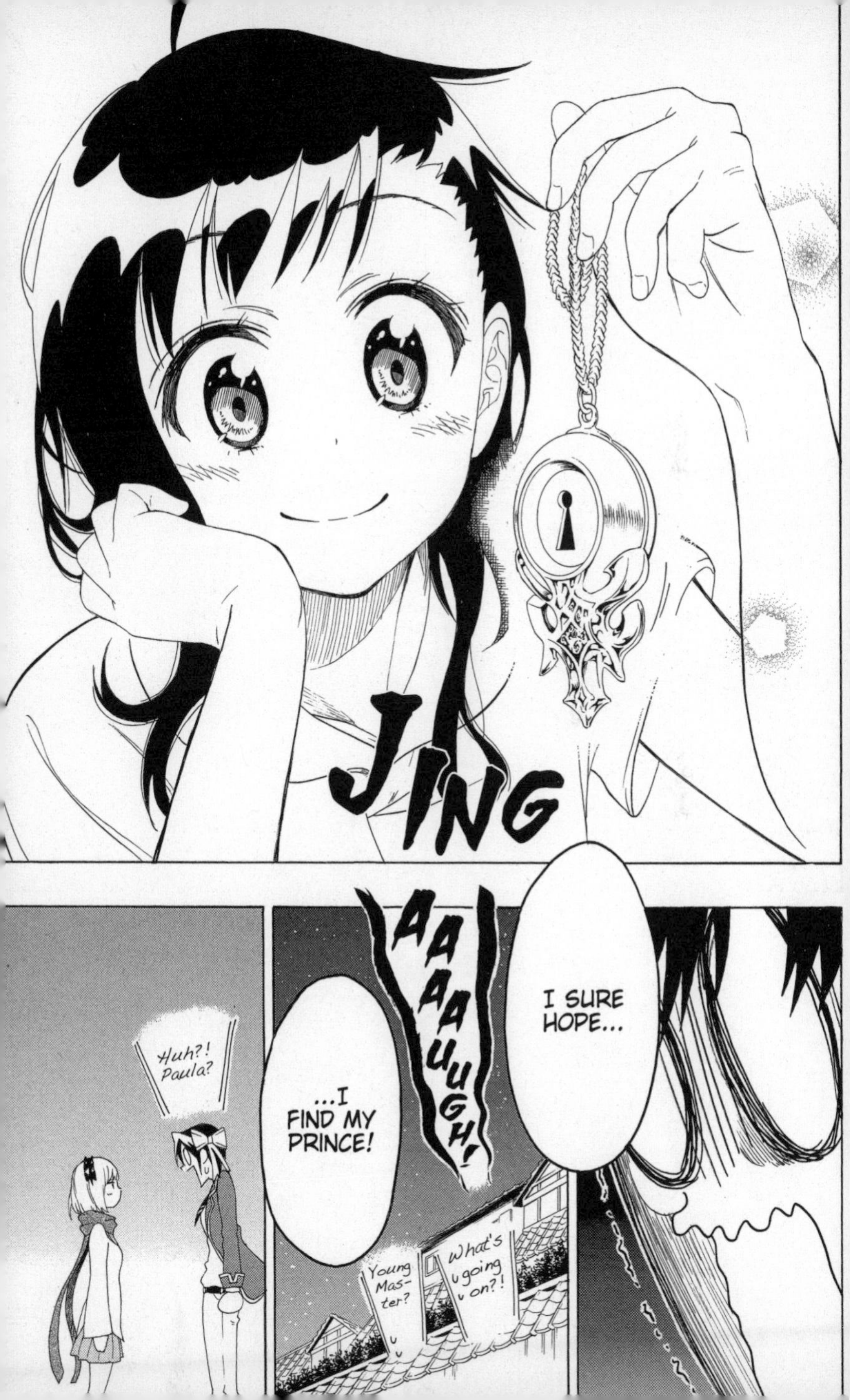
JING
I SURE HOPE...
AAAAAUUGH!
...I FIND MY PRINCE!
What's going on?!
Young Master?
Huh?! Paula?

Menagerie Resident No. 126
Cyclops Gengar
Vermilion Bird

Sparkle!!

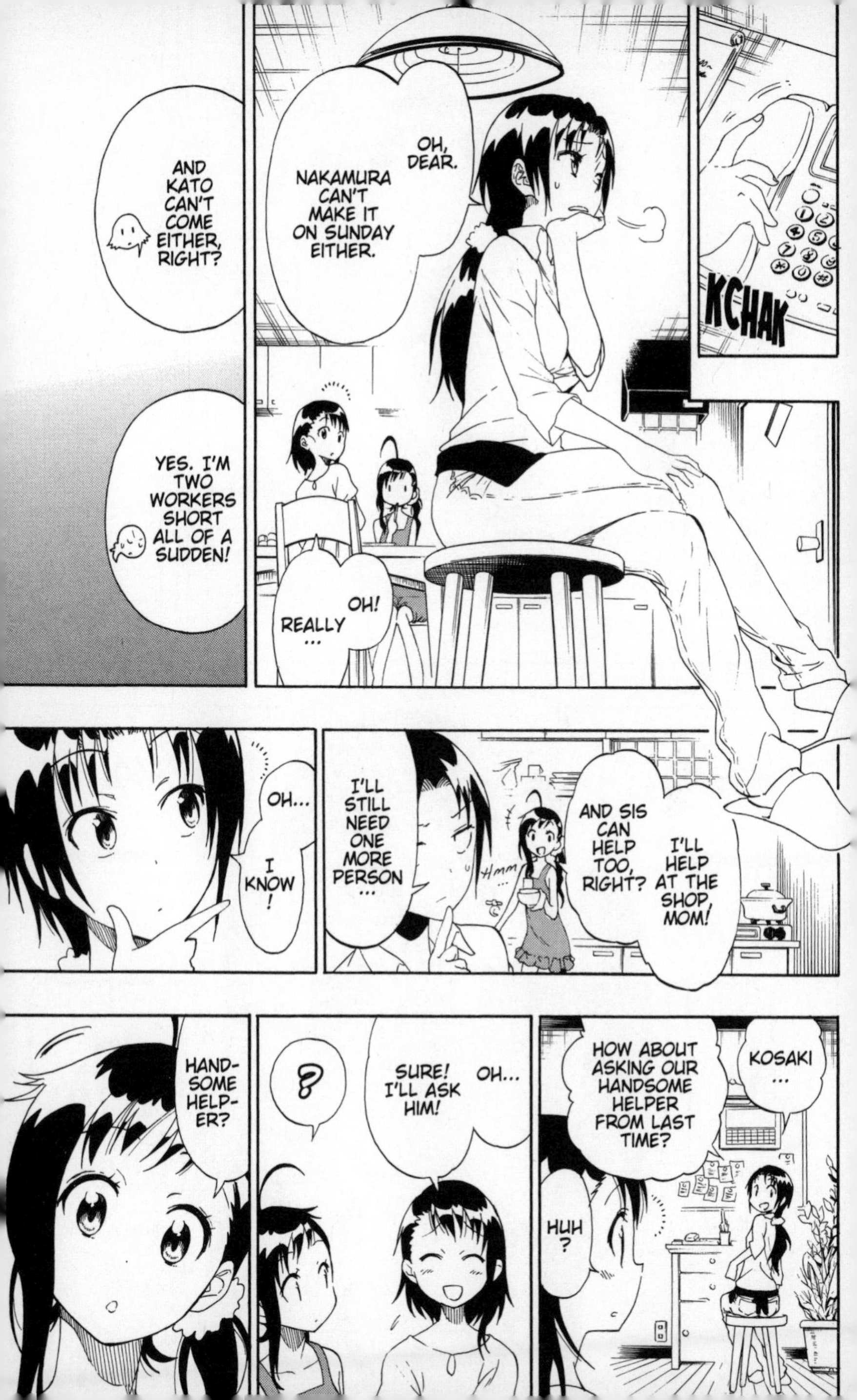
KCHAK
OH, DEAR.
NAKAMURA CAN'T MAKE IT ON SUNDAY EITHER.
OH! REALLY...
AND KATO CAN'T COME EITHER, RIGHT?
YES. I'M TWO WORKERS SHORT ALL OF A SUDDEN!
I'LL HELP AT THE SHOP, MOM!
AND SIS CAN HELP TOO, RIGHT?
Hmm...
I'LL STILL NEED ONE MORE PERSON...
OH...
I KNOW!
KOSAKI...
HOW ABOUT ASKING OUR HANDSOME HELPER FROM LAST TIME?
HUH?
OH...
SURE! I'LL ASK HIM!
?
HAND-SOME HELP-ER?

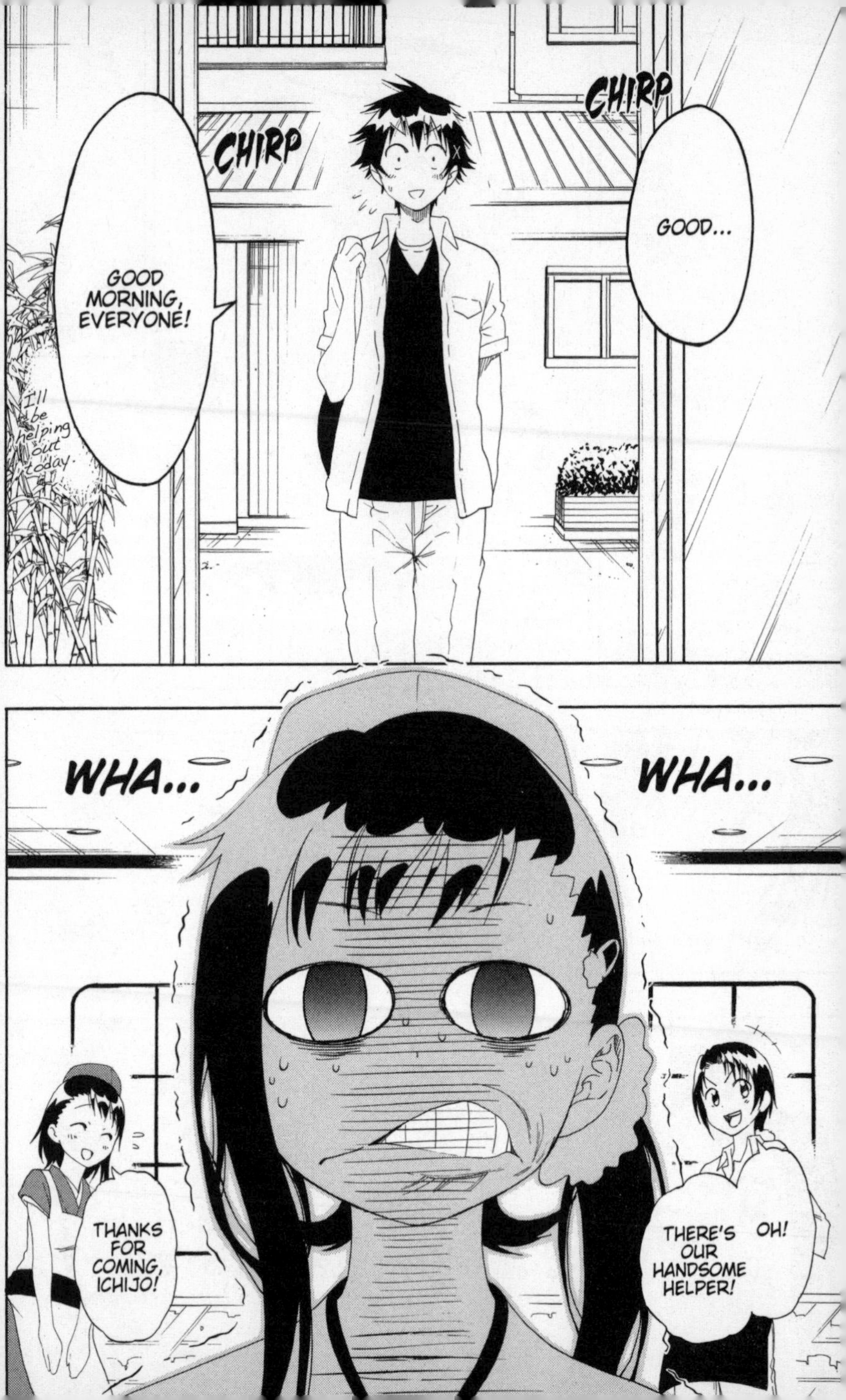
CHIRP
GOOD...
CHIRP
GOOD MORNING, EVERYONE!
I'll be helping out today.
WHA...
WHA...
OH!
THERE'S OUR HANDSOME HELPER!
THANKS FOR COMING, ICHIJO!

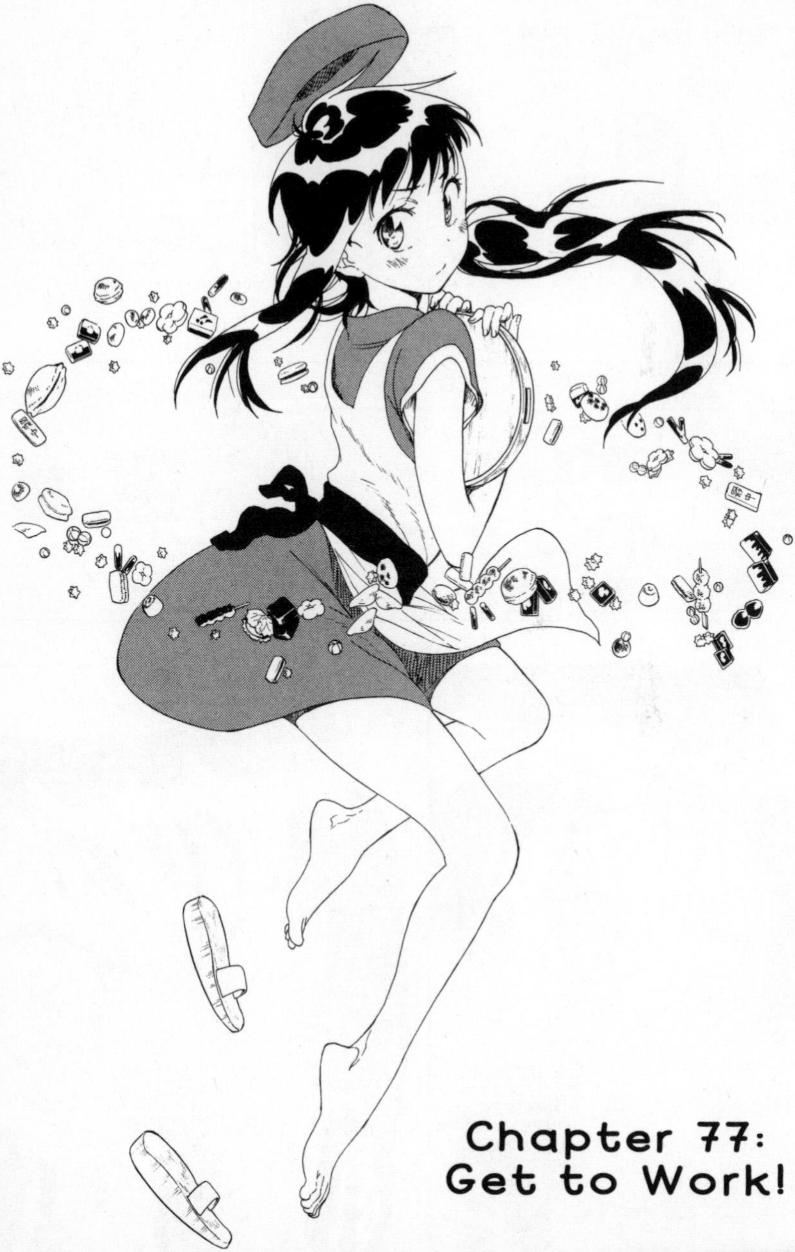

Chapter 77: Get to Work!

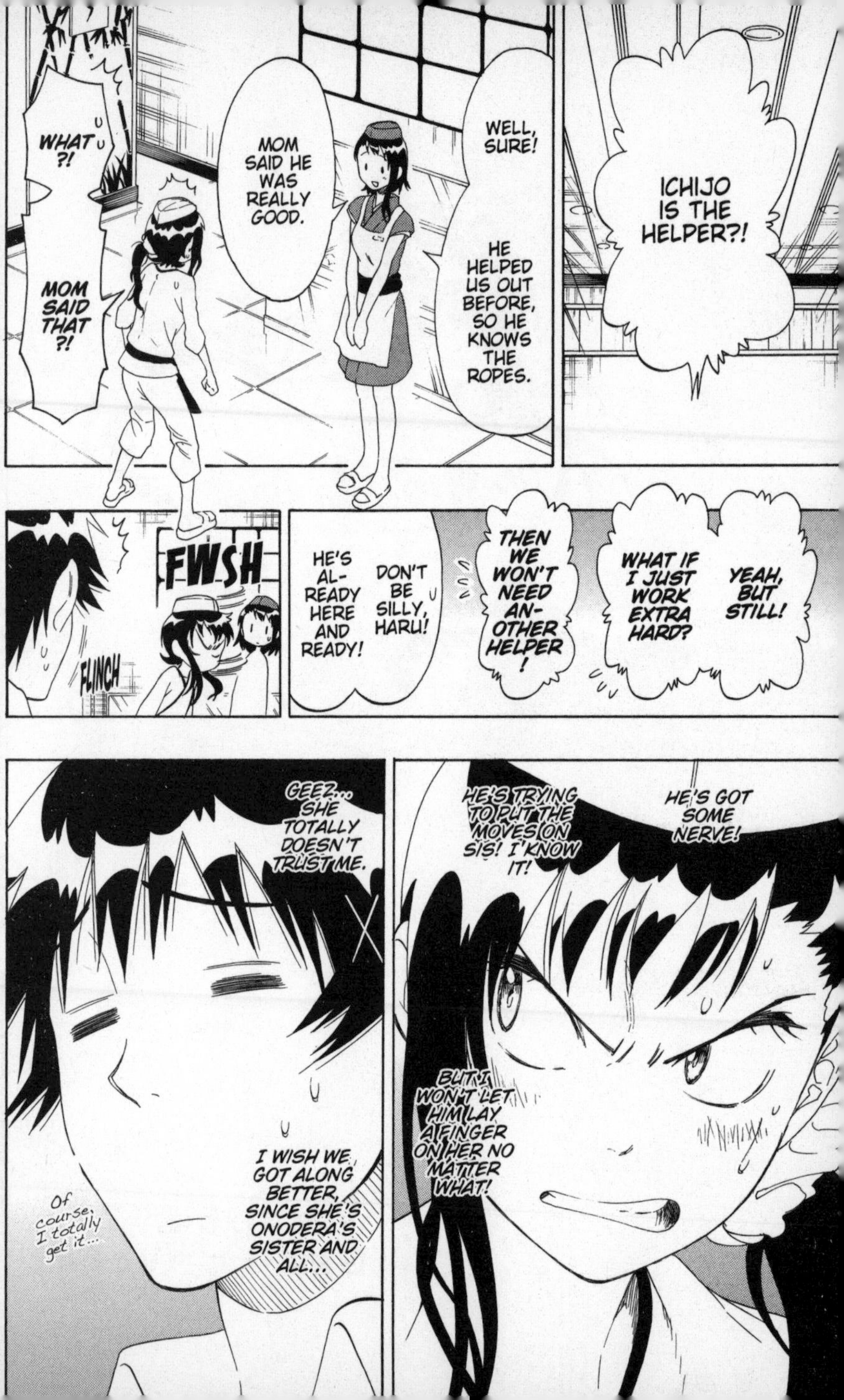
ICHIJO IS THE HELPER?!
WELL, SURE!
HE HELPED US OUT BEFORE, SO HE KNOWS THE ROPES.
MOM SAID HE WAS REALLY GOOD.
WHAT?!
MOM SAID THAT?!
YEAH, BUT STILL!
WHAT IF I JUST WORK EXTRA HARD?
THEN WE WON'T NEED ANOTHER HELPER!
DON'T BE SILLY, HARU!
HE'S ALREADY HERE AND READY!
FWSH
FLINCH
HE'S GOT SOME NERVE!
HE'S TRYING TO PUT THE MOVES ON SIS! I KNOW IT!
BUT I WON'T LET HIM LAY A FINGER ON HER NO MATTER WHAT!
GEEZ... SHE TOTALLY DOESN'T TRUST ME.
I WISH WE GOT ALONG BETTER, SINCE SHE'S ONODERA'S SISTER AND ALL...
Of course. I totally get it...

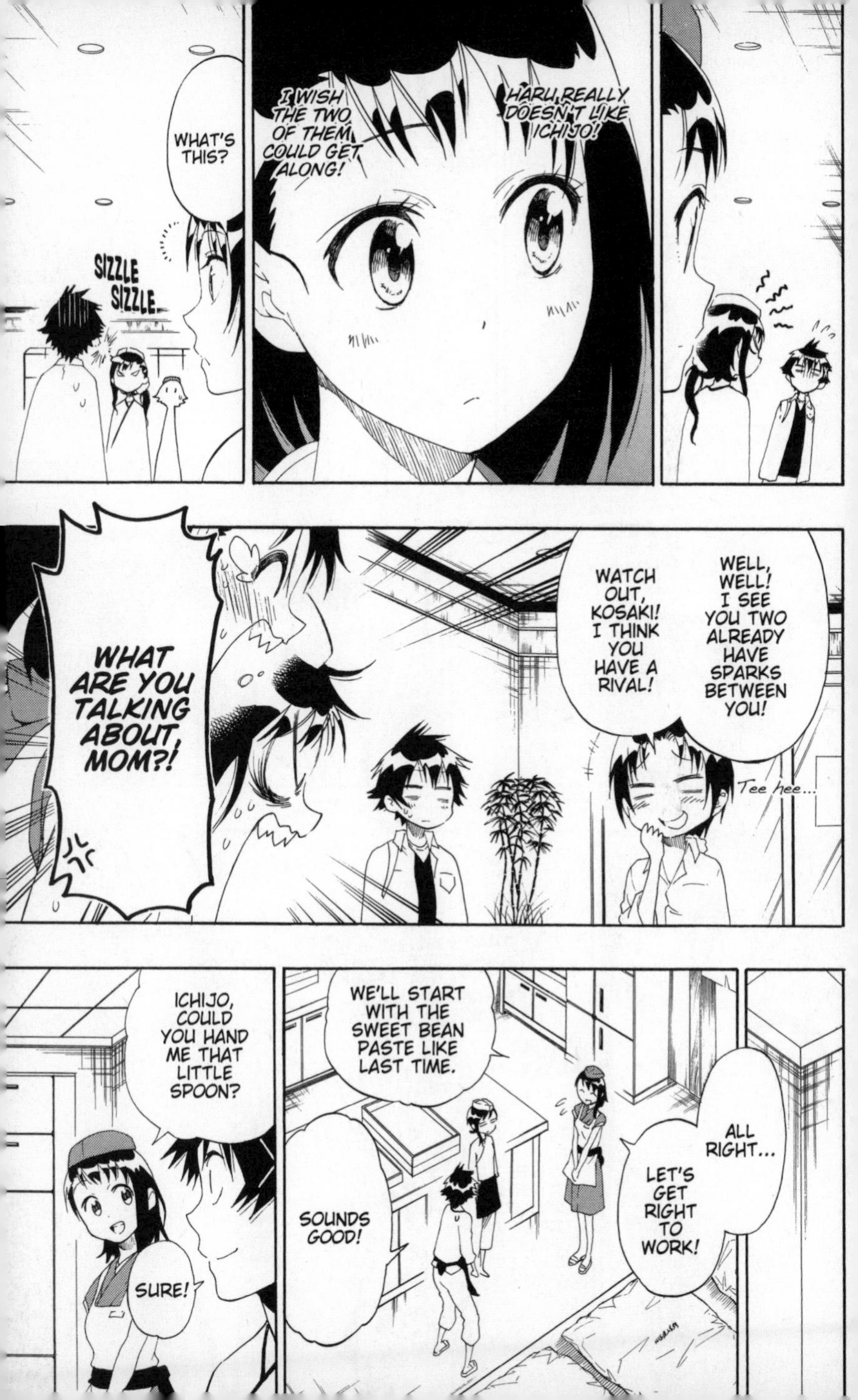
HARU REALLY DOESN'T LIKE ICHIJO!
I WISH THE TWO OF THEM COULD GET ALONG!
WHAT'S THIS?
SIZZLE SIZZLE
WELL, WELL! I SEE YOU TWO ALREADY HAVE SPARKS BETWEEN YOU!
WATCH OUT, KOSAKI! I THINK YOU HAVE A RIVAL!
Tee hee...
WHAT ARE YOU TALKING ABOUT, MOM?!
ALL RIGHT... LET'S GET RIGHT TO WORK!
WE'LL START WITH THE SWEET BEAN PASTE LIKE LAST TIME.
SOUNDS GOOD!
ICHIJO, COULD YOU HAND ME THAT LITTLE SPOON?
SURE!

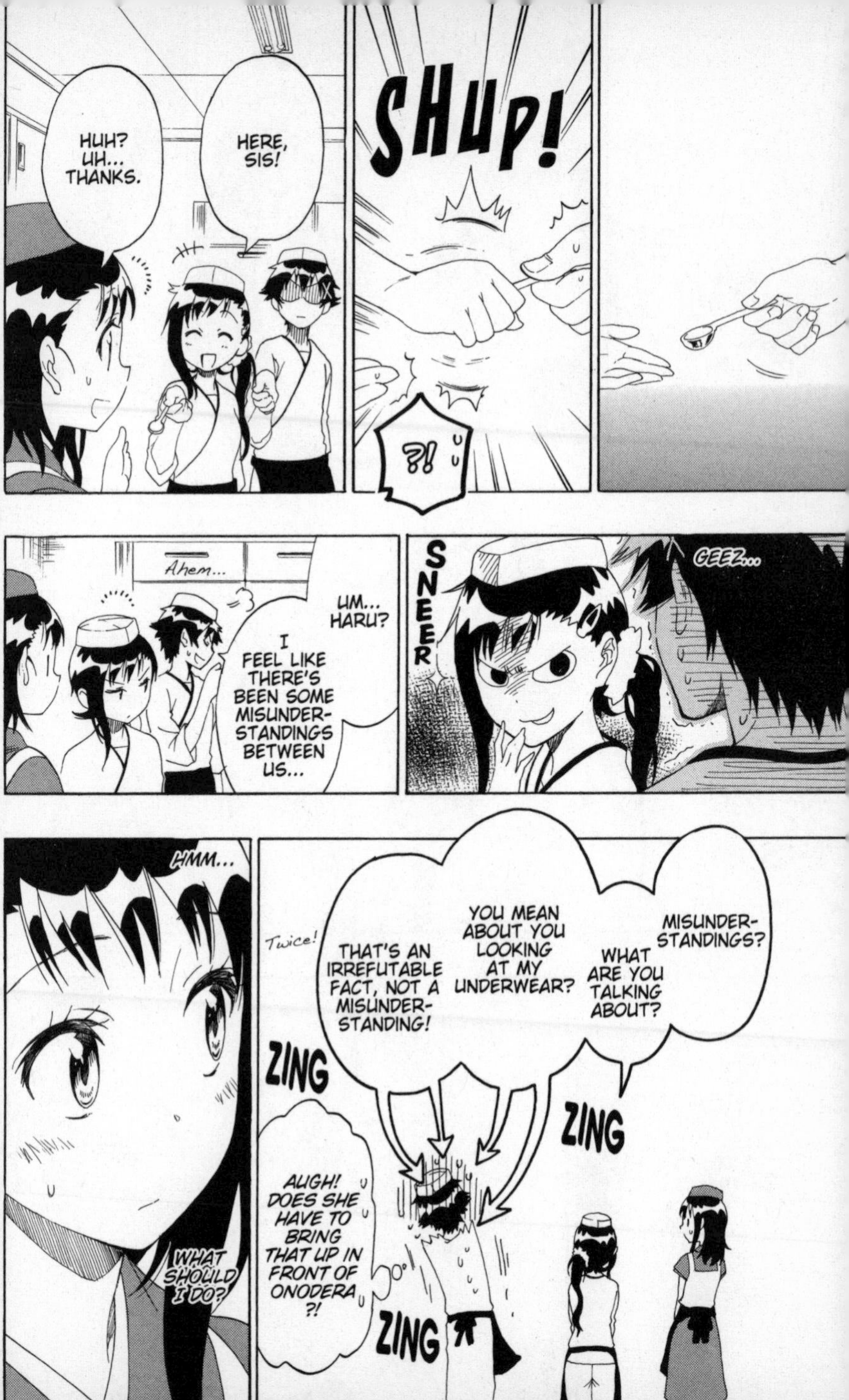
SHUP!
?!
HERE, SIS!
HUH? UH... THANKS.
GEEZ...
SNEER
UM... HARU?
I FEEL LIKE THERE'S BEEN SOME MISUNDER-STANDINGS BETWEEN US...
Ahem...
MISUNDER-STANDINGS? WHAT ARE YOU TALKING ABOUT?
YOU MEAN ABOUT YOU LOOKING AT MY UNDERWEAR?
THAT'S AN IRREFUTABLE FACT, NOT A MISUNDER-STANDING!
Twice!
ZING
ZING
AUGH! DOES SHE HAVE TO BRING THAT UP IN FRONT OF ONODERA?!
ZING
HMM...
WHAT SHOULD I DO?

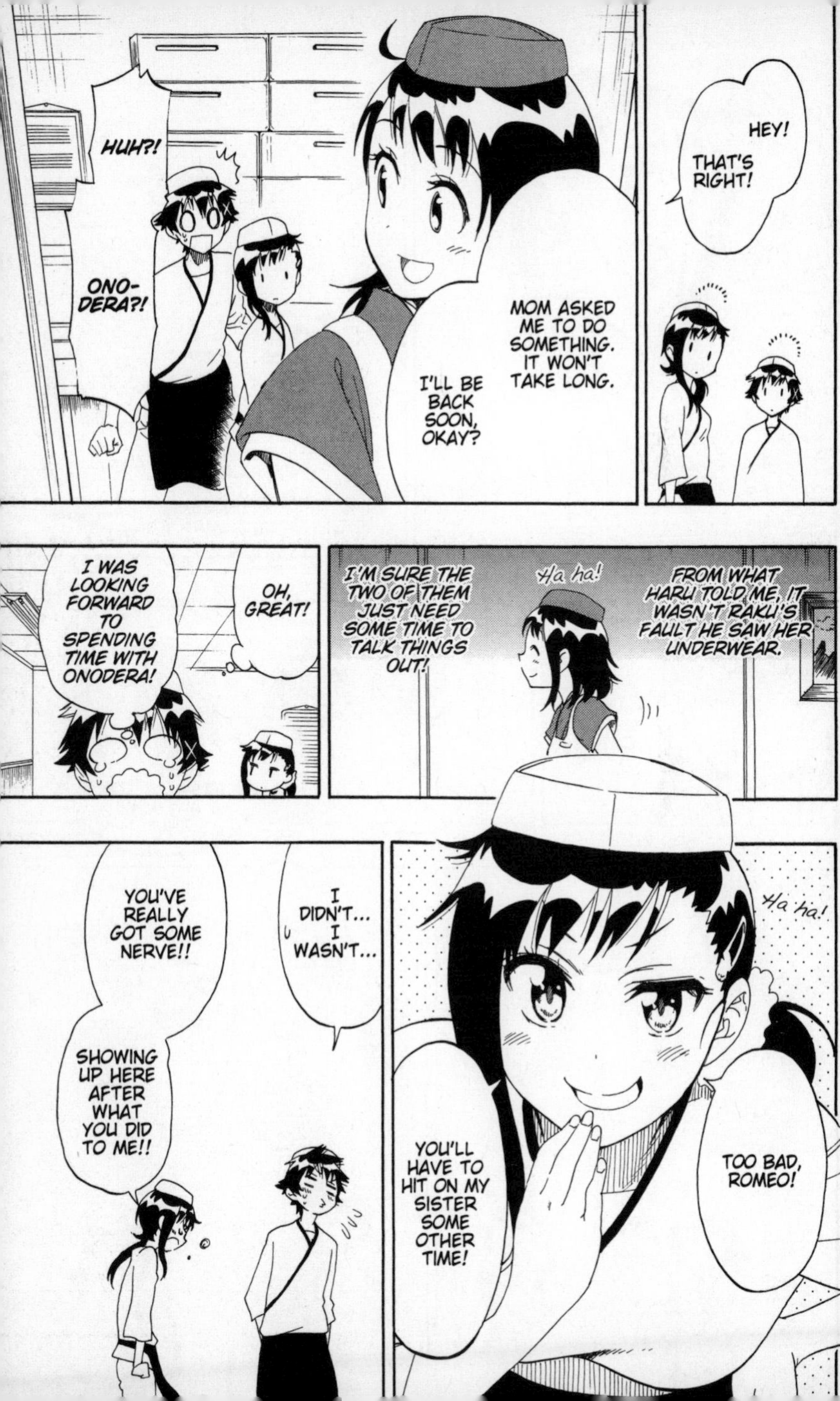
HEY! THAT'S RIGHT!
MOM ASKED ME TO DO SOMETHING. IT WON'T TAKE LONG.
I'LL BE BACK SOON, OKAY?
HUH?!
ONO-DERA?!
FROM WHAT HARU TOLD ME, IT WASN'T RAKU'S FAULT HE SAW HER UNDERWEAR.
Ha ha!
I'M SURE THE TWO OF THEM JUST NEED SOME TIME TO TALK THINGS OUT!
OH, GREAT!
I WAS LOOKING FORWARD TO SPENDING TIME WITH ONODERA!
Ha ha!
TOO BAD, ROMEO!
YOU'LL HAVE TO HIT ON MY SISTER SOME OTHER TIME!
I DIDN'T... I WASN'T...
YOU'VE REALLY GOT SOME NERVE!!
SHOWING UP HERE AFTER WHAT YOU DID TO ME!!

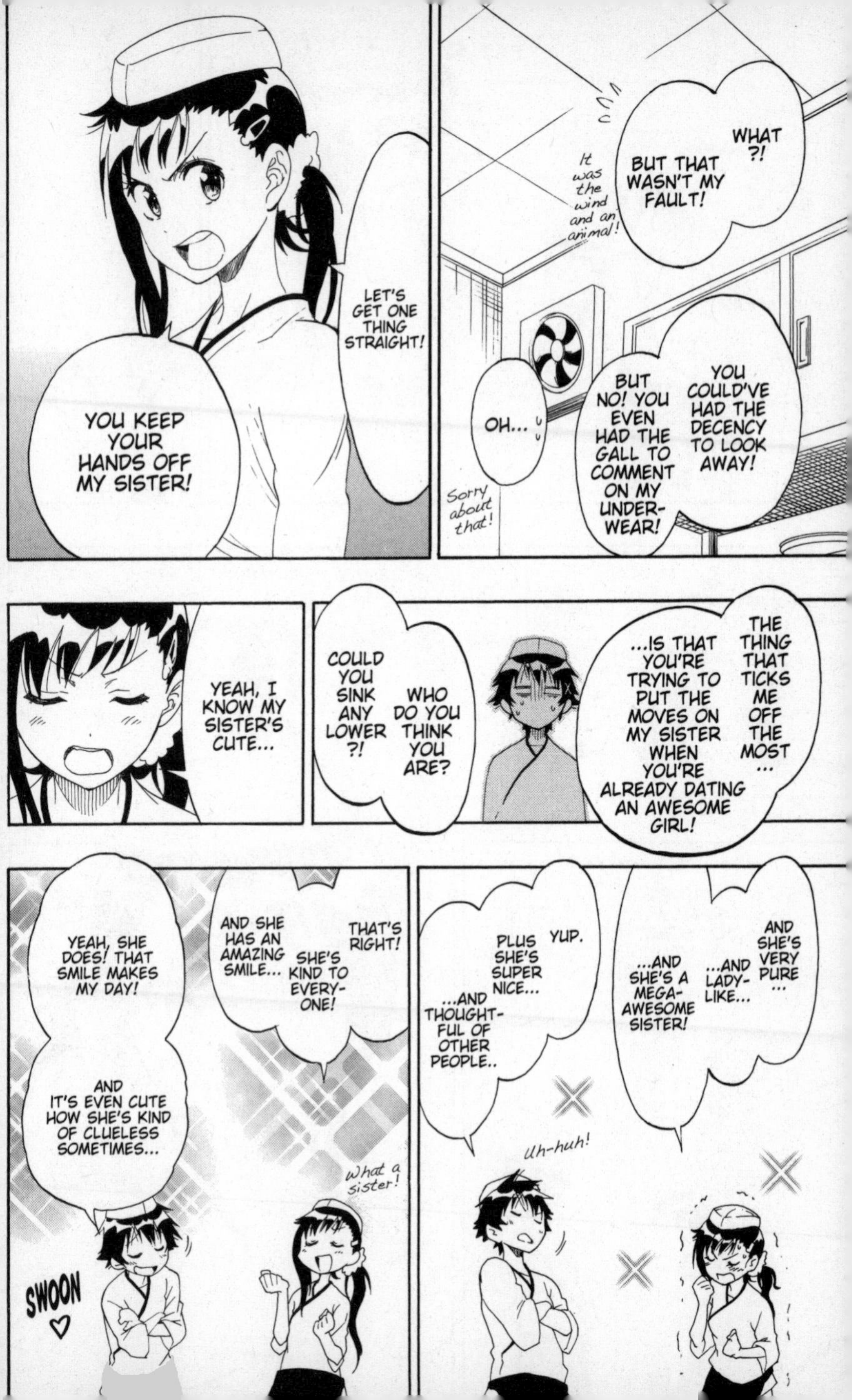
WHAT?!
BUT THAT WASN'T MY FAULT!
It was the wind and an animal!
YOU COULD'VE HAD THE DECENCY TO LOOK AWAY!
BUT NO! YOU EVEN HAD THE GALL TO COMMENT ON MY UNDER-WEAR!
OH...
Sorry about that!
LET'S GET ONE THING STRAIGHT!
YOU KEEP YOUR HANDS OFF MY SISTER!
THE THING THAT TICKS ME OFF THE MOST...
...IS THAT YOU'RE TRYING TO PUT THE MOVES ON MY SISTER WHEN YOU'RE ALREADY DATING AN AWESOME GIRL!
WHO DO YOU THINK YOU ARE?
COULD YOU SINK ANY LOWER?!
YEAH, I KNOW MY SISTER'S CUTE...
AND SHE'S VERY PURE...
...AND LADY-LIKE...
...AND SHE'S A MEGA-AWESOME SISTER!
YUP.
PLUS SHE'S SUPER NICE...
...AND THOUGHT-FUL OF OTHER PEOPLE..
Uh-huh!
THAT'S RIGHT!
SHE'S KIND TO EVERY-ONE!
AND SHE HAS AN AMAZING SMILE...
YEAH, SHE DOES! THAT SMILE MAKES MY DAY!
AND IT'S EVEN CUTE HOW SHE'S KIND OF CLUELESS SOMETIMES...
What a sister!
SWOON

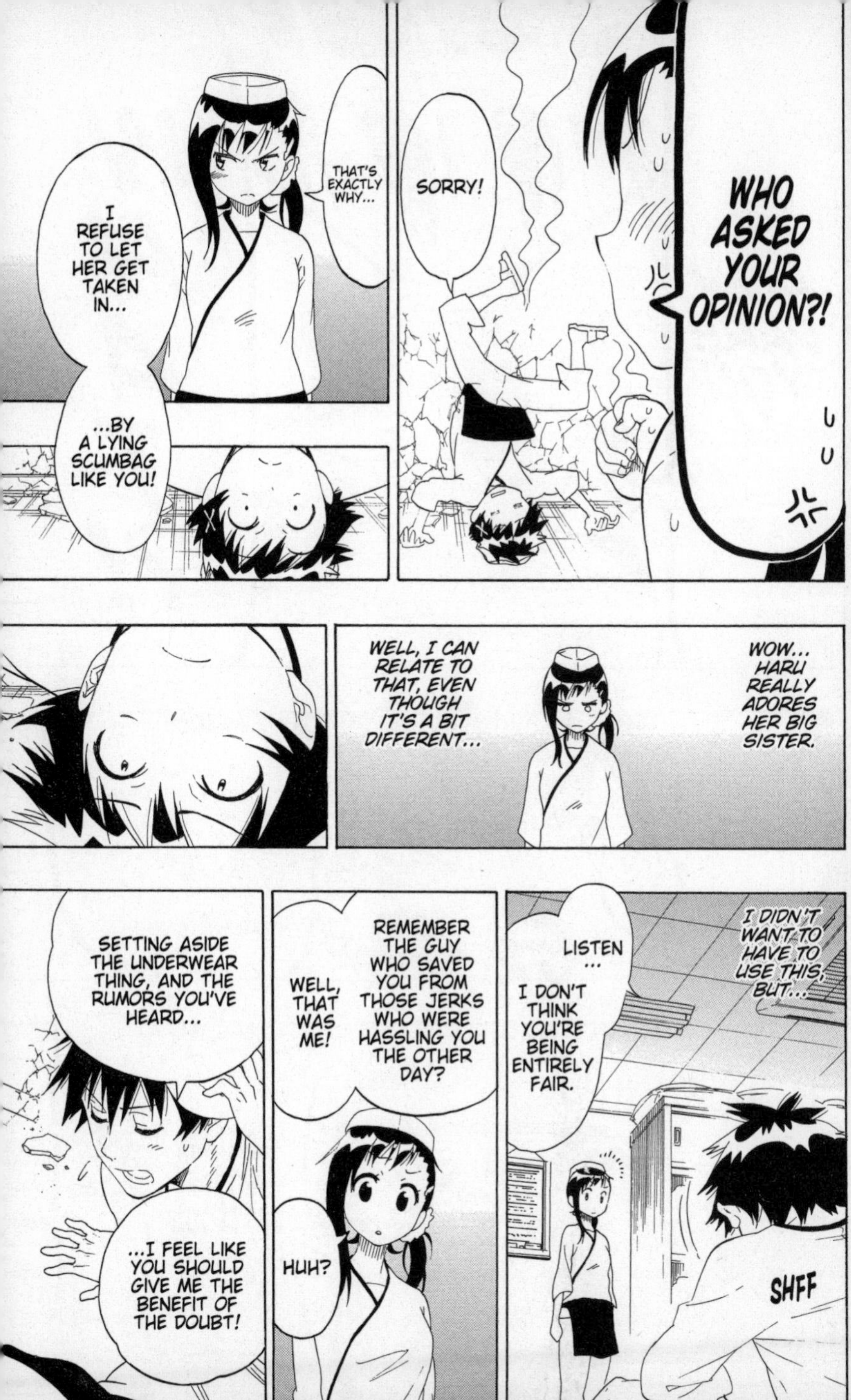
WHO ASKED YOUR OPINION?!
SORRY!
THAT'S EXACTLY WHY...
I REFUSE TO LET HER GET TAKEN IN...
...BY A LYING SCUMBAG LIKE YOU!
WOW... HARU REALLY ADORES HER BIG SISTER.
WELL, I CAN RELATE TO THAT, EVEN THOUGH IT'S A BIT DIFFERENT...
I DIDN'T WANT TO HAVE TO USE THIS, BUT...
SHFF
LISTEN...
I DON'T THINK YOU'RE BEING ENTIRELY FAIR.
REMEMBER THE GUY WHO SAVED YOU FROM THOSE JERKS WHO WERE HASSLING YOU THE OTHER DAY?
WELL, THAT WAS ME!
HUH?
SETTING ASIDE THE UNDERWEAR THING, AND THE RUMORS YOU'VE HEARD...
...I FEEL LIKE YOU SHOULD GIVE ME THE BENEFIT OF THE DOUBT!

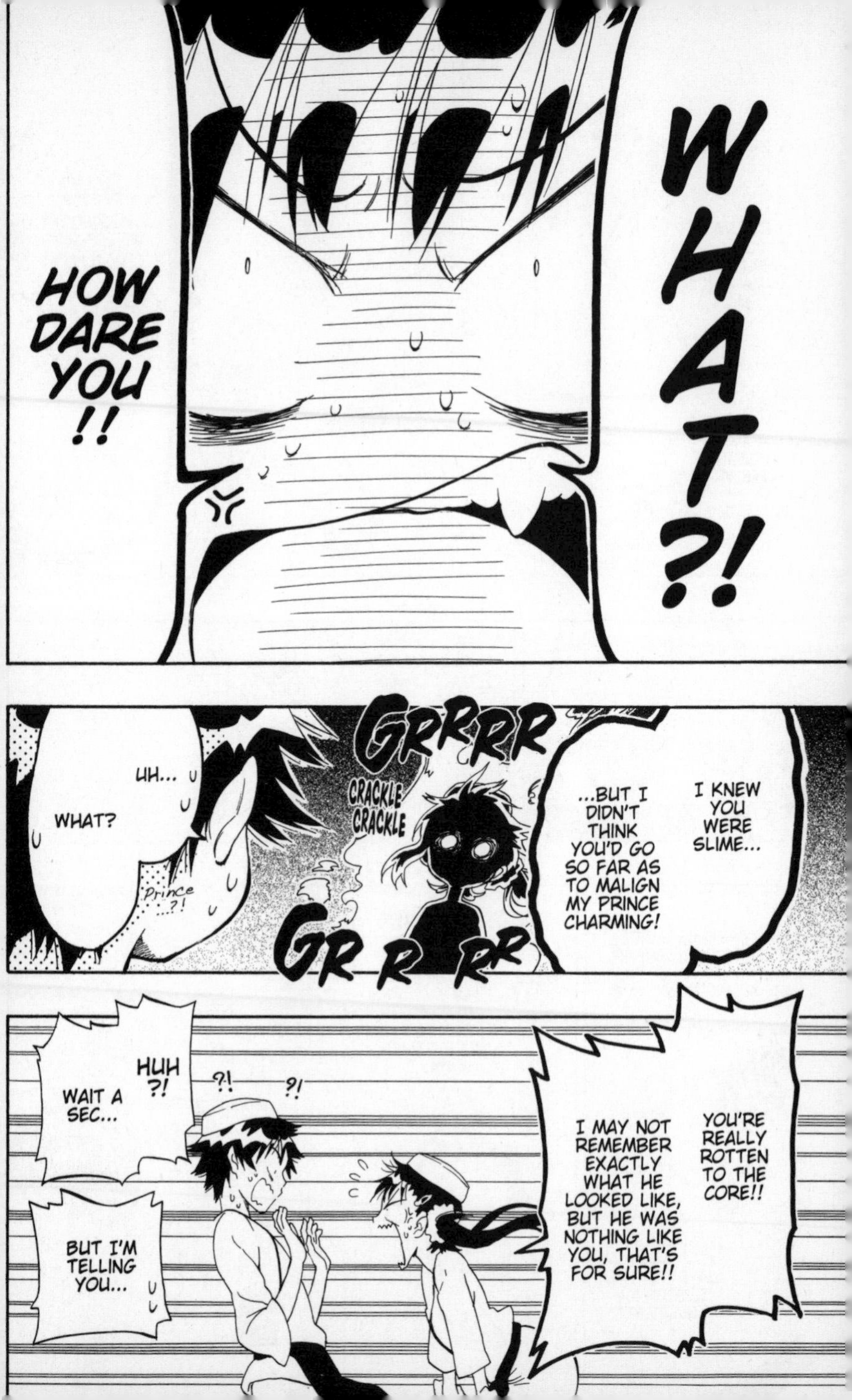
WHAT?!
HOW DARE YOU!!
I KNEW YOU WERE SLIME...
...BUT I DIDN'T THINK YOU'D GO SO FAR AS TO MALIGN MY PRINCE CHARMING!
GRRRR
CRACKLE CRACKLE
GR R RR
UH...
WHAT?
Prince...?!
YOU'RE REALLY ROTTEN TO THE CORE!!
I MAY NOT REMEMBER EXACTLY WHAT HE LOOKED LIKE, BUT HE WAS NOTHING LIKE YOU, THAT'S FOR SURE!!
?!
?!
HUH?!
WAIT A SEC...
BUT I'M TELLING YOU...

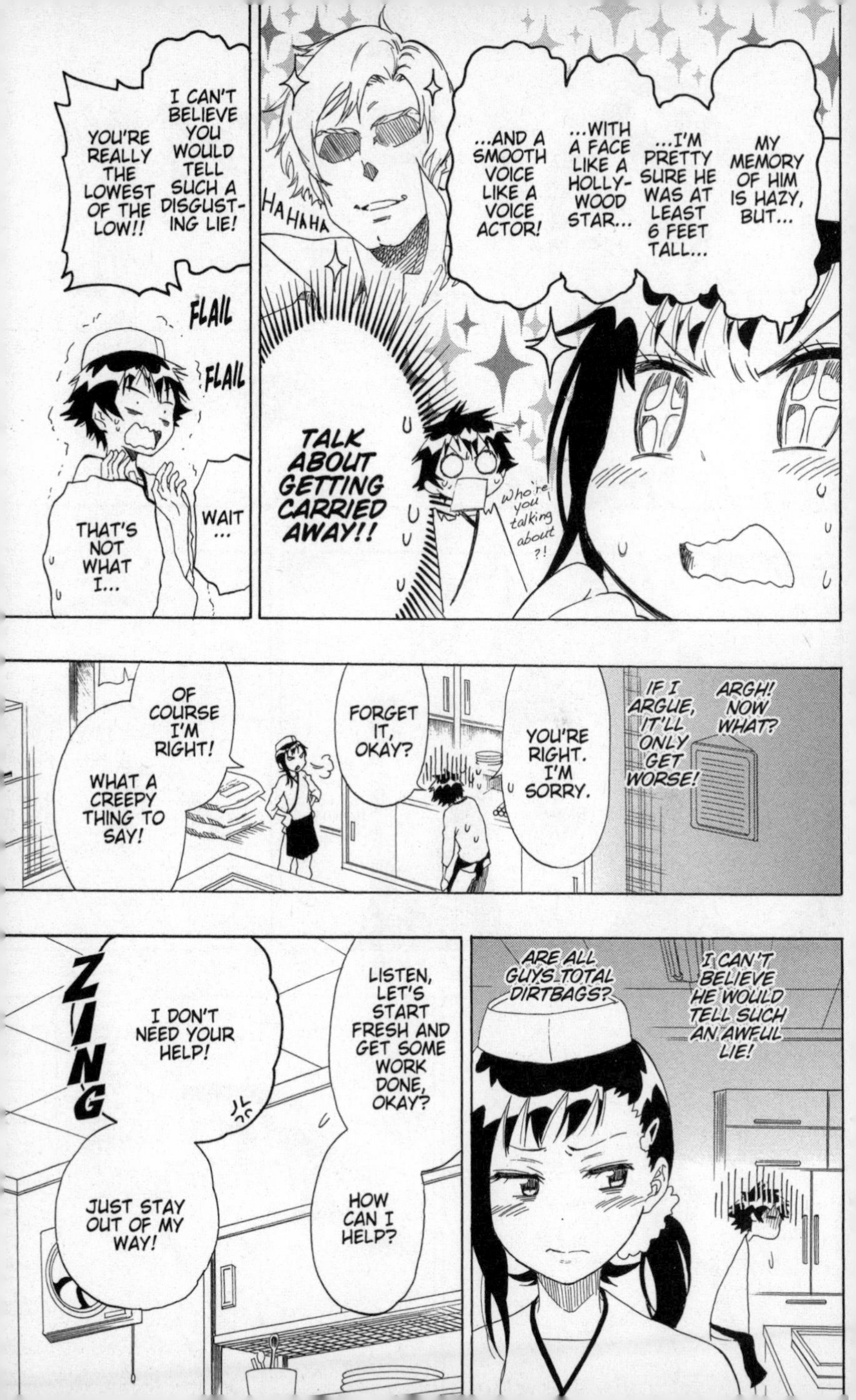
MY MEMORY OF HIM IS HAZY, BUT...
...I'M PRETTY SURE HE WAS AT LEAST 6 FEET TALL...
...WITH A FACE LIKE A HOLLYWOOD STAR...
...AND A SMOOTH VOICE LIKE A VOICE ACTOR!
HAHAHA
TALK ABOUT GETTING CARRIED AWAY!!
Who're you talking about?!
I CAN'T BELIEVE YOU WOULD TELL SUCH A DISGUSTING LIE!
YOU'RE REALLY THE LOWEST OF THE LOW!!
FLAIL
FLAIL
WAIT...
THAT'S NOT WHAT I...
ARGH! NOW WHAT?
IF I ARGUE, IT'LL ONLY GET WORSE!
YOU'RE RIGHT. I'M SORRY.
FORGET IT, OKAY?
OF COURSE I'M RIGHT!
WHAT A CREEPY THING TO SAY!
I CAN'T BELIEVE HE WOULD TELL SUCH AN AWFUL LIE!
ARE ALL GUYS TOTAL DIRTBAGS?
LISTEN, LET'S START FRESH AND GET SOME WORK DONE, OKAY?
HOW CAN I HELP?
I DON'T NEED YOUR HELP!
ZING
JUST STAY OUT OF MY WAY!

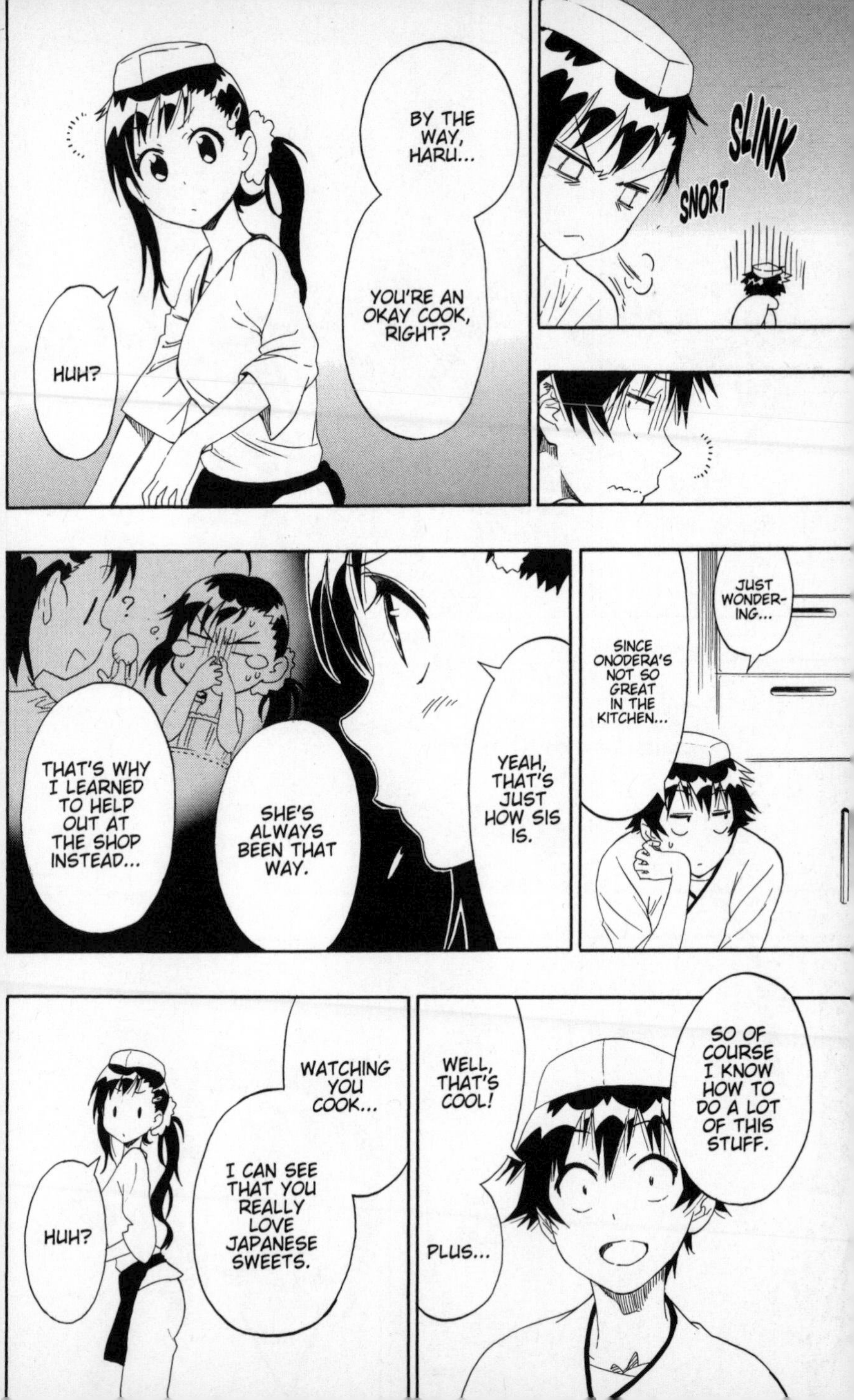
SLINK
SNORT
BY THE WAY, HARU...
YOU'RE AN OKAY COOK, RIGHT?
HUH?
JUST WONDERING...
SINCE ONODERA'S NOT SO GREAT IN THE KITCHEN...
YEAH, THAT'S JUST HOW SIS IS.
SHE'S ALWAYS BEEN THAT WAY.
THAT'S WHY I LEARNED TO HELP OUT AT THE SHOP INSTEAD...
SO OF COURSE I KNOW HOW TO DO A LOT OF THIS STUFF.
WELL, THAT'S COOL!
PLUS...
WATCHING YOU COOK...
I CAN SEE THAT YOU REALLY LOVE JAPANESE SWEETS.
HUH?

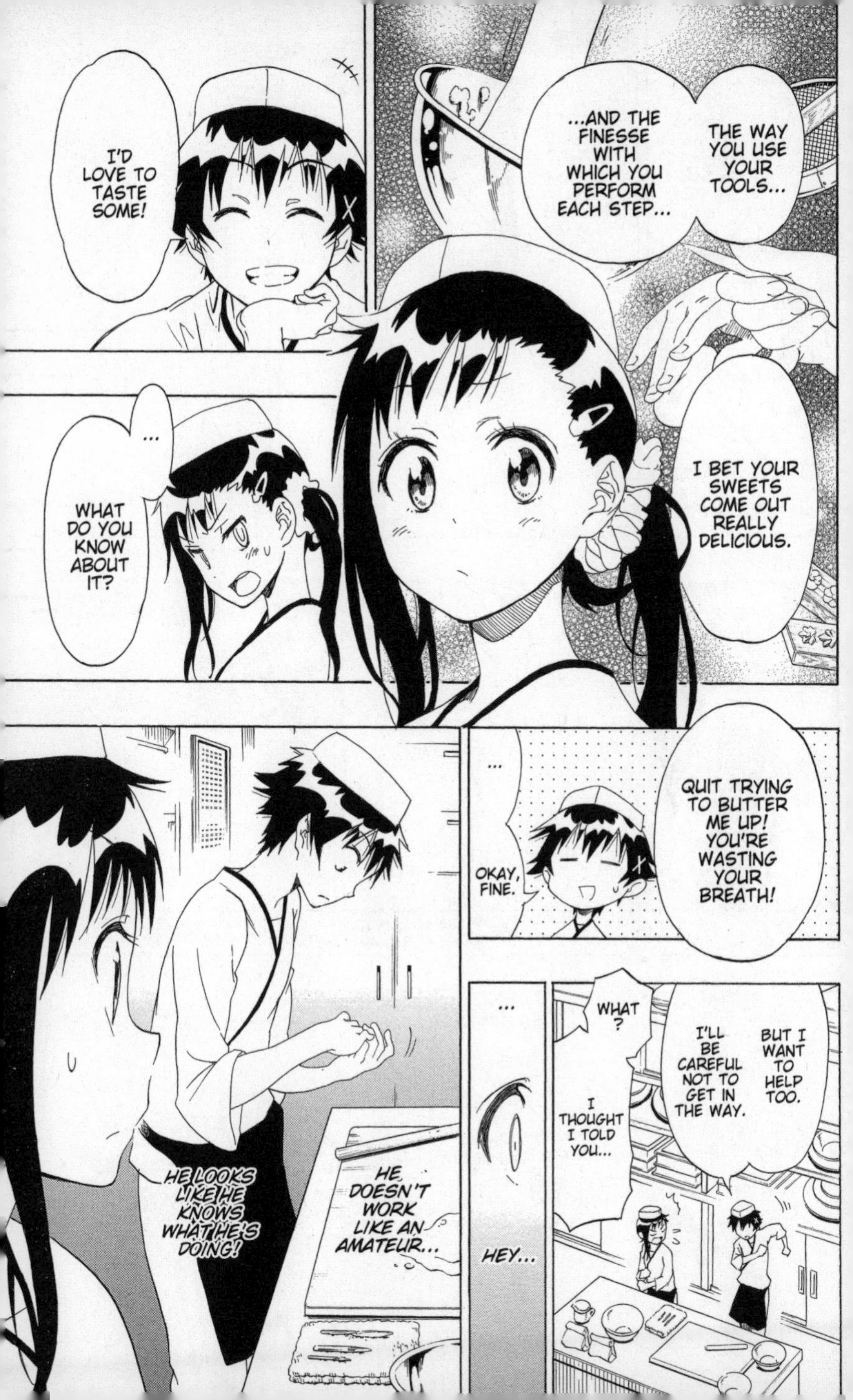
THE WAY YOU USE YOUR TOOLS...
...AND THE FINESSE WITH WHICH YOU PERFORM EACH STEP...
I BET YOUR SWEETS COME OUT REALLY DELICIOUS.
I'D LOVE TO TASTE SOME!
...
WHAT DO YOU KNOW ABOUT IT?
QUIT TRYING TO BUTTER ME UP! YOU'RE WASTING YOUR BREATH!
...
OKAY, FINE.
BUT I WANT TO HELP TOO.
I'LL BE CAREFUL NOT TO GET IN THE WAY.
WHAT?
I THOUGHT I TOLD YOU...
...
HEY...
HE DOESN'T WORK LIKE AN AMATEUR...
HE LOOKS LIKE HE KNOWS WHAT HE'S DOING!

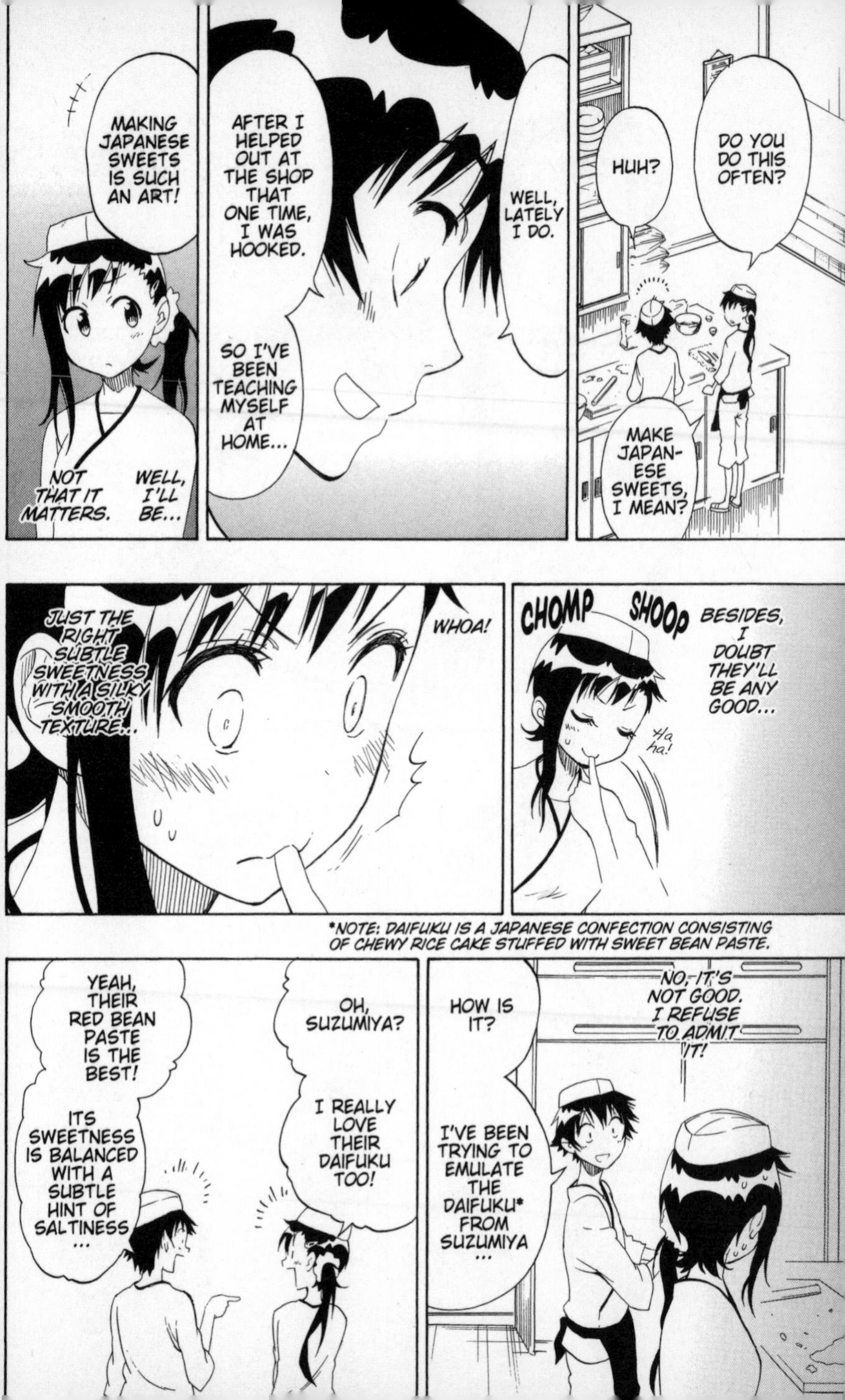
DO YOU DO THIS OFTEN?
HUH?
MAKE JAPANESE SWEETS, I MEAN?
WELL, LATELY I DO.
AFTER I HELPED OUT AT THE SHOP THAT ONE TIME, I WAS HOOKED.
SO I'VE BEEN TEACHING MYSELF AT HOME...
MAKING JAPANESE SWEETS IS SUCH AN ART!
WELL, I'LL BE...
NOT THAT IT MATTERS.
CHOMP
SHOOP
BESIDES, I DOUBT THEY'LL BE ANY GOOD...
Ha ha!
WHOA!
JUST THE RIGHT SUBTLE SWEETNESS WITH A SILKY SMOOTH TEXTURE...
NO, IT'S NOT GOOD. I REFUSE TO ADMIT IT!
HOW IS IT?
I'VE BEEN TRYING TO EMULATE THE DAIFUKU* FROM SUZUMIYA...
OH, SUZUMIYA?
I REALLY LOVE THEIR DAIFUKU TOO!
YEAH, THEIR RED BEAN PASTE IS THE BEST!
ITS SWEETNESS IS BALANCED WITH A SUBTLE HINT OF SALTINESS...

*NOTE: DAIFUKU IS A JAPANESE CONFECTION CONSISTING OF CHEWY RICE CAKE STUFFED WITH SWEET BEAN PASTE.

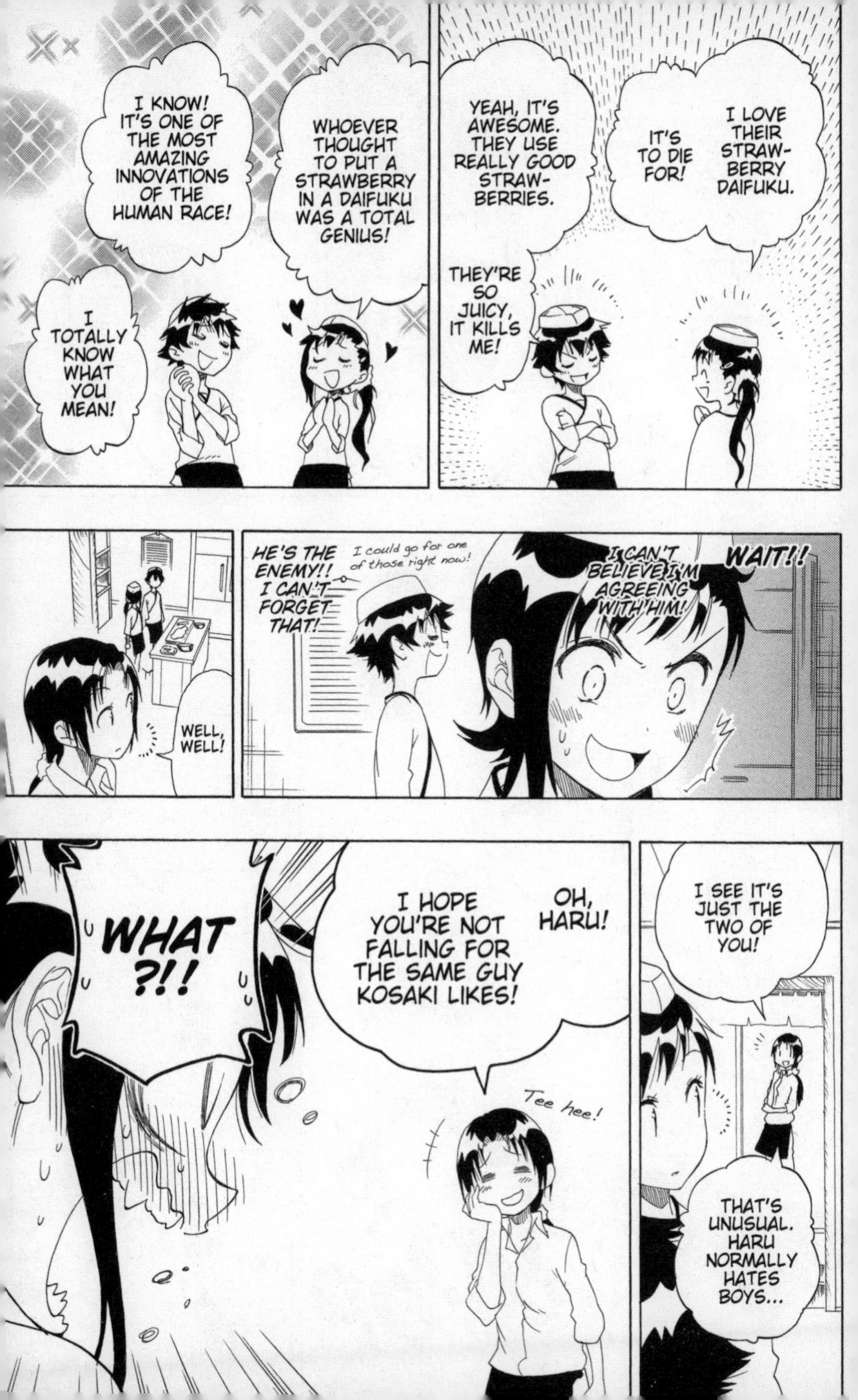
I LOVE THEIR STRAWBERRY DAIFUKU.
IT'S TO DIE FOR!
YEAH, IT'S AWESOME. THEY USE REALLY GOOD STRAWBERRIES.
THEY'RE SO JUICY, IT KILLS ME!
WHOEVER THOUGHT TO PUT A STRAWBERRY IN A DAIFUKU WAS A TOTAL GENIUS!
I KNOW! IT'S ONE OF THE MOST AMAZING INNOVATIONS OF THE HUMAN RACE!
I TOTALLY KNOW WHAT YOU MEAN!
WAIT!!
I CAN'T BELIEVE I'M AGREEING WITH HIM!
HE'S THE ENEMY!! I CAN'T FORGET THAT!
I could go for one of those right now!
WELL, WELL!
I SEE IT'S JUST THE TWO OF YOU!
THAT'S UNUSUAL. HARU NORMALLY HATES BOYS...
OH, HARU!
I HOPE YOU'RE NOT FALLING FOR THE SAME GUY KOSAKI LIKES!
Tee hee!
WHAT?!!

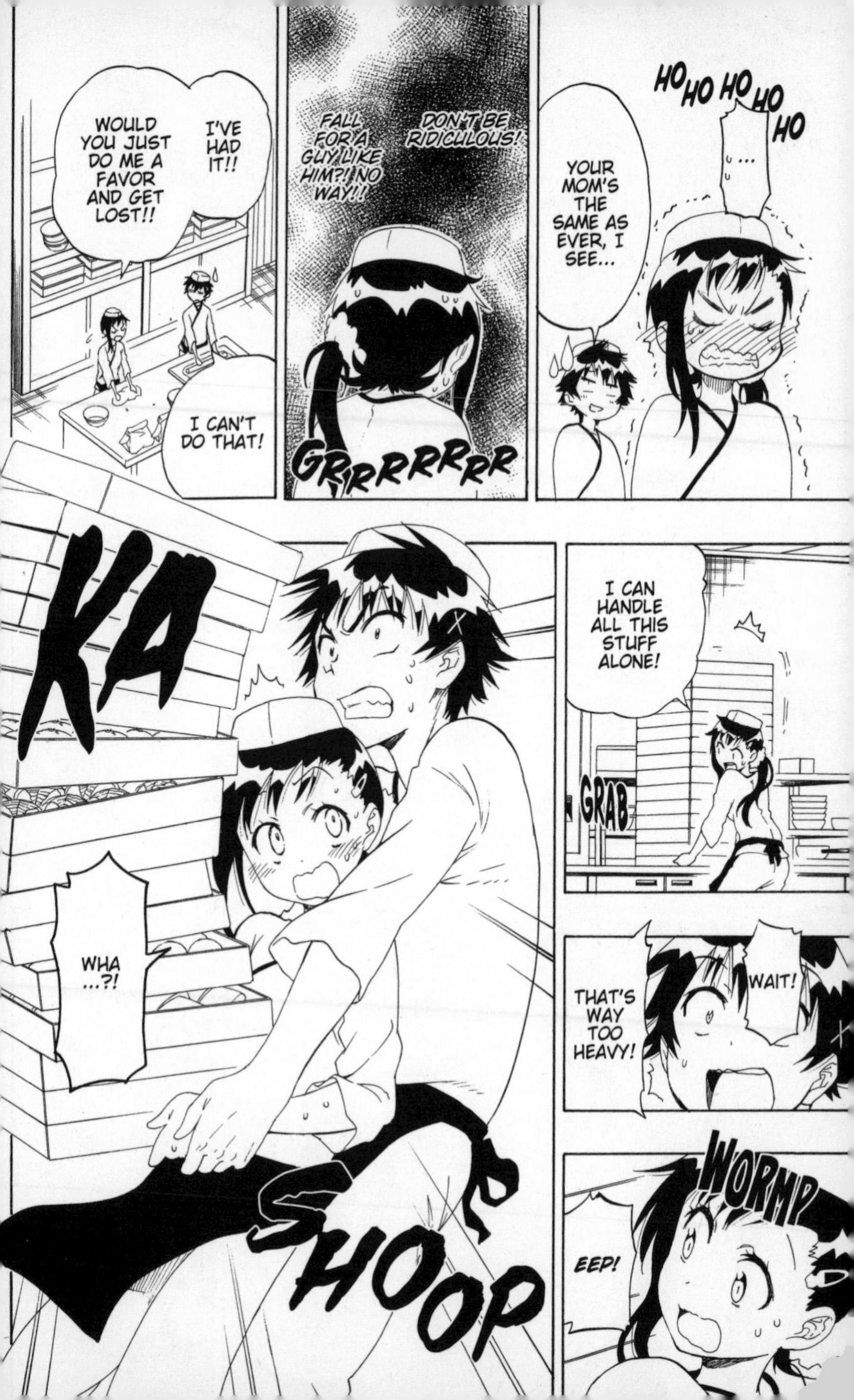
HO HO HO HO HO
...
YOUR MOM'S THE SAME AS EVER, I SEE...
DON'T BE RIDICULOUS!
FALL FOR A GUY LIKE HIM?! NO WAY!!
GRRRRRRR
I'VE HAD IT!!
WOULD YOU JUST DO ME A FAVOR AND GET LOST!!
I CAN'T DO THAT!
I CAN HANDLE ALL THIS STUFF ALONE!
GRAB
WAIT!
THAT'S WAY TOO HEAVY!
WORMP
EEP!
KA
WHA ...?!
SHOOP

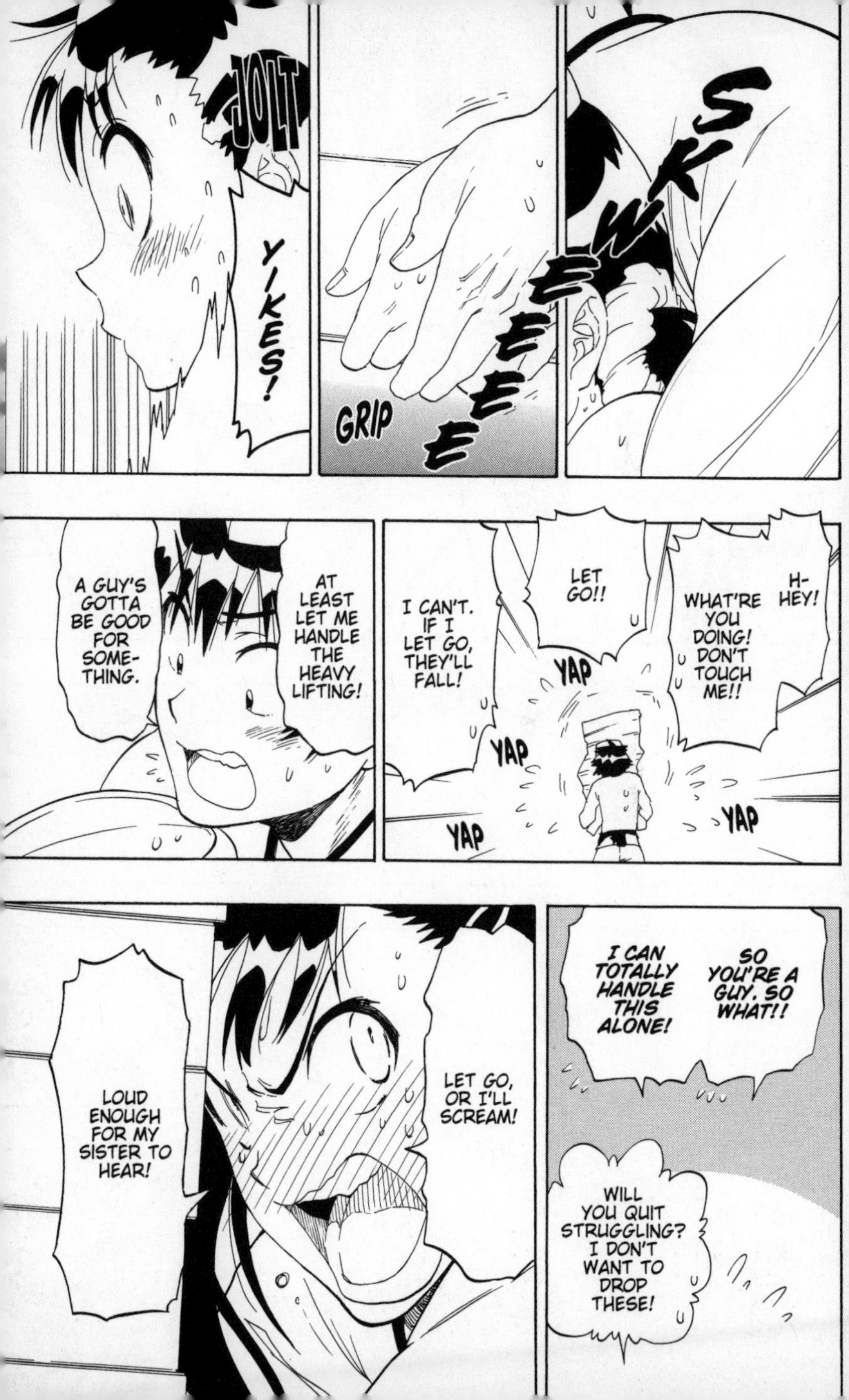
SKWEEEEE
GRIP
JOLT
YIKES!
H-HEY!
WHAT'RE YOU DOING! DON'T TOUCH ME!!
LET GO!!
YAP
YAP
YAP
YAP
I CAN'T. IF I LET GO, THEY'LL FALL!
AT LEAST LET ME HANDLE THE HEAVY LIFTING!
A GUY'S GOTTA BE GOOD FOR SOMETHING.
SO YOU'RE A GUY. SO WHAT!!
I CAN TOTALLY HANDLE THIS ALONE!
WILL YOU QUIT STRUGGLING? I DON'T WANT TO DROP THESE!
LET GO, OR I'LL SCREAM!
LOUD ENOUGH FOR MY SISTER TO HEAR!

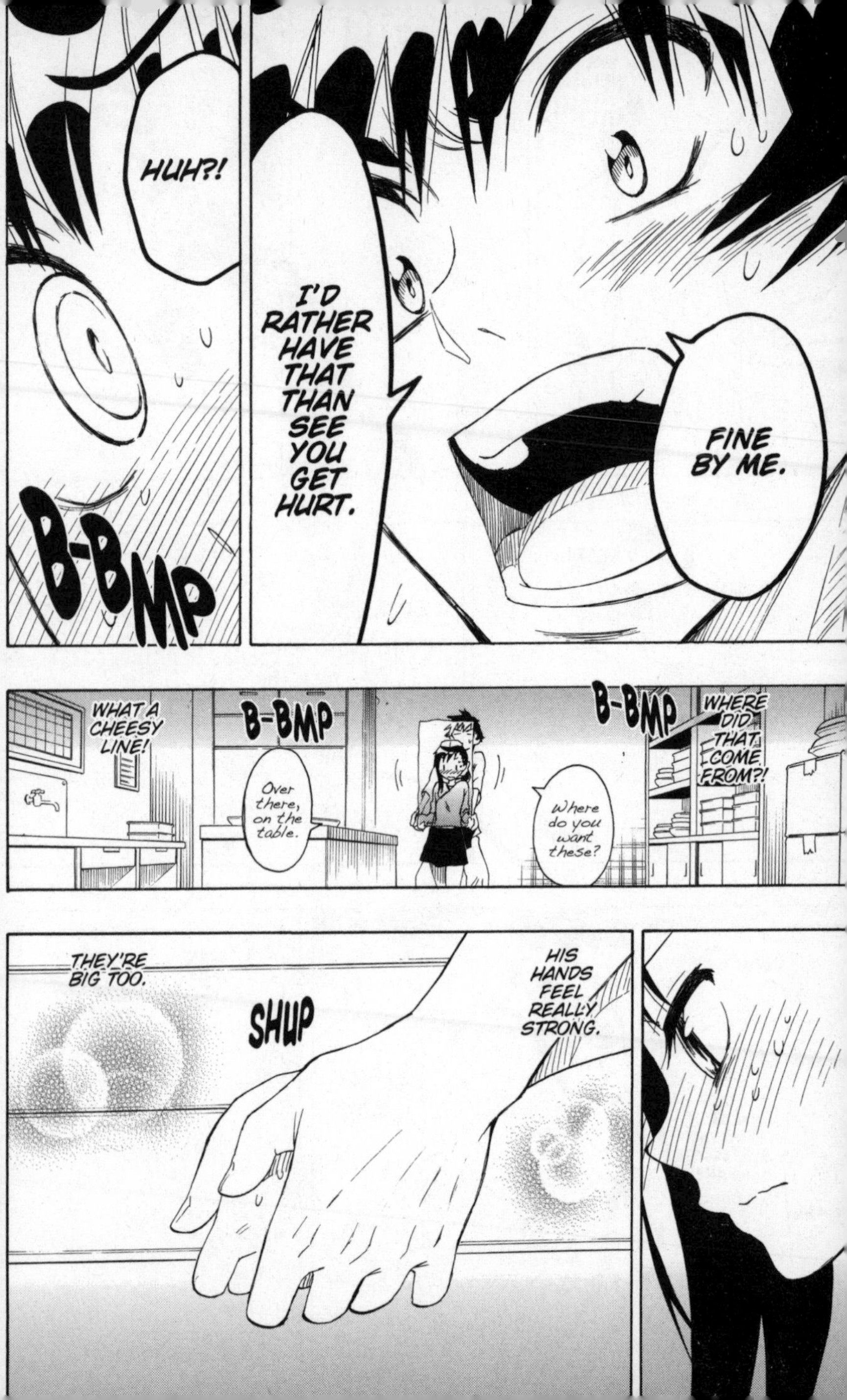
FINE BY ME.
I'D RATHER HAVE THAT THAN SEE YOU GET HURT.
HUH?!
B-BMP
WHERE DID THAT COME FROM?!
B-BMP
Where do you want these?
Over there, on the table.
B-BMP
WHAT A CHEESY LINE!
HIS HANDS FEEL REALLY STRONG.
SHUP
THEY'RE BIG TOO.

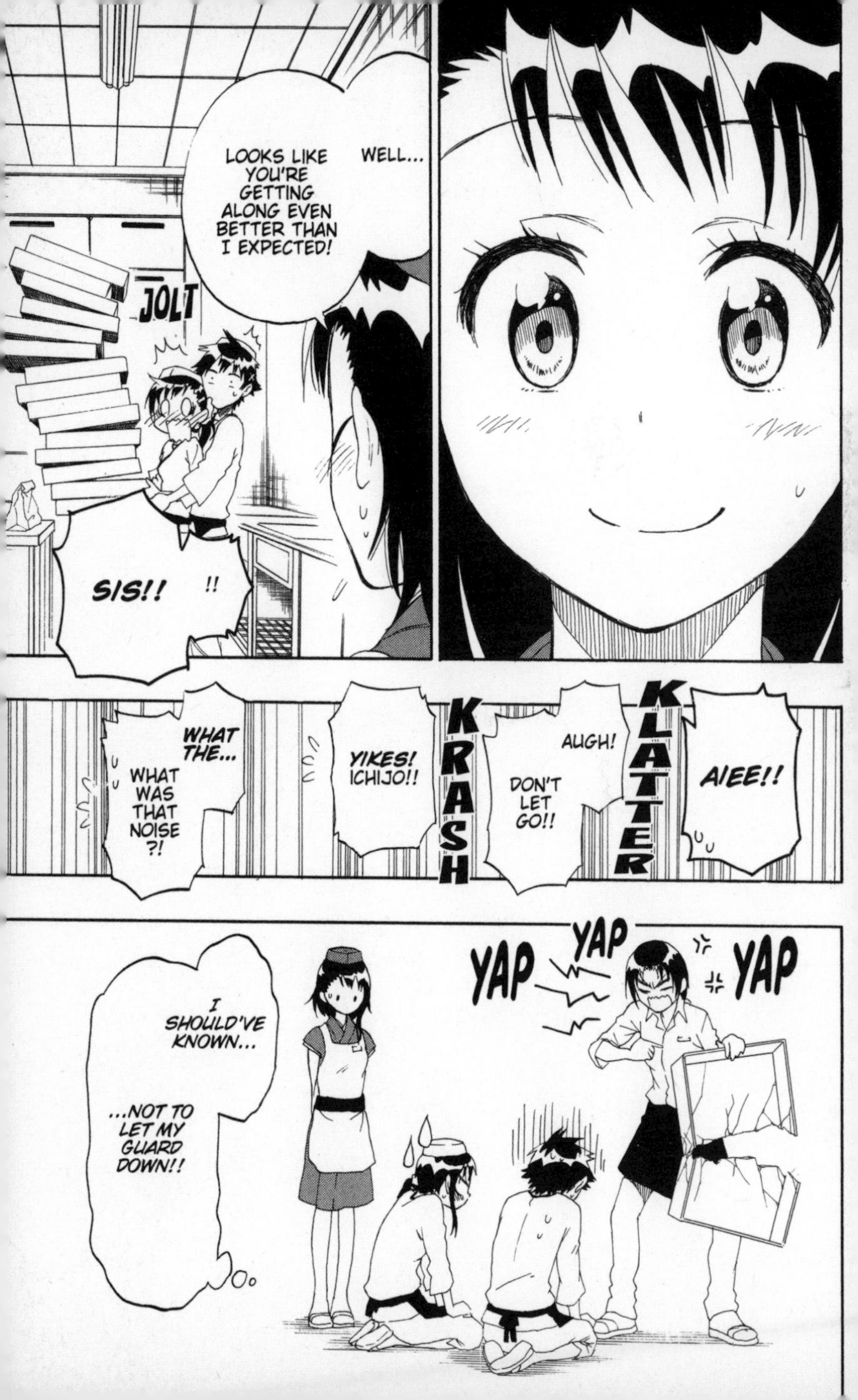
WELL...
LOOKS LIKE YOU'RE GETTING ALONG EVEN BETTER THAN I EXPECTED!
JOLT
SIS!!
!!
AIEE!!
KLATTER
AUGH!
DON'T LET GO!!
KRASH
YIKES! ICHIJO!!
WHAT THE...
WHAT WAS THAT NOISE?!
YAP
YAP
YAP
I SHOULD'VE KNOWN...
...NOT TO LET MY GUARD DOWN!!

The scent
of a love
comic!

I smell
something!

Tee hee
hee

Hee hee
hee!

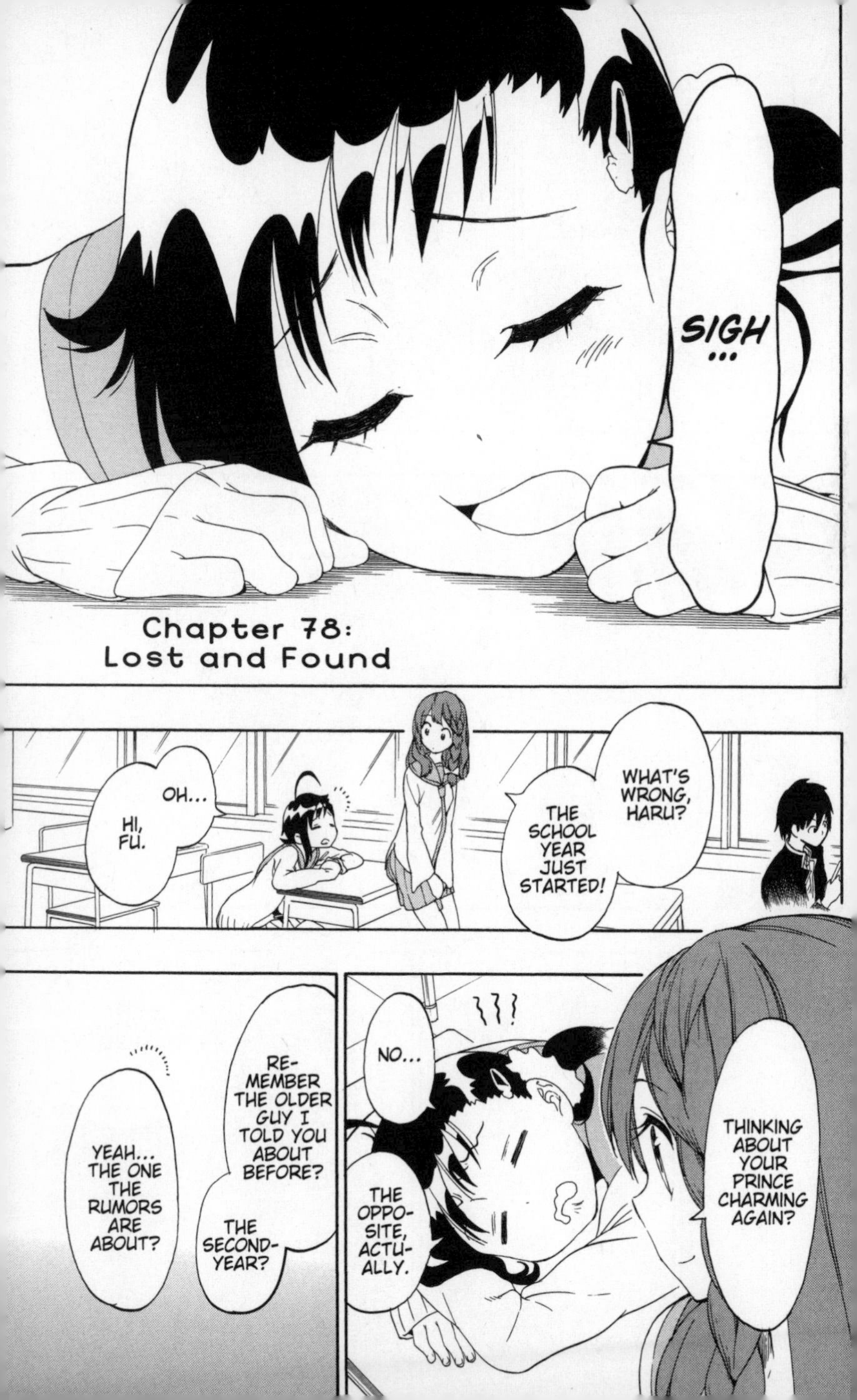
SIGH...
Chapter 78: Lost and Found
WHAT'S WRONG, HARU?
THE SCHOOL YEAR JUST STARTED!
OH...
HI, FU.
THINKING ABOUT YOUR PRINCE CHARMING AGAIN?
NO...
THE OPPOSITE, ACTUALLY.
REMEMBER THE OLDER GUY I TOLD YOU ABOUT BEFORE?
THE SECOND-YEAR?
YEAH... THE ONE THE RUMORS ARE ABOUT?

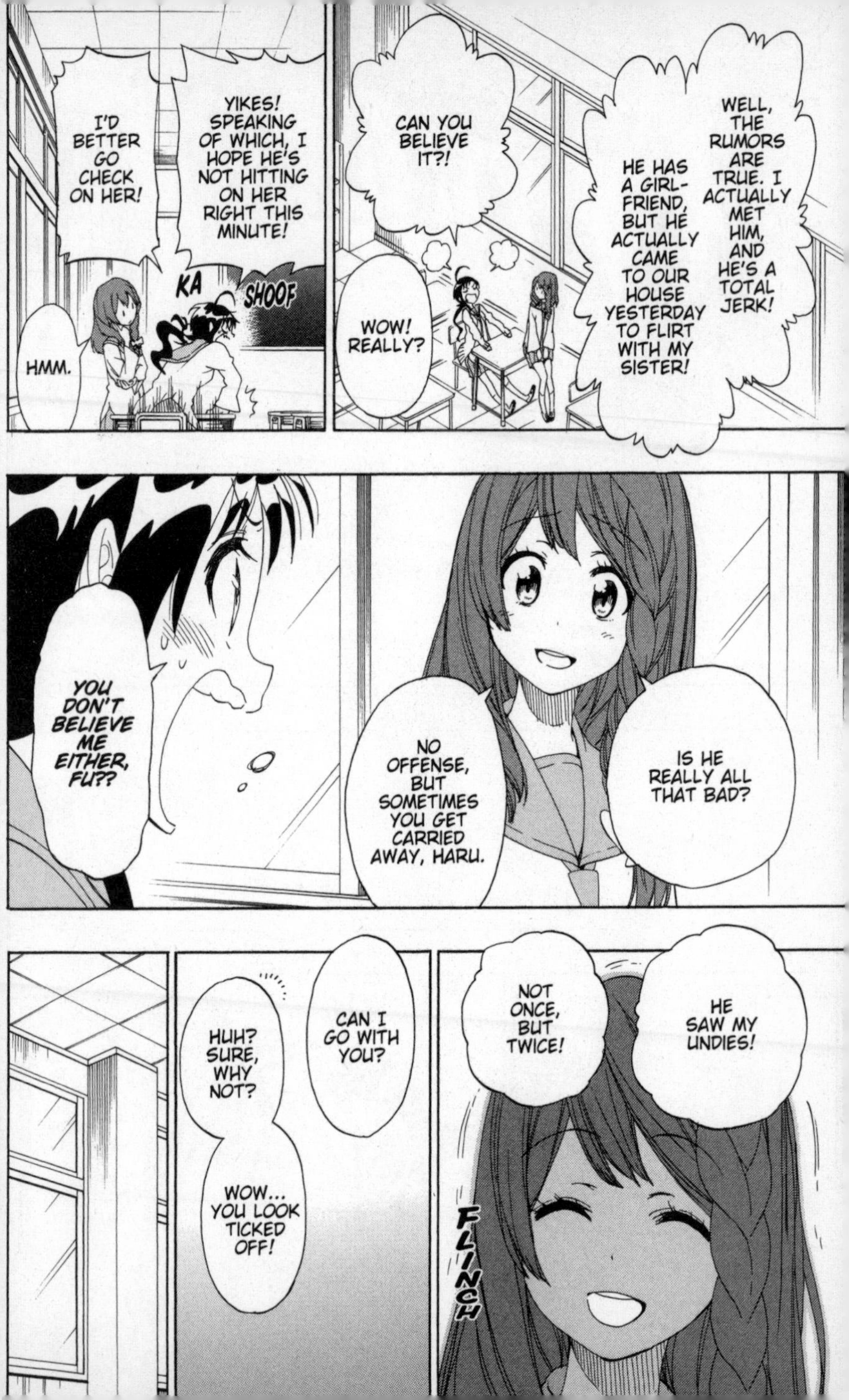
WELL, THE RUMORS ARE TRUE. I ACTUALLY MET HIM, AND HE'S A TOTAL JERK!
HE HAS A GIRL-FRIEND, BUT HE ACTUALLY CAME TO OUR HOUSE YESTERDAY TO FLIRT WITH MY SISTER!
CAN YOU BELIEVE IT?!
WOW! REALLY?
YIKES! SPEAKING OF WHICH, I HOPE HE'S NOT HITTING ON HER RIGHT THIS MINUTE!
I'D BETTER GO CHECK ON HER!
KA SHOOF
HMM.
IS HE REALLY ALL THAT BAD?
NO OFFENSE, BUT SOMETIMES YOU GET CARRIED AWAY, HARU.
YOU DON'T BELIEVE ME EITHER, FU??
HE SAW MY UNDIES!
NOT ONCE, BUT TWICE!
FLINCH
CAN I GO WITH YOU?
HUH? SURE, WHY NOT?
WOW... YOU LOOK TICKED OFF!

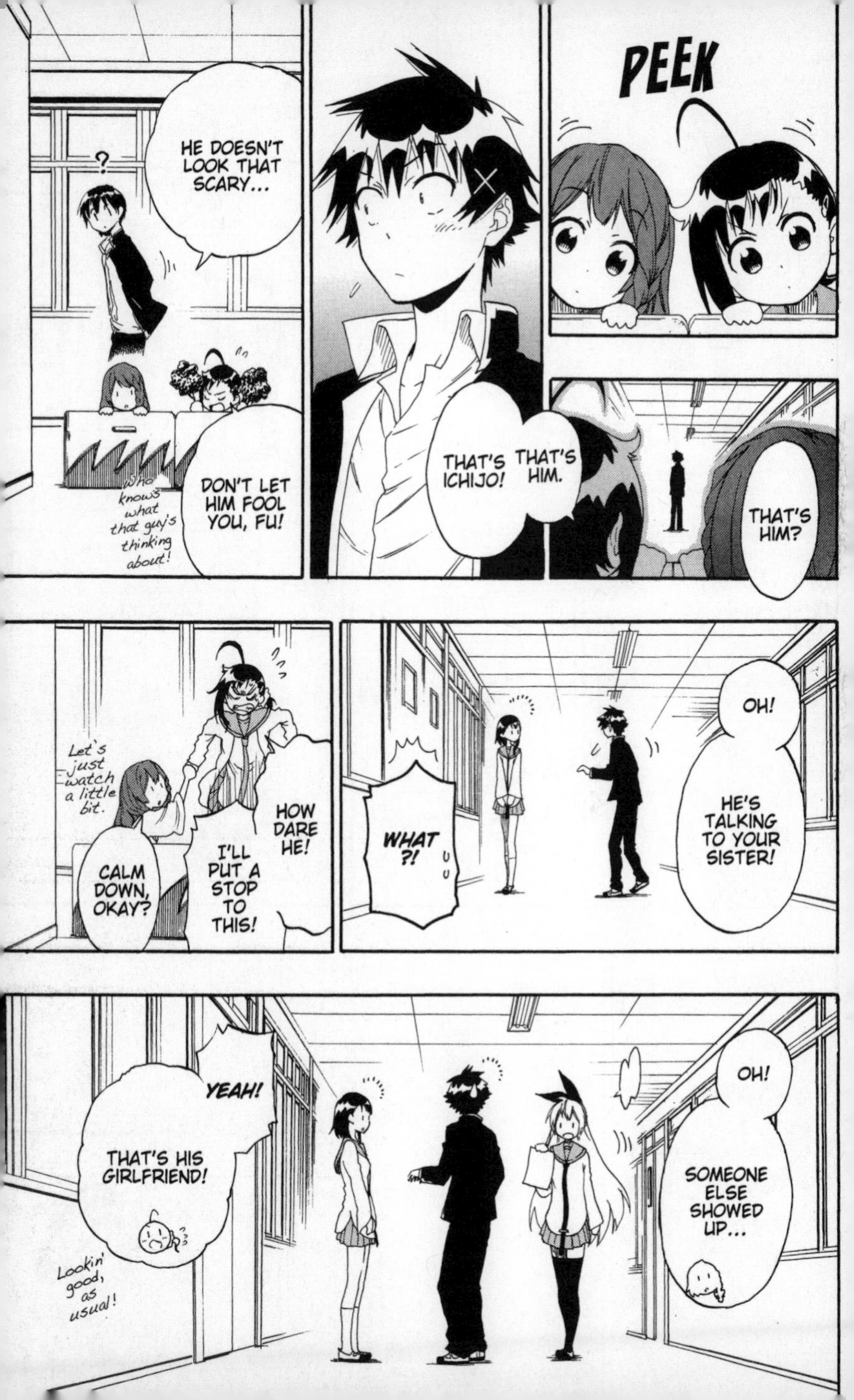
PEEK
THAT'S HIM?
THAT'S HIM.
THAT'S ICHIJO!
HE DOESN'T LOOK THAT SCARY...
DON'T LET HIM FOOL YOU, FU!
Who knows what that guy's thinking about!
OH!
HE'S TALKING TO YOUR SISTER!
WHAT?!
HOW DARE HE!
I'LL PUT A STOP TO THIS!
Let's just watch a little bit.
CALM DOWN, OKAY?
OH!
SOMEONE ELSE SHOWED UP...
YEAH!
THAT'S HIS GIRLFRIEND!
Lookin' good, as usual!

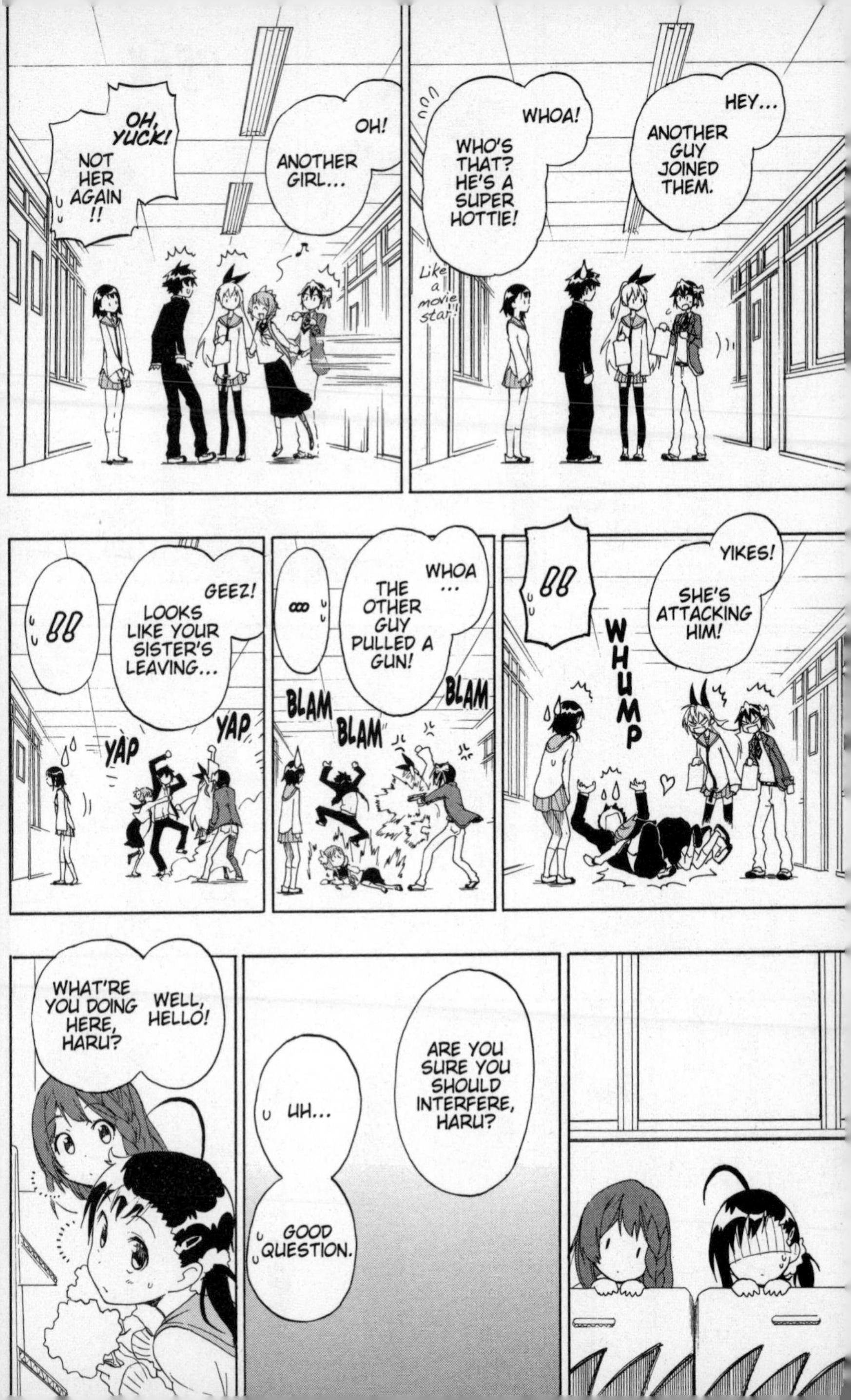
HEY...
ANOTHER GUY JOINED THEM.
WHOA!
WHO'S THAT? HE'S A SUPER HOTTIE!
Like a movie star!!
OH!
ANOTHER GIRL...
OH, YUCK!
NOT HER AGAIN!!
YIKES!
SHE'S ATTACKING HIM!
!!
WHUMP
WHOA...
THE OTHER GUY PULLED A GUN!
...
BLAM
BLAM
BLAM
GEEZ!
LOOKS LIKE YOUR SISTER'S LEAVING...
!!
YAP
YAP
ARE YOU SURE YOU SHOULD INTERFERE, HARU?
UH...
GOOD QUESTION.
WELL, HELLO!
WHAT'RE YOU DOING HERE, HARU?

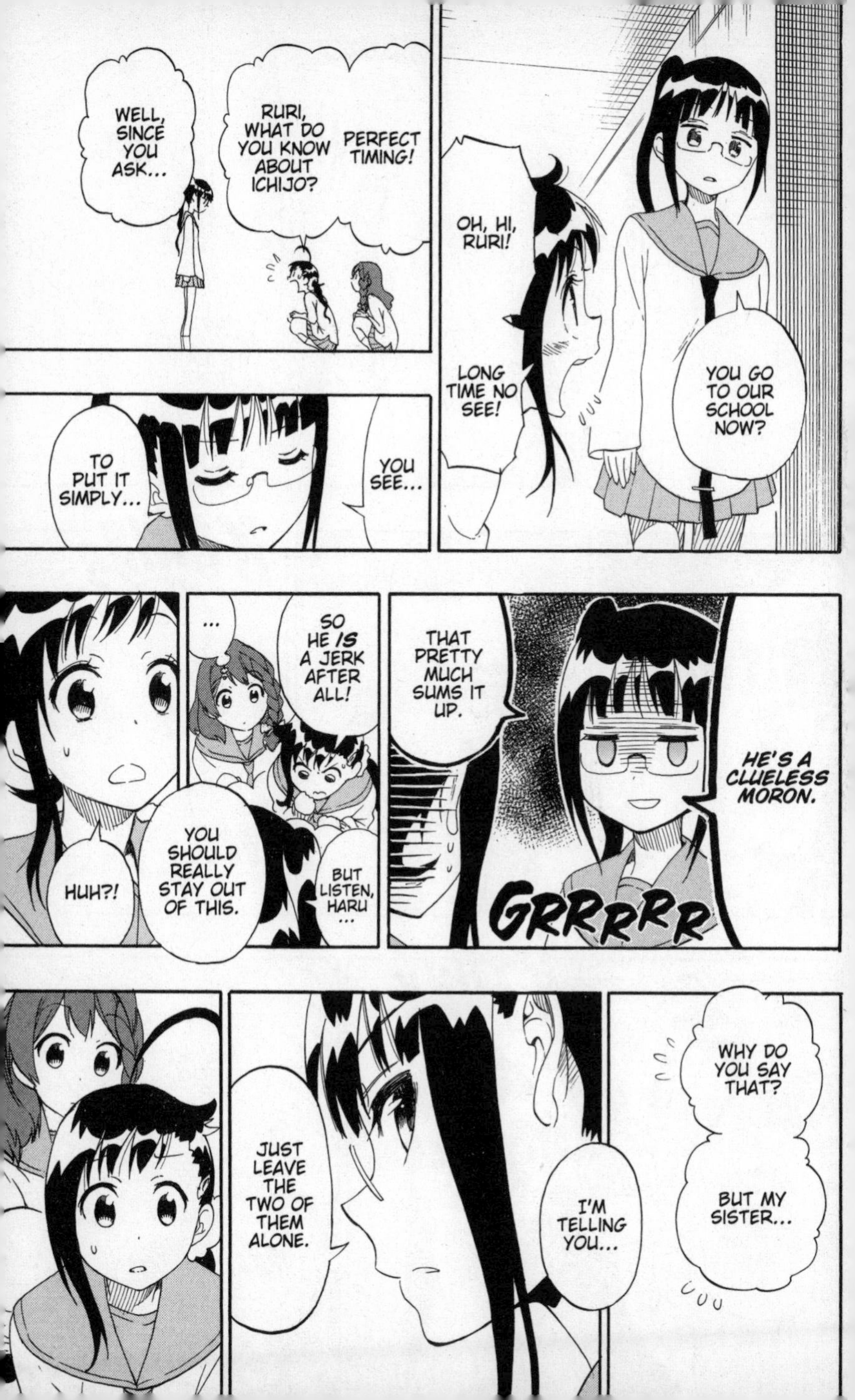
OH, HI, RURI!
LONG TIME NO SEE!
YOU GO TO OUR SCHOOL NOW?
PERFECT TIMING!
RURI, WHAT DO YOU KNOW ABOUT ICHIJO?
WELL, SINCE YOU ASK...
YOU SEE...
TO PUT IT SIMPLY...
HE'S A CLUELESS MORON.
GRRRRR
THAT PRETTY MUCH SUMS IT UP.
SO HE *IS* A JERK AFTER ALL!
...
BUT LISTEN, HARU...
YOU SHOULD REALLY STAY OUT OF THIS.
HUH?!
WHY DO YOU SAY THAT?
BUT MY SISTER...
I'M TELLING YOU...
JUST LEAVE THE TWO OF THEM ALONE.

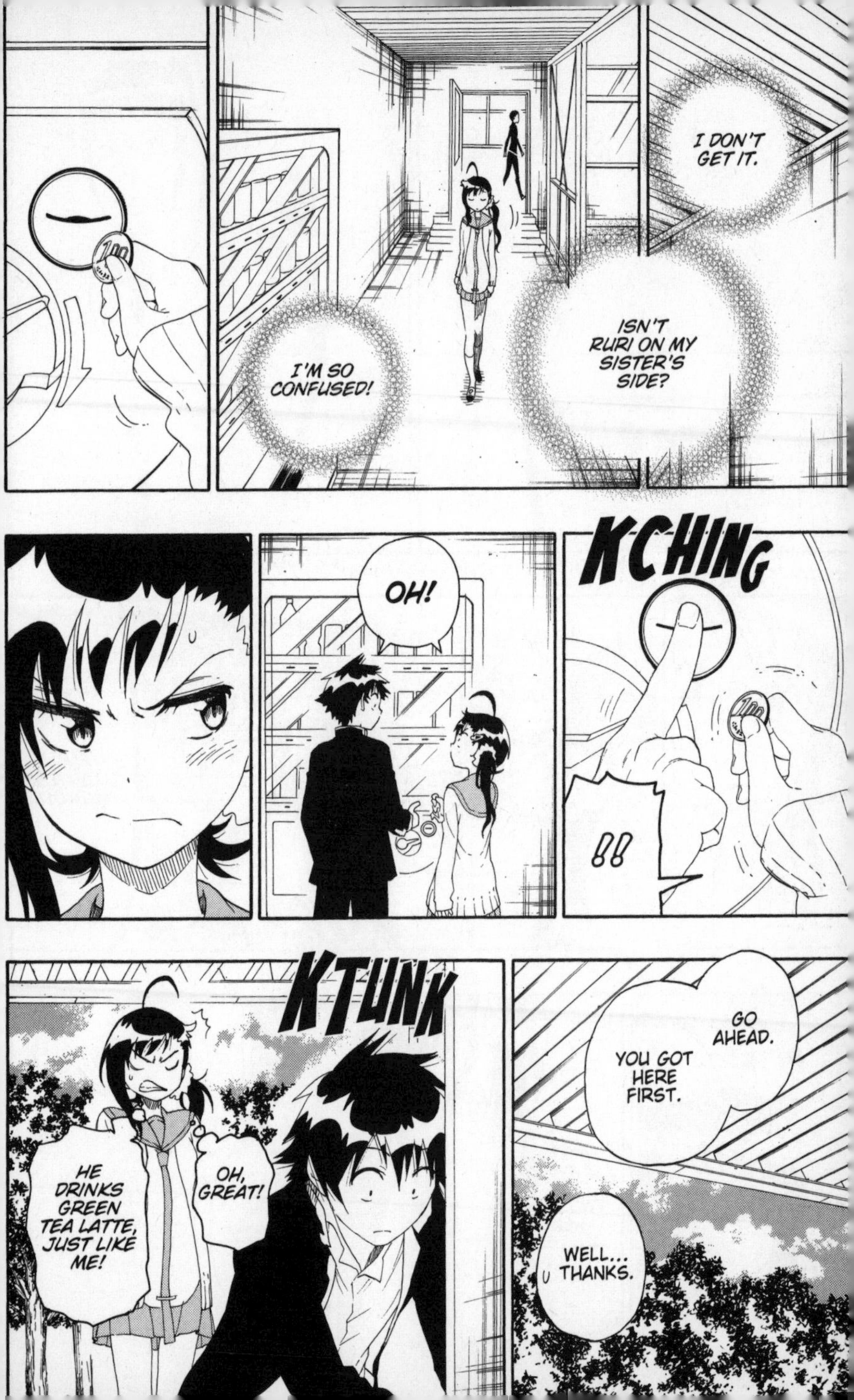
I DON'T GET IT.
ISN'T RURI ON MY SISTER'S SIDE?
I'M SO CONFUSED!
KCHING
!!
OH!
GO AHEAD.
YOU GOT HERE FIRST.
WELL... THANKS.
KTUNK
OH, GREAT!
HE DRINKS GREEN TEA LATTE, JUST LIKE ME!

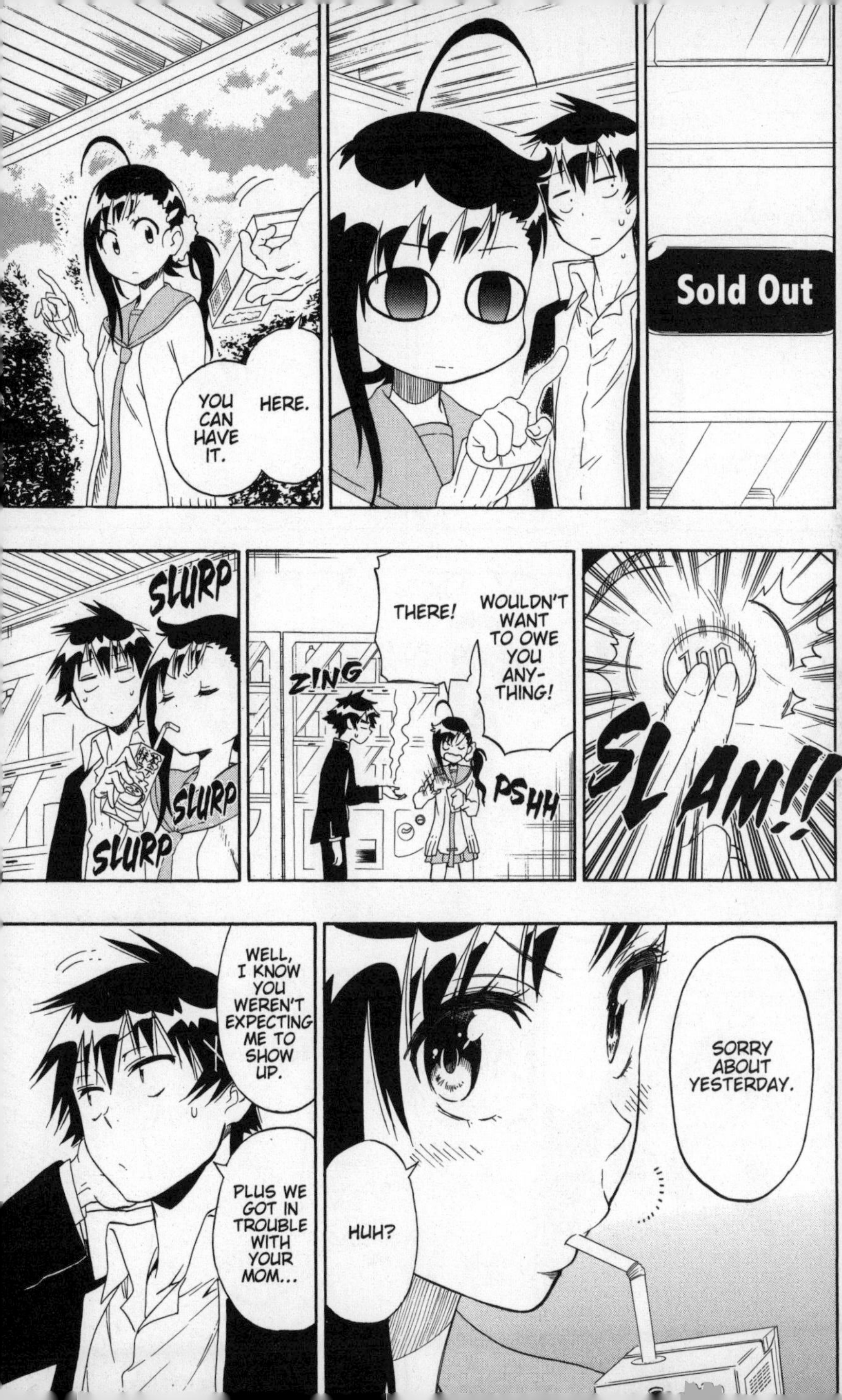
Sold Out
HERE.
YOU CAN HAVE IT.
SLAM!!
WOULDN'T WANT TO OWE YOU ANYTHING!
THERE!
ZING
PSHH
SLURP
SLURP
SLURP
SORRY ABOUT YESTERDAY.
HUH?
WELL, I KNOW YOU WEREN'T EXPECTING ME TO SHOW UP.
PLUS WE GOT IN TROUBLE WITH YOUR MOM...

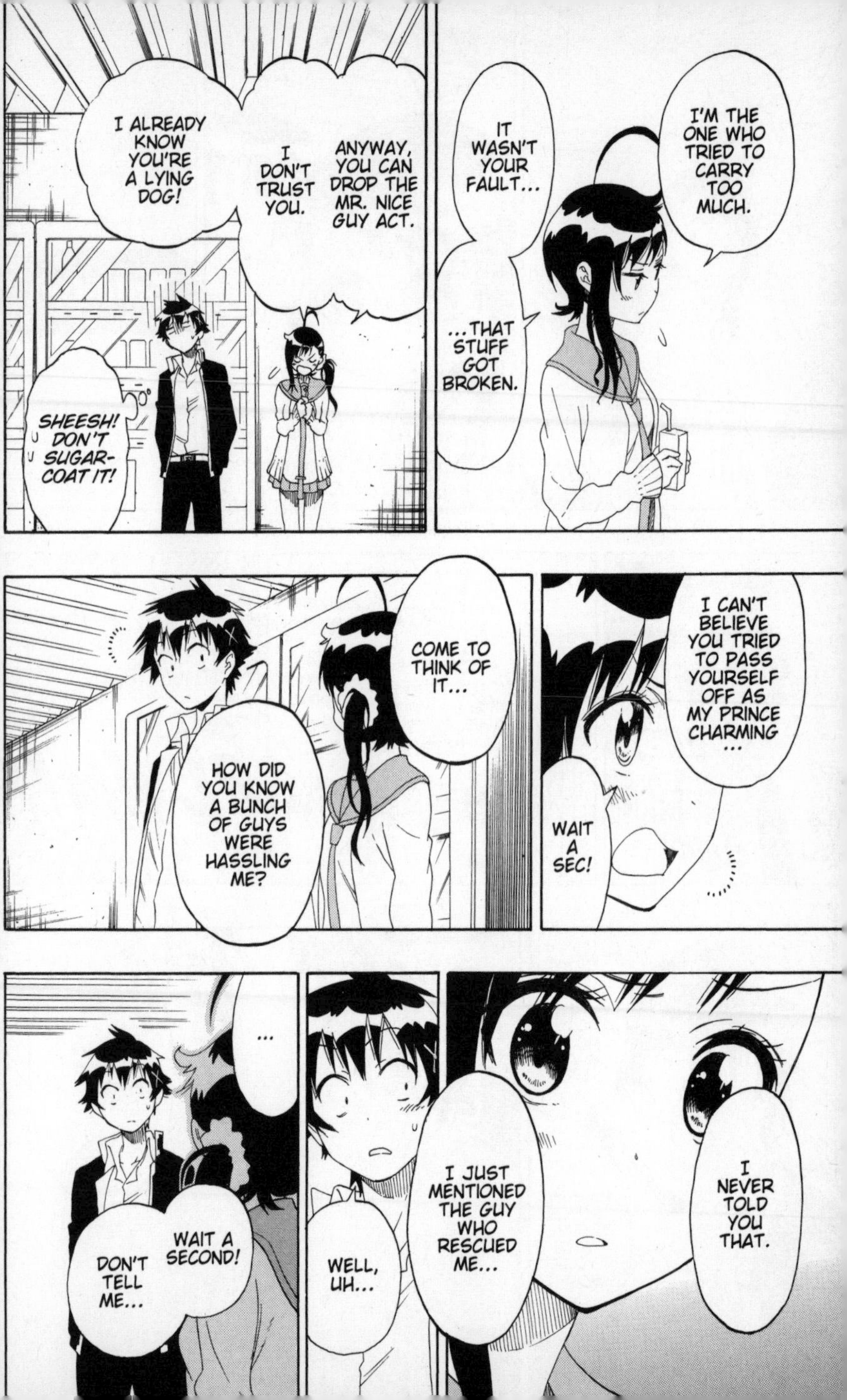
I'M THE ONE WHO TRIED TO CARRY TOO MUCH.
IT WASN'T YOUR FAULT...
...THAT STUFF GOT BROKEN.
ANYWAY, YOU CAN DROP THE MR. NICE GUY ACT.
I DON'T TRUST YOU.
I ALREADY KNOW YOU'RE A LYING DOG!
SHEESH! DON'T SUGAR-COAT IT!
I CAN'T BELIEVE YOU TRIED TO PASS YOURSELF OFF AS MY PRINCE CHARMING...
WAIT A SEC!
COME TO THINK OF IT...
HOW DID YOU KNOW A BUNCH OF GUYS WERE HASSLING ME?
I NEVER TOLD YOU THAT.
I JUST MENTIONED THE GUY WHO RESCUED ME...
WELL, UH...
...
WAIT A SECOND!
DON'T TELL ME...

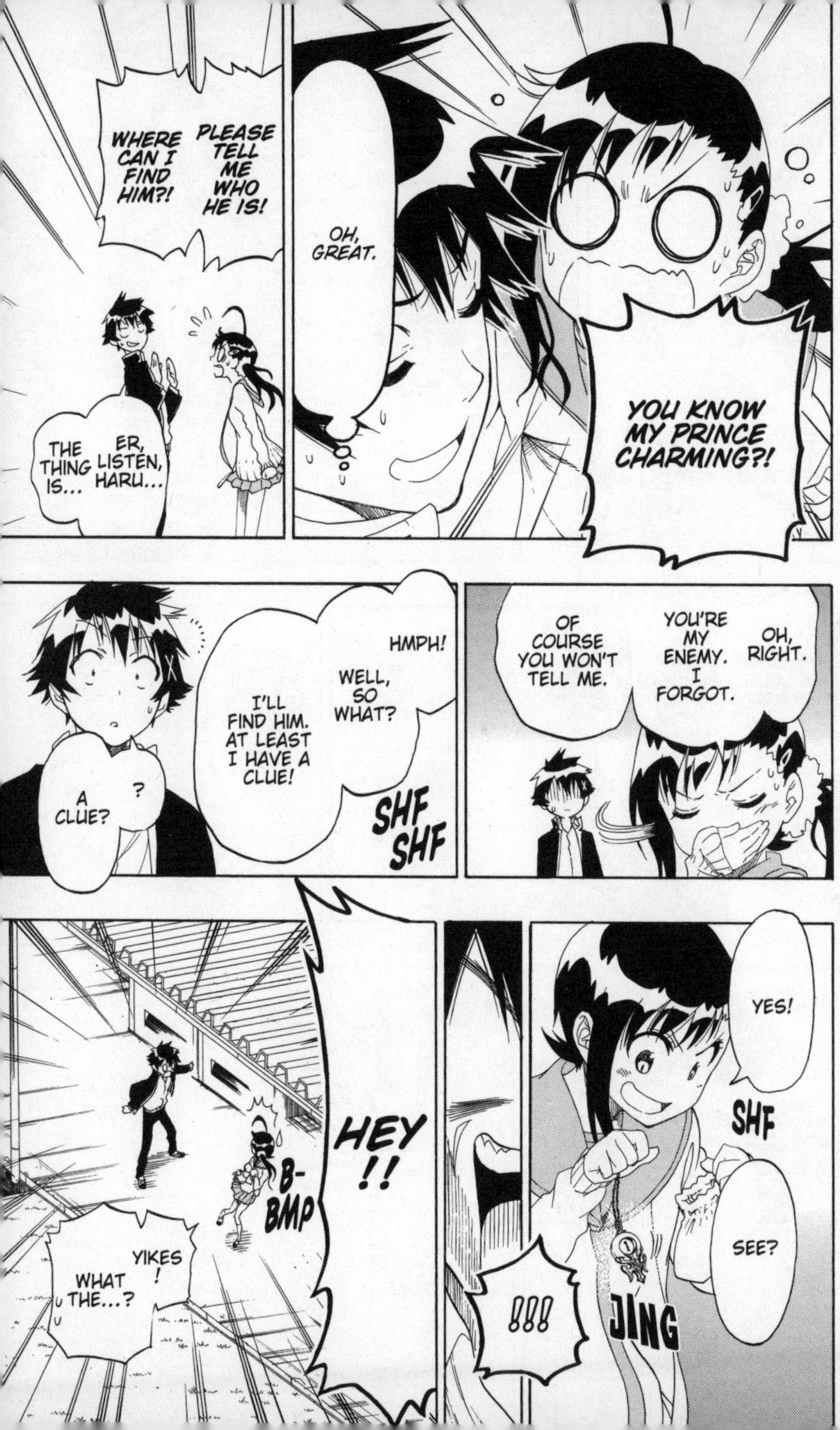
YOU KNOW MY PRINCE CHARMING?!
OH, GREAT.
PLEASE TELL ME WHO HE IS!
WHERE CAN I FIND HIM?!
ER, LISTEN, HARU...
THE THING IS...
OH, RIGHT.
YOU'RE MY ENEMY. I FORGOT.
OF COURSE YOU WON'T TELL ME.
HMPH!
WELL, SO WHAT?
I'LL FIND HIM. AT LEAST I HAVE A CLUE!
SHF SHF
?
A CLUE?
YES!
SHF
SEE?
JING
!!!
HEY!!
B-BMP
YIKES!
WHAT THE...?

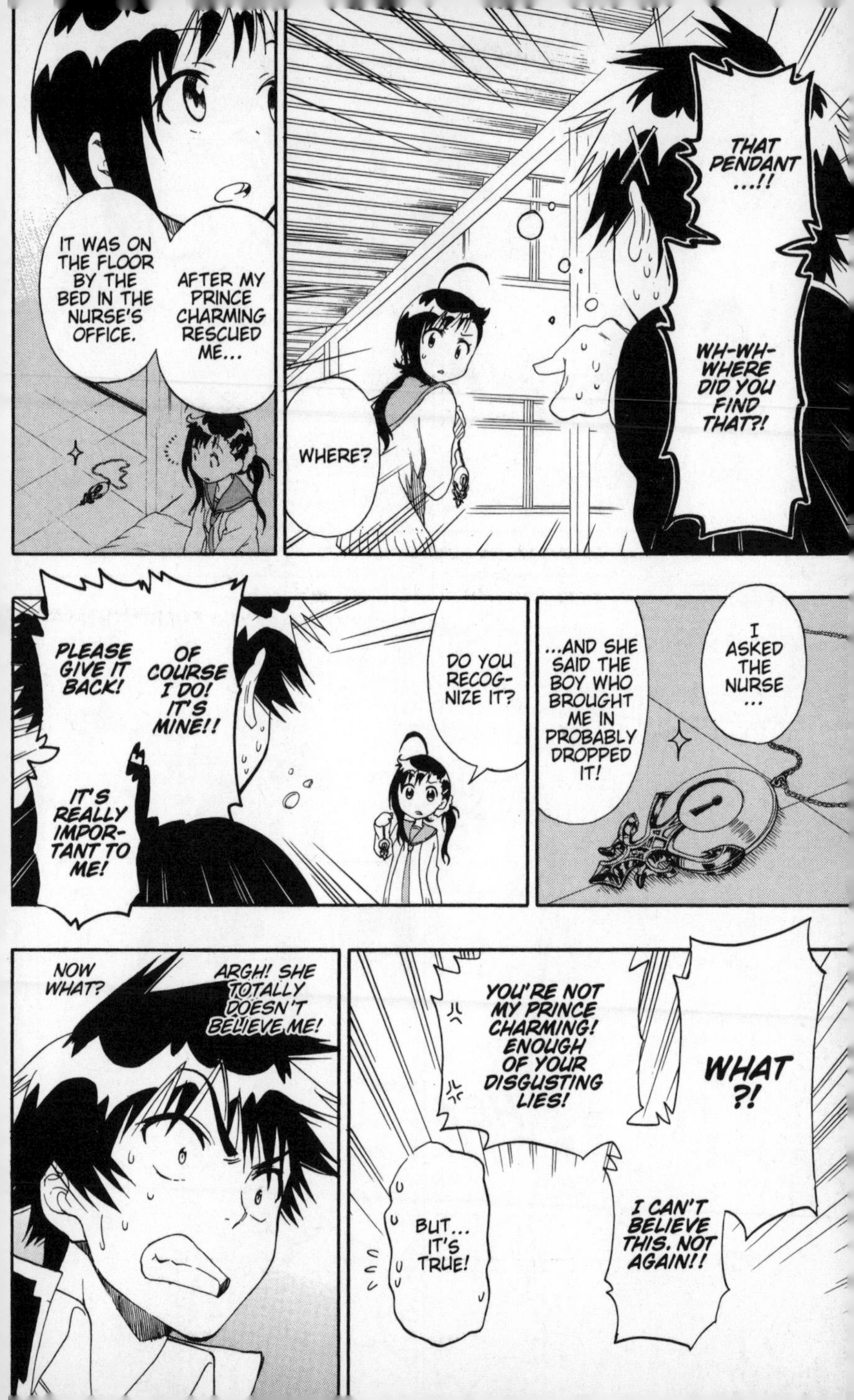
THAT PENDANT...!!
WH-WH-WHERE DID YOU FIND THAT?!
WHERE?
AFTER MY PRINCE CHARMING RESCUED ME...
IT WAS ON THE FLOOR BY THE BED IN THE NURSE'S OFFICE.
I ASKED THE NURSE...
...AND SHE SAID THE BOY WHO BROUGHT ME IN PROBABLY DROPPED IT!
DO YOU RECOGNIZE IT?
OF COURSE I DO! IT'S MINE!!
PLEASE GIVE IT BACK!
IT'S REALLY IMPORTANT TO ME!
WHAT?!
YOU'RE NOT MY PRINCE CHARMING! ENOUGH OF YOUR DISGUSTING LIES!
I CAN'T BELIEVE THIS. NOT AGAIN!!
BUT... IT'S TRUE!
ARGH! SHE TOTALLY DOESN'T BELIEVE ME!
NOW WHAT?

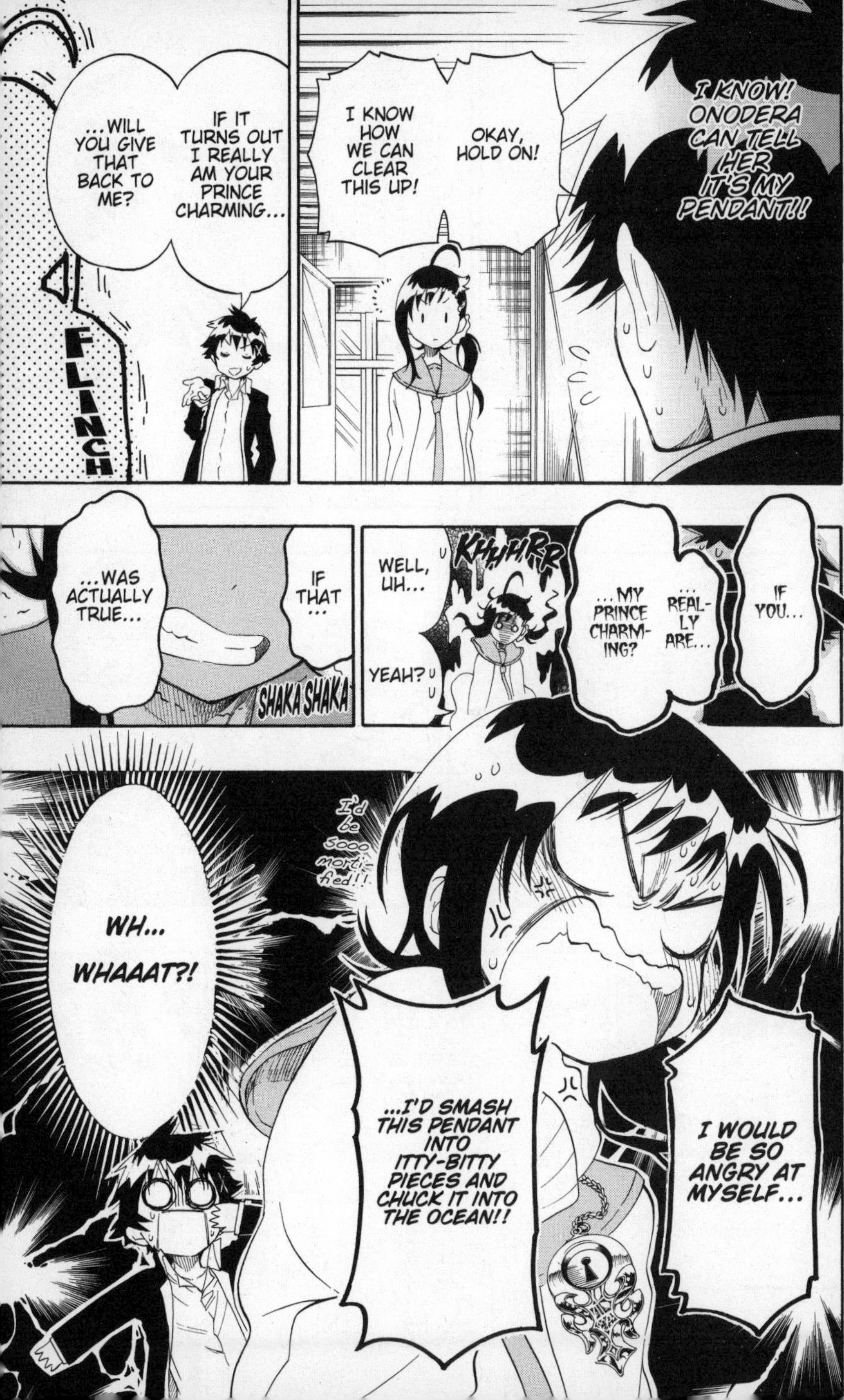

I KNOW! ONODERA CAN TELL HER IT'S MY PENDANT!!
OKAY, HOLD ON!
I KNOW HOW WE CAN CLEAR THIS UP!
IF IT TURNS OUT I REALLY AM YOUR PRINCE CHARMING...
...WILL YOU GIVE THAT BACK TO ME?
FLINCH
IF YOU...
...REALLY ARE...
...MY PRINCE CHARMING?
KHUHRR
WELL, UH...
YEAH?
IF THAT...
...WAS ACTUALLY TRUE...
SHAKA SHAKA
I WOULD BE SO ANGRY AT MYSELF...
...I'D SMASH THIS PENDANT INTO ITTY-BITTY PIECES AND CHUCK IT INTO THE OCEAN!!
I'd be sooo mortified!!
WH... WHAAAT?!

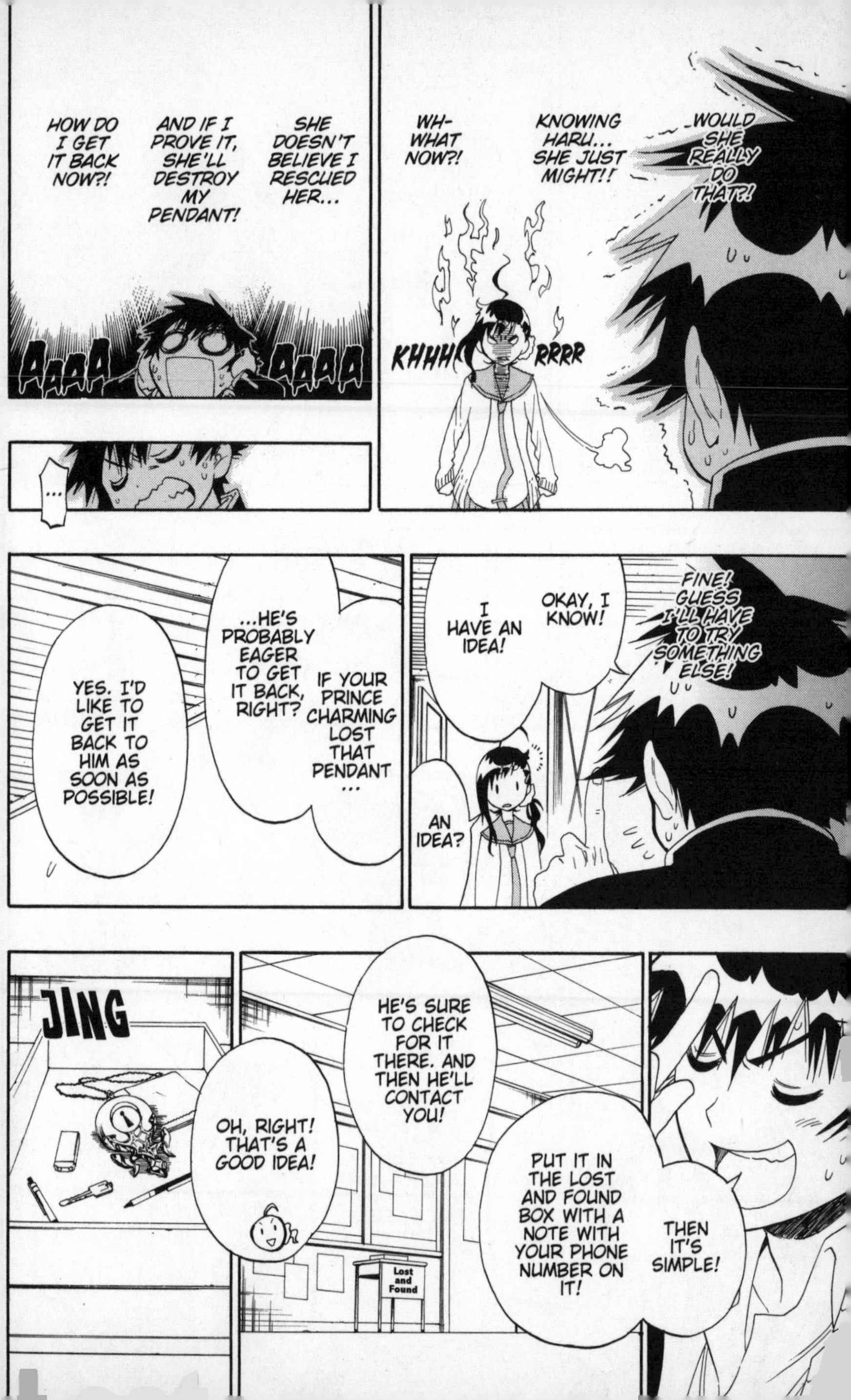
WOULD SHE REALLY DO THAT?!
KNOWING HARU... SHE JUST MIGHT!!
WH- WHAT NOW?!
KHHH RRRR
SHE DOESN'T BELIEVE I RESCUED HER...
AND IF I PROVE IT, SHE'LL DESTROY MY PENDANT!
HOW DO I GET IT BACK NOW?!
AAAA AAAA
...
FINE! GUESS I'LL HAVE TO TRY SOMETHING ELSE!
OKAY, I KNOW!
I HAVE AN IDEA!
AN IDEA?
IF YOUR PRINCE CHARMING LOST THAT PENDANT...
...HE'S PROBABLY EAGER TO GET IT BACK, RIGHT?
YES. I'D LIKE TO GET IT BACK TO HIM AS SOON AS POSSIBLE!
THEN IT'S SIMPLE!
PUT IT IN THE LOST AND FOUND BOX WITH A NOTE WITH YOUR PHONE NUMBER ON IT!
HE'S SURE TO CHECK FOR IT THERE. AND THEN HE'LL CONTACT YOU!
OH, RIGHT! THAT'S A GOOD IDEA!
Lost and Found
JING

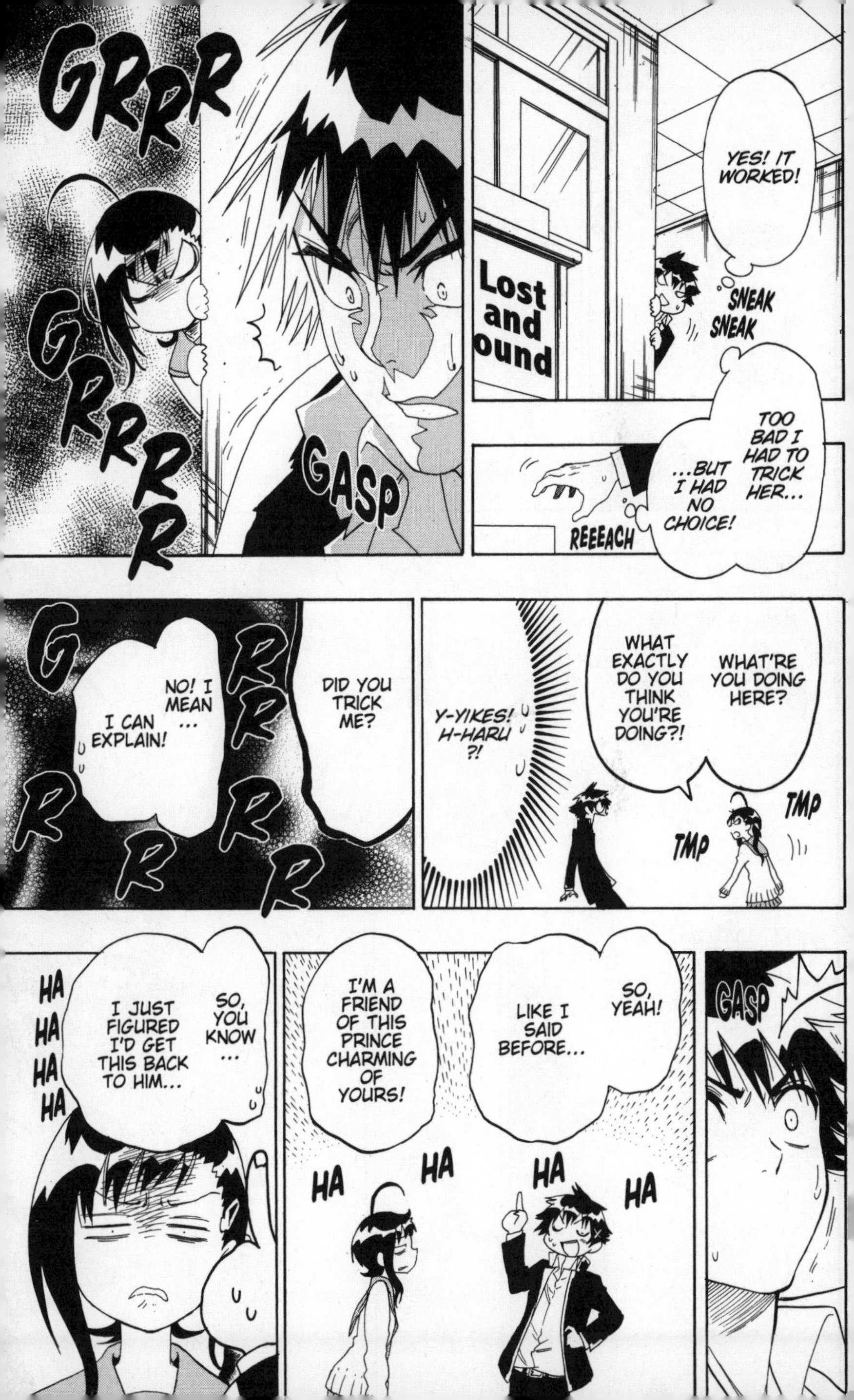
YES! IT WORKED!
SNEAK SNEAK
Lost
and
ound
TOO BAD I HAD TO TRICK HER...
...BUT I HAD NO CHOICE!
REEEACH
GASP
GRRR
GRRRRR
WHAT'RE YOU DOING HERE?
WHAT EXACTLY DO YOU THINK YOU'RE DOING?!
Y-YIKES! H-HARU?!
TMP
TMP
DID YOU TRICK ME?
NO! I MEAN...
I CAN EXPLAIN!
GRRRRRRRR
GASP
SO, YEAH!
LIKE I SAID BEFORE...
I'M A FRIEND OF THIS PRINCE CHARMING OF YOURS!
HA
HA
HA
HA
SO, YOU KNOW...
I JUST FIGURED I'D GET THIS BACK TO HIM...
HA HA HA HA

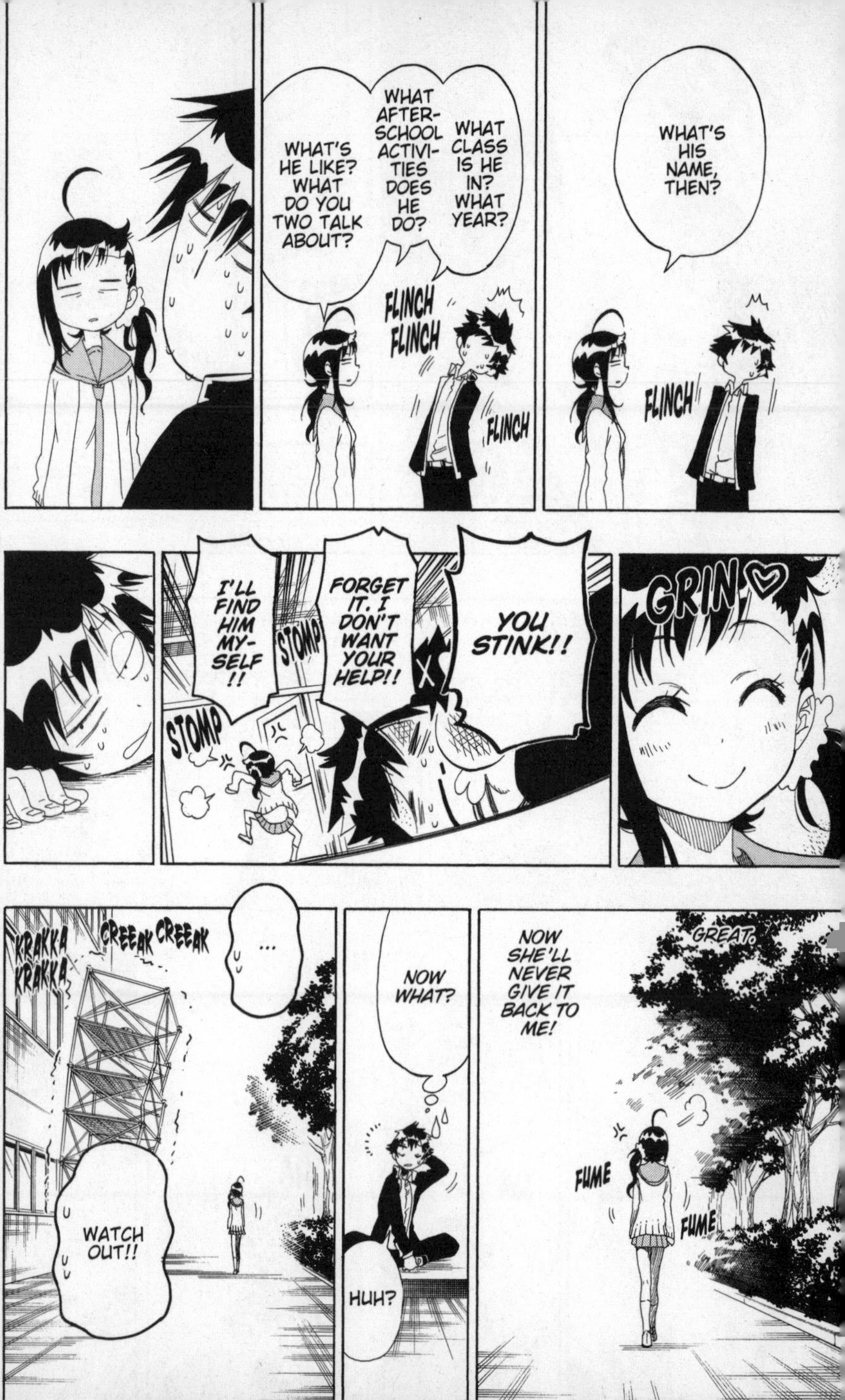
WHAT'S HIS NAME, THEN?
FLINCH
WHAT CLASS IS HE IN? WHAT YEAR?
WHAT AFTER-SCHOOL ACTIVITIES DOES HE DO?
WHAT'S HE LIKE? WHAT DO YOU TWO TALK ABOUT?
FLINCH FLINCH
FLINCH
GRIN♡
YOU STINK!!
FORGET IT. I DON'T WANT YOUR HELP!!
I'LL FIND HIM MYSELF!!
STOMP
STOMP
GREAT.
NOW SHE'LL NEVER GIVE IT BACK TO ME!
FUME
FUME
NOW WHAT?
HUH?
...
CREEAK CREEAK
KRAKKA KRAKKA
WATCH OUT!!

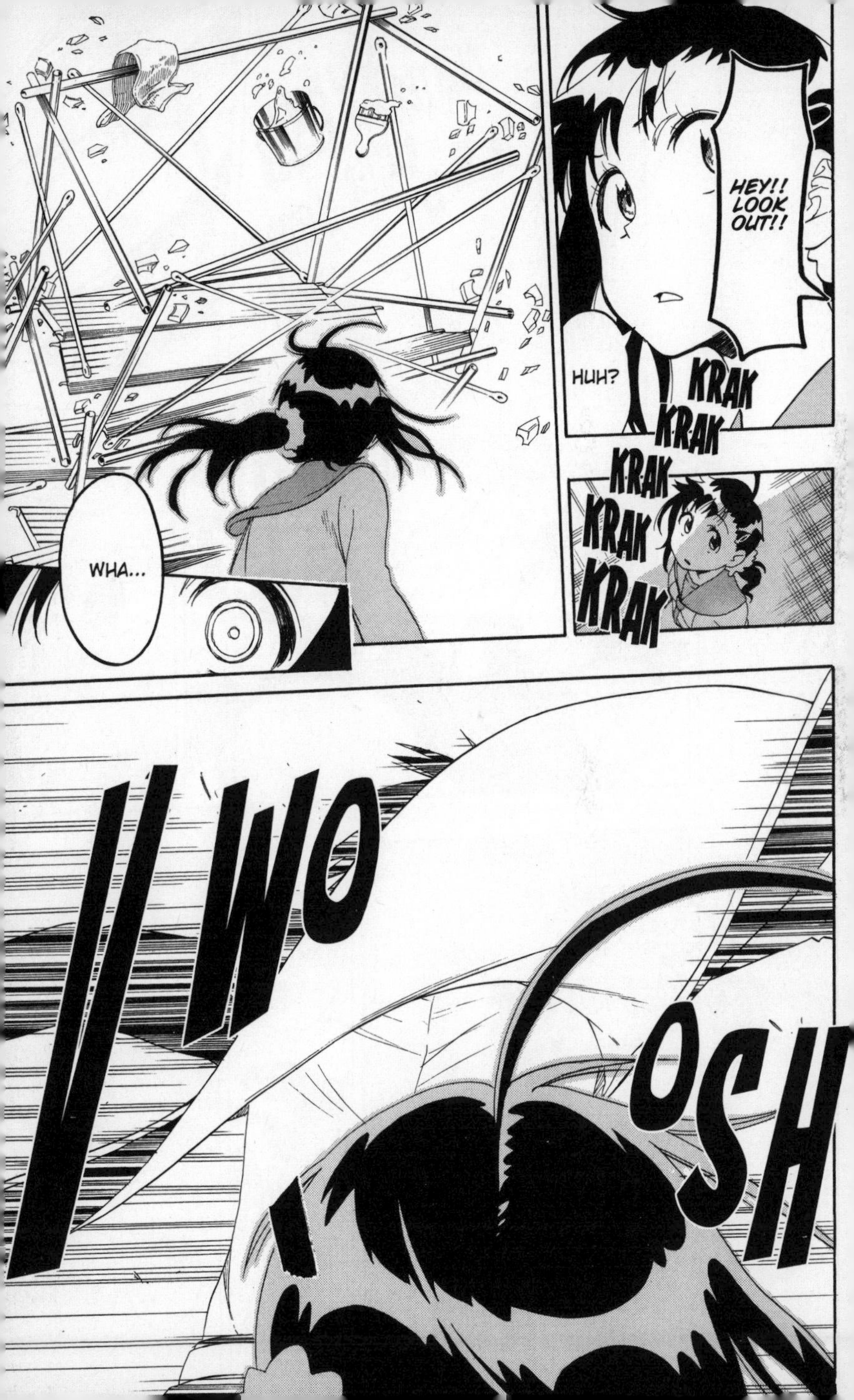
HEY!! LOOK OUT!!
HUH?
KRAK
KRAK
KRAK
KRAK
KRAK
WHA...
WOOSH

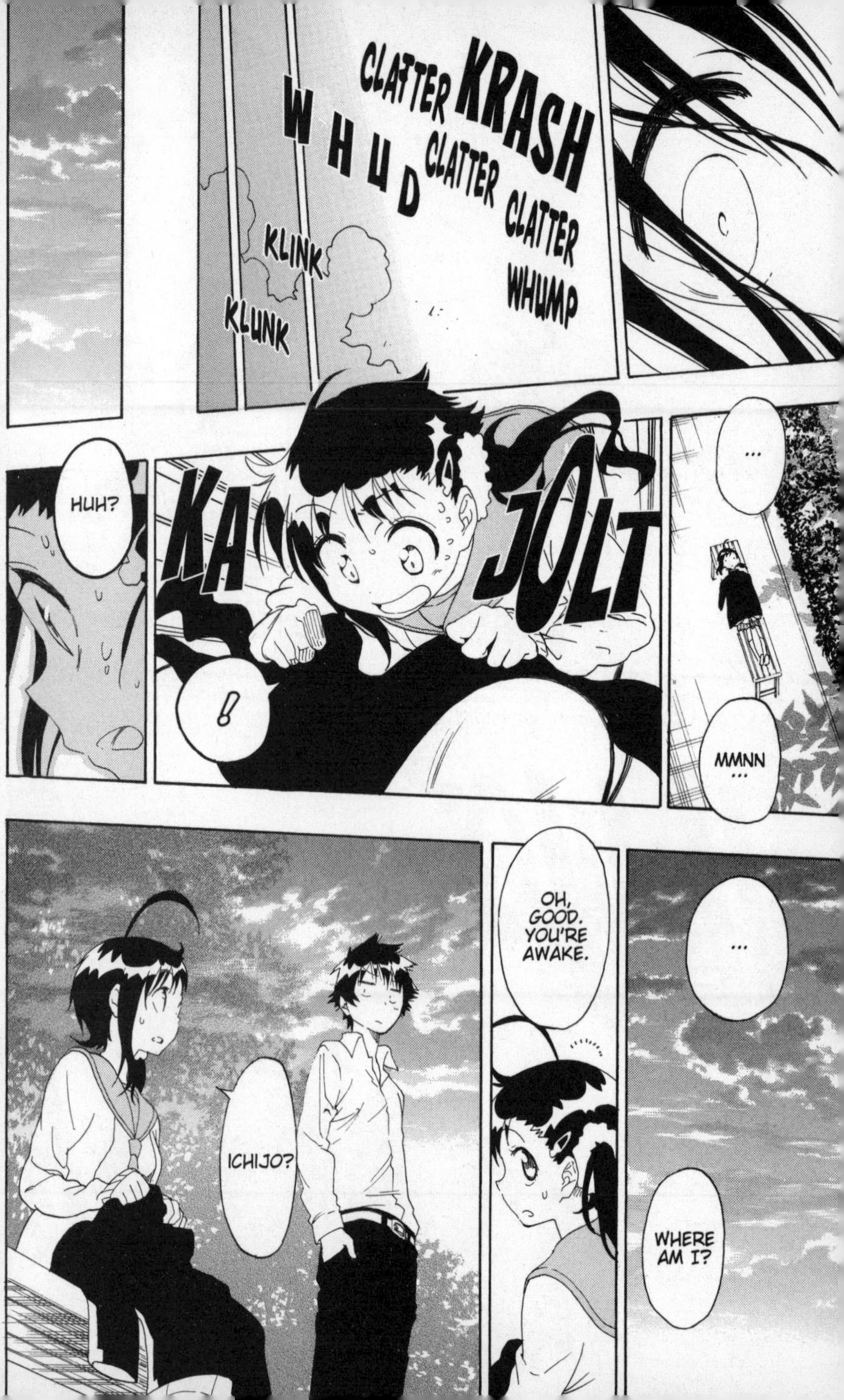
KRASH
CLATTER
CLATTER
CLATTER
WHUMP
W H U D
KLINK
KLUNK
...
MMNN ...
KA
JOLT
!
HUH?
...
WHERE AM I?
OH, GOOD. YOU'RE AWAKE.
ICHIJO?

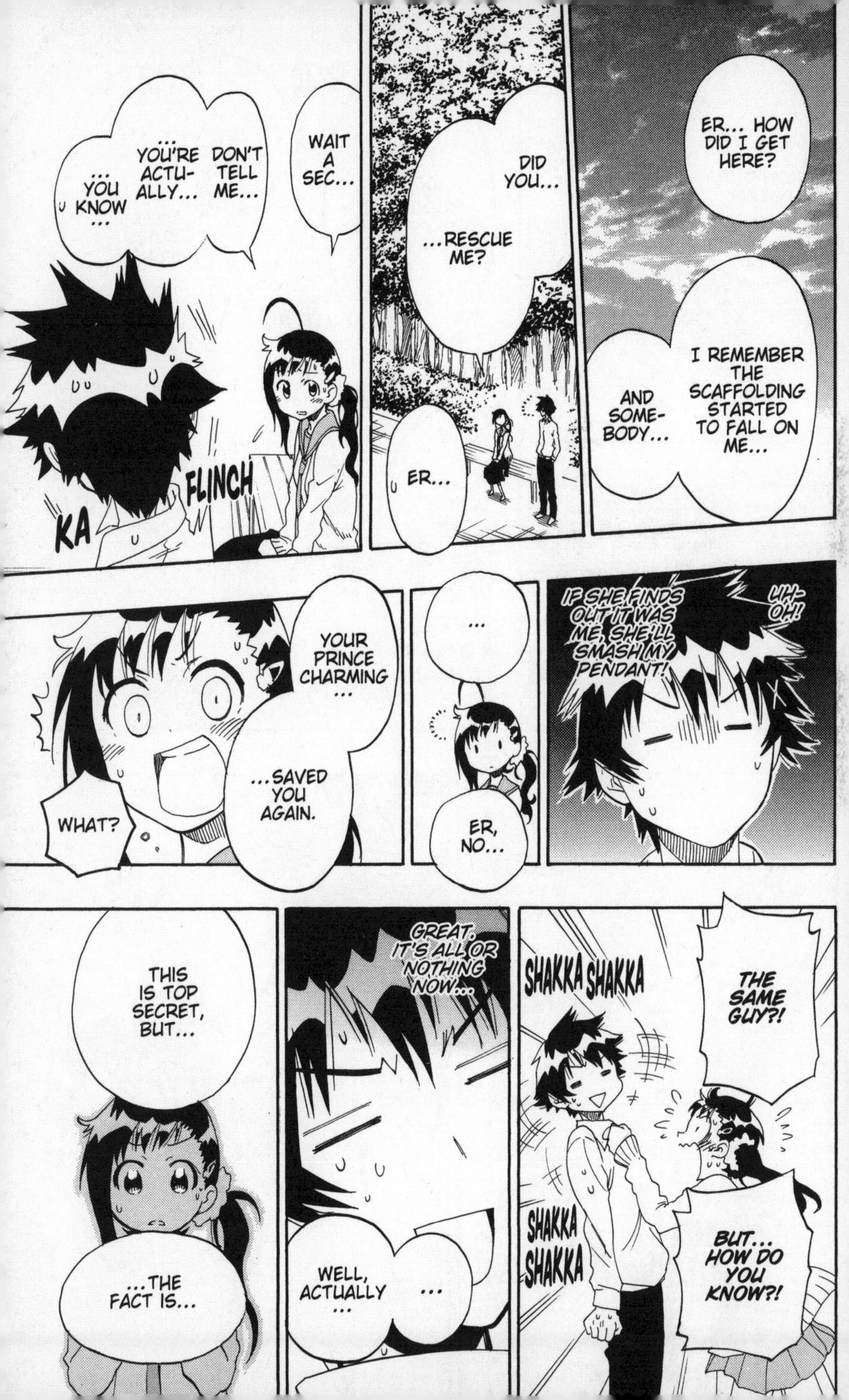
ER... HOW DID I GET HERE?
I REMEMBER THE SCAFFOLDING STARTED TO FALL ON ME...
AND SOMEBODY...
DID YOU...
...RESCUE ME?
ER...
WAIT A SEC...
... DON'T TELL ME... YOU'RE ACTUALLY... ... YOU KNOW ...
FLINCH
KA
UH-OH!
IF SHE FINDS OUT IT WAS ME, SHE'LL SMASH MY PENDANT!
...
ER, NO...
YOUR PRINCE CHARMING ...
...SAVED YOU AGAIN.
WHAT?
THE SAME GUY?!
SHAKKA SHAKKA
SHAKKA SHAKKA
BUT... HOW DO YOU KNOW?!
GREAT. IT'S ALL OR NOTHING NOW...
...
WELL, ACTUALLY ...
THIS IS TOP SECRET, BUT...
...THE FACT IS...

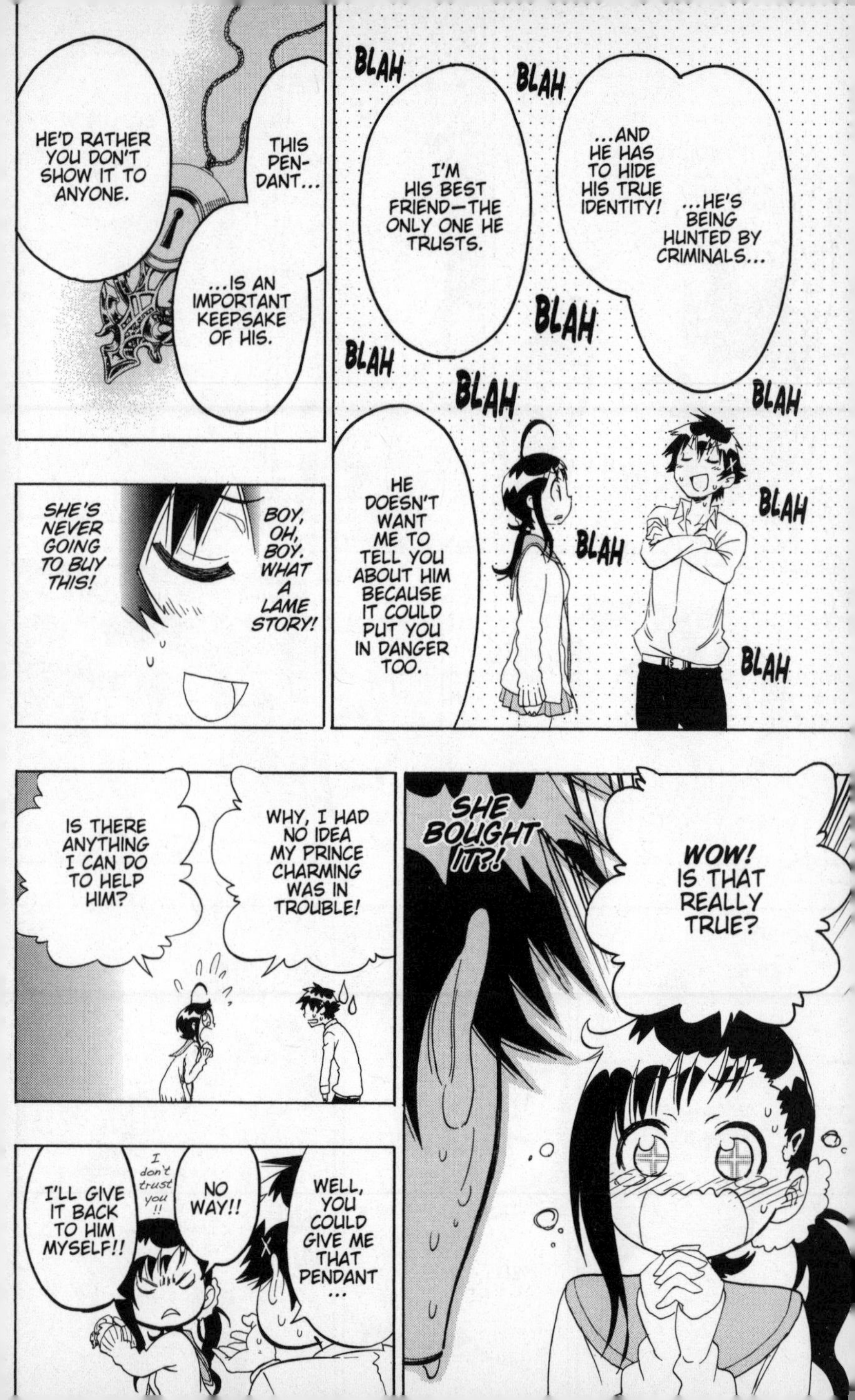
BLAH
BLAH
...HE'S BEING HUNTED BY CRIMINALS...
...AND HE HAS TO HIDE HIS TRUE IDENTITY!
I'M HIS BEST FRIEND—THE ONLY ONE HE TRUSTS.
BLAH
BLAH
BLAH
BLAH
HE DOESN'T WANT ME TO TELL YOU ABOUT HIM BECAUSE IT COULD PUT YOU IN DANGER TOO.
BLAH
BLAH
BLAH
BLAH
THIS PENDANT...
...IS AN IMPORTANT KEEPSAKE OF HIS.
HE'D RATHER YOU DON'T SHOW IT TO ANYONE.
BOY, OH, BOY. WHAT A LAME STORY!
SHE'S NEVER GOING TO BUY THIS!
WOW! IS THAT REALLY TRUE?
SHE BOUGHT IT?!
WHY, I HAD NO IDEA MY PRINCE CHARMING WAS IN TROUBLE!
IS THERE ANYTHING I CAN DO TO HELP HIM?
WELL, YOU COULD GIVE ME THAT PENDANT...
NO WAY!!
I don't trust you!!
I'LL GIVE IT BACK TO HIM MYSELF!!

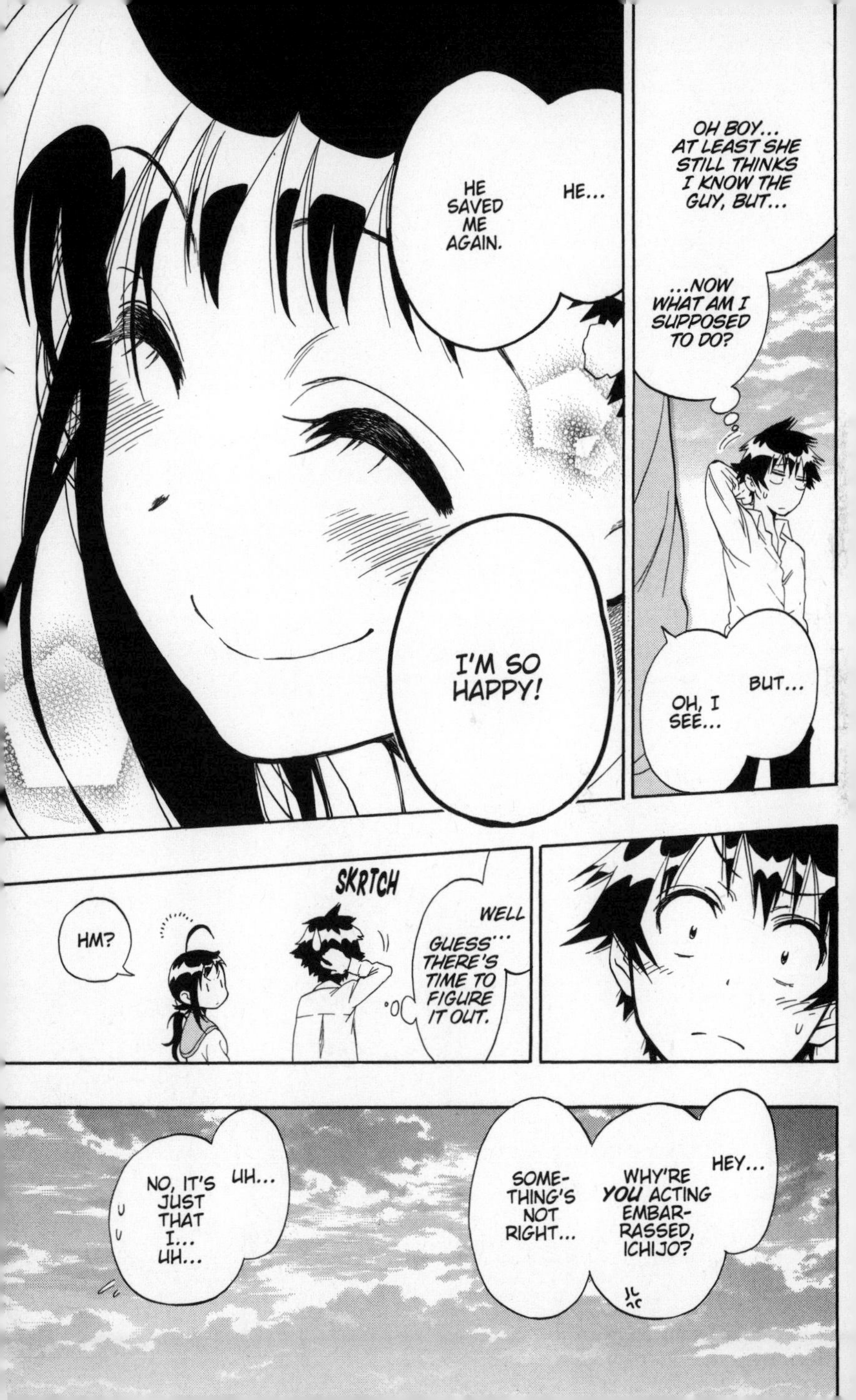
OH BOY... AT LEAST SHE STILL THINKS I KNOW THE GUY, BUT...
...NOW WHAT AM I SUPPOSED TO DO?
BUT... OH, I SEE...
HE...
HE SAVED ME AGAIN.
I'M SO HAPPY!
WELL... GUESS THERE'S TIME TO FIGURE IT OUT.
SKRTCH
HM?
HEY... WHY'RE *YOU* ACTING EMBARRASSED, ICHIJO?
SOMETHING'S NOT RIGHT...
UH... NO, IT'S JUST THAT I... UH...

Your...

...undies?!

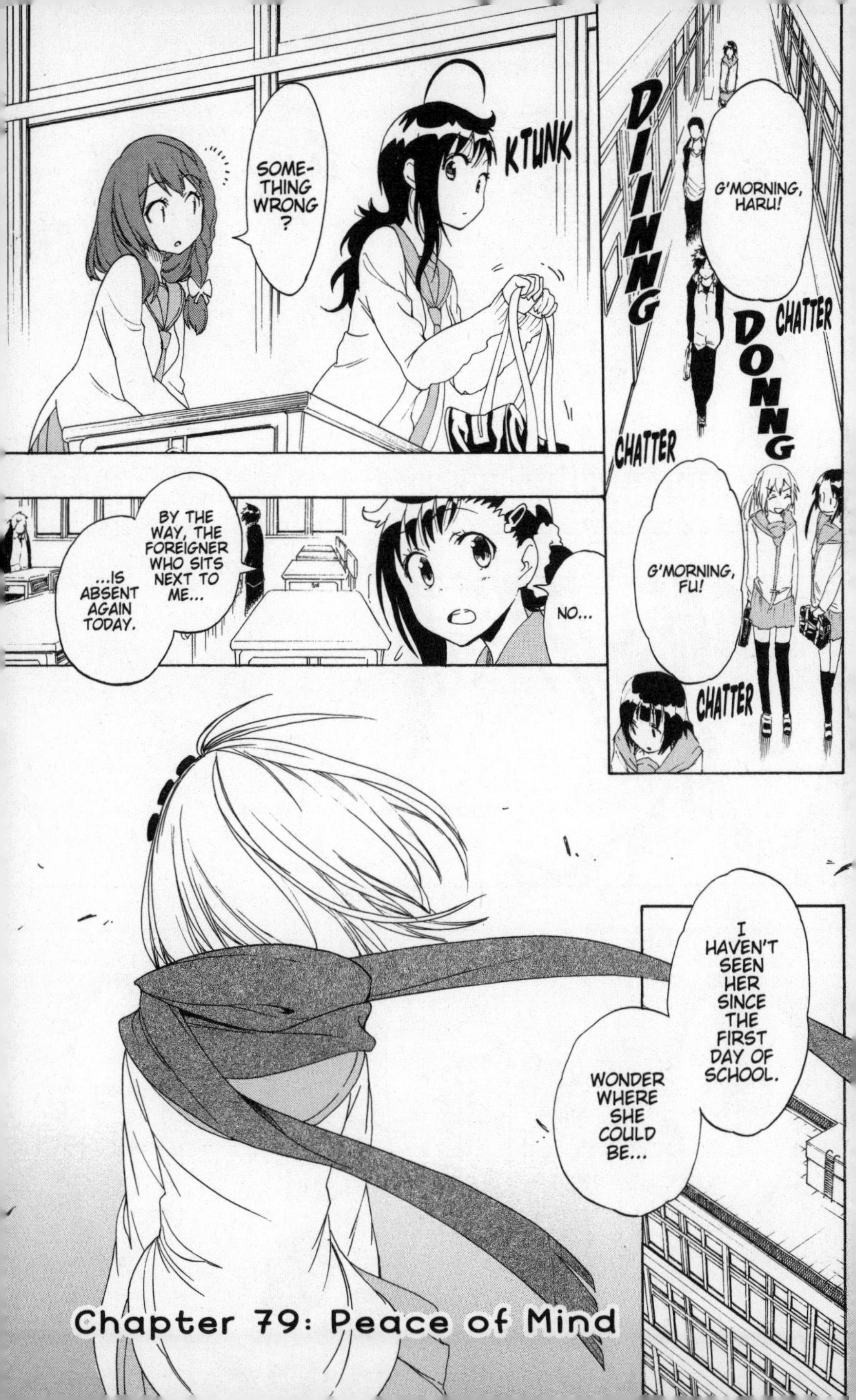
DIIING
G'MORNING, HARU!
CHATTER
DONNG
CHATTER
G'MORNING, FU!
CHATTER
KTUNK
SOME-THING WRONG?
NO...
BY THE WAY, THE FOREIGNER WHO SITS NEXT TO ME...
...IS ABSENT AGAIN TODAY.
I HAVEN'T SEEN HER SINCE THE FIRST DAY OF SCHOOL.
WONDER WHERE SHE COULD BE...
Chapter 79: Peace of Mind

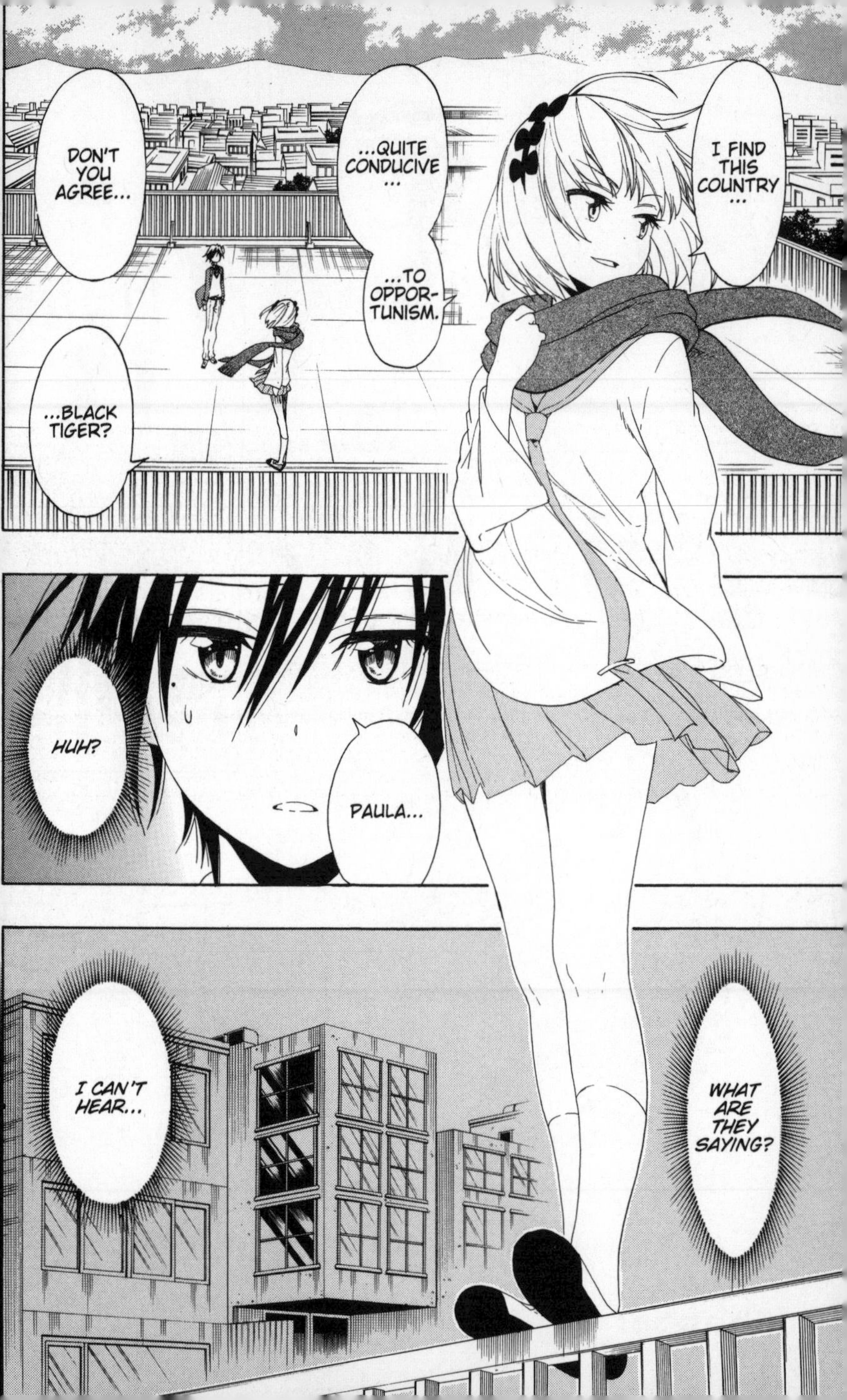
I FIND THIS COUNTRY...
...QUITE CONDUCIVE...
...TO OPPORTUNISM.
DON'T YOU AGREE...
...BLACK TIGER?
PAULA...
HUH?
WHAT ARE THEY SAYING?
I CAN'T HEAR...

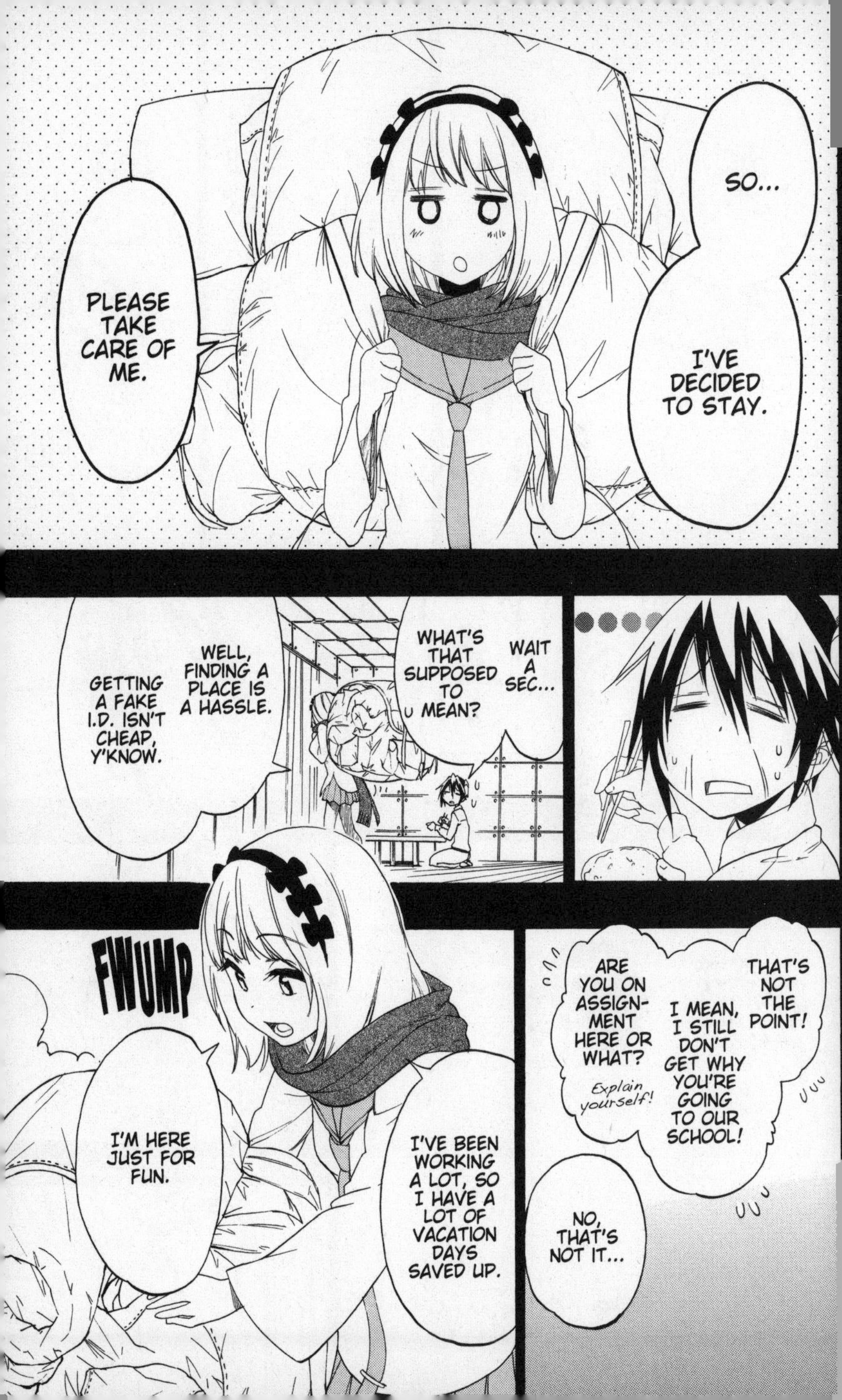
SO... I'VE DECIDED TO STAY.
PLEASE TAKE CARE OF ME.
WAIT A SEC...
WHAT'S THAT SUPPOSED TO MEAN?
WELL, FINDING A PLACE IS A HASSLE.
GETTING A FAKE I.D. ISN'T CHEAP, Y'KNOW.
THAT'S NOT THE POINT!
I MEAN, I STILL DON'T GET WHY YOU'RE GOING TO OUR SCHOOL!
ARE YOU ON ASSIGNMENT HERE OR WHAT?
Explain yourself!
NO, THAT'S NOT IT...
FWUMP
I'VE BEEN WORKING A LOT, SO I HAVE A LOT OF VACATION DAYS SAVED UP.
I'M HERE JUST FOR FUN.

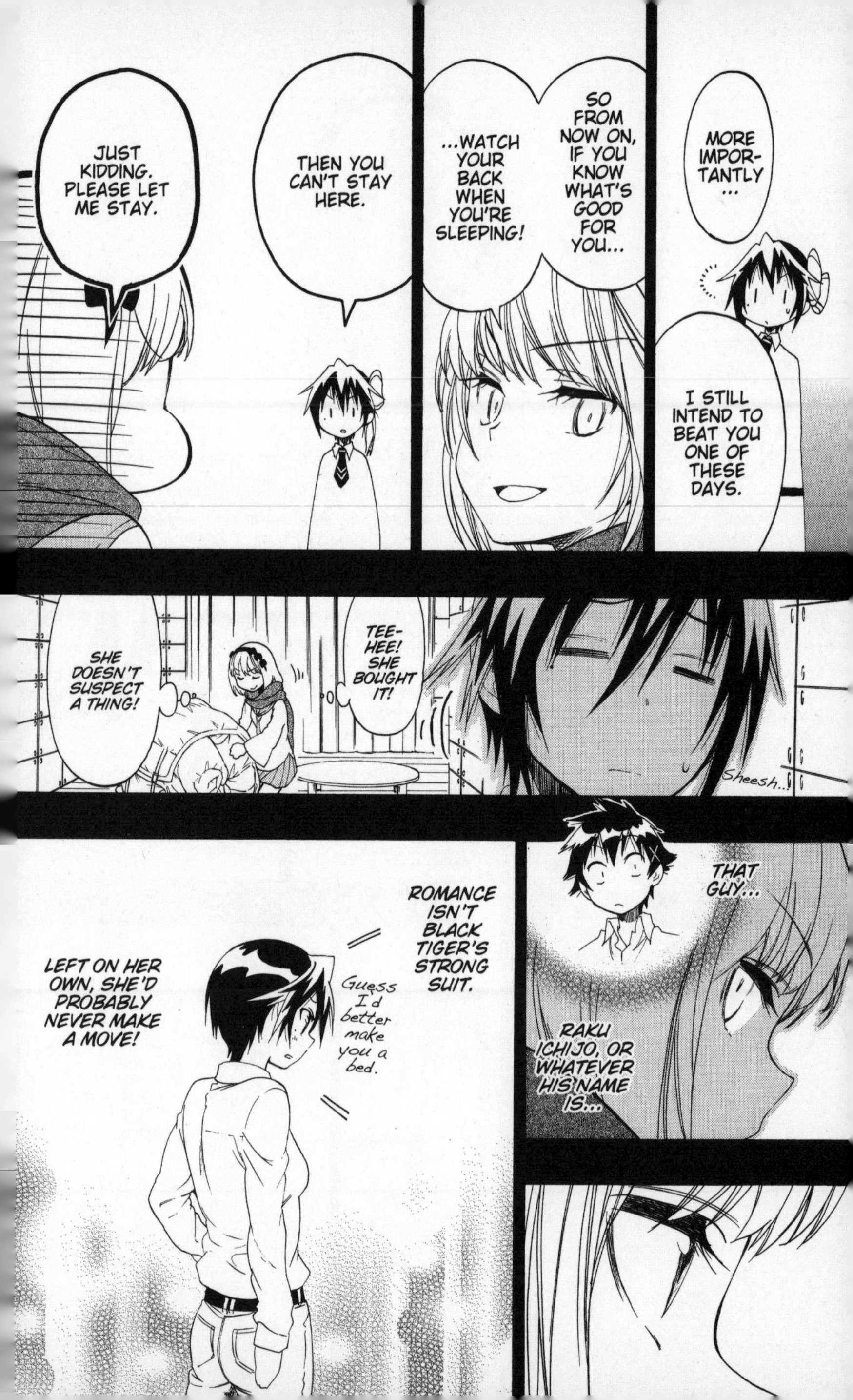
MORE IMPORTANTLY...
I STILL INTEND TO BEAT YOU ONE OF THESE DAYS.
SO FROM NOW ON, IF YOU KNOW WHAT'S GOOD FOR YOU...
...WATCH YOUR BACK WHEN YOU'RE SLEEPING!
THEN YOU CAN'T STAY HERE.
JUST KIDDING. PLEASE LET ME STAY.
Sheesh...
TEE-HEE! SHE BOUGHT IT!
SHE DOESN'T SUSPECT A THING!
THAT GUY...
RAKU ICHIJO, OR WHATEVER HIS NAME IS...
ROMANCE ISN'T BLACK TIGER'S STRONG SUIT.
Guess I'd better make you a bed.
LEFT ON HER OWN, SHE'D PROBABLY NEVER MAKE A MOVE!

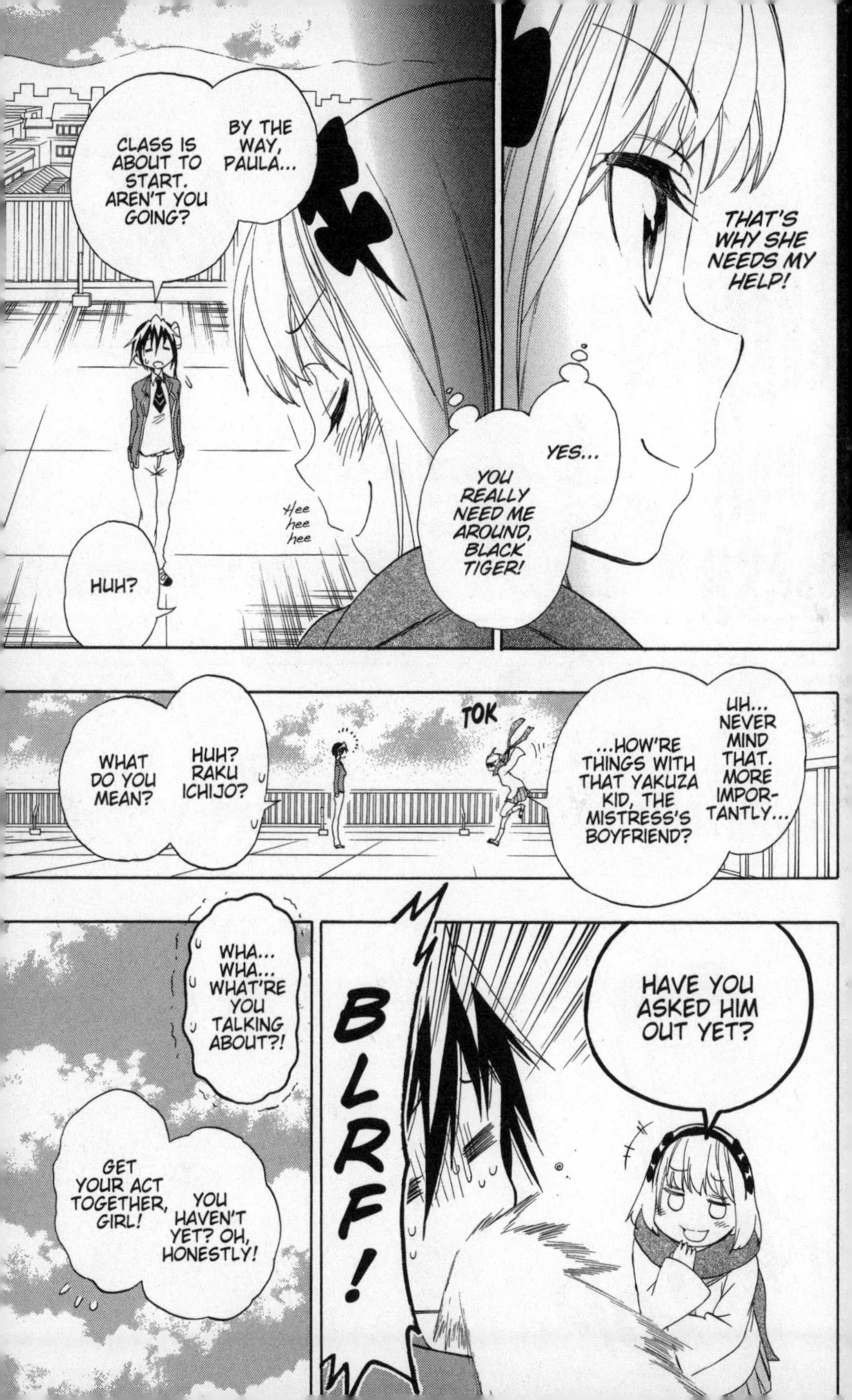
THAT'S WHY SHE NEEDS MY HELP!
YES...
YOU REALLY NEED ME AROUND, BLACK TIGER!
BY THE WAY, PAULA...
CLASS IS ABOUT TO START. AREN'T YOU GOING?
Hee hee hee
HUH?
UH... NEVER MIND THAT. MORE IMPOR-TANTLY...
...HOW'RE THINGS WITH THAT YAKUZA KID, THE MISTRESS'S BOYFRIEND?
TOK
HUH? RAKU ICHIJO?
WHAT DO YOU MEAN?
HAVE YOU ASKED HIM OUT YET?
BLRF!
WHA... WHA... WHAT'RE YOU TALKING ABOUT?!
YOU HAVEN'T YET? OH, HONESTLY!
GET YOUR ACT TOGETHER, GIRL!

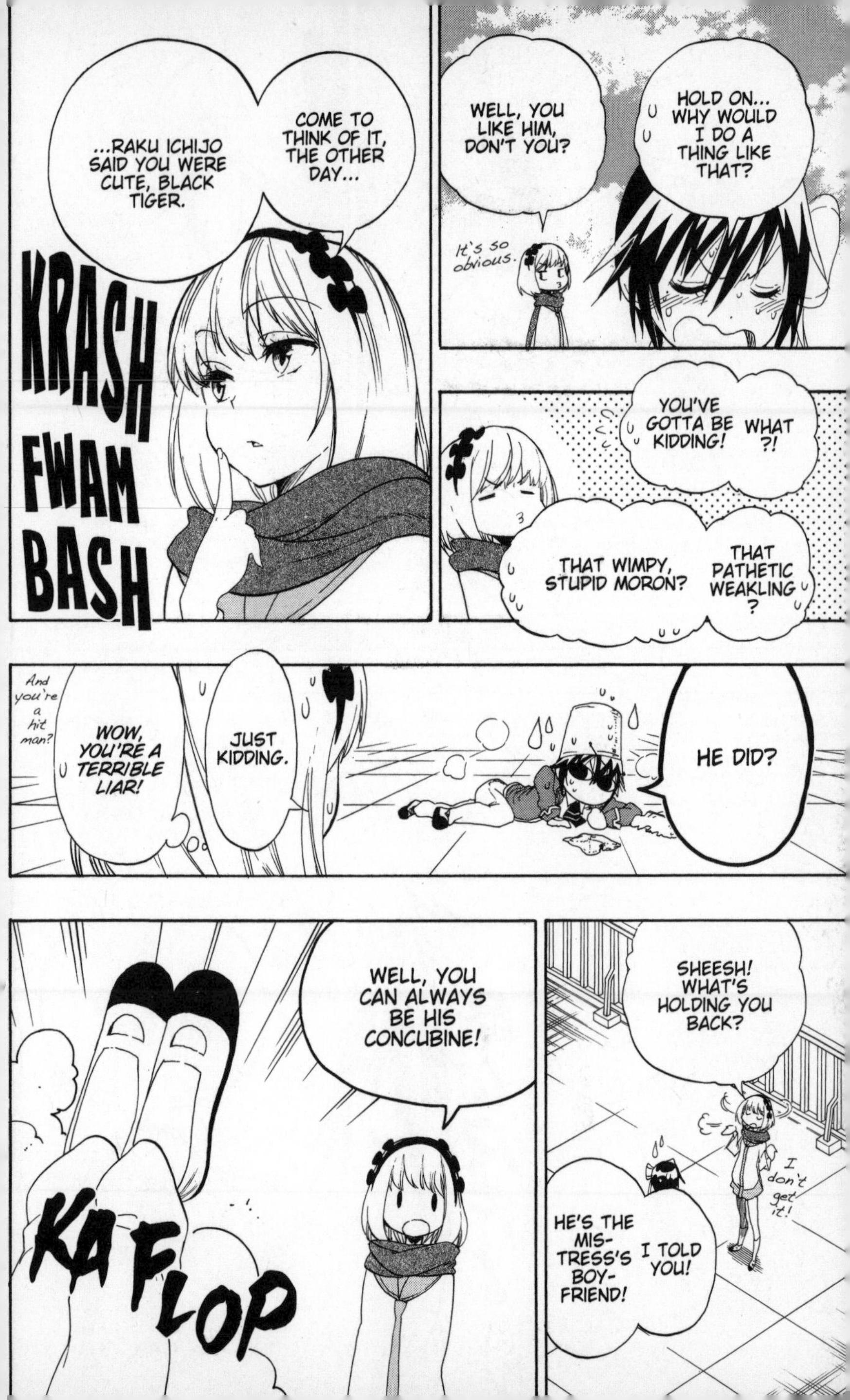
HOLD ON... WHY WOULD I DO A THING LIKE THAT?
WELL, YOU LIKE HIM, DON'T YOU?
It's so obvious.
WHAT?!
YOU'VE GOTTA BE KIDDING!
THAT PATHETIC WEAKLING?
THAT WIMPY, STUPID MORON?
COME TO THINK OF IT, THE OTHER DAY...
...RAKU ICHIJO SAID YOU WERE CUTE, BLACK TIGER.
KRASH
FWAM
BASH
HE DID?
JUST KIDDING.
WOW, YOU'RE A TERRIBLE LIAR!
And you're a hit man?
SHEESH! WHAT'S HOLDING YOU BACK?
I don't get it!
I TOLD YOU!
HE'S THE MIS-TRESS'S BOY-FRIEND!
WELL, YOU CAN ALWAYS BE HIS CONCUBINE!
KA FLOP

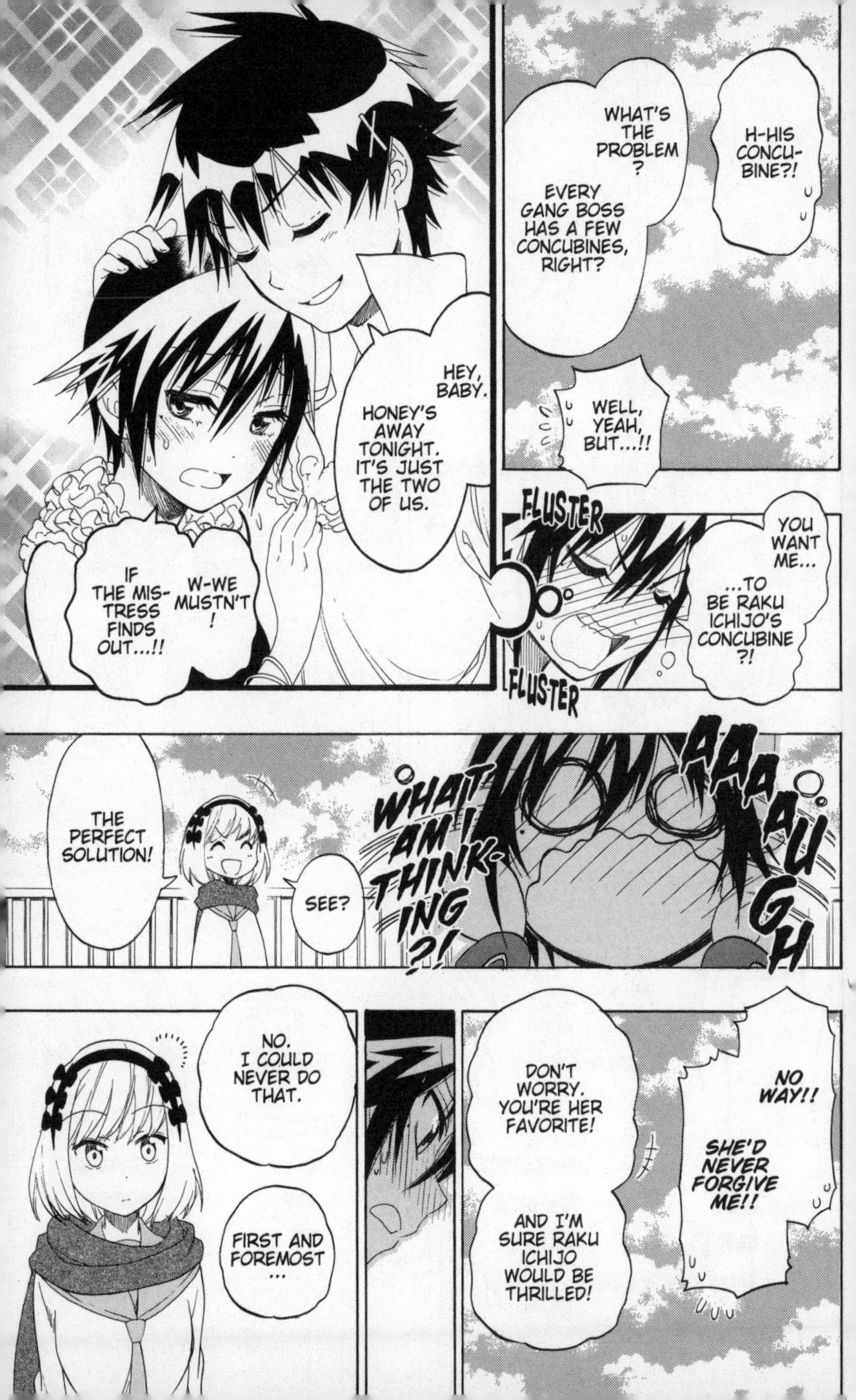
H-HIS CONCUBINE?!
WHAT'S THE PROBLEM?
EVERY GANG BOSS HAS A FEW CONCUBINES, RIGHT?
WELL, YEAH, BUT...!!
FLUSTER
FLUSTER
YOU WANT ME...
...TO BE RAKU ICHIJO'S CONCUBINE?!
HEY, BABY.
HONEY'S AWAY TONIGHT. IT'S JUST THE TWO OF US.
W-WE MUSTN'T!
IF THE MISTRESS FINDS OUT...!!
AAAAAUGH
WHAT AM I THINKING?!
SEE?
THE PERFECT SOLUTION!
NO WAY!!
SHE'D NEVER FORGIVE ME!!
DON'T WORRY. YOU'RE HER FAVORITE!
AND I'M SURE RAKU ICHIJO WOULD BE THRILLED!
NO. I COULD NEVER DO THAT.
FIRST AND FOREMOST...

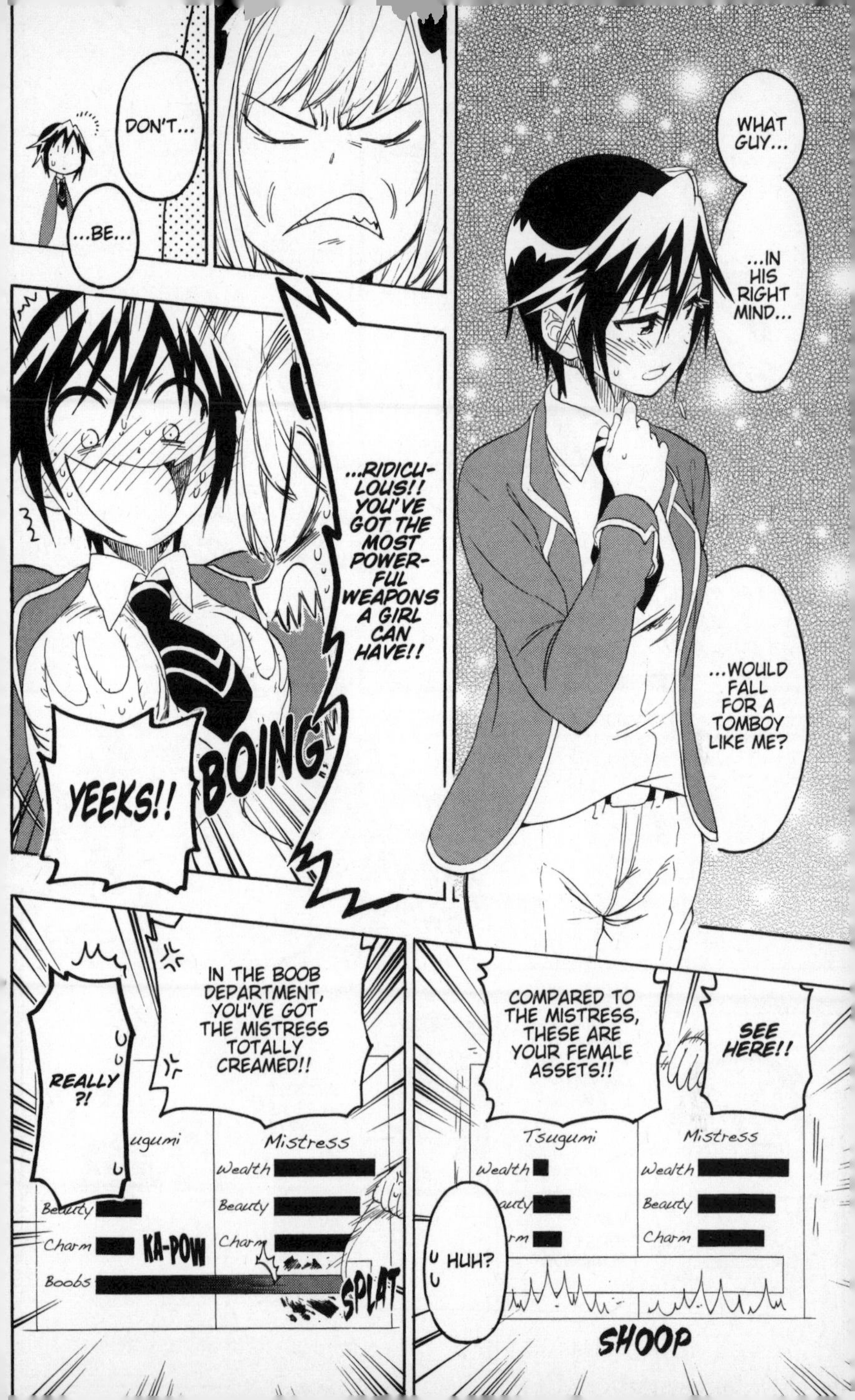
WHAT GUY...
...IN HIS RIGHT MIND...
...WOULD FALL FOR A TOMBOY LIKE ME?
DON'T...
...BE...
...RIDICULOUS!! YOU'VE GOT THE MOST POWERFUL WEAPONS A GIRL CAN HAVE!!
BOING
YEEKS!!
SEE HERE!!
COMPARED TO THE MISTRESS, THESE ARE YOUR FEMALE ASSETS!!
Tsugumi
Wealth
Mistress
Wealth
Beauty
Charm
HUH?
SHOOP
IN THE BOOB DEPARTMENT, YOU'VE GOT THE MISTRESS TOTALLY CREAMED!!
REALLY?!
Mistress
Wealth
Beauty
Charm
Beauty
Charm
Boobs
KA-POW
SPLAT

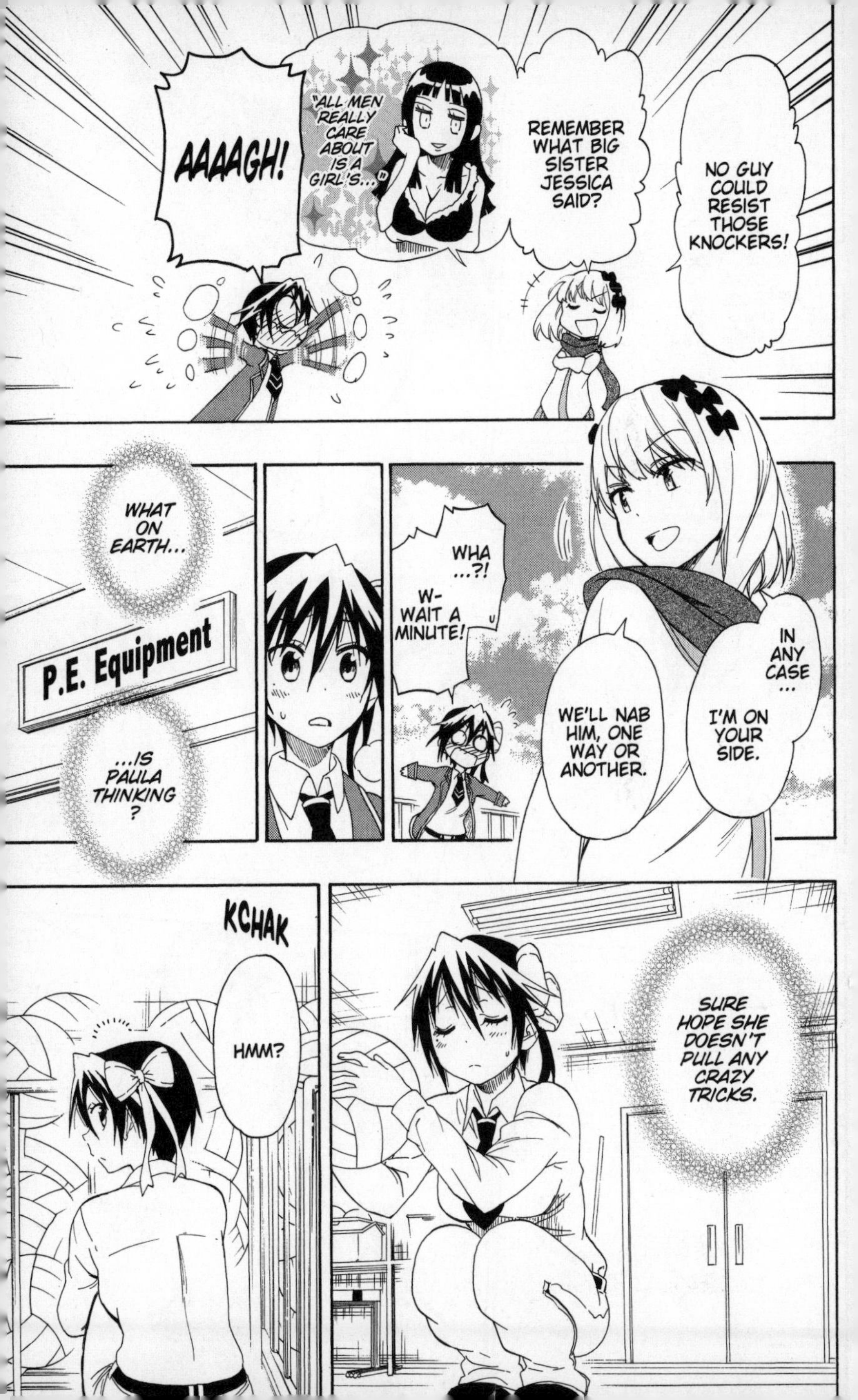
NO GUY COULD RESIST THOSE KNOCKERS!
REMEMBER WHAT BIG SISTER JESSICA SAID?
"ALL MEN REALLY CARE ABOUT IS A GIRL'S..."
AAAAGH!
IN ANY CASE...
I'M ON YOUR SIDE.
WE'LL NAB HIM, ONE WAY OR ANOTHER.
WHA...?!
W-WAIT A MINUTE!
WHAT ON EARTH...
P.E. Equipment
...IS PAULA THINKING?
SURE HOPE SHE DOESN'T PULL ANY CRAZY TRICKS.
KCHAK
HMM?

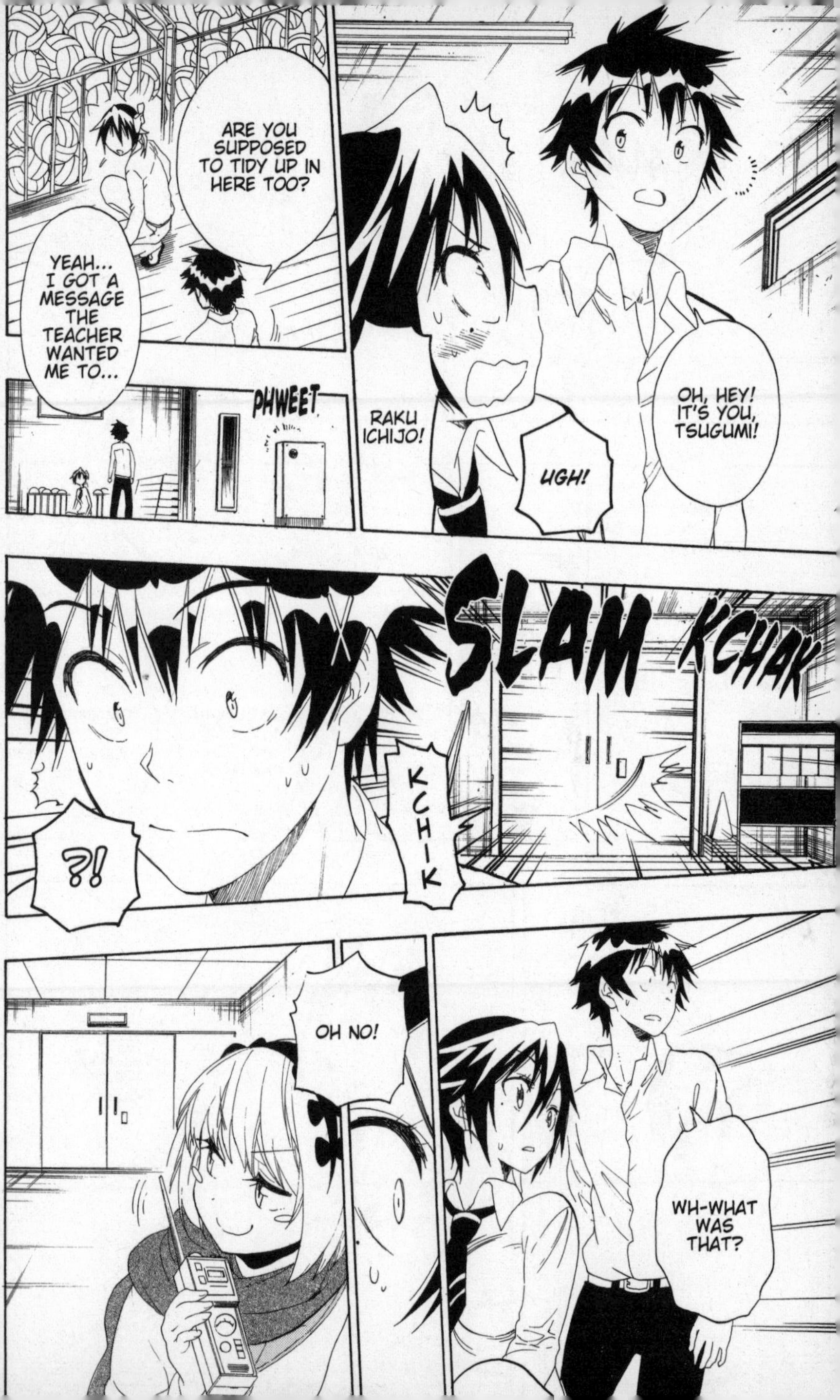
OH, HEY! IT'S YOU, TSUGUMI!
UGH!
RAKU ICHIJO!
ARE YOU SUPPOSED TO TIDY UP IN HERE TOO?
YEAH... I GOT A MESSAGE THE TEACHER WANTED ME TO...
PHWEET
KCHAK
SLAM
KCHIK
?!
WH-WHAT WAS THAT?
OH NO!

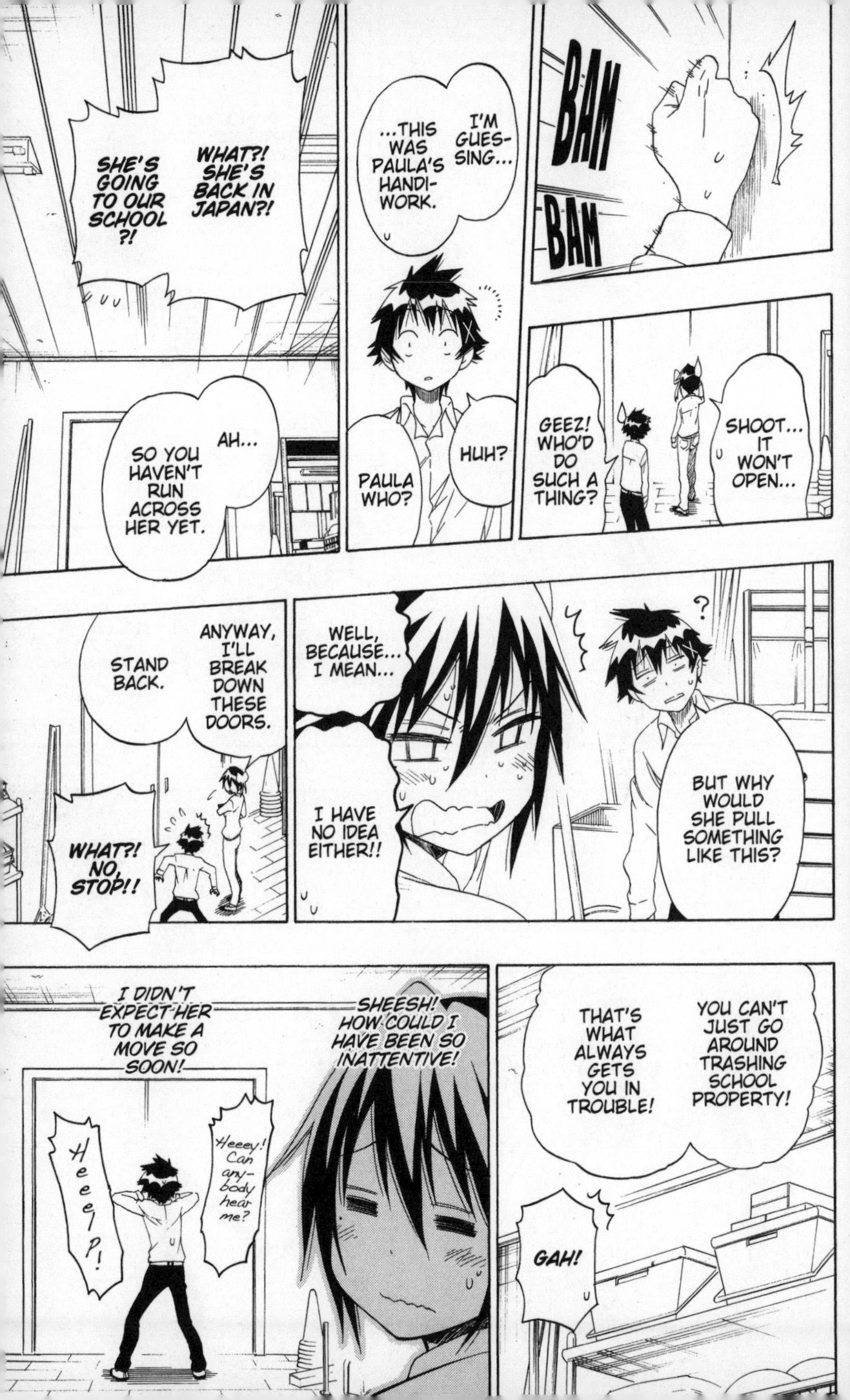
BAM
BAM
SHOOT... IT WON'T OPEN...
GEEZ! WHO'D DO SUCH A THING?
I'M GUESSING... ...THIS WAS PAULA'S HANDIWORK.
HUH?
PAULA WHO?
WHAT?! SHE'S BACK IN JAPAN?!
SHE'S GOING TO OUR SCHOOL?!
AH...
SO YOU HAVEN'T RUN ACROSS HER YET.
?
BUT WHY WOULD SHE PULL SOMETHING LIKE THIS?
WELL, BECAUSE... I MEAN...
I HAVE NO IDEA EITHER!!
ANYWAY, I'LL BREAK DOWN THESE DOORS.
STAND BACK.
WHAT?! NO, STOP!!
YOU CAN'T JUST GO AROUND TRASHING SCHOOL PROPERTY!
THAT'S WHAT ALWAYS GETS YOU IN TROUBLE!
GAH!
SHEESH! HOW COULD I HAVE BEEN SO INATTENTIVE!
I DIDN'T EXPECT HER TO MAKE A MOVE SO SOON!
Heeeey! Can anybody hear me?
Heeelp!

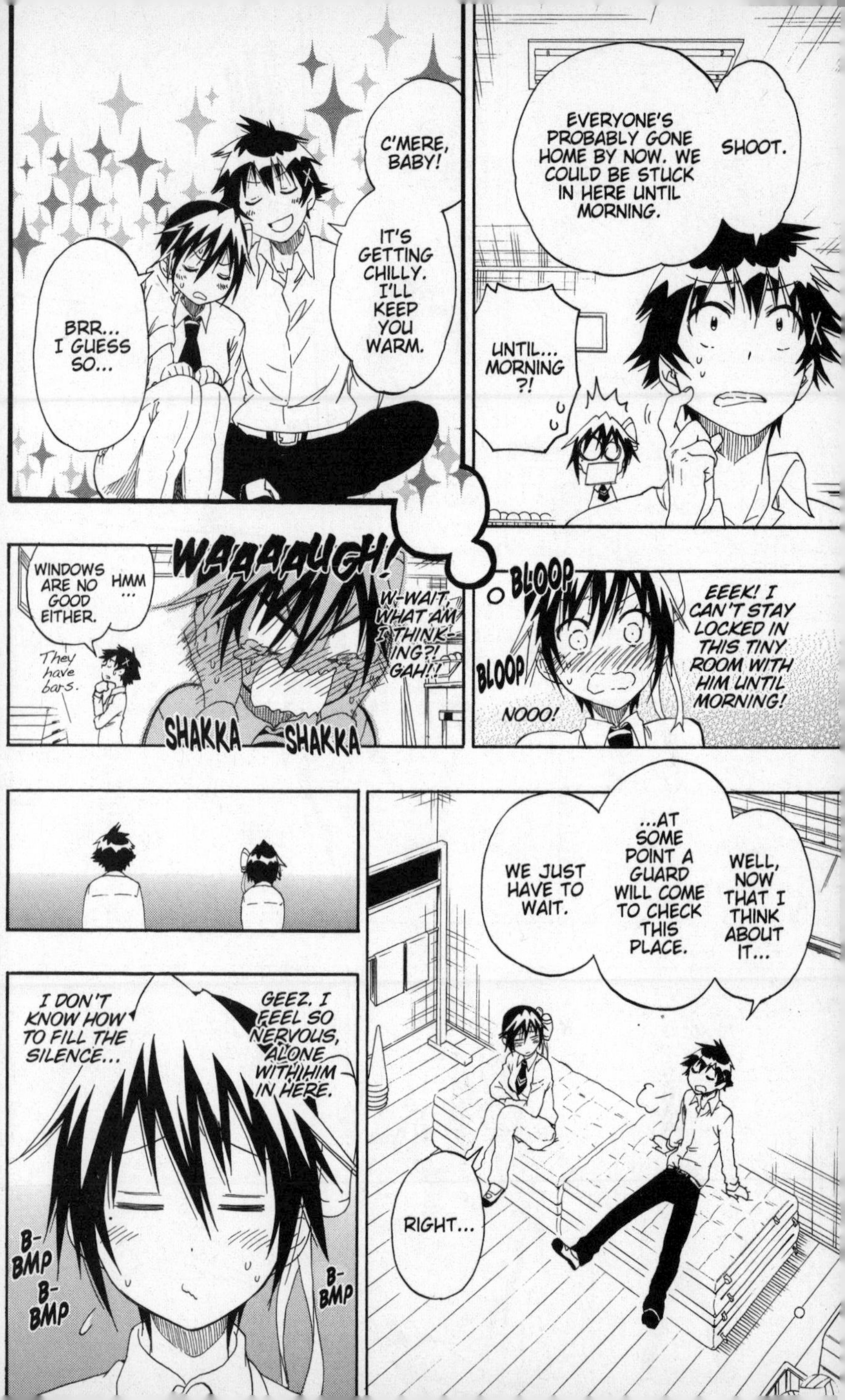
SHOOT.
EVERYONE'S PROBABLY GONE HOME BY NOW. WE COULD BE STUCK IN HERE UNTIL MORNING.
UNTIL... MORNING ?!
C'MERE, BABY!
IT'S GETTING CHILLY. I'LL KEEP YOU WARM.
BRR... I GUESS SO...
BLOOP
BLOOP
EEEK! I CAN'T STAY LOCKED IN THIS TINY ROOM WITH HIM UNTIL MORNING!
NOOO!
WAAAAAUGH!
W-WAIT, WHAT AM I THINKING?! GAH!!
SHAKKA SHAKKA
HMM ...
WINDOWS ARE NO GOOD EITHER.
They have bars.
WELL, NOW THAT I THINK ABOUT IT...
...AT SOME POINT A GUARD WILL COME TO CHECK THIS PLACE.
WE JUST HAVE TO WAIT.
RIGHT...
GEEZ. I FEEL SO NERVOUS, ALONE WITH HIM IN HERE.
I DON'T KNOW HOW TO FILL THE SILENCE...
B-BMP B-BMP
B-BMP

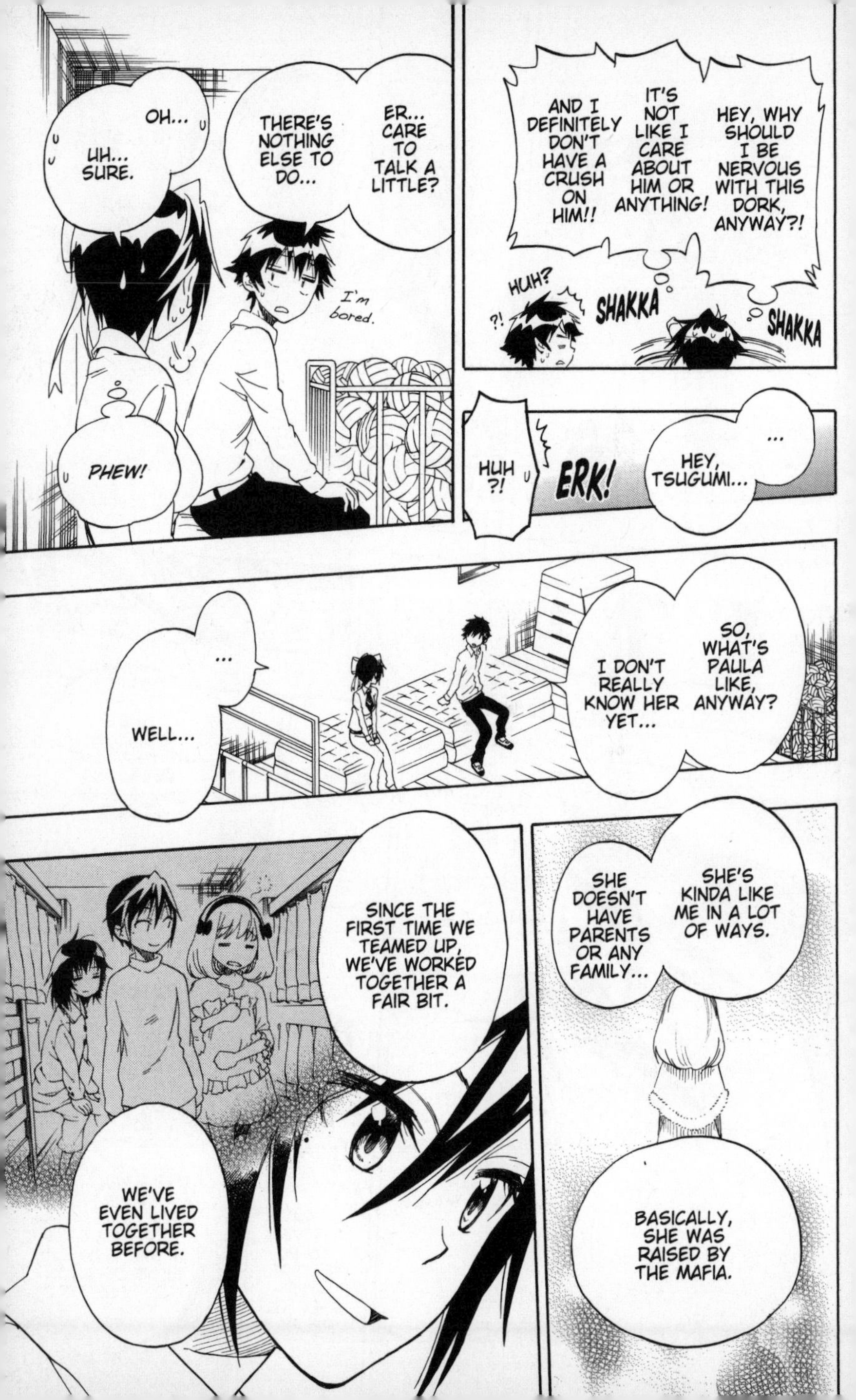
HEY, WHY SHOULD I BE NERVOUS WITH THIS DORK, ANYWAY?!
IT'S NOT LIKE I CARE ABOUT HIM OR ANYTHING!
AND I DEFINITELY DON'T HAVE A CRUSH ON HIM!!
SHAKKA
SHAKKA
HUH?
?!
...
HEY, TSUGUMI...
ERK!
HUH ?!
ER... CARE TO TALK A LITTLE?
THERE'S NOTHING ELSE TO DO...
I'm bored.
OH...
UH... SURE.
PHEW!
SO, WHAT'S PAULA LIKE, ANYWAY?
I DON'T REALLY KNOW HER YET...
...
WELL...
SHE'S KINDA LIKE ME IN A LOT OF WAYS.
SHE DOESN'T HAVE PARENTS OR ANY FAMILY...
BASICALLY, SHE WAS RAISED BY THE MAFIA.
SINCE THE FIRST TIME WE TEAMED UP, WE'VE WORKED TOGETHER A FAIR BIT.
WE'VE EVEN LIVED TOGETHER BEFORE.

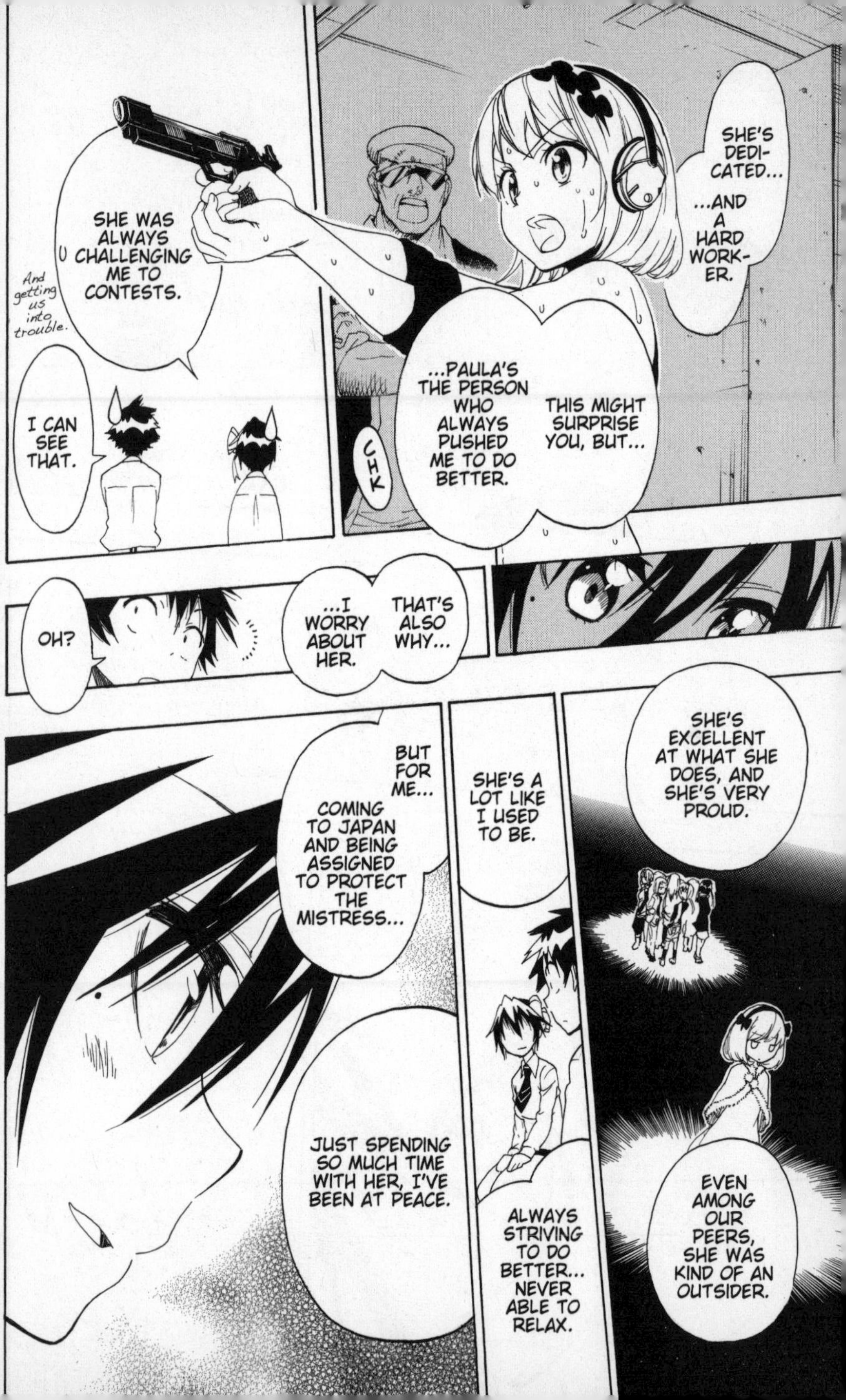
SHE'S DEDICATED...
...AND A HARD WORKER.
THIS MIGHT SURPRISE YOU, BUT...
...PAULA'S THE PERSON WHO ALWAYS PUSHED ME TO DO BETTER.
CHK
SHE WAS ALWAYS CHALLENGING ME TO CONTESTS.
And getting us into trouble.
I CAN SEE THAT.
THAT'S ALSO WHY...
...I WORRY ABOUT HER.
OH?
SHE'S EXCELLENT AT WHAT SHE DOES, AND SHE'S VERY PROUD.
EVEN AMONG OUR PEERS, SHE WAS KIND OF AN OUTSIDER.
SHE'S A LOT LIKE I USED TO BE.
ALWAYS STRIVING TO DO BETTER... NEVER ABLE TO RELAX.
BUT FOR ME...
COMING TO JAPAN AND BEING ASSIGNED TO PROTECT THE MISTRESS...
JUST SPENDING SO MUCH TIME WITH HER, I'VE BEEN AT PEACE.

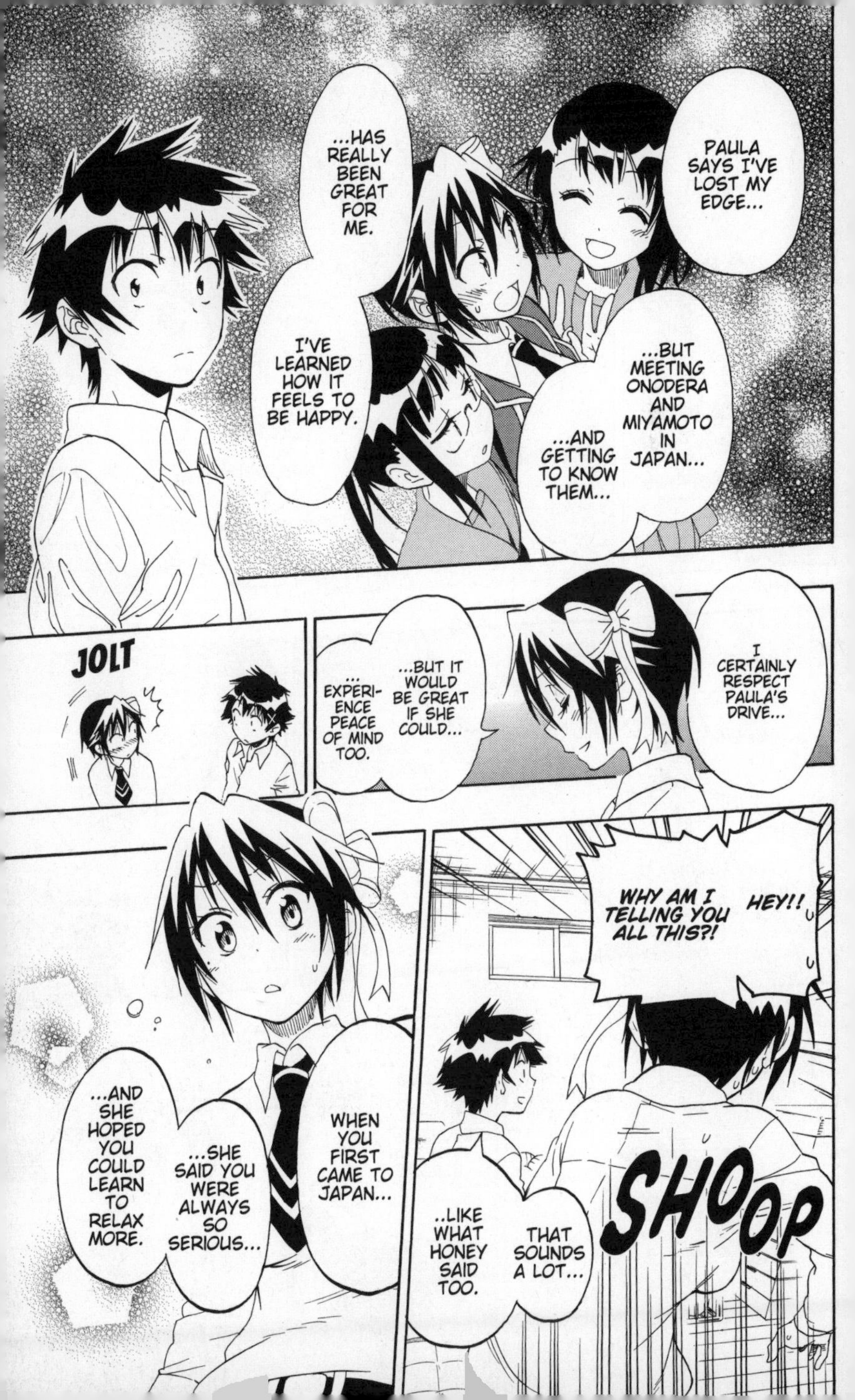
PAULA SAYS I'VE LOST MY EDGE...
...BUT MEETING ONODERA AND MIYAMOTO IN JAPAN...
...AND GETTING TO KNOW THEM...
...HAS REALLY BEEN GREAT FOR ME.
I'VE LEARNED HOW IT FEELS TO BE HAPPY.
I CERTAINLY RESPECT PAULA'S DRIVE...
...BUT IT WOULD BE GREAT IF SHE COULD...
...EXPERIENCE PEACE OF MIND TOO.
JOLT
HEY!!
WHY AM I TELLING YOU ALL THIS?!
SHOOP
THAT SOUNDS A LOT...
..LIKE WHAT HONEY SAID TOO.
WHEN YOU FIRST CAME TO JAPAN...
...SHE SAID YOU WERE ALWAYS SO SERIOUS...
...AND SHE HOPED YOU COULD LEARN TO RELAX MORE.

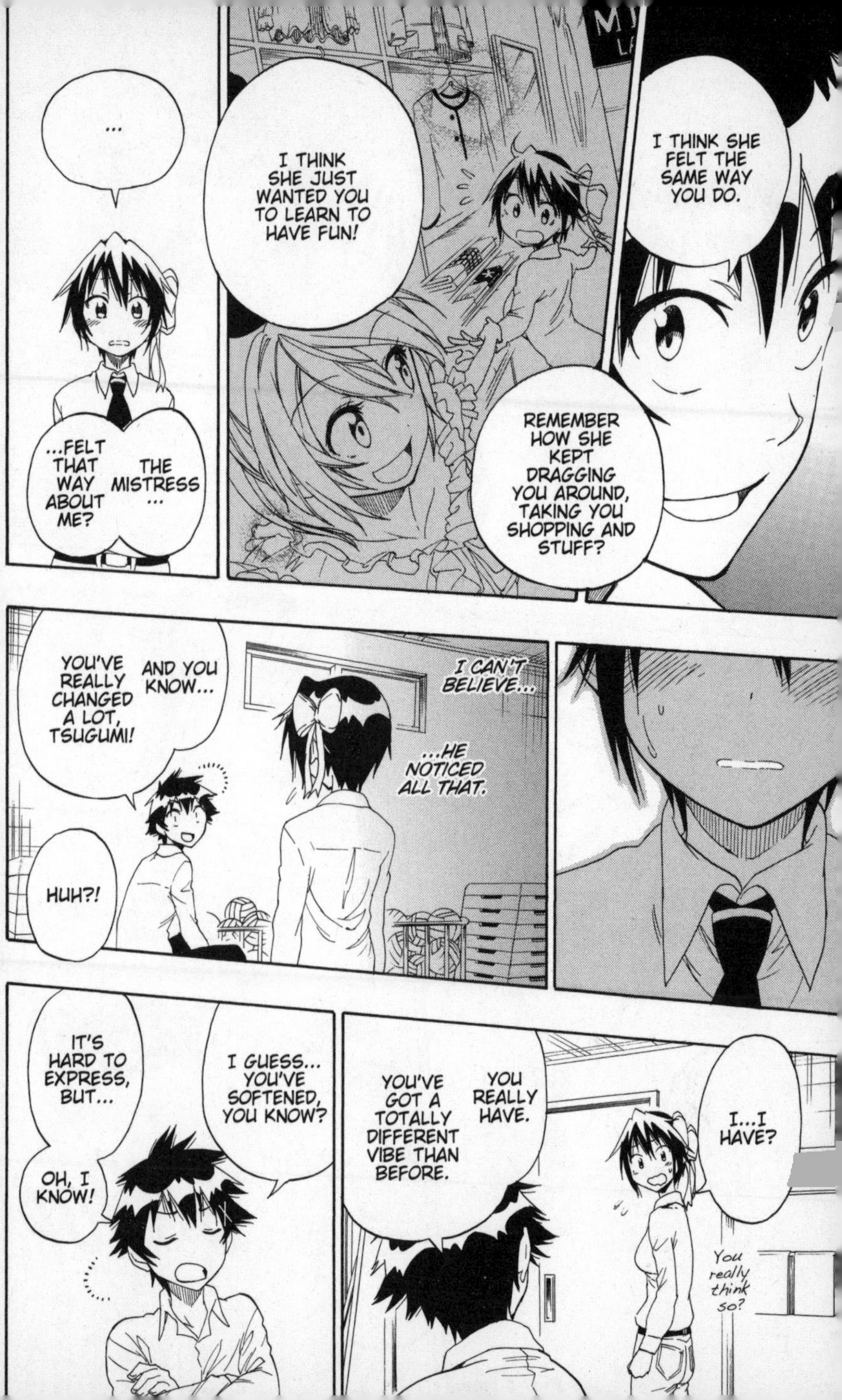
I THINK SHE FELT THE SAME WAY YOU DO.
REMEMBER HOW SHE KEPT DRAGGING YOU AROUND, TAKING YOU SHOPPING AND STUFF?
I THINK SHE JUST WANTED YOU TO LEARN TO HAVE FUN!
...
THE MISTRESS...
...FELT THAT WAY ABOUT ME?
I CAN'T BELIEVE...
...HE NOTICED ALL THAT.
AND YOU KNOW...
YOU'VE REALLY CHANGED A LOT, TSUGUMI!
HUH?!
I...I HAVE?
YOU REALLY HAVE.
YOU'VE GOT A TOTALLY DIFFERENT VIBE THAN BEFORE.
You really think so?
I GUESS... YOU'VE SOFTENED, YOU KNOW?
IT'S HARD TO EXPRESS, BUT...
OH, I KNOW!

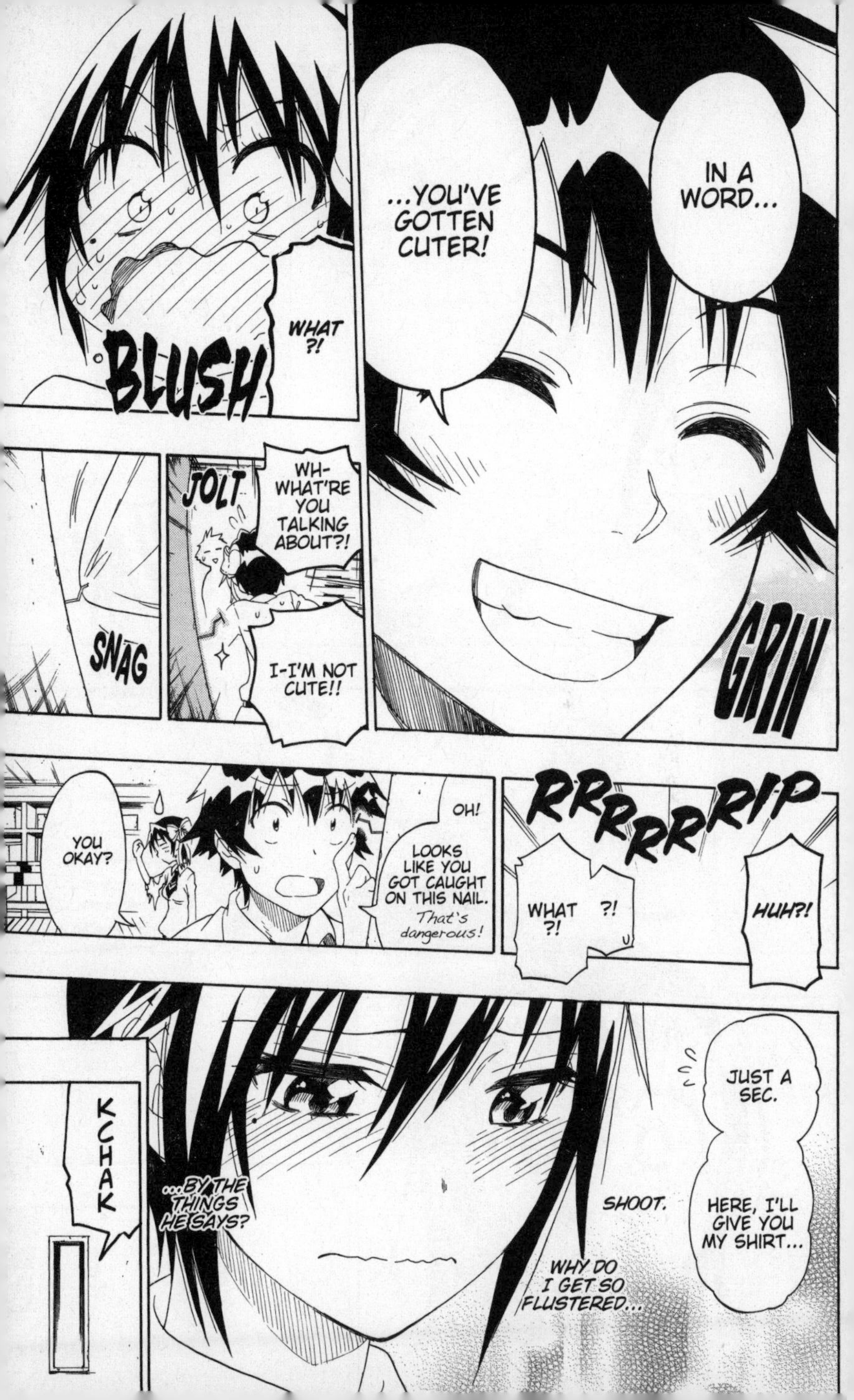
IN A WORD...
...YOU'VE GOTTEN CUTER!
GRIN
WHAT ?!
BLUSH
JOLT
WH- WHAT'RE YOU TALKING ABOUT?!
I-I'M NOT CUTE!!
SNAG
RRRRRRRIP
HUH?!
WHAT ?! ?!
OH!
LOOKS LIKE YOU GOT CAUGHT ON THIS NAIL.
That's dangerous!
YOU OKAY?
JUST A SEC.
HERE, I'LL GIVE YOU MY SHIRT...
SHOOT.
WHY DO I GET SO FLUSTERED...
...BY THE THINGS HE SAYS?
KCHAK

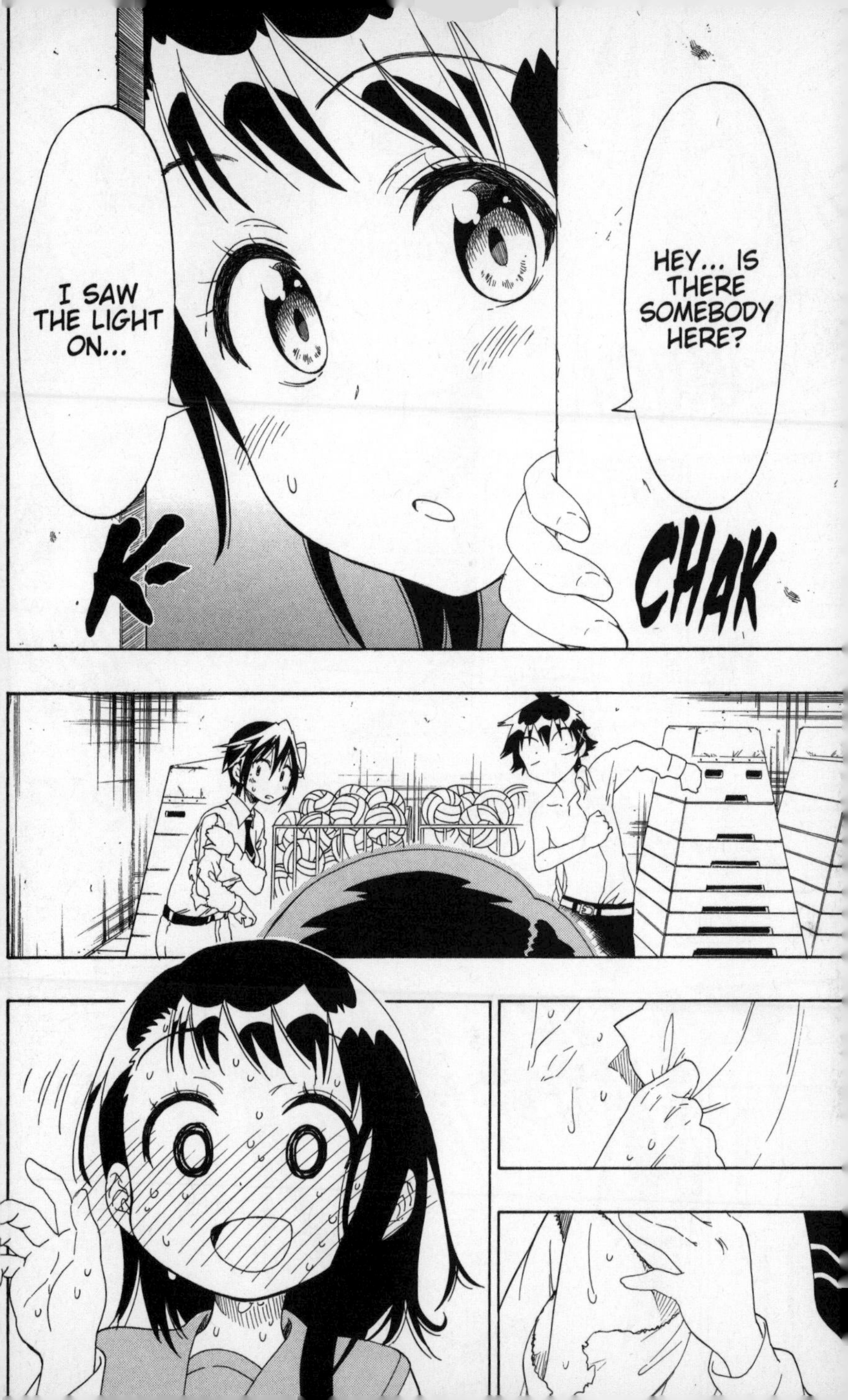
HEY... IS THERE SOMEBODY HERE?
I SAW THE LIGHT ON...
CHAK
K-

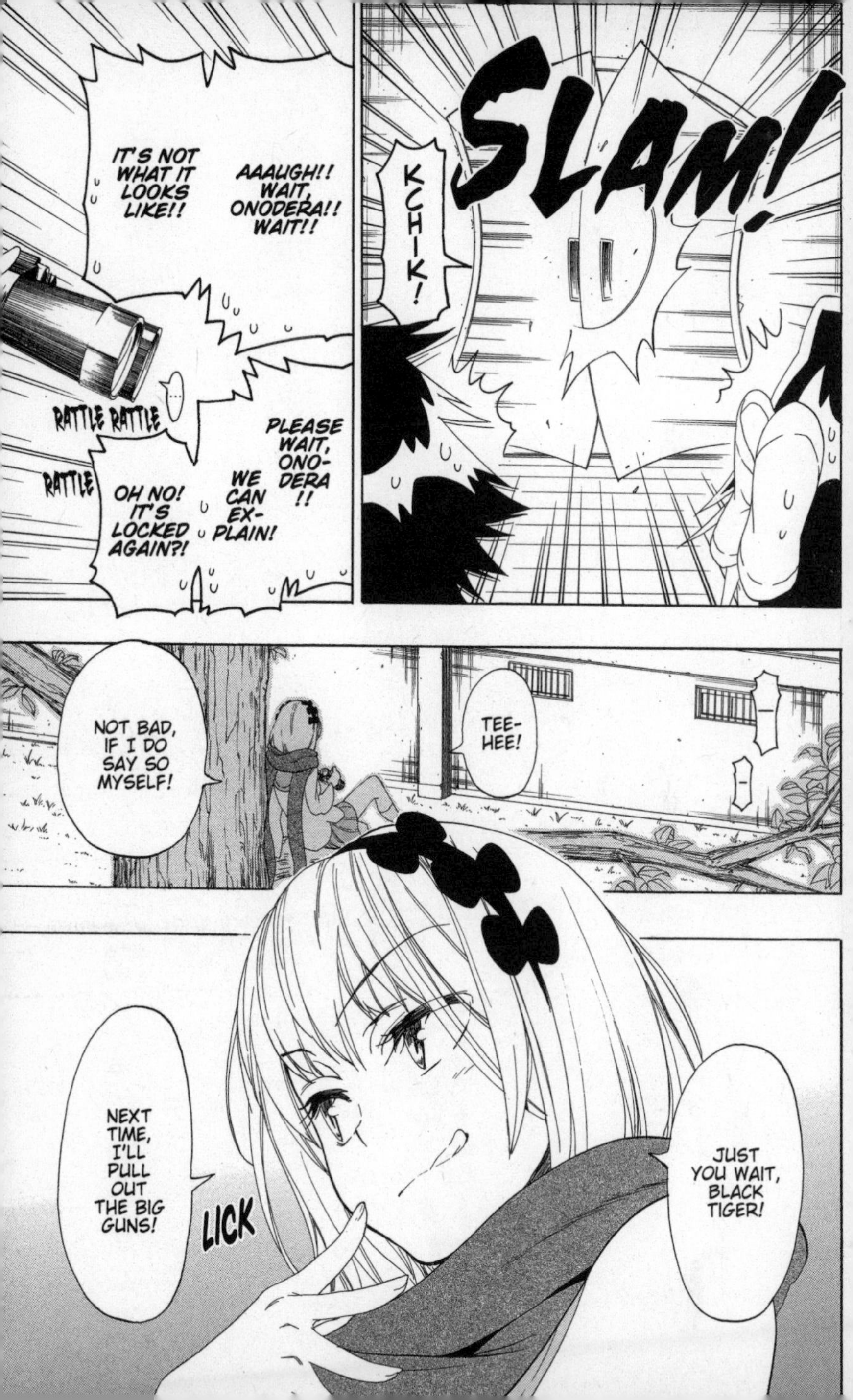
SLAM!
KCHIK!
AAAUGH!! WAIT, ONODERA!! WAIT!!
IT'S NOT WHAT IT LOOKS LIKE!!
...
PLEASE WAIT, ONODERA!!
WE CAN EXPLAIN!
RATTLE RATTLE
OH NO! IT'S LOCKED AGAIN?!
RATTLE
TEE-HEE!
NOT BAD, IF I DO SAY SO MYSELF!
JUST YOU WAIT, BLACK TIGER!
LICK
NEXT TIME, I'LL PULL OUT THE BIG GUNS!

Paula's Effort

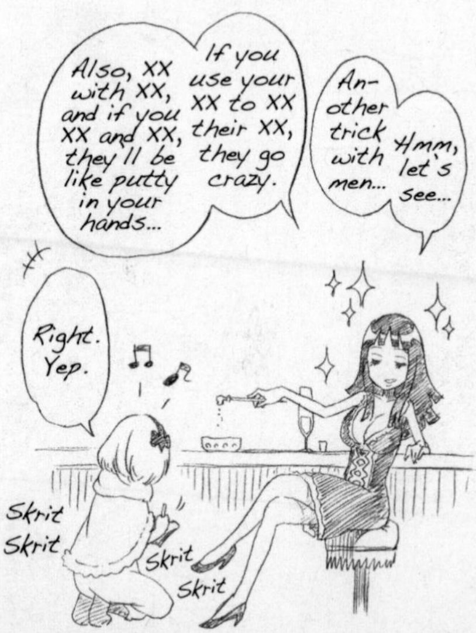
Hmm, let's see...
Another trick with men...
If you use your XX to XX their XX, they go crazy.
Also, XX with XX, and if you XX and XX, they'll be like putty in your hands...
Right. Yep.
Skrit Skrit
Skrit Skrit

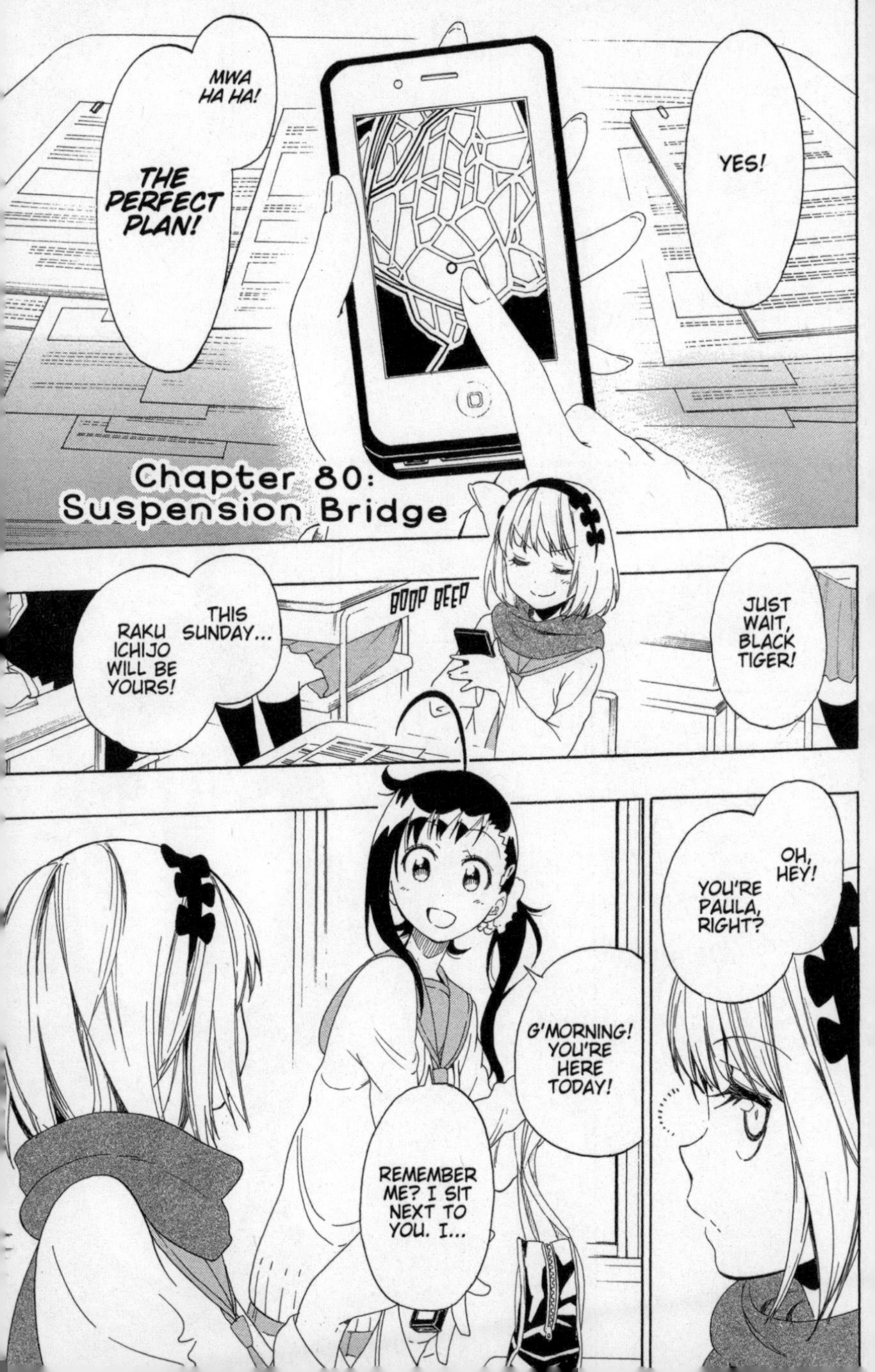
YES!
MWA HA HA! THE PERFECT PLAN!
Chapter 80: Suspension Bridge
JUST WAIT, BLACK TIGER!
BOOP BEEP
THIS SUNDAY... RAKU ICHIJO WILL BE YOURS!
OH, HEY! YOU'RE PAULA, RIGHT?
G'MORNING! YOU'RE HERE TODAY!
REMEMBER ME? I SIT NEXT TO YOU. I...

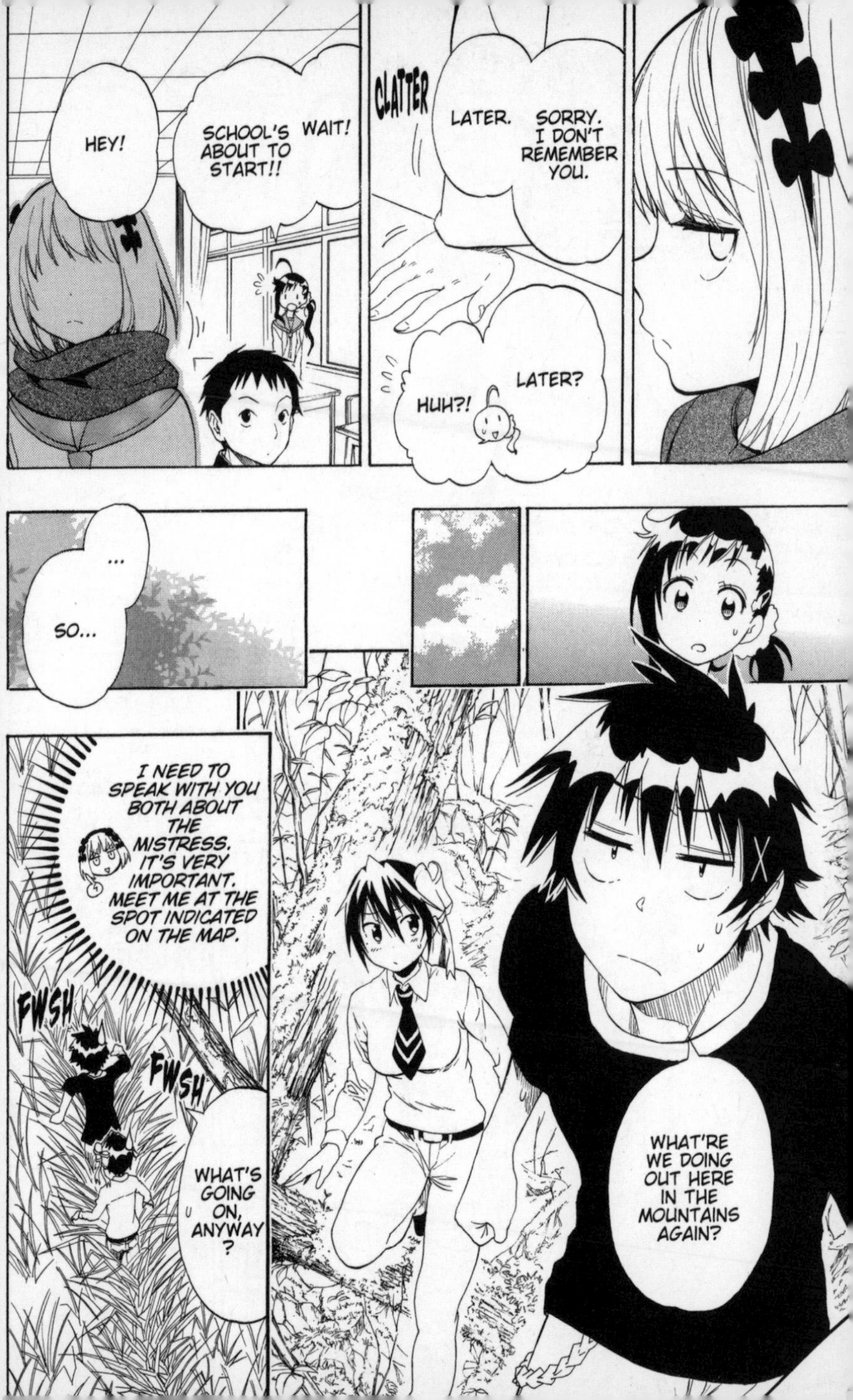
SORRY. I DON'T REMEMBER YOU.
LATER.
CLATTER
LATER?
HUH?!
WAIT!
SCHOOL'S ABOUT TO START!!
HEY!
...
SO...
WHAT'RE WE DOING OUT HERE IN THE MOUNTAINS AGAIN?
I NEED TO SPEAK WITH YOU BOTH ABOUT THE MISTRESS. IT'S VERY IMPORTANT. MEET ME AT THE SPOT INDICATED ON THE MAP.
FWSH
FWSH
WHAT'S GOING ON, ANYWAY?

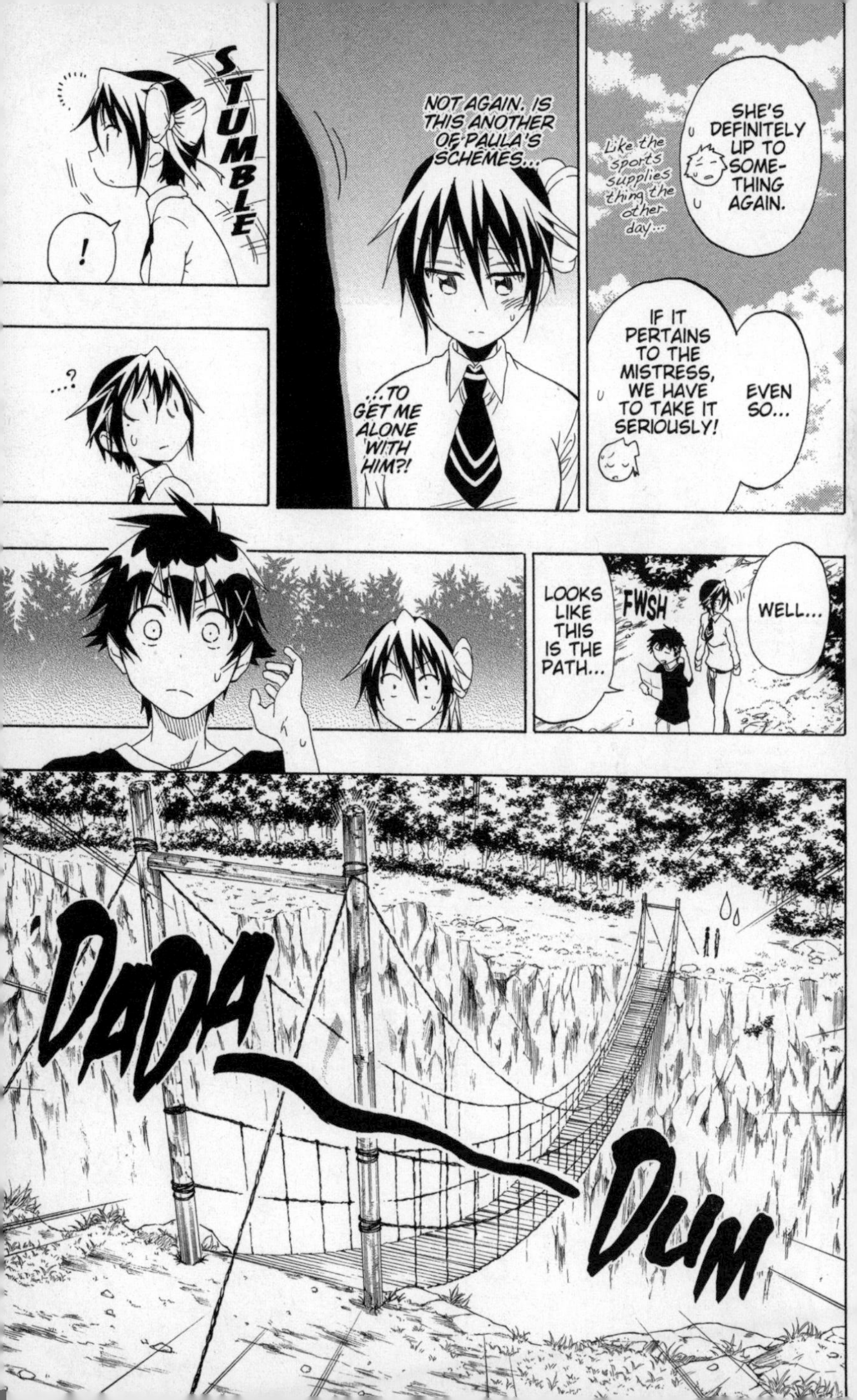
SHE'S DEFINITELY UP TO SOME-THING AGAIN.
Like the sports supplies thing the other day...
EVEN SO...
IF IT PERTAINS TO THE MISTRESS, WE HAVE TO TAKE IT SERIOUSLY!
NOT AGAIN. IS THIS ANOTHER OF PAULA'S SCHEMES...
...TO GET ME ALONE WITH HIM?!
STUMBLE
!
...?
WELL...
FWSH
LOOKS LIKE THIS IS THE PATH...
DADA—DUM

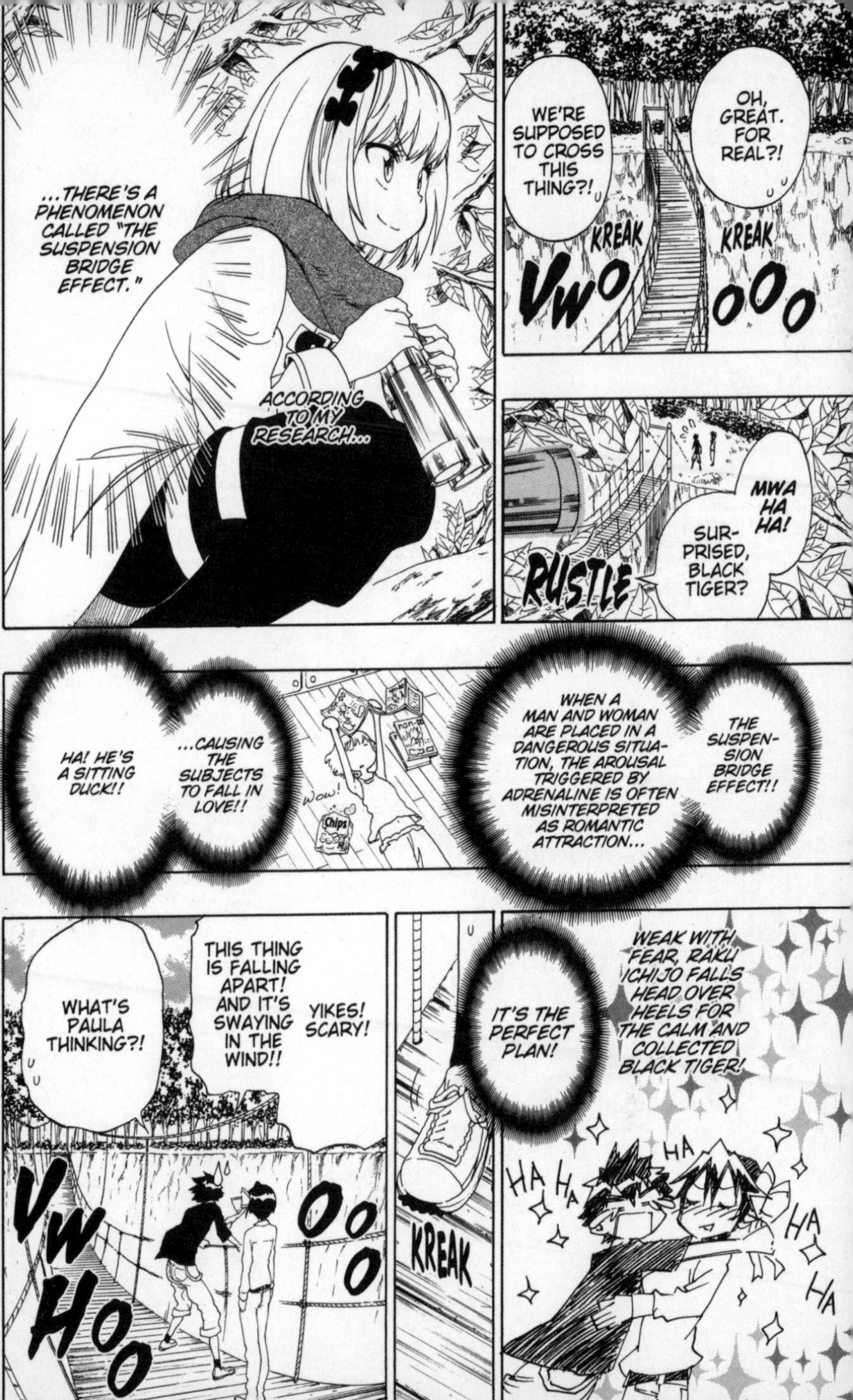
OH, GREAT. FOR REAL?!
WE'RE SUPPOSED TO CROSS THIS THING?!
KREAK
KREAK
VWOOOO
MWA HA HA!
SURPRISED, BLACK TIGER?
RUSTLE
ACCORDING TO MY RESEARCH...
...THERE'S A PHENOMENON CALLED "THE SUSPENSION BRIDGE EFFECT."
THE SUSPENSION BRIDGE EFFECT!!
WHEN A MAN AND WOMAN ARE PLACED IN A DANGEROUS SITUATION, THE AROUSAL TRIGGERED BY ADRENALINE IS OFTEN MISINTERPRETED AS ROMANTIC ATTRACTION...
...CAUSING THE SUBJECTS TO FALL IN LOVE!!
HA! HE'S A SITTING DUCK!!
WOW!
Chips
WEAK WITH FEAR, RAKU ICHIJO FALLS HEAD OVER HEELS FOR THE CALM AND COLLECTED BLACK TIGER!
IT'S THE PERFECT PLAN!
HA HA HA HA HA HA
KREAK
YIKES! SCARY!
THIS THING IS FALLING APART! AND IT'S SWAYING IN THE WIND!!
WHAT'S PAULA THINKING?!
VWHOOOO

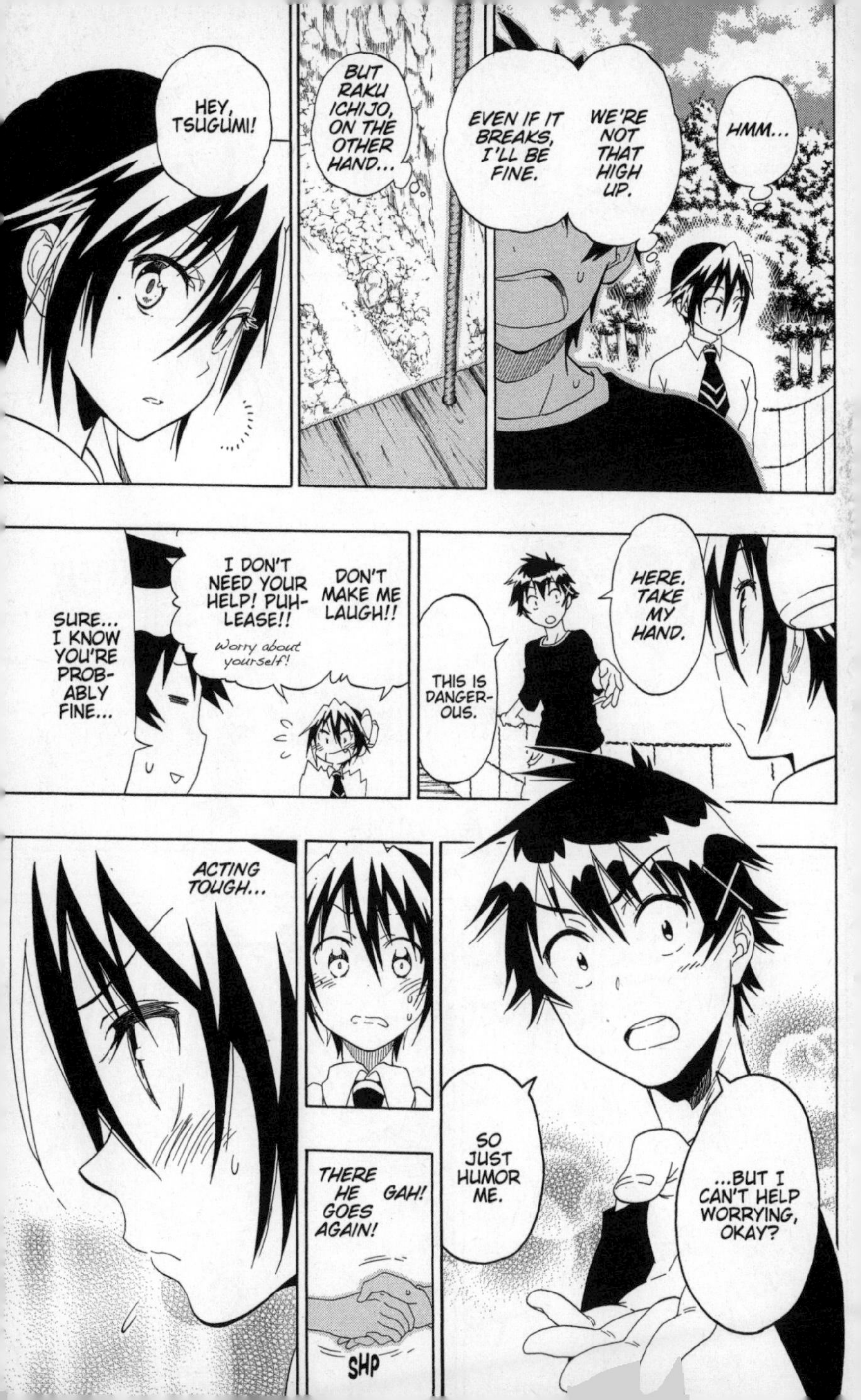
HMM...
WE'RE NOT THAT HIGH UP.
EVEN IF IT BREAKS, I'LL BE FINE.
BUT RAKU ICHIJO, ON THE OTHER HAND...
HEY, TSUGUMI!
HERE. TAKE MY HAND.
THIS IS DANGEROUS.
DON'T MAKE ME LAUGH!!
I DON'T NEED YOUR HELP! PUH-LEASE!!
Worry about yourself!
SURE... I KNOW YOU'RE PROBABLY FINE...
...BUT I CAN'T HELP WORRYING, OKAY?
SO JUST HUMOR ME.
GAH!
THERE HE GOES AGAIN!
SHP
ACTING TOUGH...

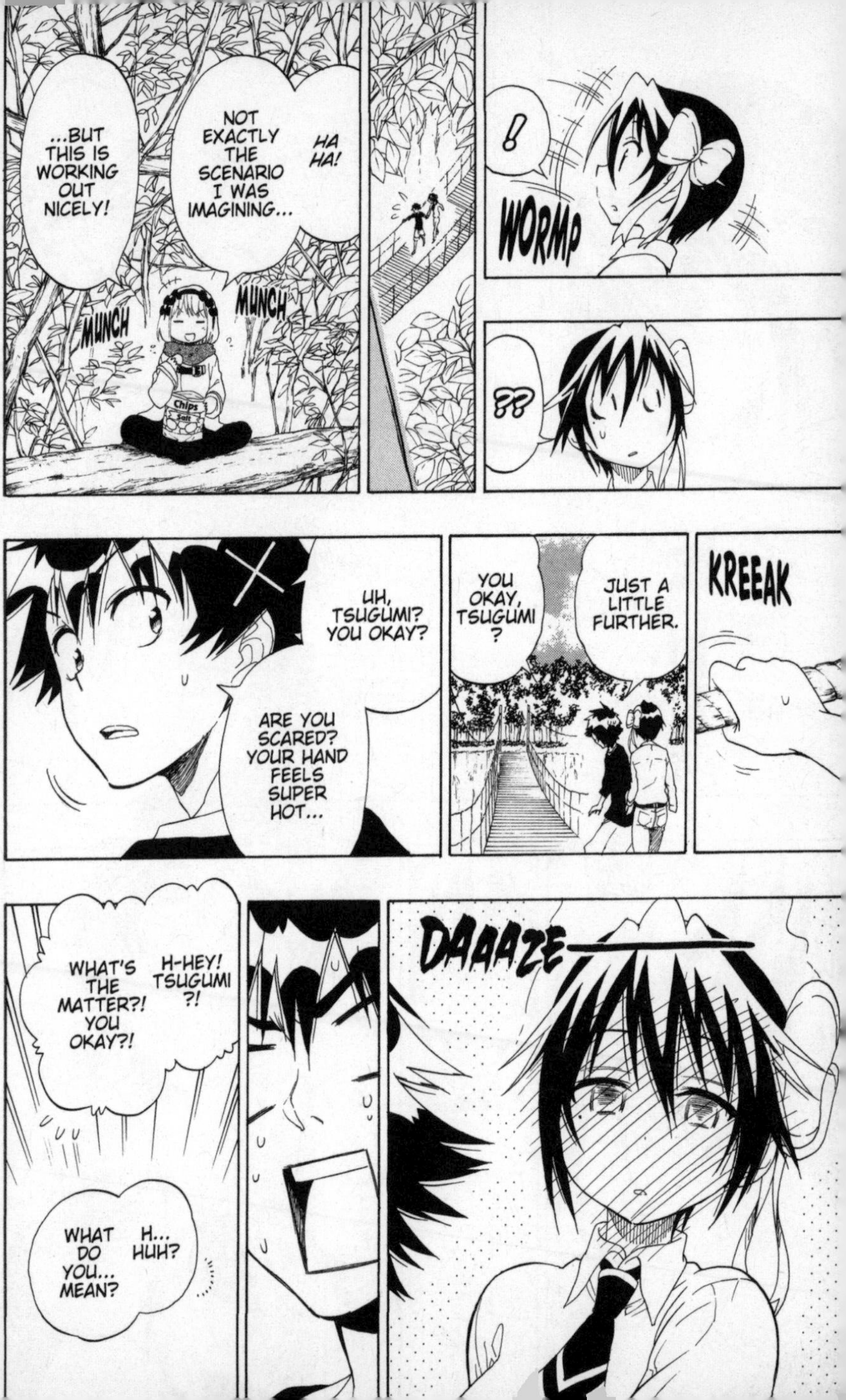
!
WORMP
??
HA HA!
NOT EXACTLY THE SCENARIO I WAS IMAGINING...
...BUT THIS IS WORKING OUT NICELY!
MUNCH
MUNCH
Chips Salt
KREEAK
JUST A LITTLE FURTHER.
YOU OKAY, TSUGUMI?
UH, TSUGUMI? YOU OKAY?
ARE YOU SCARED? YOUR HAND FEELS SUPER HOT...
DAAAZE
H-HEY! TSUGUMI?!
WHAT'S THE MATTER?! YOU OKAY?!
H... HUH?
WHAT DO YOU... MEAN?

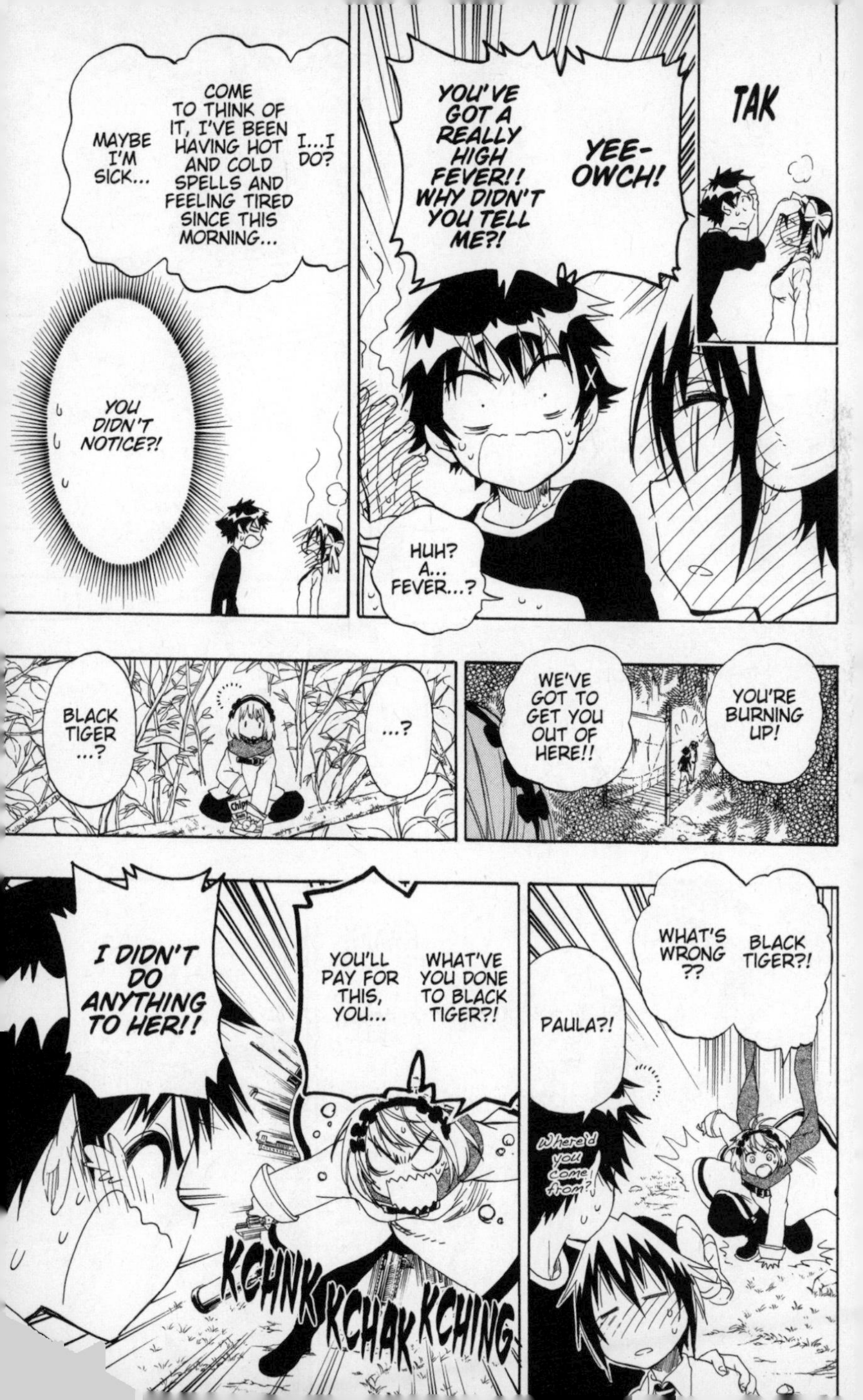
TAK
YEE-OWCH!
YOU'VE GOT A REALLY HIGH FEVER!! WHY DIDN'T YOU TELL ME?!
HUH? A... FEVER...?
I...I DO?
COME TO THINK OF IT, I'VE BEEN HAVING HOT AND COLD SPELLS AND FEELING TIRED SINCE THIS MORNING...
MAYBE I'M SICK...
YOU DIDN'T NOTICE?!
YOU'RE BURNING UP!
WE'VE GOT TO GET YOU OUT OF HERE!!
...?
BLACK TIGER ...?
BLACK TIGER?!
WHAT'S WRONG ??
PAULA?!
Where'd you come from?!
WHAT'VE YOU DONE TO BLACK TIGER?!
YOU'LL PAY FOR THIS, YOU...
KCHNK KCHAK KCHING
I DIDN'T DO ANYTHING TO HER!!

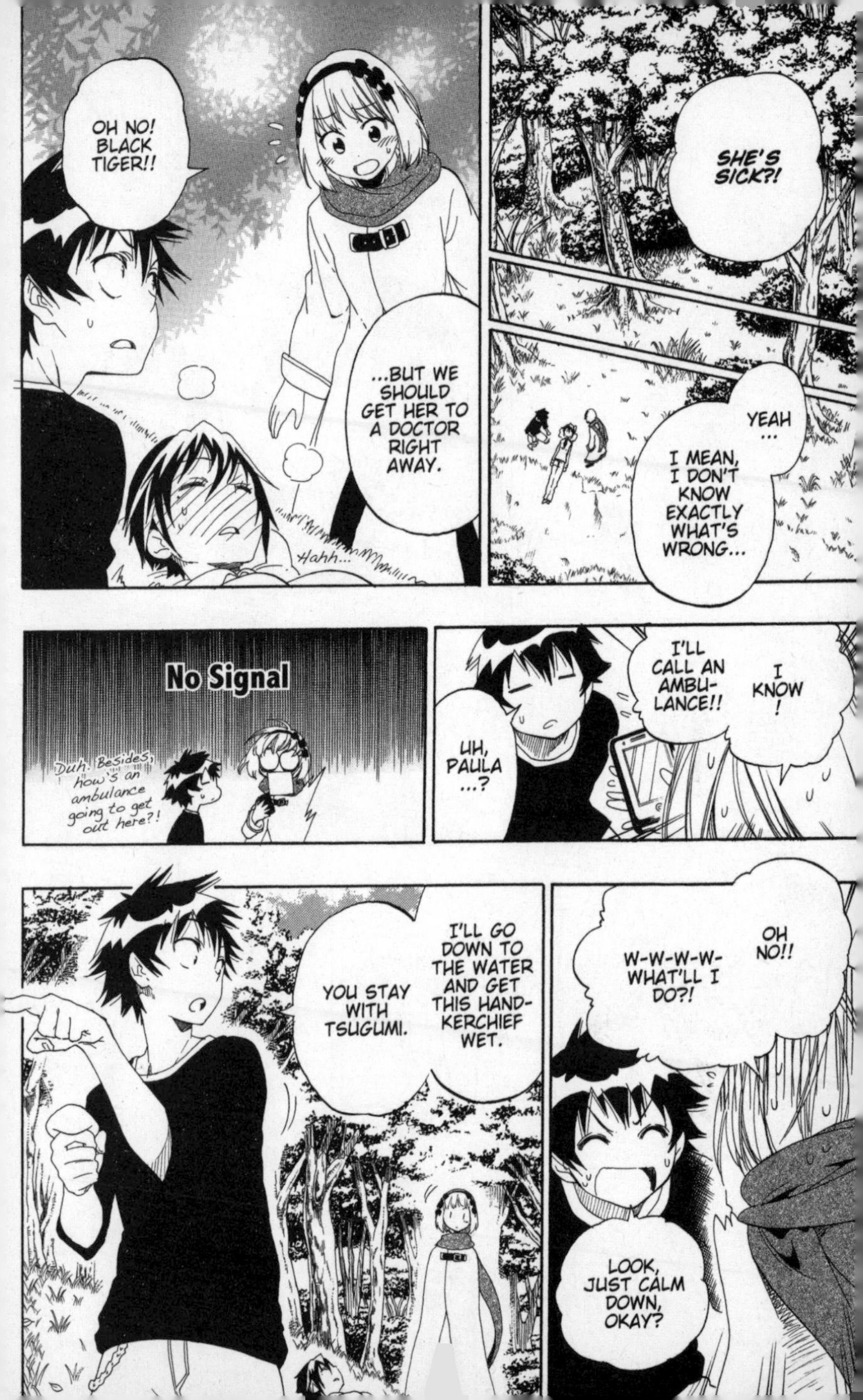
SHE'S SICK?!
YEAH...
I MEAN, I DON'T KNOW EXACTLY WHAT'S WRONG...
OH NO! BLACK TIGER!!
...BUT WE SHOULD GET HER TO A DOCTOR RIGHT AWAY.
Hahh...
I KNOW!
I'LL CALL AN AMBULANCE!!
UH, PAULA...?
No Signal
Duh. Besides, how's an ambulance going to get out here?!
OH NO!!
W-W-W-W-WHAT'LL I DO?!
LOOK, JUST CALM DOWN, OKAY?
I'LL GO DOWN TO THE WATER AND GET THIS HAND-KERCHIEF WET.
YOU STAY WITH TSUGUMI.

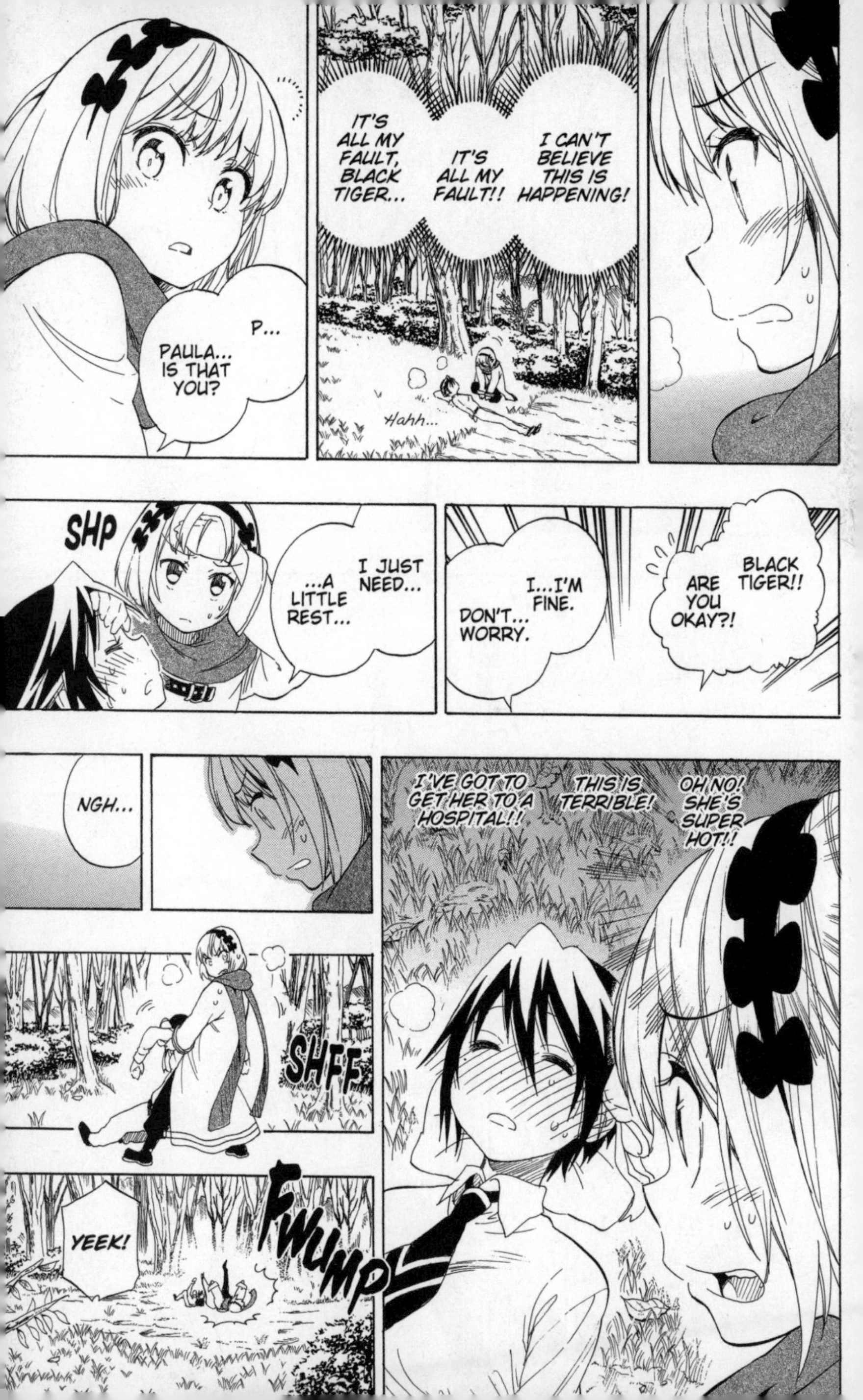
I CAN'T BELIEVE THIS IS HAPPENING!
IT'S ALL MY FAULT!!
IT'S ALL MY FAULT, BLACK TIGER...
Hahh...
P...
PAULA... IS THAT YOU?
BLACK TIGER!! ARE YOU OKAY?!
I...I'M FINE. DON'T... WORRY.
I JUST NEED... ...A LITTLE REST...
SHP
OH NO! SHE'S SUPER HOT!!
THIS IS TERRIBLE!
I'VE GOT TO GET HER TO A HOSPITAL!!
NGH...
SHFF
FWUMP
YEEK!

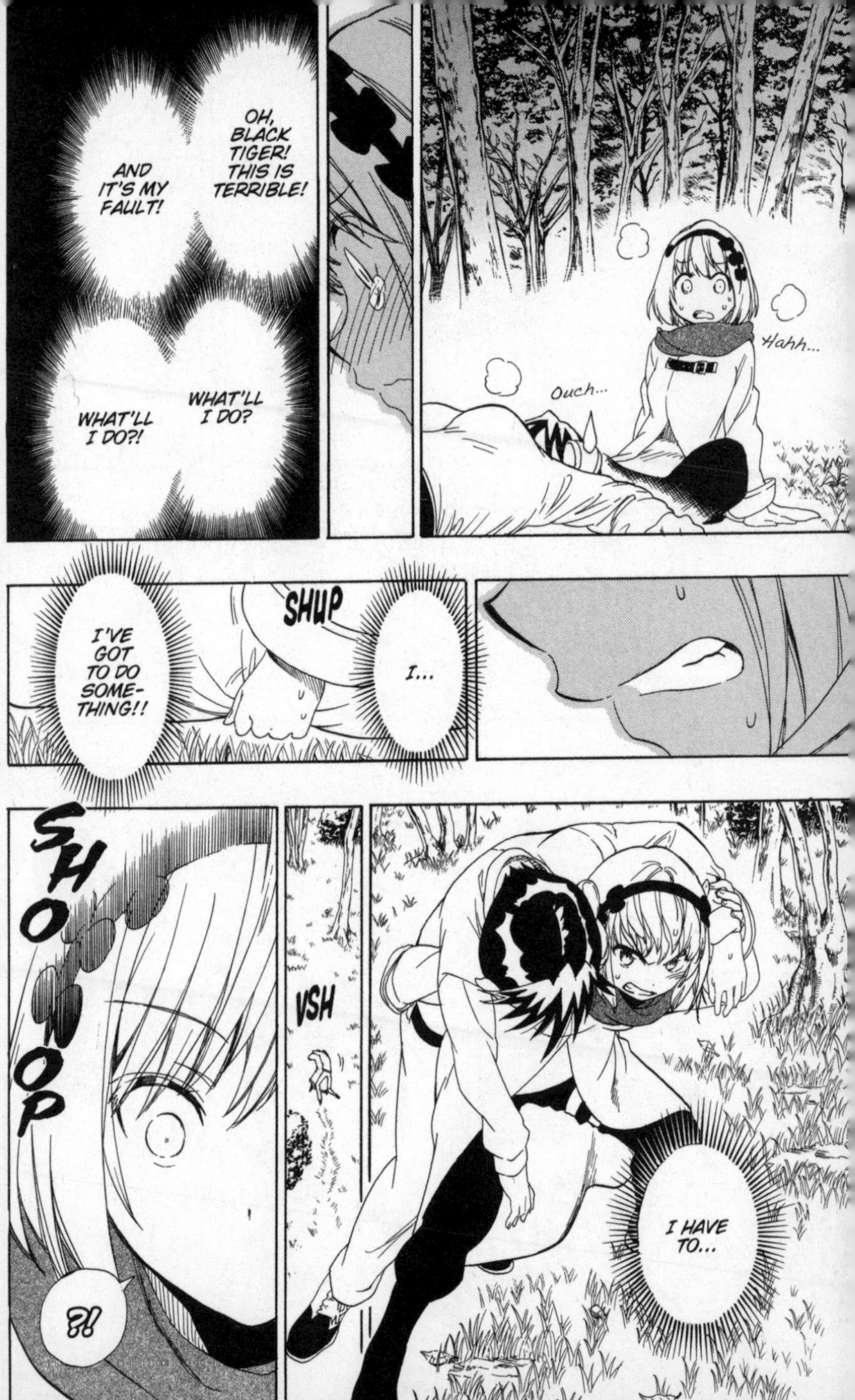

Hahh...
Ouch...
OH, BLACK TIGER! THIS IS TERRIBLE!
AND IT'S MY FAULT!
WHAT'LL I DO?
WHAT'LL I DO?!
SHUP
I...
I'VE GOT TO DO SOME-THING!!
I HAVE TO...
VSH
SHOWOP
?!

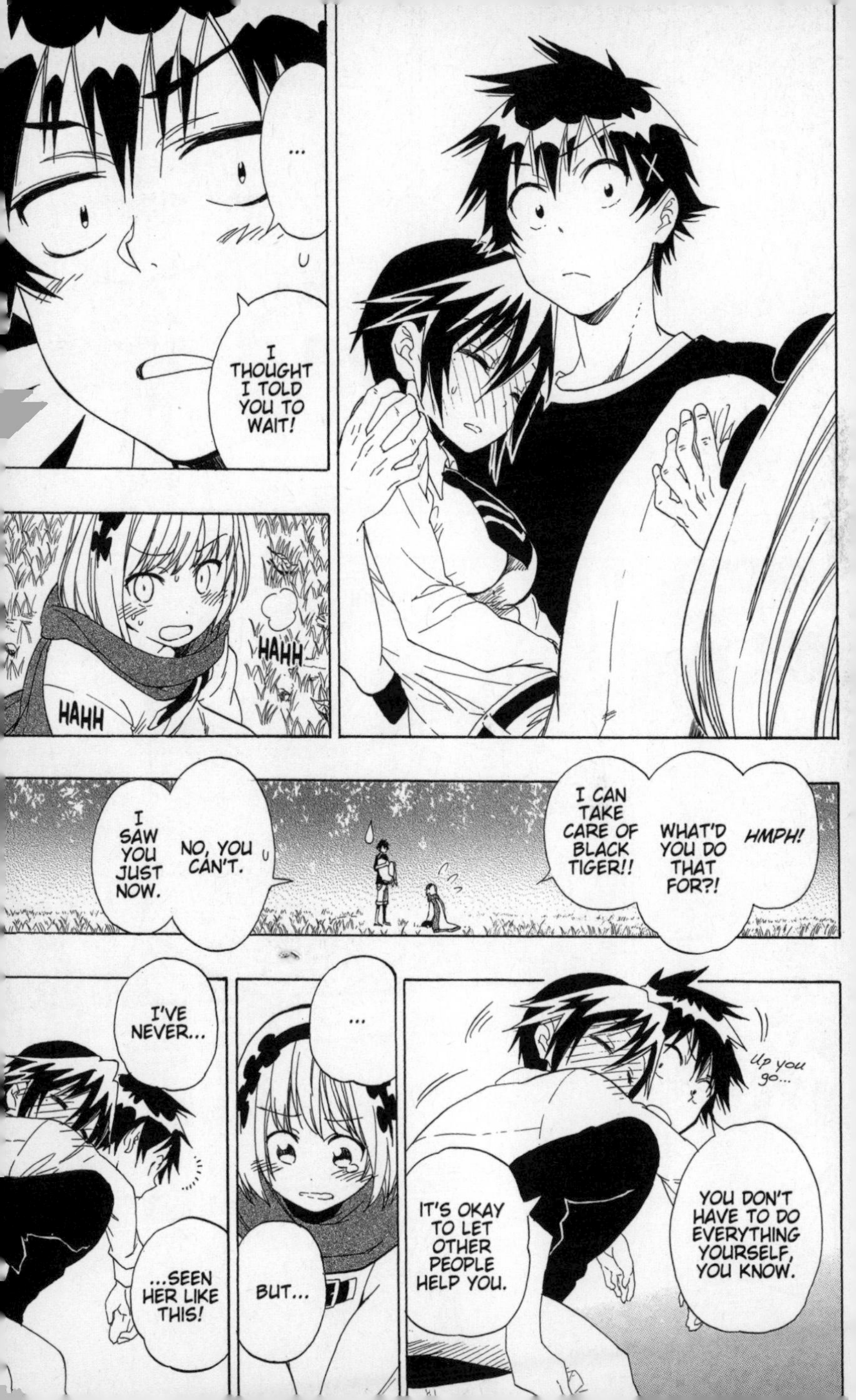
...
I THOUGHT I TOLD YOU TO WAIT!
HAHH
HAHH
HMPH!
WHAT'D YOU DO THAT FOR?!
I CAN TAKE CARE OF BLACK TIGER!!
NO, YOU CAN'T.
I SAW YOU JUST NOW.
Up you go...
YOU DON'T HAVE TO DO EVERYTHING YOURSELF, YOU KNOW.
IT'S OKAY TO LET OTHER PEOPLE HELP YOU.
...
BUT...
I'VE NEVER...
...SEEN HER LIKE THIS!

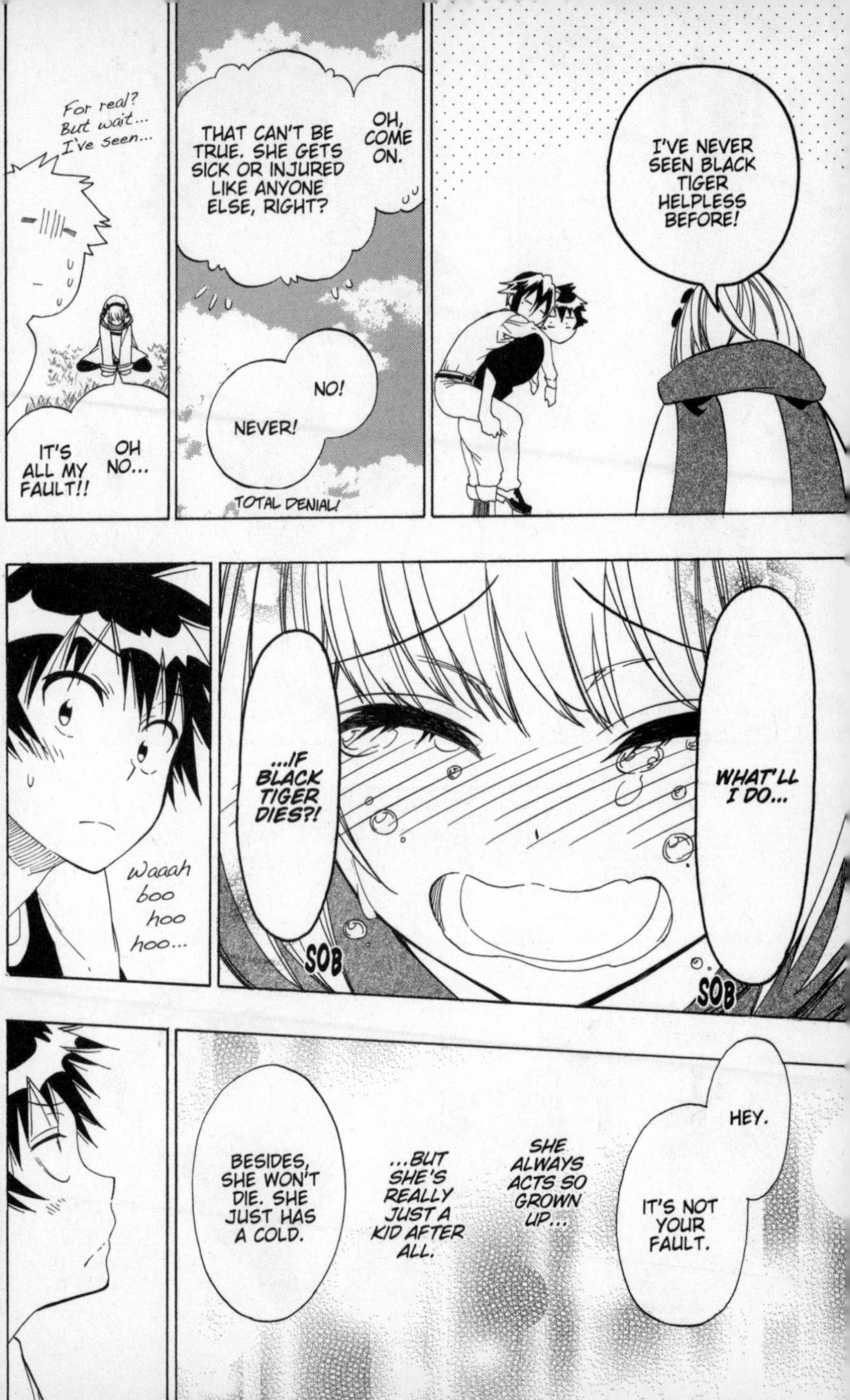
I'VE NEVER SEEN BLACK TIGER HELPLESS BEFORE!
OH, COME ON.
THAT CAN'T BE TRUE. SHE GETS SICK OR INJURED LIKE ANYONE ELSE, RIGHT?
NO!
NEVER!
TOTAL DENIAL!
For real? But wait... I've seen...
OH NO...
IT'S ALL MY FAULT!!
WHAT'LL I DO...
...IF BLACK TIGER DIES?!
SOB
SOB
Waaah boo hoo hoo...
HEY.
IT'S NOT YOUR FAULT.
SHE ALWAYS ACTS SO GROWN UP...
...BUT SHE'S REALLY JUST A KID AFTER ALL.
BESIDES, SHE WON'T DIE. SHE JUST HAS A COLD.

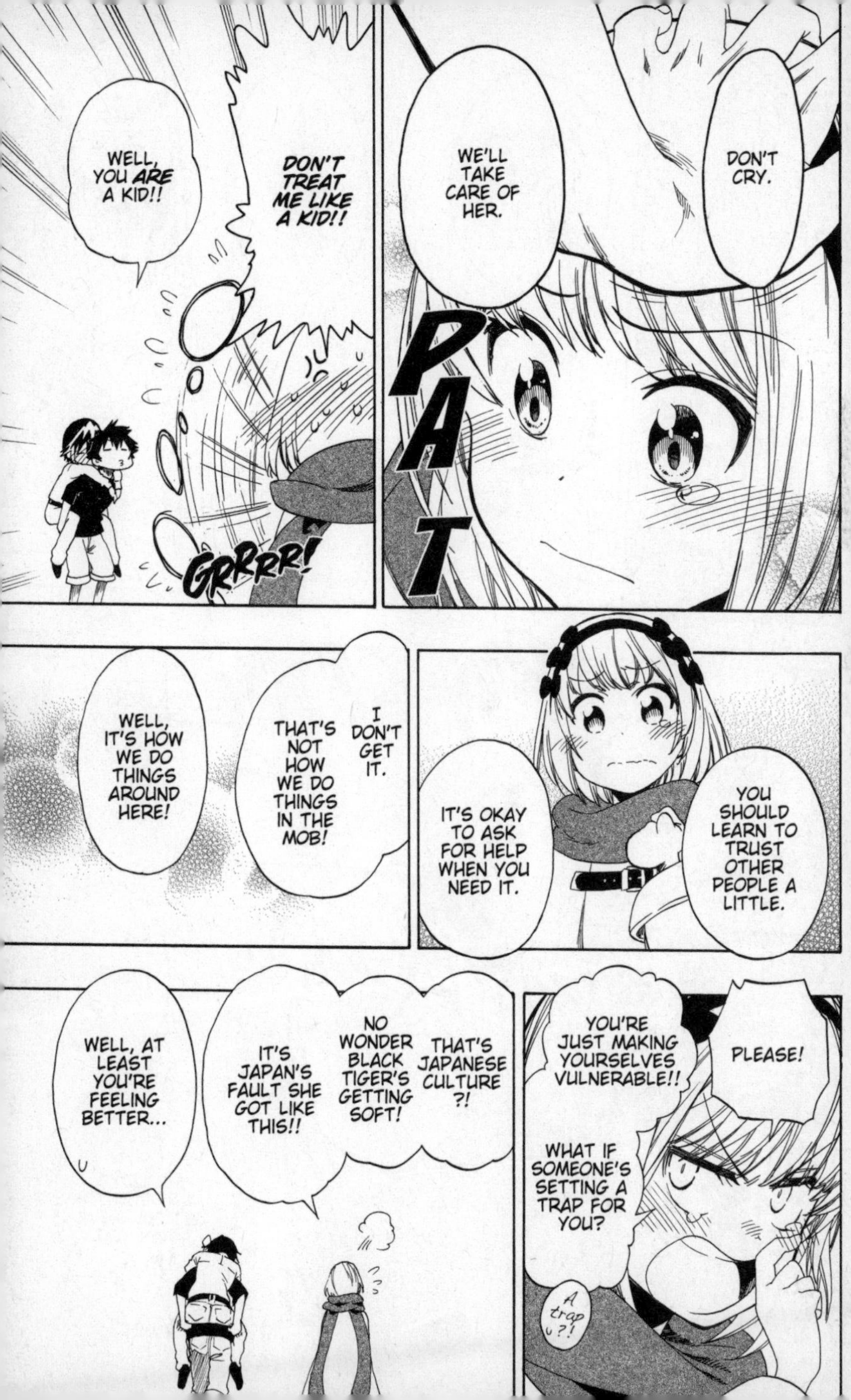

DON'T CRY.
WE'LL TAKE CARE OF HER.
PAT
DON'T TREAT ME LIKE A KID!!
WELL, YOU ARE A KID!!
GRRRR!
YOU SHOULD LEARN TO TRUST OTHER PEOPLE A LITTLE.
IT'S OKAY TO ASK FOR HELP WHEN YOU NEED IT.
I DON'T GET IT.
THAT'S NOT HOW WE DO THINGS IN THE MOB!
WELL, IT'S HOW WE DO THINGS AROUND HERE!
PLEASE!
YOU'RE JUST MAKING YOURSELVES VULNERABLE!!
WHAT IF SOMEONE'S SETTING A TRAP FOR YOU?
A trap?!
THAT'S JAPANESE CULTURE?!
NO WONDER BLACK TIGER'S GETTING SOFT!
IT'S JAPAN'S FAULT SHE GOT LIKE THIS!!
WELL, AT LEAST YOU'RE FEELING BETTER...

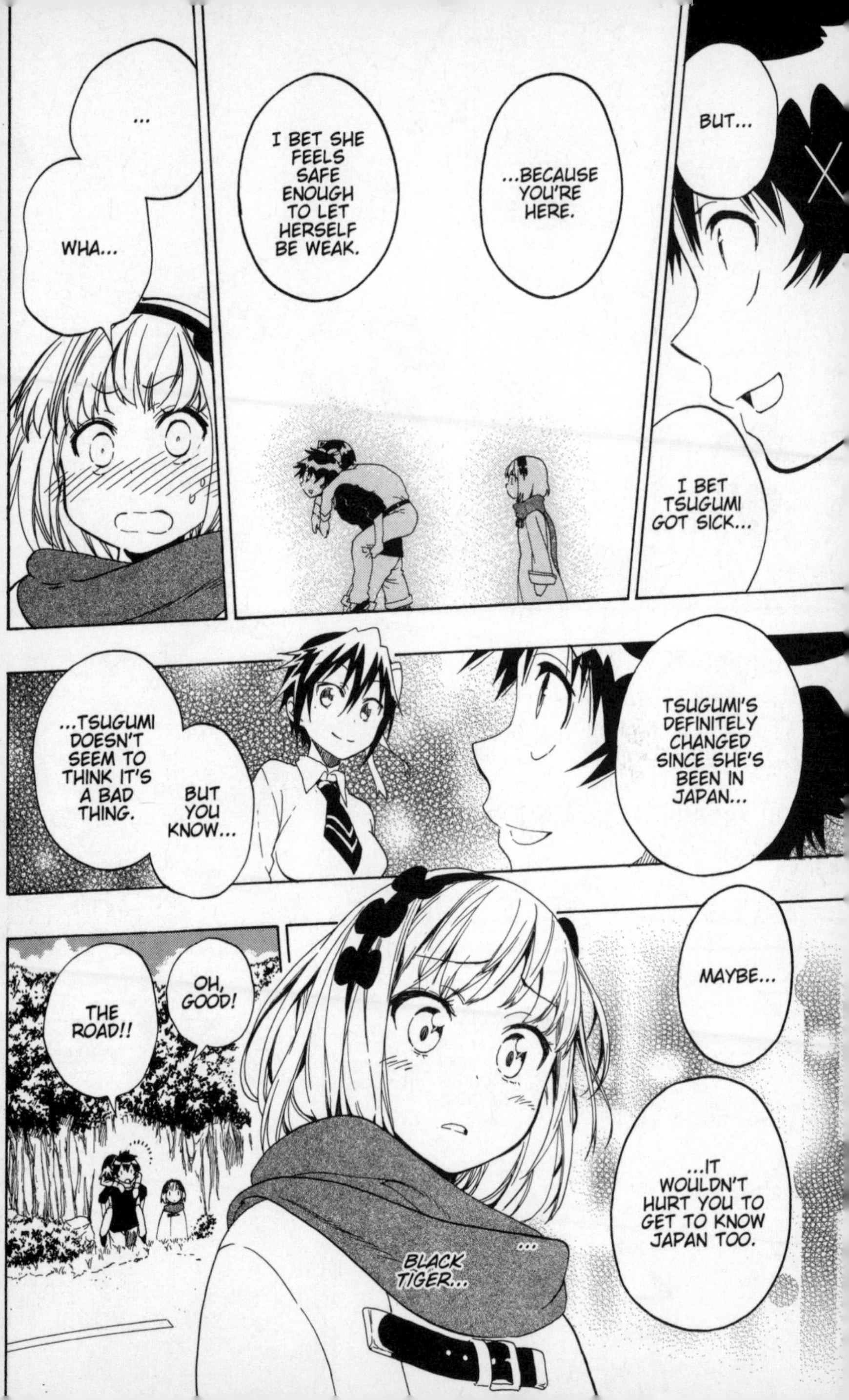
BUT...
I BET TSUGUMI GOT SICK...
...BECAUSE YOU'RE HERE.
I BET SHE FEELS SAFE ENOUGH TO LET HERSELF BE WEAK.
...
WHA...
TSUGUMI'S DEFINITELY CHANGED SINCE SHE'S BEEN IN JAPAN...
BUT YOU KNOW...
...TSUGUMI DOESN'T SEEM TO THINK IT'S A BAD THING.
MAYBE...
...IT WOULDN'T HURT YOU TO GET TO KNOW JAPAN TOO.
...
BLACK TIGER...
OH, GOOD!
THE ROAD!!

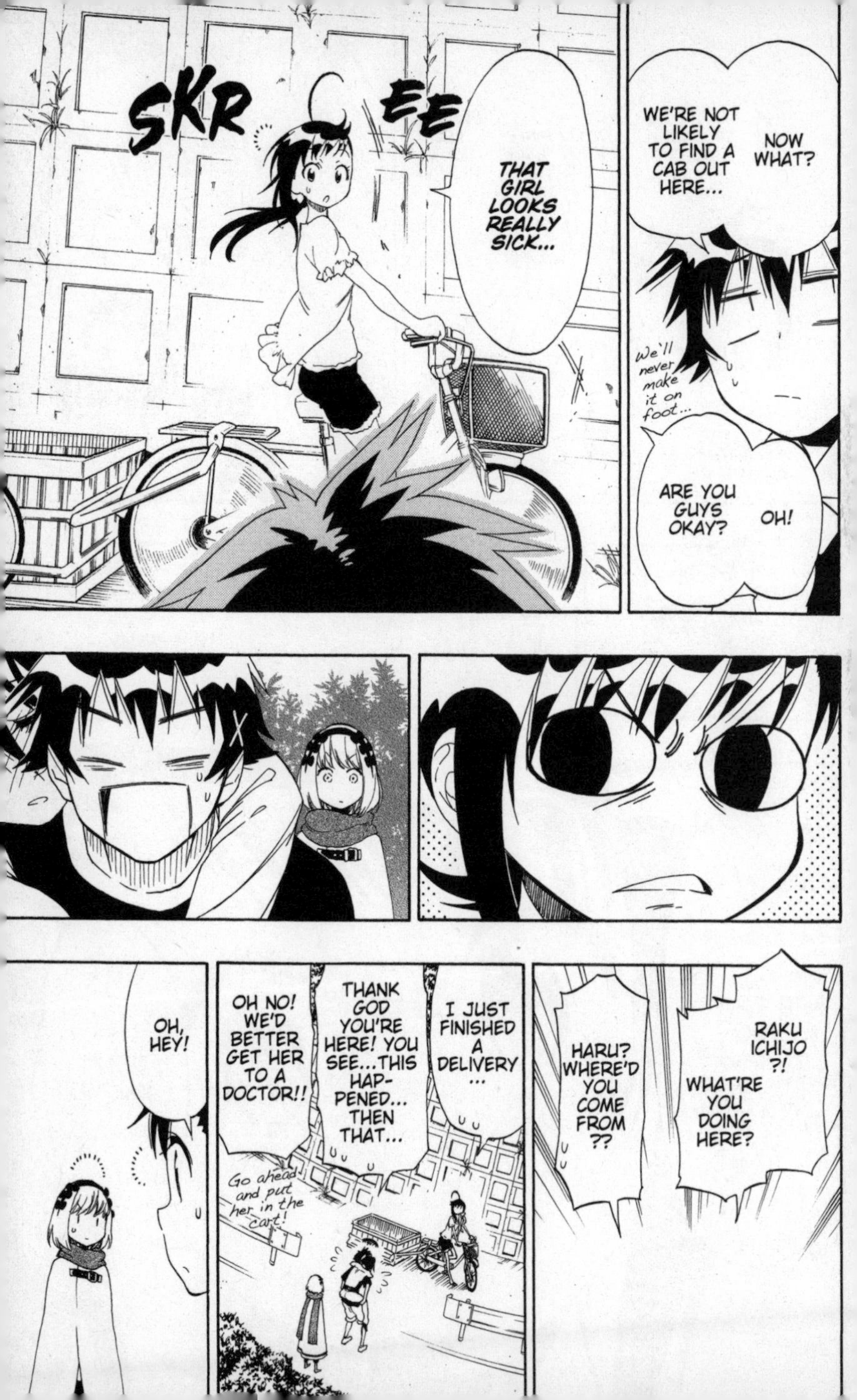
NOW WHAT?
WE'RE NOT LIKELY TO FIND A CAB OUT HERE...
We'll never make it on foot...
OH!
ARE YOU GUYS OKAY?
SKREE
THAT GIRL LOOKS REALLY SICK...
RAKU ICHIJO?!
WHAT'RE YOU DOING HERE?
HARU? WHERE'D YOU COME FROM??
I JUST FINISHED A DELIVERY...
THANK GOD YOU'RE HERE! YOU SEE...THIS HAP-PENED... THEN THAT...
OH NO! WE'D BETTER GET HER TO A DOCTOR!!
Go ahead and put her in the cart!
OH, HEY!

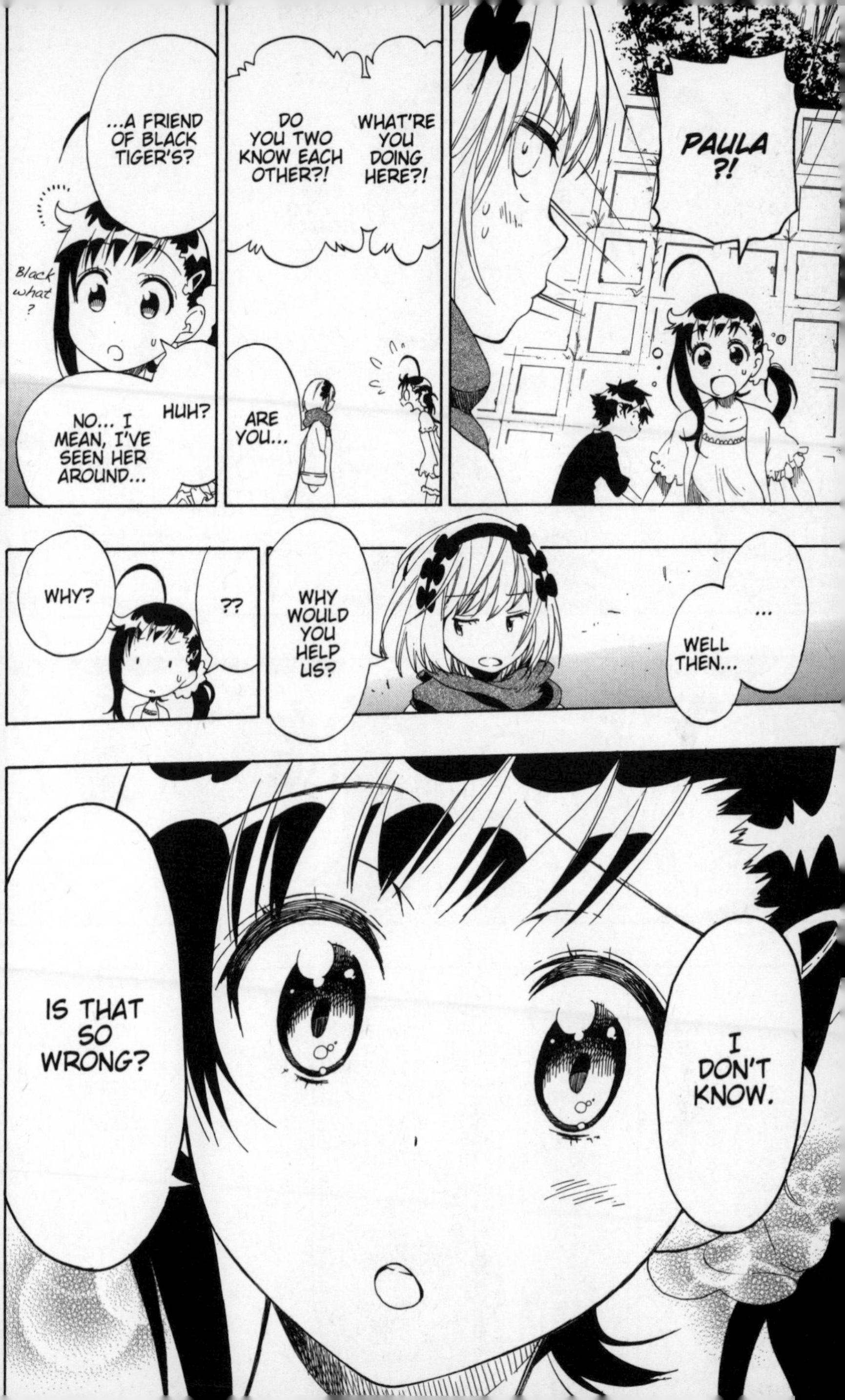
PAULA ?!
WHAT'RE YOU DOING HERE?!
DO YOU TWO KNOW EACH OTHER?!
ARE YOU...
...A FRIEND OF BLACK TIGER'S?
Black what ?
HUH?
NO... I MEAN, I'VE SEEN HER AROUND...
...
WELL THEN...
WHY WOULD YOU HELP US?
??
WHY?
I DON'T KNOW.
IS THAT SO WRONG?

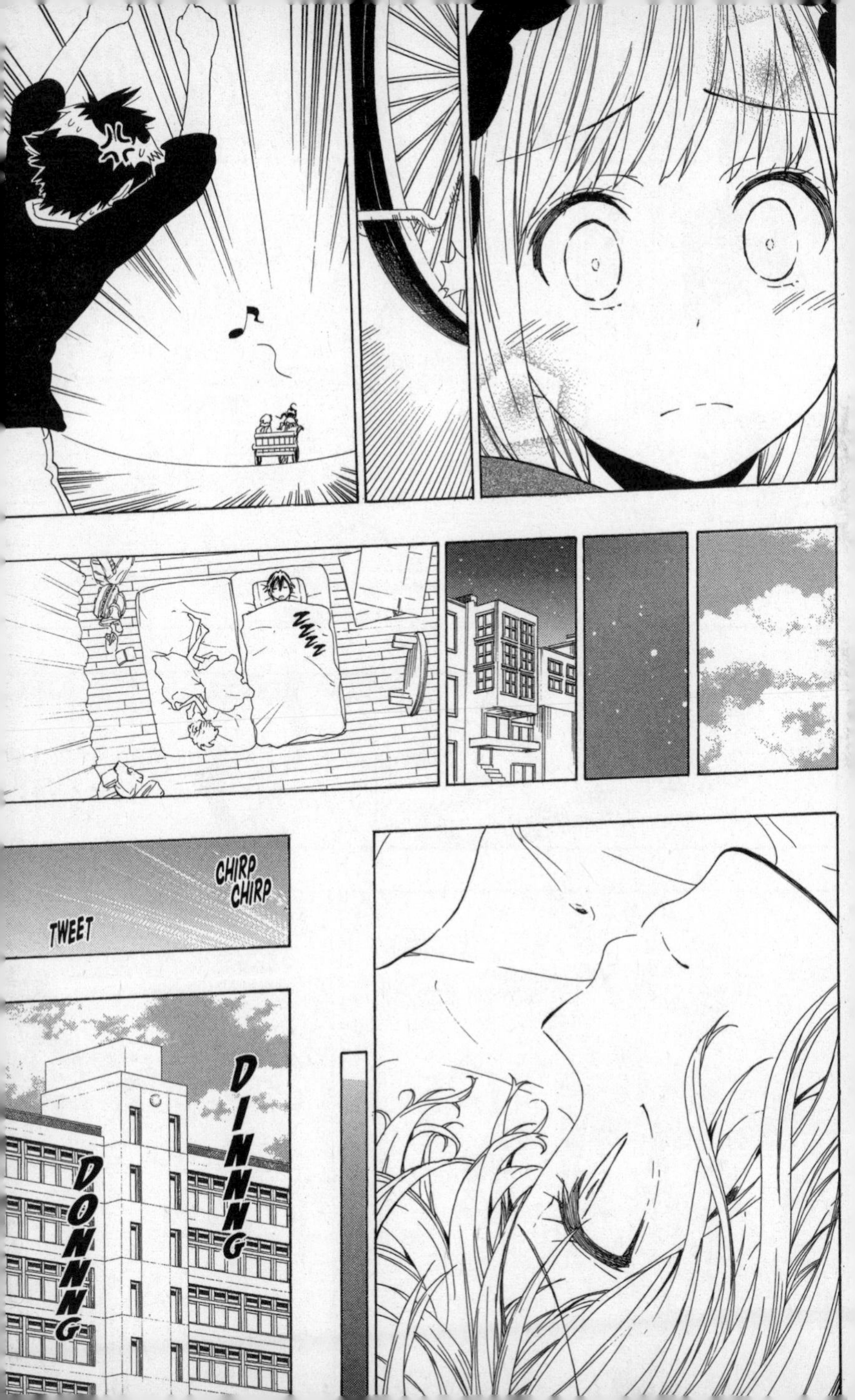
ZZZZ
CHIRP CHIRP
TWEET
DINNNG
DONNNG

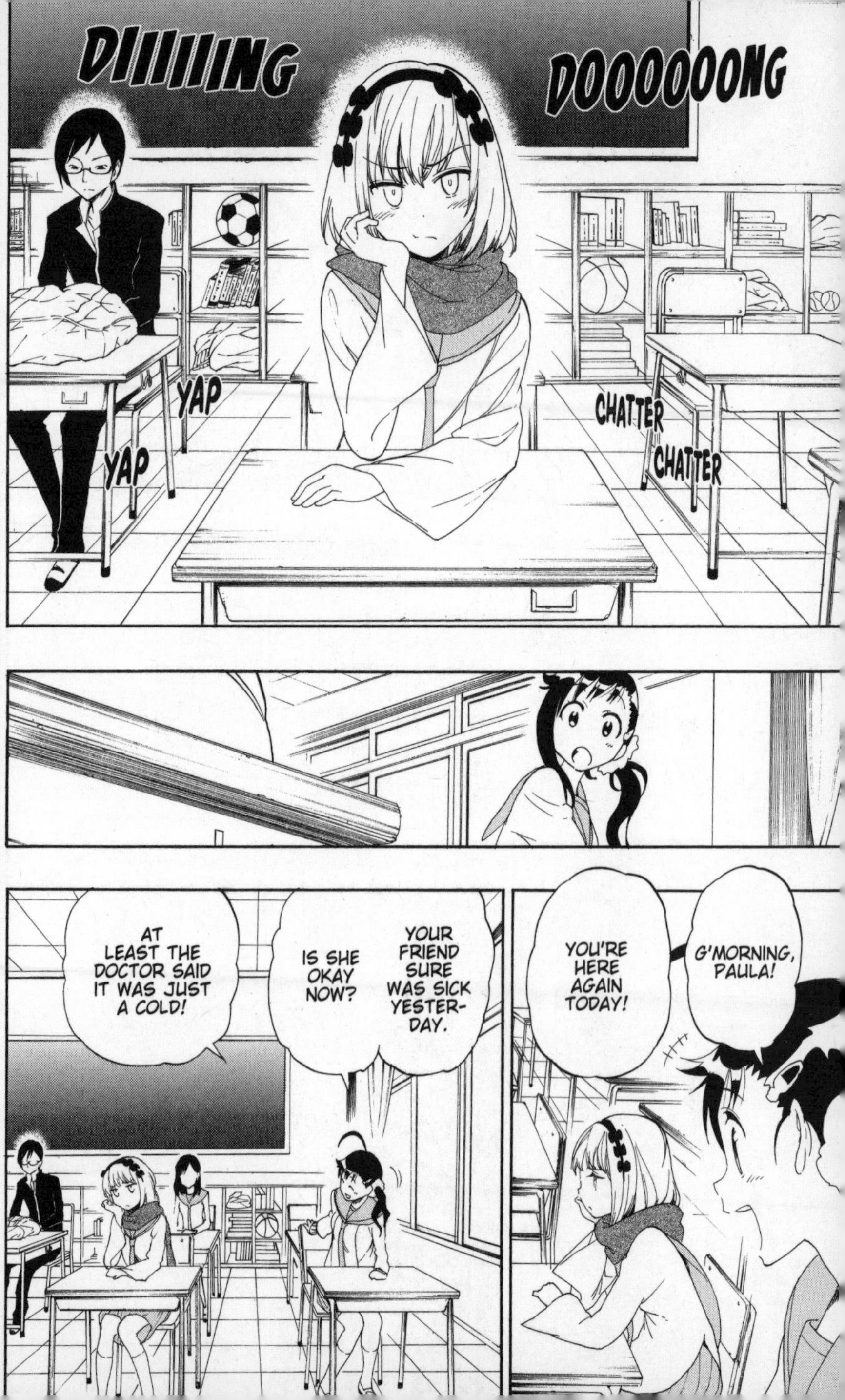
DIIIIIING
DOOOOOONG
CHATTER CHATTER
YAP YAP
G'MORNING, PAULA!
YOU'RE HERE AGAIN TODAY!
YOUR FRIEND SURE WAS SICK YESTER-DAY.
IS SHE OKAY NOW?
AT LEAST THE DOCTOR SAID IT WAS JUST A COLD!

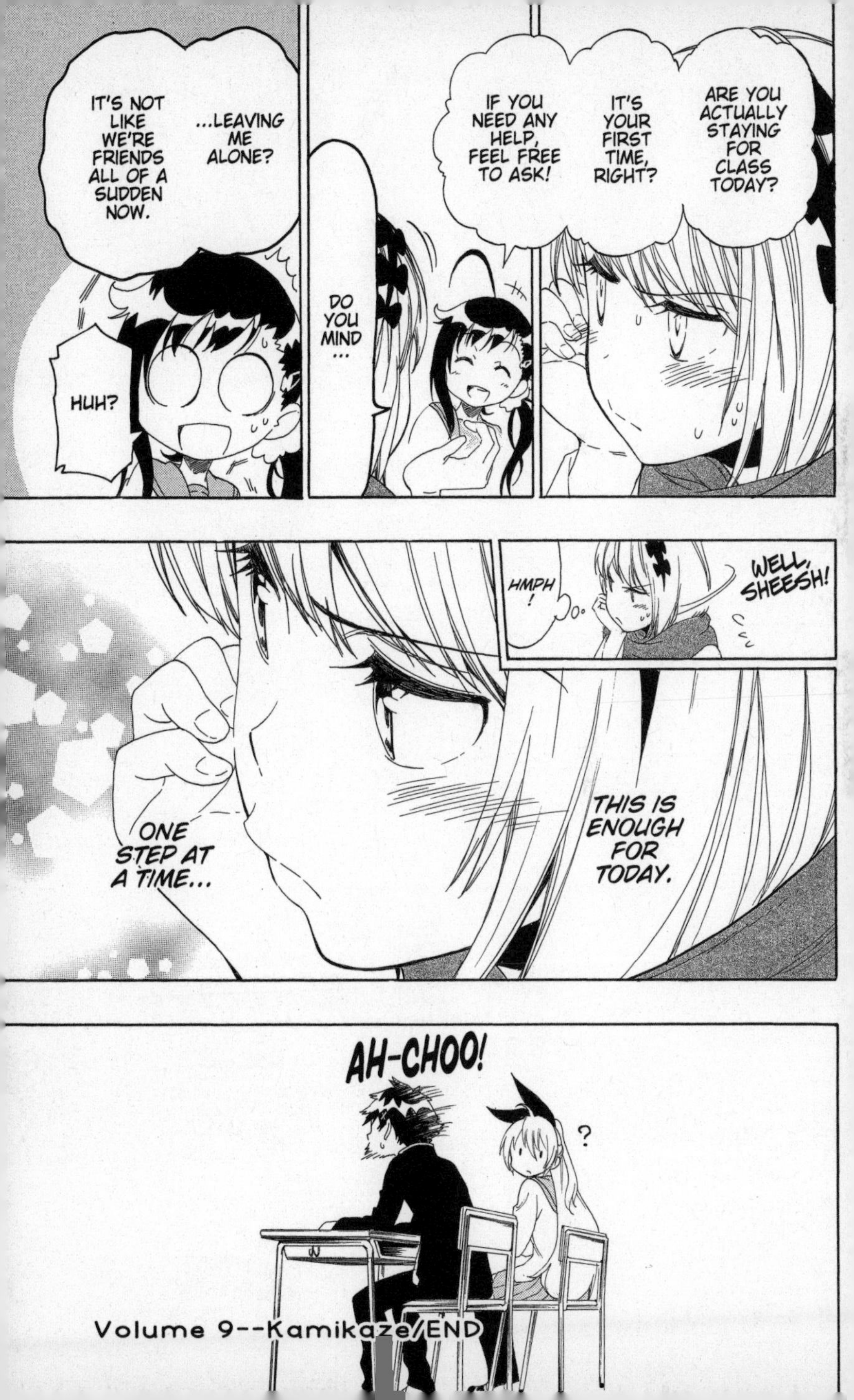
ARE YOU ACTUALLY STAYING FOR CLASS TODAY?
IT'S YOUR FIRST TIME, RIGHT?
IF YOU NEED ANY HELP, FEEL FREE TO ASK!
DO YOU MIND...
...LEAVING ME ALONE?
IT'S NOT LIKE WE'RE FRIENDS ALL OF A SUDDEN NOW.
HUH?
WELL, SHEESH!
HMPH!
THIS IS ENOUGH FOR TODAY.
ONE STEP AT A TIME...
AH-CHOO!
?
Volume 9--Kamikaze/END

Paula's Favorite
Magazine
Kosmo

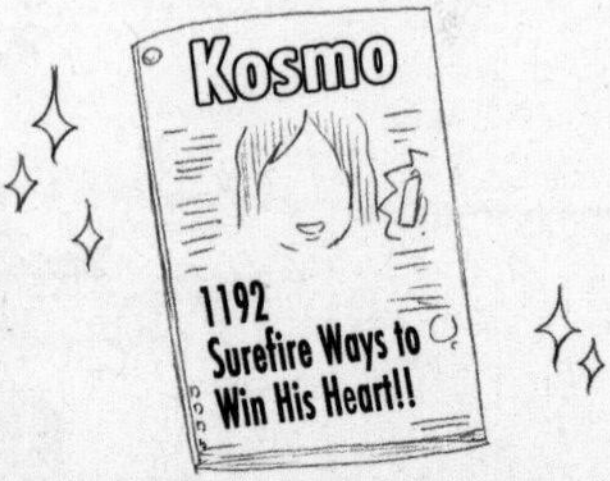
Kosmo
1192
Surefire Ways to
Win His Heart!!

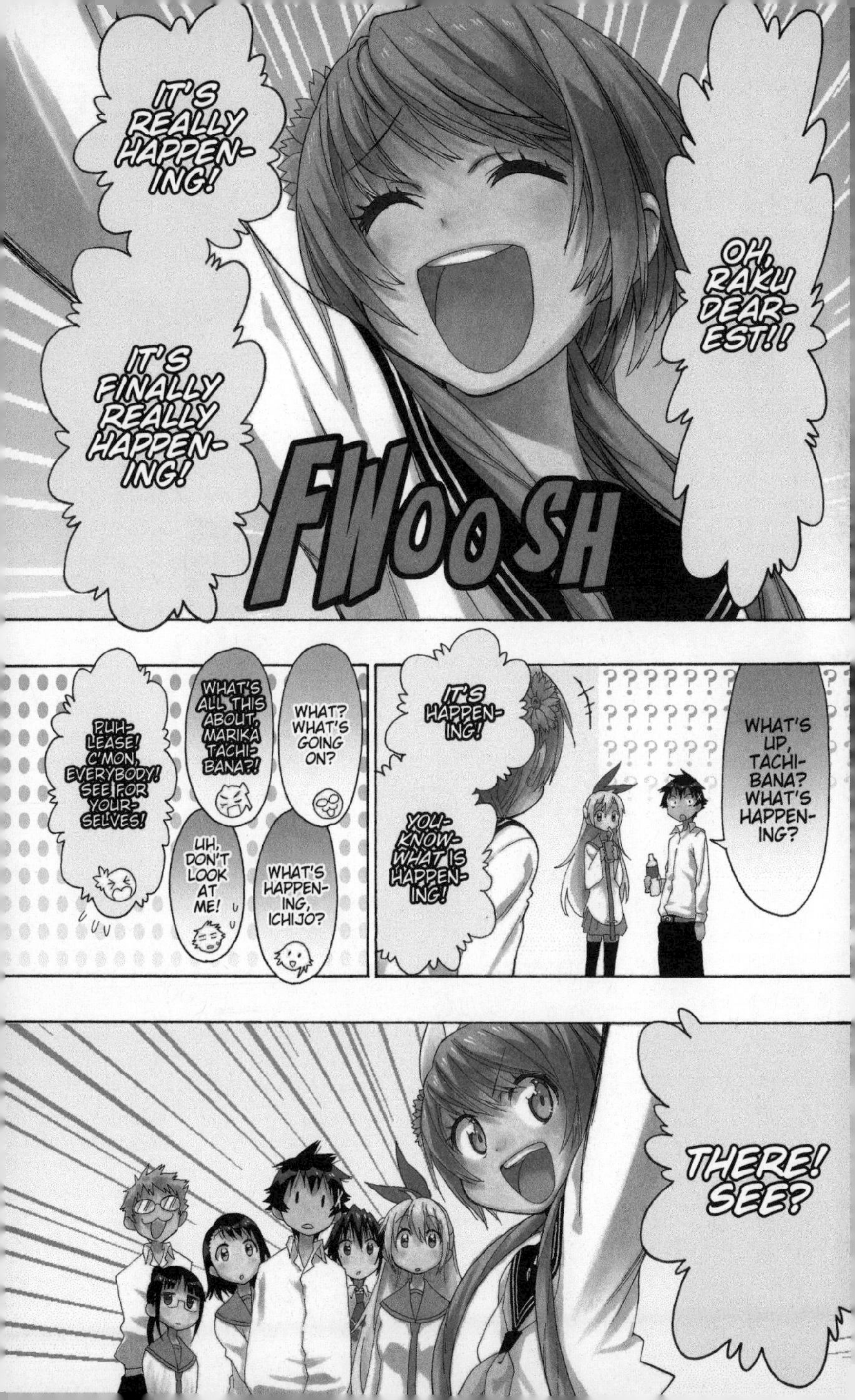
OH, RAKU DEAR-EST!!
IT'S REALLY HAPPEN-ING!
IT'S FINALLY REALLY HAPPEN-ING!
FWOOSH
WHAT'S UP, TACHI-BANA? WHAT'S HAPPEN-ING?
IT'S HAPPEN-ING!
YOU-KNOW-WHAT IS HAPPEN-ING!
WHAT? WHAT'S GOING ON?
WHAT'S ALL THIS ABOUT, MARIKA TACHI-BANA?!
WHAT'S HAPPEN-ING, ICHIJO?
UH, DON'T LOOK AT ME!
PUH-LEASE! C'MON, EVERYBODY! SEE FOR YOUR-SELVES!
THERE! SEE?

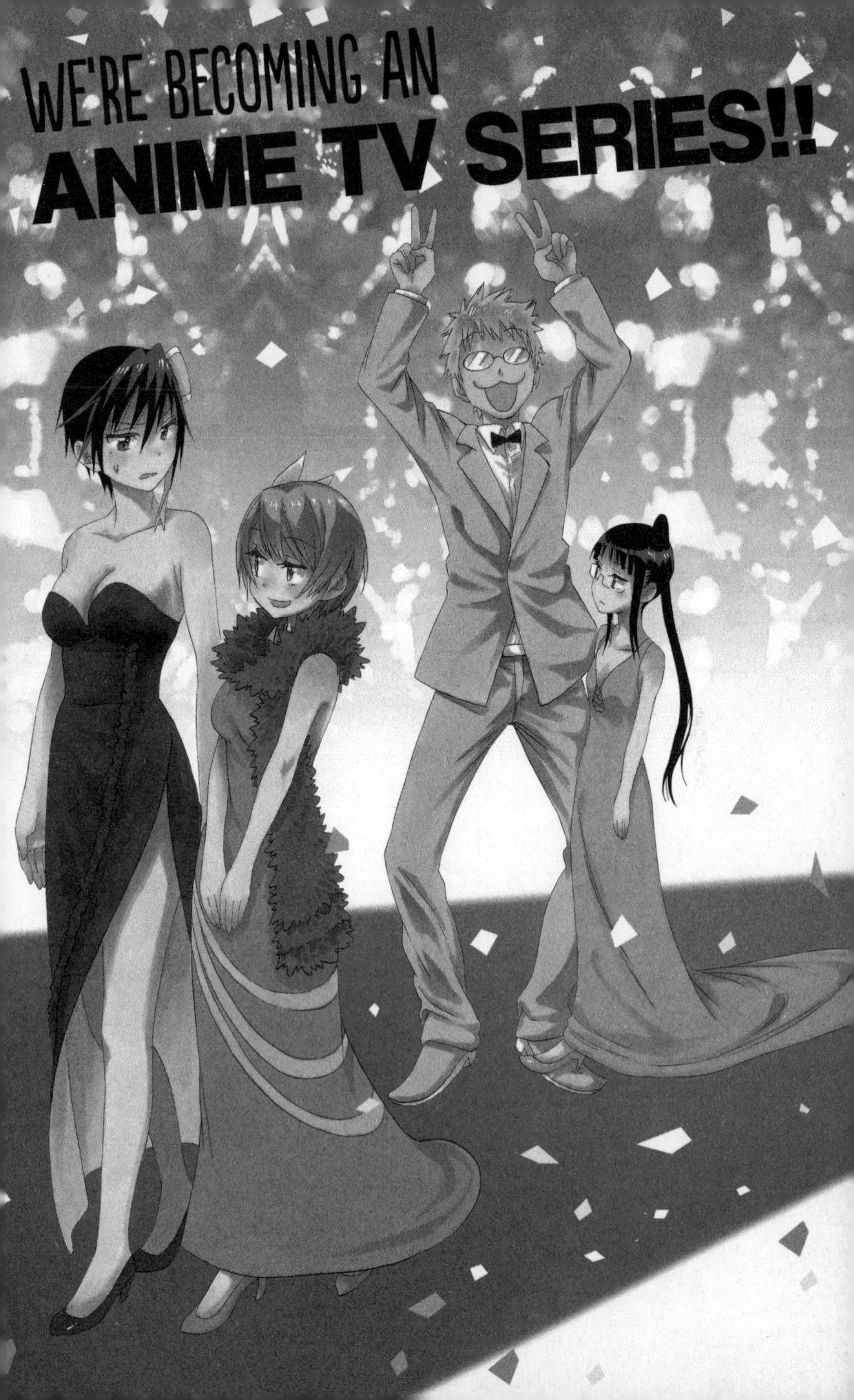
WE'RE BECOMING AN
ANIME TV SERIES!!

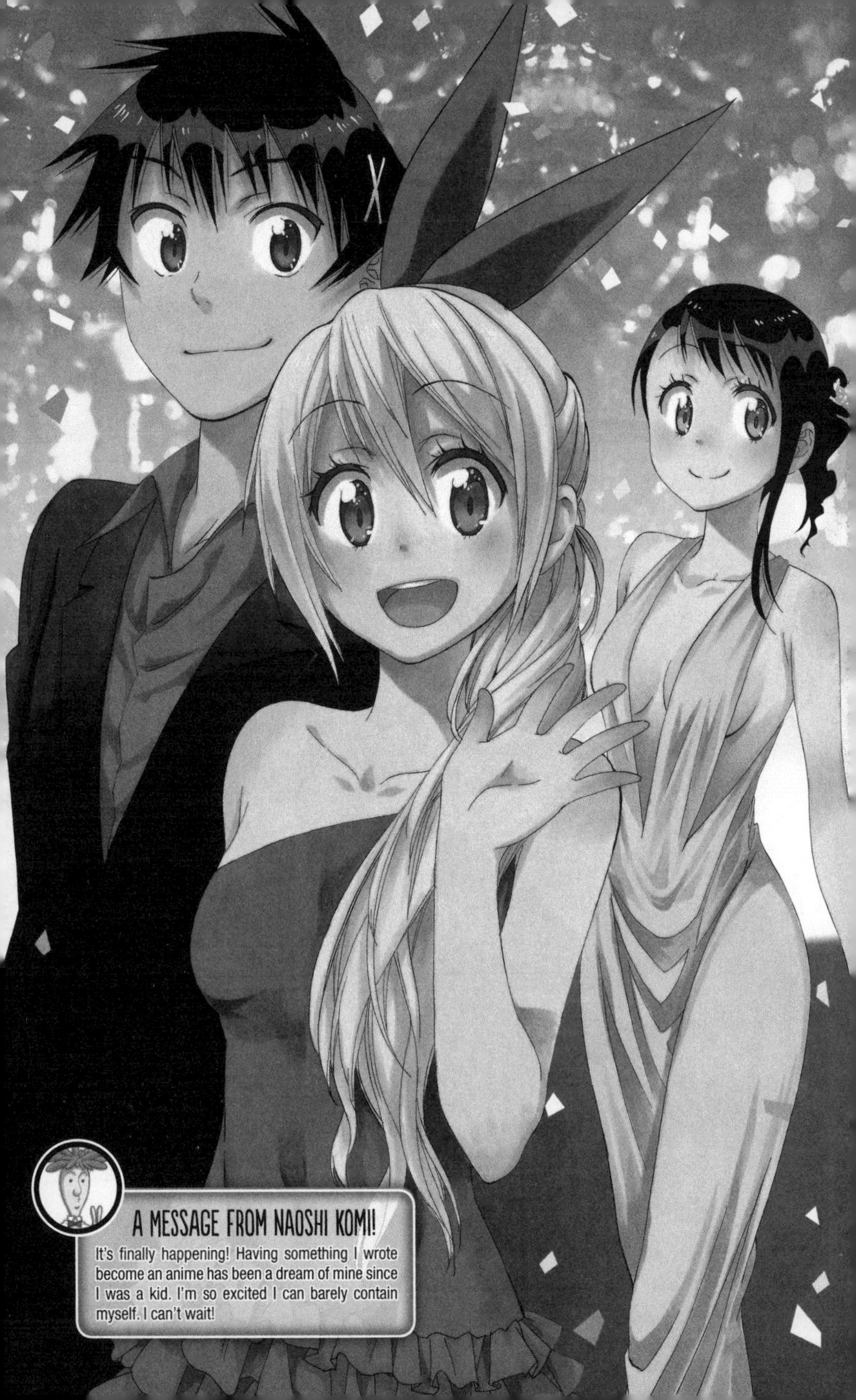
A MESSAGE FROM NAOSHI KOMI!
It's finally happening! Having something I wrote become an anime has been a dream of mine since I was a kid. I'm so excited I can barely contain myself. I can't wait!

☆ Bonus Comic!! ☆

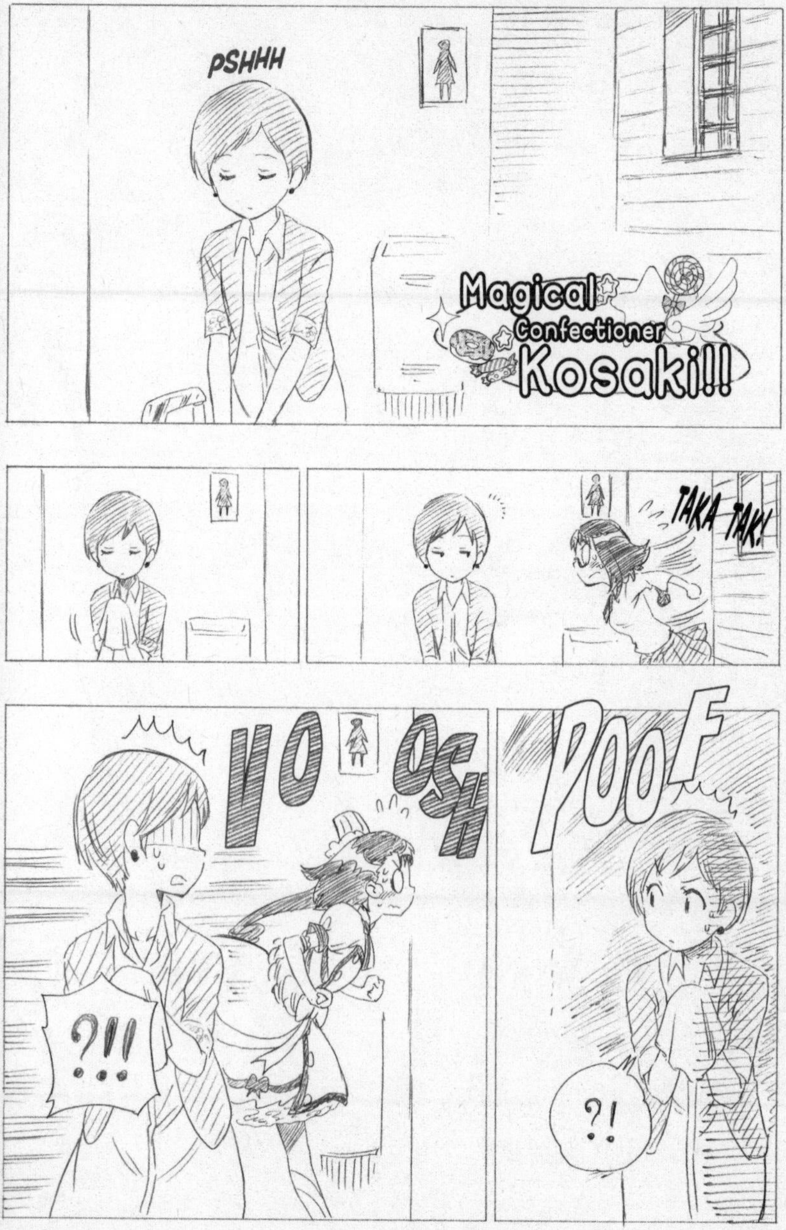

PSHHH
Magical Confectioner Kosaki!!
TAKA TAK!
POOF
?!
VOOSH
?!!

You need to quit running to the bathroom every time you transform.
You're wasting valuable time!
Yeah, but I don't want everyone to see me naked!
Who cares?
Whatcha got to lose?
Everything!
It's embarrassing, okay?
Well, how 'bout this?
If you wrap a cloth around your whole body, you can transform anytime, anywhere!
FORMATION
TRANS
POOF
Oh! I get it!
Okay, let's try it out!
Trans-form, Kosaki!
Okay!

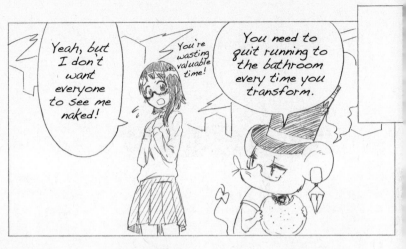

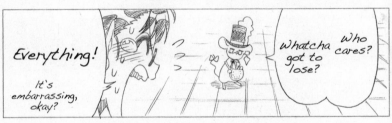

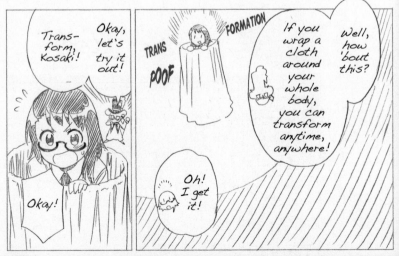

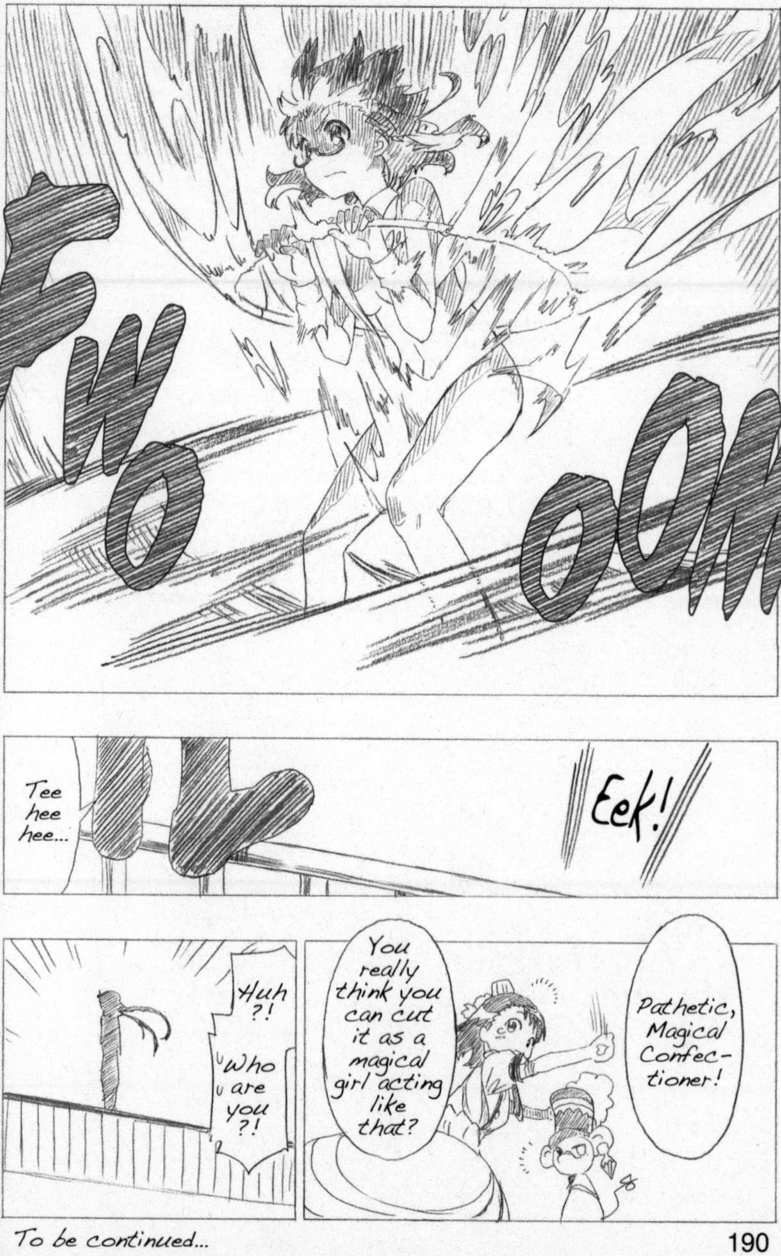
FWOOOM
Eek!
Tee hee hee...
Pathetic, Magical Confectioner!
You really think you can cut it as a magical girl acting like that?
Huh?!
Who are you?!

To be continued...